MERCY!

MERCY!

A CELEBRATION OF FENWAY PARK'S CENTENNIAL TOLD THROUGH **RED SOX** RADIO AND TV

CURT SMITH

Potomac Books
Washington, D.C.

Library of Congress Cataloging-in-Publication Data
Smith, Curt.
  Mercy! : a celebration of Fenway Park's centennial told through Red Sox Radio and TV / Curt Smith. — 1st ed.
     p. cm.
  Includes bibliographical references and index.
  ISBN 978-1-59797-935-1 (hardcover)
  ISBN 978-1-59797-936-8 (electronic)
  1. Fenway Park (Boston, Mass.)—Anecdotes. 2. Boston Red Sox (Baseball team)—Anecdotes. 3. Radio broadcasting of sports—Massachusetts—Boston—Anecdotes. 4. Television broadcasting—Massachusetts—Boston—Anecdotes. I. Title.
  GV416.B674S548 2012
  796.357'640974461—dc23

(alk. paper)

Printed in the United States of America on acid-free paper that meets the American National Standards Institute Z39-48 Standard.

Potomac Books
22841 Quicksilver Drive
Dulles, Virginia 20166

First Edition

10 9 8 7 6 5 4 3 2 1

For my mother—

who introduced me
to the Red Sox

"'Mercy. . . .' If that word has no meaning,
you haven't had your Sox on."

—*Boston Globe* columnist Jack Craig,
on Ned Martin's signature phrase

CONTENTS

ACKNOWLEDGMENTS

"So we beat on, boats against the current, borne back ceaselessly into the past," wrote F. Scott Fitzgerald. A book beats on against deadline, borne back to its start. Many people pitched *Mercy! A Celebration of Fenway Park's Centennial Told Through Red Sox Radio and TV* from spring training to final game. They were generous with their help and time, and I am grateful to them.

Narrating 1967's *The Impossible Dream* long-playing record, Ken Coleman hailed an "affair twixt a town and a team." His voice will always be synonymous with that year. Other mikemen to thank, their Fenway suzerainty long or brief, include Oscar Baez, Uri Berenguer, Joe Castiglione, Glenn Geffner, Ken Harrelson, Sean McDonough, Jon Miller, Dave O'Brien, Don Orsillo, Rico Petrocelli, Jerry Remy, Dick Stockton, Jerry Trupiano, and late Curt Gowdy, Ned Martin, Bob Murphy, Bob Starr, J. P. Villaman, and Jim Woods.

The Red Sox front office was especially helpful. I met current president and chief executive officer Larry Lucchino in the early 1990s, when he owned the Orioles, built Oriole Park at Camden Yards, and beat the Olde Towne Team more than was necessary. Red Sox Nation long ago forgave him: saving Fenway Park, taking a 2004 title, and encoring in 2007 helped. As at Baltimore, Lucchino has forged a staff adverse to bragging, gloating, or thinking they have it made.

Let me thank Sam Kennedy, executive vice president/chief operating officer: also Lawrence Cancro, senior VP/Fenway affairs; Sarah C. Coffin, photo archival assistant; Pam Ganley, manager of media relations; Susan Goodenow, senior VP/ public affairs and marketing; Debbie Matson, director of publications; Dan Rea, coordinator, alumni and team archives; Fay Scheer, assistant to the president; and

John Shestakofsky, media relations coordinator. Dick Bresciani, vice president/ emeritus and team historian, is *the* Soxopedia from Don Aase to Al Zarilla. Jim Healy, former VP, broadcasting and technology, detailed the late-1990s plan for a new ballpark to replace John Updike's "lyric little bandbox."

Many have covered Fenway long and well, including Nick Cafardo, Gordon Edes, Peter Gammons, Tony Massarotti, Martin Nolan, Bob Ryan, and Dan Shaughnessy. Mort Bloomberg profiled Jim Britt for the Society for American Baseball Research (SABR) biography project. Shaun L. Kelly's boston.com article on Ned Martin etched a truly literate man. The late Jack Craig was baseball's first true radio/TV critic, his "SporTView" a *Boston Globe*, then *The Sporting News*, landmark. Jack was kind, thoughtful, and incorruptible. I hope he would have liked *Mercy!*—as my generation admired him.

I am indebted to Tom Shaer, former WITS Boston radio reporter and talk host, now head, Chicago's Tom Shaer Media, for play-by-play, material about Ned Martin's and Jim Woods's 1978 firing, and other invaluable behind-the-scenes archive. Archivist John Miley and WEEI Radio executive sports producer Jon Albanese contributed other play-by-play. I wish to also thank NBC TV's late Scotty Connal, Harry Coyle, and Carl Lindemann—and longtime friend Ken Samelson, who reviewed the manuscript. George Mitrovich, chairman, The Great Fenway Park Writers Series, supplied insight and vignette.

National Radio Hall of Fame president Bruce DuMont officially endorsed the book. A statue of 6-foot-4 Ted Williams—elegant as a stallion, long-limbed as a pelican, and jittery as a colt: to poet Donald Hall, "turn[ing] on himself like a barber's pole in its shapely curving"—gilds the National Baseball Hall of Fame and Museum. Its staff is as tall, including senior library associate Bill Francis; librarian Jim Gates; senior director, communications and education, Brad Horn; president Jeff Idelson; photo archivist Pat Kelly; manager, museum programs, Stephen Light; and communications director Greg Mudder.

Potomac Books' Laura Briggs, Hilary Claggett, Elizabeth Demers, Sam Dorrance, Elizabeth Norris, and Kathryn Owens conceived this project. Also helpful were my agent Andrew Blauner and counselor Phil Hochberg. My wife, Sarah, a Houstonian, grasps the Red Sox' Texas-sized sorcery. Having been to Fenway, our children, Olivia, 13, and Travis, 12, know that it is not wasted on the young.

I did 125 interviews, relived hundreds of broadcast hours—"Slaughter scores!" "One of the greatest catches we've ever seen by Yastrzemski!" "Carlton Fisk . . . is the happiest guy in Massachusetts!" "In foul ground is Nettles!" "Ortiz has done it again!"—and physically or electronically visited the Baseball Hall, Library of Congress, *Sports Illustrated*, *The Sporting News*, BostonGlobe.com, and the Sports Museum in Boston: Rusty Sullivan, executive director, and Richard Johnson, curator.

I wrote where I am privileged to teach: the University of Rochester in Upstate New York. Students Steve Huber and Nate Mulberg were as diligent in research as in the classroom. I am pleased that my undergraduate alma mater, the State University of New York at Geneseo, will receive half of all royalties accrued from the sales of this book. Finally, let me thank the citizens of the Nation—a term *Boston Globe* feature writer Nathan Cobb coined in 1986—without whom the Red Sox would not be the Red Sox.

1 PROLOGUE

In 1971, former secretary of state Dean Acheson wrote a memoir, *Present at the Creation: My Years in the State Department*. An army, not a diplomat, was present at this book's creation, *Mercy! A Celebration of Fenway Park's Centennial Told Through Red Sox Radio and TV*. Onward, Red Sox Nation, marching as to war.

In July 2009, I spoke at the Baltimore Sports Museum, then walked a short pop-up to the Hilton Harbor Hotel: in turn, a fly ball from Oriole Park at Camden Yards. The Orioles–Red Sox game was scheduled for 7:05 p.m. Suddenly, at 5 o'clock—gates opened at 5:30—a battalion left nearby hotels to occupy the park.

Hand in hand, soldiers of the Nation in pink and red shirts, pants, and hats filled West Pratt Street. "We travel well," broadcaster Joe Castiglione described the diaspora, packing the Yard, Big A, and Safeco Field: near or at the top of major-league away attendance. Colleague Dave O'Brien says, "There may be somewhere without Sox fans, but I haven't found it." In 2010, *Forbes* magazine wrote, "[They] are so devoted they top our list of 'America's Best Sports Fans.'"

In 1975, a then record 124 million people viewed all or part of the Red Sox–Reds World Series. In 1986, Game Seven of the Mets-Sox Fall Classic wooed 81 million, still baseball's most watched-ever match. In our cable television–fractured age, the 2004 Olde Towne Team had the highest Series audience since 1995. Crucial to its lure is New England's cabaret.

Fenway Park "draws people at home, to the Sox on the road, and above all, to TV," said the legendary late NBC producer Harry Coyle. In person, the red brick facade, scarce foul turf, long and short distances, and low and high walls—highest, 37-foot-2 left-field Green Monster—evoke stadia pre- and post-modernism. On

1

television, drop-dead coverage shows angled blocks, nooks, and planes and seats near the field, rolling away, row upon row.

Born in nearby Cambridge, Tip O'Neill "went to games there as a kid. I'd see a pop-fly homer down the line, or ball ricocheting off the [left-field] door. A guy'd make a circus catch, or miss an inside-the-parker." Later, he became Speaker of the U.S. House of Representatives, finding politics like Fenway. "Since nothing was uniform, anything could happen." Pause. "Let me tell ya, pal, that was [is] the beauty of the place."

Deem Old Yankee Stadium baseball's most famous park; Ebbets Field, mourned; Camden Yards, prophetic. As I wrote in 1999, between Carlton Fisk and Bill Buckner Fenway Park became "the most beloved." Other books hail its hundredth birthday bash. Only *Mercy!*—announcer Ned Martin's term for a piquant moment between or beyond the lines—uses the canvas of radio and TV. "Over the years you remember the ups and downs, but above all the excitement of this boundless, confounded team," Martin said. "Remember them and weep, or laugh, or sing. And wrap yourself in this Red Sox thing."

The "thing" consists of the three Rs: rise, regress, and recovery. Rise: The Townies won five of baseball's first 15 World Series. Regress: Paul Simon hymned, "I would not give you false hope." False hope sustained the Red Sox for 86 years after 1918, when the Twenty-Sixth (Yankee) Division entered France. Recovery: Only St. Louis has won as many twenty-first-century Series—two. Here broadcast lives, tales, and calls wrap like vines around a trellis: memory's soundtrack on the page.

Gus Rooney began Townies radio on Opening Day 1926. Fred Hoey's firsts fused 1927 and 1933: daily American League play-by-play and being dropped from the Series, respectively—"bombed, like the ['20s second-division] Sox," mused a friend. "The only thing worse than watching them drunk was watching them sober." Successor Jim Britt was baseball's *Roget's*, airing the Red Sox TV debut, 1948 AL playoff, and 1949 last/lost weekend in New York. On the train back to Boston, pitcher Ellis Kinder punched equally soused skipper Joe McCarthy in the mouth.

In 1951, Curt Gowdy became the Cowboy behind the mike, "that ever-so-soothing and sensible voice," John Updike wrote, "with its guileless hint of Wyoming twang." Bob Murphy soon joined him, voice rising an octave on a dribbler past the mound. The Kid exited like a deity in 1960: "Ted Williams has homered in his last time at bat in a Red Sox uniform!" Curt said. Straightaway

Ted retired, the Red Sox sinking southward. In 1966, Gowdy left for a decade as NBC's sports paradigm. Three Voices succeeded him, often disbelieving what they saw.

Ken Coleman never split an infinitive, dangled a participle, or felt magic to match 1967's. "People mention upsets," he said of the 100-to-1ers. "They're nothing compared to that." The Impossible Dream spun the first Red Sox pennant since 1946, revived the Boston American League Baseball Company, and even after 2004 is to many its finest hour. Coleman was born in North Quincy, 15 minutes from the Sox sanctorum. Raised 18 miles northwest of Center City, Ned Martin, deciding not to be in Philadelphia, relocated to the Fens.

"Petrocelli's back, he's got it!" Martin said of 1967's final regular-season pitch. "The Red Sox win! And there's pandemonium on the field!" One night he called Williams "Big Guy." The next might invoke the Bard: "Good night, sweet prince. May flights of angels sing thee to thy rest." An inning might reference "pool-cue shot," "peeled foul," and *Macbeth*'s "Out, damn'd spot." In 1975, Ned aired a one rip-roarious-play-after-another Series Game Six. "Fisk swings. Long drive, left field!" The ball was far enough, but fair or foul? "Home run! The Red Sox win!" It is how millions still remember him.

In 1956, Enos Slaughter, eyeing Jim Woods's slight overbite and gray buzz cut, jibed, "I've seen better heads on a possum." Poss and Martin's 1970s travelogue bagged New England: Ned, wry and wistful; Jim, a bullhorn behind the mike. "There are a reported fifteen thousand people at the game this afternoon," Woods said. "If that's true, then at least twelve thousand of them are disguised as empty seats." His last Sox game with Martin was Bucky Dent's Yanks-Townies playoff. "It's over," Jim said simply, 1978 needing no embroidery—a Woodstock or Waterloo, Sputnik or Gallipoli.

By then, Ken Harrelson was the Red Sox southern-fried TV analyst, Hawkspeak his specialty. Later, Jon Miller used anecdote, mimed Vin Scully in English, Spanish, and Japanese, and joined the Orioles, Giants, and ESPN. Sean McDonough was never unprepared. Dick Stockton made even statistics muse. Bob Starr had a gentle lummox William Bendix kind of charm. In the evaluating of the Red Sox post-second-third of the century, all cherished a game less slam-bang than ballet.

Castiglione left a Connecticut Yankees' baseball boyhood to become the Townies' radio leitmotif; Don Orsillo, his father's New Hampshire farm for 4 Yawkey Way; Jerry Remy, the Sox infield to "talk a good game," said the *Globe*.

Dave O'Brien later joined Castiglione, having heard Starr punctuate a loss by saying, "My partner [Joe] is sitting here, looking like he's been harpooned." With the club required study, most took defeat hard.

Thirteen times the Towne Team lost a pennant or World Series on the next-to-last or final day from 1946 through 2003. Depending on your view, Johnny Pesky does or does not hold the ball. Luis Aparicio loses a division by falling down rounding third. Dent homers above the Monster. The Grounder goes under Bill Buckner's glove. Aaron Boone goes deep at The Stadium. The Law of Averages (things even out) fell to Murphy's Law (if things can go wrong, they will).

Then, in 2004, the Yankees took a 3-0 best-of-seven game League Championship Series (LCS); whereupon Boston won the next four; after which it swept St. Louis in the Series. "Swing and a ground ball!" Castiglione said. "Stabbed by [reliever Keith] Foulke! He has it! He underhands to first! And the Boston Red Sox are the world champions!"—the first time since before the first Armistice Day. Pigs flew. The Charles River reversed course. Walt Dropo became Jacoby Ellsbury.

Numbed and stunned, the Nation anointed Pedro and Big Papi's bat and Curt Schilling's Bloody Sock and Manny being Manny—or was it Smoky Joe and the Silent Captain of the Red Sox and Gentleman Jim and the Man They Called Yaz? Each was family, though as recently as the late 1990s their house seemed old-timey: too few luxury boxes and concession stands, too little parking; above all, too small.

Rebuilding would be prohibitive, even the Sox had said. Suites couldn't squeeze into a Wilsonian shoebox. The foundation was built to house one deck, not two. "Build a new park if you must. Get your new deck, loges, the better amenities," Ken Coleman, 1978–1984 executive director of the Sox official charity, the Jimmy Fund, benefiting the Children's Cancer Research Foundation (now Dana-Farber Cancer Institute), said. "But keep the outfield exactly as it is from one pole to another. That's how people know Fenway, what they see on the tube."

The Red Sox kept the Green Monster, center-field Triangle, and low right-field wall—"Fenway's height, distance, look, feel," said Coleman—exactly as they were. The real change came off the field, the Sox enlarging and renovating—baseball's oldest park improbably preserved. The Townies entered 2012 with the major leagues' longest-ever sellout streak: 712 straight games. More than ever, going there meant coming home.

In 1948, ten-year-old A. Bartlett Giamatti of South Hadley, near Springfield, Massachusetts, entered Fenway for the first time. Leaving the tunnel, baseball's future seventh commissioner saw "emerald grass and bases whiter than I'd ever seen. As I grew up, I knew that as a building it was on the level of Mount Olympus, the Pyramid at Giza, the nation's Capitol, the czar's Winter Palace, and the Louvre—except, of course, that it was better than all those inconsequential places." As *Mercy!* suggests, it still is.

2

BEFORE THE FENS
(CIRCA 1850–1911)

However memory flags, baseball coverage began with print. As early as 1859, writers—"scribes," in the age's cant—described amateur teams playing at the White Lot between the White House and Washington Monument. In 1861, recently elected president Abraham Lincoln played hooky to watch ball on the Ellipse. Later, amateur pitcher William Howard Taft pined for the big leagues, settled for Lincoln's post, and saw his first game as president in 1909. "It was interrupted by cheering," read the *Washington Post*, "which spread from the grandstand to the bleachers as the crowd recognized him"—at three hundred pounds, hard to miss. Both governed as America shed wilderness for settlement. In 1876, nearly 8 in 10 lived on farms or in towns that relied on agriculture. By 1900, an immigrant tide swelled the urban postwar boom, Boston reaching nearly six hundred thousand people. To succeed, you needed to learn English. The best way was to read.

To Leonard Koppett, who emigrated from Russia and later authored the classic *A Thinking Man's Guide to Baseball*, the sport became the "essential and dominant feature of my Americanization," providing "the main opportunity to learn the new language and practice arithmetic."

Born in 1894 near Framingham, a Boston suburb, another future sportswriter hit fungos, traded American Tobacco Company four-color playing cards, and studied inning-by-inning scores in a telegraph office window. "[It's] how I learned baseball," said Fred Hoey, "and to read. To grasp Boston's love for the spoken word you need to know its written word."

For those keeping score, the geometry of the late-nineteenth and early-twentieth-century diamond bred the *Saturday Evening Post*, *Collier's*, and month-

6

ly *Baseball Magazine*. You could buy the annual *DeWitt's* and *Bull Durham* and *Spalding's Official Baseball Guide* and *Beadle's Dime Base-Ball Player*, edited by Henry Chadwick, "The Father of Baseball," which included rules, regulations, a scorebook diagram, and a plea not to gamble. The weekly *Sporting Life* and St. Louis–based *The Sporting News* (*TSN*) took a fractured game and somehow made it whole. "You'd inhale it all," said Ken Coleman, another to-be Sox Voice, "then go back to the daily writers." There were many to return to.

In New York, Grantland Rice was aka Grannie, the courser of the press box. Damon Runyon, a Salieri of the short story, inspired the musical *Guys and Dolls*. Heywood C. Broun wrote the syndicated "It Seems to Me." James Isaminger's "Tips from the Sporting Ticker" was penned in Philadelphia. Detroiter Harry G. Salsinger's "The Umpire" stemmed from the old French word *nom-pere*, meaning "one who is without peer." Charles Dryden coined "Washington: First in War, First in Peace, and Last in the American League." Each let you see faces harden, hear players jabber, feel pressure creep.

In Boston, the printed page disproportionately made baseball *our* game, bub, and don't you forget it. Jacob Morse (Harvard 1881) wrote for the *Daily Globe*, *Herald*, and *Post*, became secretary of the New England Baseball League, and helped found *Baseball Magazine*. From 1883 to 1937, William Sullivan (Harvard 1882) was *Globe* sports editor, city editor, and managing editor. In 1898, Edward Stevens, former *Boston Times* man and 18-year *Herald* baseball editor, died at 48: to the *Globe*, "one of the widest known writers on the national game in the country," siring "the custom of going away with the home team on its trips to other cities." All would have liked to be paid by the pitch.

By 1911, the new Baseball Writers' Association of America listed eleven Hub scribes from seven daily papers. Walter Barnes Jr., Boston's "local representative," and R. E. McMillan wrote for the *Herald*. Others were Morse, the *American's* I. S. Clark and A. H. C. Mitchell; *Journal's* Herman Nickerson; *Post's* Arthur Cooper and Paul Shannon; *Record and Advertiser's* Carl Barrett; and *Globe's* Melville Webb and BBWAA treasurer Tim H. Murnane. In 1978, Murnane became a Hall of Fame J. G. Spink award recipient for "meritorious contributions to baseball writing." Jack Kavanagh wrote in *Sports Heritage*: "Never before had such a baseball reporter won such affection, such renown."

A quarter century earlier, actor Robert Young had said, "I feel drawn to television like a man to the falls in a canoe." Hyperbole drew Murnane. Born June 4, 1851, in Naugatuck, Connecticut, of Irish émigrés, he signed a contract at 18 to catch with Stamford, later pitched and played outfield with nearby Middletown, Philadelphia, Boston, and Providence, and retired with the 1880 Capitol City Club of Albany, New York. Murnane was "a very fast runner and a sure catch," a writer said. The *Globe* noted his "peculiar style of running. It was not so much running as bounding. He went along in a series of lopes, covering ground at a wonderful rate," leap-frogging one fielder set to tag him near the bag.

In 1873, Murnane toured Europe with the Philadelphia Athletics of the National Association of Professional Baseball *Players*: baseball's first pay-for-play league. Kavanagh hailed "masterly fielding . . . against the British cricketers," whom Tim twitted for "well tried, old chap"—politesse toward an error. In Philadelphia, "they would have cried, 'take him out, the bonehead!'" Murnane created and managed the Union Association Boston Unions, headed the New England League, was first vice president of the National Association of Minor Leagues, and served the National Board of Arbitration: funny, sunny, burly, broad, white-maned, and Irish-brogued—the Silver King.

In 1885, His Majesty founded the local sports *Boston Referee*. In 1888, hired by the *Globe*, Murnane wrote until his death in 1917, becoming, author Louise Lyons said, "baseball's best-known name. The copy desk wrestled his spectacular inventiveness of baseball language into a semblance of English." Tim had perspective, tolerance, and charm. "After all, boys will be boys," he said, "and you know we're none of us perfect."

Boston's "patriarch of the national pastime," Kavanagh wrote, was atypical of the era. Many reporters were pleased to have any team buy food, drink, and dame. "The saloon and the brothel are the evils of the baseball world at the present day," said Chadwick. Coverage was quid pro quo; writer, as hack and flack, covering up, not covering, a player's fast-lane life. As *Sports Illustrated* (*SI*) later said, such consensus fueled "America's great *divertissement*." Few complained, not knowing what they missed.

Murnane's Industrial Age baseball was quite different than his country. From 1865 to 1901, national income quadrupled. Alaska hailed its first major gold strike. George Westinghouse and George Eastman built empires based on generators and film, respectively. "People here are far less raw and provincial than their fathers," said *The Nation* of America at age 100. By contrast, primitive baseball parks and grounds linked cow dung, a single deck, no bleachers, and fences at a lot's edge.

The game had begun in 1845 with Alexander Cartwright's first town team of amateur gentlemen: the Knickerbockers of New York. "No wonder," said Hall of Fame librarian Jim Gates, "he was called his game's founder." By the early 1850s, most cities along the Eastern Seaboard had one club, even two. In 1862, William Cammeyer opened the first fenced—enclosed—field in Brooklyn's Williamsburg section: Union Grounds augured Flatbush as a franchise more byzantine than most. Outfield distances were five hundred feet. The exception: a one-story building, 350 feet from home plate, in play *inside* the right-field fence.

The 1866 national champion A's were said to pay three players. In 1869, the Cincinnati Red Stockings became the first solely professional team. "With pros, you had to pay them," Gates continued. "That meant getting people to watch, which demanded wooden parks," including bleachers. By 1871, the new National Association (NA) had eight enclosed parks, and America 93,252 miles of railroad track. In Boston, rail lines to Hartford and Providence intersected the NA charter Red Stockings' South End Grounds—aka Boston Baseball, Union Baseball, or Walpole Street Grounds.

A Hall plaque reads, "Boston is the only major league city to field a team every year since professional baseball's start." In 1876, the NA succumbed to the National League of Professional Baseball *Clubs*—the distinction counts—inking players by contract. The Red Stockings, Reds, or Red Caps, later called Beaneaters and Braves, stayed at South End Grounds as a National League (NL) charter member: the only team beside Chicago continuously active to this day.

Optimist: The glass is half full.

Pessimist: The glass is half empty.

Cubs' fan: When's the glass going to spill?

The Hub's NL glass was full until a new century replaced the old.

Boston manager Harry Wright waved each 1872–1875 NA pennant. On April 22, 1876, he beat Philadelphia, 6-5, in the National League's debut. Next week the Red Caps uncorked their first game at home, losing to Hartford, 3-2. A year later Arthur H. Soden became president, 1877–1878 and 1883 titles preceding the first of six park renovations, including scrapping the press box to bulge capacity, writers something to take or leave. Even had the Red Sox then existed, the Nationals would have likely reigned.

1879: Tommy Bond forged his third straight 40-victory market—"the big cheese," wrote Murnane. 1894: Hugh Duffy batted .438: baseball's highest single-year average. Five 1891–1898 flags fueled interest, Charles (Kid) Nichols seven times taking 30 games. "[Jimmy Collins] reinvented third base," said Ken Coleman, "first to play away from the bag." Tommy McCarthy dropped flies on purpose to force runners: ergo, the infield fly rule. "Sliding Billy" Hamilton popularized the stolen base. Even accident begot precedent. A Detroit batter's two-strike foul tip lodged in catcher Mike Hines's mask. Umpire Van Court called him out, saying Hines snared strike three. Canning convention, NL Boston changed the game.

Its funhouse was 6,800-seat South End Grounds II: "a breakthrough," noted TV's History Channel *Ballparks* of a twin-spired roof and six spires above the upper deck. "For the first time attention was paid to architecture. It looked like a place where armored knights, not players, fought." Sullivan Tower dwarfed right field, spectators watching gratis: When Soden raised the *wall*, freeloaders raised the *tower*. On May 15, 1894, it joined 20 other wooden parks to catch fire in the decade, most begun accidentally by discarded cigars or matches. The Beaneaters moved to Dartmouth, or Boston Congress Street, Grounds, their Everest Bobby Lowe's big-league first four homers in a game. "The fans went wild," Murnane wrote. "They stopped the game and showered $160 worth of silver on Bobby." When Lowe singled in the eighth, a wiseacre jibed, "What's the matter, Bobby? Getting weak?"

On July 20, the Red Stockings returned to find South End Grounds III shrunk by an insurance shortfall: damage valued at more than $75,000 but covered for barely half. "What a difference!" added future *Herald* writer and Sox announcer Leo Egan of the spartan one deck, right-field incline, and cigar factory behind the bank. It presaged a turning of the page. Hubball was about to mean a very different team.

In 1889, Rutherford B. Hayes mused, "If Napoleon ever became president, he could make the office what he wished to make it." A decade later, with William McKinley president, baseball's newest major league wished to dent the National. Since 1884, the UA, AA, and Players' League had folded. Surviving: the Western League of Detroit, Milwaukee, Minneapolis, and St. Paul; Ban Johnson, president. In 1900, he renamed it (American League), put a club in Chicago (White Sox), moved Grand Rapids to Cleveland (vacated by the "Senior Circuit"), and swiped other ex-NL parks (Baltimore and St. Louis). The Americans needed only to build fields in Chicago, Philadelphia, and Washington. "New parks usually cost a lot of money," Johnson thanked extinct NL teams. "We got theirs by default."

Originally Ban intended to ban the AL in Boston. Instead, learning that the NL hoped to revive the AA, make *it* the second major league, and put a team there, he relocated his proposed Buffalo club and added the charter Pilgrims to new owner Charles Somers's three other clubs: "something of a Mr. Money Bags to the new league," wrote Henry Berry. In 1901, the Pilgrims (later Puritans, Plymouth Rocks, Somersets, Speed Boys, Americans, and 1908– Red Sox) opened 11,500-seat Huntington Avenue Grounds. Owned by the New Haven Railroad, it had an in-play tool shed, popgun right field (280, later 320, feet), and un–Fenway Park footage (left, 350 feet; left-center, 365 feet; center, 530, ultimately 635; and right, 280, later 424).

Pilgrims' progress depended on definition. The team flunked the 1906–1908 and 1911 first division. In apposition was Denton True Young, or Cyclone (Cy), referring to his fast ball, starting Boston's 1901 (10-6 loss at Baltimore) and Huntington's investiture (Pilgrims 12, A's 4). Young still ranks one-two all-time in Sox wins (192), losses (112), earned run average (2.00), complete games (275), and shutouts (38). One reason: Somers's coal, lumber, and shipping balance sheet. Like Hessians, Young, pitcher Bill Dinneen, catcher Lou Criger, infielders Fred Parent and Hobe Ferris, and outfielders Chick Stahl and Buck Freeman left other teams to hurl, bat, and field. The NL Hub's Jimmy Collins crossed over to play third and manage. "[Braves' ownership] don't like to pay players much," Stahl said. The future Sox, who also didn't, did.

In 1903, Somers sold to Milwaukee lawyer Henry Killilea, whose first game foretold a 1970s announcer: "Here we are in the bottom of the fifth. Boy, I wish I was *at* the bottom of a fifth." Boston faced alcoholic A's pitcher Rube Waddell, just off "a bender," Collins said. "We're going to bunt the hell out of him—run his arse all over the park." The first-place Pilgrims domineered the AL leader board: Freeman, in homers, total bases, and RBI; Patsy Dougherty, hits and runs scored; Young, victories a third straight year. On October 1, baseball commenced its then-best-of-nine first World Series.

"We can beat Pittsburgh no matter *how* good [Honus] Wagner is," shrilled regulars at Boston's McGreevy's 3rd Base Saloon. "Enough said," railed owner Michael McGreevy, renamed Nuf Ced, who on occasion danced atop the dugout. The Sox fan club—the Royal Rooters—traded jibes, sang for a glad hand, and did not discriminate. They drank alone, with strangers, and with friends.

Merriam-Webster's defines *fan*, derived from the Greek *fanatic*, as "a person whose extreme zeal, piety, etc. goes beyond what is reasonable." The Royal Rooters were not always reasonable, though their intuition was in tune. "Honus, why do you hit so badly!" they jeered to the song "Tessie." "Take a back seat and sit down. Honus, at bat you look so sadly. Hey, why don't you get out of town?" At 36, Young threw the first-ever Series pitch. Before Game Five, up 3-1, a Pirates player gave Nuf Ced an umbrella, saying, "You'll need this to ward off our base hits. Who are you going to beat us with, that farmer Young?" Cy tilled an 11-2 rout, pivoting the Classic. Boston won, five games to three—to Berry, "one of baseball's greatest upsets"—given later history, a Sisyphean boulder pushed up the hill.

In 1904, Theodore Roosevelt was reelected president—to one of his six children, "a mix of St. Vitas and St. Paul." That April *Globe* owner Gen. Charles Taylor bought the Pilgrims to busy his saintless son, John—said a columnist, "a habitué of the fleshpots of Boston." Ironically, Taylor Sr. turned Murnane from unfriendly fire to friendly witness. "Tim had favored the Braves," the *Globe's* William Sullivan said. "Now his coverage changed. He loved the military, and that's what the General was."

On April 19, Boston's American League Patriots Day twin-bill outdrew a same-month Braves home double-header, 36,034 *v.* 5,667. Closing Day inverted 2003's Tim Wakefield *v.* Aaron Boone: The New York Yankees' (née Highlanders) Jack Chesbro, 41-12, wild-pitched Lou Criger home with the Pilgrims' flag-waving run. Such a year deserved, and got, a postscript. Giants manager John McGraw had won the NL pennant. "We don't play minor leaguers," he now said, killing the Series. *The Sporting News* crowned the future Sox "world champions" by default.

"Plan for the next year and make a devil laugh," a Czech proverb says. By 1907, Boston's plan starred a divine Pilgrim Landing. Roger Angell described Roberto Clemente "playing . . . close to the level of absolute perfection, playing to win but also . . . as if it were a form of punishment for everyone else on the field." He could have meant Tris Speaker, at 19 trading his hometown of Hubbard, Texas, for the Hub, later Cleveland, and .345 lifetime average, 3,514 hits, 792 doubles, 436 stolen bases, 449 assists, and 4 unassisted double plays—a record for an outfielder. "The Grey Eagle" played in 1,065 Sox games. Nuf Ced's regulars barely missed a day.

By 1900, the NL had juggled 31 franchises. Boston's 1876 charter team changed nicknames as dizzily: Beaneaters became Doves (for owners George and John

Dovey), Rustlers (W. Hepburn Russell), and Braves (after James Gaffney bought them in 1913. "Gaffney was a fearless Tammany Hall pol," said O'Neill, "so people called him a Brave"). The team became the Bees (1936), Braves redux (1941), built Braves Field (1915), named it the Bee Hive (1936–1940), and in 1953 left Boston for Milwaukee. In late 1907, the Pilgrims appropriated an ex-NL Hub moniker: "From now on, we'll wear red stockings and I'm grabbing that name Red Sox," John I. Taylor said, planning a new mostly steel, concrete reinforced house on the property of the Fenway Realty Company.

On September 24, 1908, another park, Harvard Stadium, staged the Old-Time Professionals *v.* Old-Time Amateurs, teams including Worcester, Harvard, Yale, MIT, and Lowells and Boston Nationals, after "Boston business and professional men decided a game between pros and novices would be a good attraction," read the *Post*. A photo shows Murnane, son Horace, and future Hall of Famers Tommy McCarthy, Jim O'Rourke, and A. G. Spalding. In 1910, Murnane began editing the *Wright & Ditson Baseball Guide*, saying that "after a lapse of a quarter century we appear once more in the baseball world." It cost 10 cents, advertised in the Red Sox scorebook, and relapsed after 1912.

Huntington Avenue Grounds closed October 7, 1911—Red Sox 8, Senators 1—before what the *Washington Post* termed "a few hundred thoroughly chilled" of the wistful and devout. Northeastern University's athletic facility now occupies the site. A plaque marks the former left-field foul line. A bronze statue identifies old home plate: "Cy Young. At this site in October 1903 baseball's winningest pitcher led Boston to victory in the first World Series."

The World Series Exhibit Room, in the Cabot Cage, recalls historian Allan Nevins, in another context, daubing "an America now so far lost in time and change that it is hard to believe it ever existed. But it did"—and does, one mile to the north and west.

3 THE HUB'S NEW HUB
(1912–1919)

Eye an American football field: 53½ yards wide and 100 yards from one goal line to another. Study a pro basketball court: 94 feet long by 50 feet wide, its basket 10 feet high. A tennis court is 78 feet by 36 feet, net height and service box size identical. Baseball only decrees 90 feet between bases and 60 feet, 6 inches from home plate to the mound. Elsewhere, look backward, angel. "Thanks to Alexander Cartwright," said former commissioner Bowie Kuhn, "the outfield distance, fence height, and space between the seats and lines vary." Parks could do as they liked. Some were liked better.

In 1908, vaudevillian Jack Norworth wrote "Take Me Out to the Ball Game." Baseball's first steel and concrete ballpark, Shibe Park, opened next year in Philadelphia. By 1923, Forbes Field, Comiskey Park, Fenway Park, League Park, Griffith Stadium, the Polo Grounds, Crosley Field, Navin Field, Ebbets Field, Wrigley Field, Braves Field, Sportsman's Park, and Yankee Stadium—in all, 14— also rose from the grid of city streets. "Each fit on an urban parcel, which made for some unique angles," said the late author Michael Gershman. "Ballparks assumed a symmetrical form as they took on the lines of their property."

Brooklyn USA resembled a pinball machine. A berm flanked Cincinnati's left-field wall. St. Louis's summer furnace warmed the Cardinals and Browns. For a half-century, such Xanadus of personality sired "an infinite feeling for the spirit of the past," wrote Ellen Glasgow, "and the lingering poetry of time and place." Added Gershman: "Your uncle Sid and your aunt Thelma that you love and that you see two or three times a year, well, you see John Franco 80 times a year, or Mitch Williams, or Mark McGwire. You know more about them than you know about your family. In a sense, they *are* your family." The classic park was the street where they lived.

In Jack Benny's old TV show, a bank robber, pointing a gun, demands, "Your money or your life!" Benny: "I'm thinking. I'm thinking." In the Fens, money built a grandstand and wooden wings flanking each line beyond the infield. "It's in the Fenway section, isn't it?" said John I. Taylor. "Then name it Fenway Park." On April 9, 1912, the Sox beat Harvard, 2-0, in a snowy exhibition. After two rainouts, the Townies beat New York, 7-6, in an April 20 inaugural five days after the *Titanic* sank. First pitcher: Buck O'Brien. Batter: Highlanders' Guy Zinn. Star: Tris Speaker, driving in the winning run. More than twenty-seven thousand opened a two-story drawer of oaken seats and overhung roof and jigsaw of an outfield fence.

As *Globe* political guru Martin F. Nolan has written, Fenway "was the centerpiece of the 'Emerald Necklace' of parks designed by noted architect Frederick Law Olmstead, a planned environment of babbling brooks and green vistas." Outside, the *plat* designed by architect James McLaughlin and built by the Charles Logue Building Co. for $650,000 resembled an apartment building. Like most classic parks, it abutted streets—here, Lansdowne and then-Jersey—siring asymmetry. Center field was 488 feet from the plate, falling to 1930's 468 and 1934's 389. Right-center's 380 became 1955's 383. Before 1940's 380 built-for–Ted Williams bull pen, center's deepest corner—aka the Triangle—measured 550, 593, and 420 in 1922, 1931, and 1934, respectively. "Ironically, given its reputation for offense," Ned Martin said, "at first the park liked pitchers."

Only right and left field—initially, 314 and 324 feet; now, 302 and 310— helped a pull or opposite field hitter, as Fenway's first homer showed: Hugh Bradley "clearing the improbable 10-foot [left-field] Wall because [Lansdowne] was squeezed by the multilined pathway of the Boston and Albany Railroad," wrote Nolan. It was fronted by a 10-foot incline—Duffy's Cliff, for outfielder Duffy Lewis. Smead Jolley fell chasing a carom: "They taught me how to go up the hill, but nobody taught me how to come down." Center's 18- and right-center's 9-foot height, respectively, dipped to 3 at the right-field pole. Six cleared pre-1976's center-field barrier: Hank Greenberg, May 22, 1937; Jimmie Foxx, August 12, 1937; Bill Skowron, April 20, 1957; Carl Yastrzemski, May 16, 1970; Bobby Mitchell, September 29, 1973; and Jim Rice, July 18, 1975. Incrementally, offense rose.

In 1934, ownership cut the cliff; raised the Wall to 37 feet, 2 inches; ditched wood for steel and concrete; and put tin over a framework of two-by-four wooden railroad ties. Hitting them, a ball might kangaroo toward the infield. Hitting tin, it deadened and dropped down. A new hand-operated scoreboard listed each bigs inning-by-inning game and used bulbs to signal balls, strikes, outs, hits, and errors. The 1936 Sox added a 23-foot-7 net to protect Lansdowne windows—a grounds crew ladder helping to retrieve home runs. Each seat had a good view—if you weren't behind a post. A large-for-the-age 35,000 capacity ran through 35,300 (1947) via 33,357 (1961) to 2012's night 37,495 and day 37,067.

In 1912, the Red Sox more than doubled Highlanders' attendance. Robert Lowell wrote, "If youth is a defect, it is one we outgrow too soon." Outgrowing Huntington, the Red Sox found Fenway a virtue, as long as the Olde Towne Team won. It began to straightaway.

Each decade writes stories in which baseball has been rich: 1960, Bill Mazeroski sears the Yankees; 1975, Carlton Fisk's *touché*; 1988, Kirk Gibson limps to the plate like Walter Brennan, swings like Hank Aguirre, then dings like Tom Mix; 1990s, pinstriped dynasty; post-9/11's 2001 World Series elegy; Boston's 2004. The early Red Sox treated failure like root canal, taking the 1912, 1915–1916, and 1918 Series. Then–recent Harvard graduate T. S. Eliot called April "the cruelest month." The best Sox month, October, accented pitching, defense, and speed.

In 1912, former outfielder Jim McAleer and league secretary Bob McKay replaced John I. Taylor—and player/manager Jake Stahl pious Patsy Donovan, who often said, "Tut tut, boys, don't say those words." Instead, a *Globe* account said that Catholics and Protestants "threw punches over religion." The infield yoked Stahl, Steve Yerkes, Heinie Wagner, and Larry Gardner. Lewis, Speaker, and Harry Hooper caught everything in their time zone. Batting .383, Speaker won a Chalmers car as MVP. A half-century later John F. Kennedy called a group of Nobel Prize honorees "the most extraordinary collection of talent . . . that has ever been gathered together at the White House—with the possible exception of when Thomas Jefferson dined alone." The Sox 1912 "extraordinary collection" was a Kansan-turned-paladin.

Cooperstown fetes 1905's 31-9 Christy Mathewson, 1934's 30-7 Dizzy Dean, and 1968's Bob Gibson 1.12 ERA. Smoky Joe Wood's 1912 34-5 rivals each. In September, he beat Walter Johnson, 1-0, in a huckster's beau ideal. Asked who threw faster, the Big Train laughed, "Ain't nobody faster [than Joe]." The Series opened at the Polo Grounds after the Royal Rooters marched through Times Square again singing "Tessie": "Carrigan, Carrigan, Speaker, Lewis, Wood, and Stahl. Bradley, Engle, Pape, and Hall. Wagner, Gardner, Hooper, too. Hit them! Hit them! Hit them! Do boys, do!" Wood won, 4-3, returning to Boston ahead of Rooters special railroad cars—the "John Barleycorn Excursion." The Series tied 3-3-1, Fenway oversold. The Rooters lost their seats, shouted "To hell with Queen Victoria!" and fought mounted police, crushing the bleacher fence.

A ballad says: "Being Irish means laughing at life knowing that in the end life will break your heart." The finale broke the Giants'. On October 16, Wood allowed a top of the tenth-inning 2-1 run. Leading off the bottom, Clyde Engle lofted to center-fielder Fred Snodgrass, who dropped the ball. With one out, Christy Mathewson walked Yerkes. In 1908, Fred Merkle's base-running gaffe had cost McGraw a pennant. Speaker now gift-horsed a foul pop between first baseman Merkle and catcher Chief Meyers, who froze as it dropped untouched.

Reprieved, Tris singled to tie the game. Plating Yerkes, Gardner's sacrifice fly ended it, 3-2. The ex-Pilgrims had again found shore. Already Fenway evoked a fielder crouched, batter cocked, and pitcher about to throw—above all, the belief that there was nowhere else you would rather be.

"If you want a friend in Washington," Harry Truman said famously, "get a dog." The Braves wanted their *own* classic park. In 1914, they bought the Allston Golf Course (on Gaffney Street), left South End Grounds III on August 11 (scoreless tie, called by darkness), and began to build a home (using 750 tons of steel and 8 million pounds of concrete). An infield cave-in buried a dozen horses and mules. Problematic was where to play while their $1 million playhouse rose. Raising a hand, the Sox offered Fenway. That September, 74,163 saw a separate two-team admission double-header.

On July 4, the Braves trailed by 15 games. Five-foot-five shortstop Rabbit Maranville bared the first basket catch and a .246 average. Only Joe Connolly ended the season batting over .300. Compensating, ex-Cub second baseman Johnny Evers won the last Chalmers MVP car. "They did it *slow*, but *fast*," Casey Stengel said of the 1969 champion Mets. He could have meant the '14 "Miracle Braves," waving the flag by 10½ games—a makeup of 25½. In the Series, they took a 3-0 game lead over the 1910–1911 and 1913 champion A's. "Wonder what they're doing?" skipper George Stallings mused before the final. "Packing or puking?" Likely both: Evers's single sealed a 3-1 sweep.

On August 18, 1915, Boston beat St. Louis, 3-1, in 40,000-seat Braves Field's debut, thousands turned away. Inside: an uncovered pavilion down each line, single-deck-covered grandstand behind home plate, small circa 12-man-size "Jury Box," and grass mowed high. Trolley cars on the Commonwealth Avenue line reached the park. A stucco building with ticket arches housed the business office. A ground-level scoreboard covered the left-field fence. Once New York's Johnny Rawlings and Bill Rariden hit through-the-wall homers: "gaps kept open by a lazy scoreboard boy," future Voice Jim Britt explained.

Foul lines approximated a taxi ride—402 feet. Center field seemed as far as Framingham—550. Ty Cobb did a double take: "Nobody will ever hit a baseball out of *this* park." (For two years, nobody did.) At Fenway, Larry Gardner would rather discuss his 1912 World Series–winning fly. He couldn't recall the pitch— only, what it had meant: "Four thousand twenty-four dollars and sixty-eight cents [his Series winning share] which just about doubled my earnings for the year."

In 1913, Wood fell on his throwing hand and broke a thumb. With surgery, he might now miss a month. Then, told to exercise it, Joe soon could barely lift his arm. He retired in 1915, succeeded by Ray Collins, Dutch Leonard, Babe Ruth, and Carl Mays. "If batters didn't have bad luck against the Red Sox," a writer paraphrased, "they'd have no luck at all." That year, even *fifth* starter Wood had a league-leading 1.49 ERA. The 1915 Series *v.* Philadelphia was as minimalist, each Sox victory decided by a run. Craving cash, the Townies moved Games Three and Four to larger Braves Field, Lewis nabbing Gavvy Cravath's each-day 400-foot drive. "At Fenway, both are long gone!" rued the Phillie. "Why didn't we play these games *there?*"

Boston won in five. Lewis, Speaker, and Hooper got 20 hits, had 8 RBI, and made Cobb dub "their play among the best I've seen in many a year." It had to be as good a year later, and was.

In 1913 and 1916, respectively, Joseph Lannin bought the Red Sox from Jim McAleer and dealt Speaker to the Indians. "Ban Johnson as league president wanted Cleveland to have a winning team," Bill Carrigan explained. Boston won the 1916 pennant, used Braves Field in October, and won a five-game Classic. Carrigan—the team catcher, therapist, and only Sox skipper to win two straight Series—then retired "to take care of my business affairs down in Maine." A photo shows him punching a sliding Cobb in the face with the hand that held the ball.

Ty was out—cold, removed on a stretcher. "Now you know," Carrigan said, "why they call me Rough Bill." In time, they called Ruth the Behemoth of Biff, Caliph of Clout, Colossus of Club (or Sport), Bambino (also Big Bambino), Goliath of the Grand Slam, King of Clout, Slambino, Sultan of Swat, and Wizard of Whack.

The fox taken as a naïf who ends up taking the taker first seemed comically misplaced. At one point, Boston boasted college men Hooper, Gardner, Lewis, Carrigan, Ray Collins, and skipper Jack Barry. Babe was a grade-school dropout, a teammate saying, "Look at that big ignorant ape, making all that money." To Gardner, ignorance was small potatoes: "We're all making more because of Babe." Jimmy Cannon later praised his "burst of dazzle and jingle, Santa Claus drinking whiskey straight and groggy with a bellyache caused by gluttony." In 1914, Ruth arrived in the Hub to pitch, next year turning part-time hitter. The sunny-dark legend beat Johnson five straight times, pitched 14 innings to take 1916 Series Game Two, yet wowed Murnane by his 6-foot-2 and 215-pound power. Perhaps it was personal: "Here we are," said the Silver King, "one big guy covering another."

Glendower, in *Henry IV*, Part 1: "I can call spirits from the vasty deep." Hotspur: "Why, so can I, or so can any man. But will they come when you do call them?" Murnane found the "vasty deep" February 7, 1917, going to see *Eileen*, Vincent Herbert's only Irish operetta. Entering Boston's Shubert Theatre, he tumbled to the ground. A physician told his wife, "It is useless to raise his head—he is gone," of a cerebral hemorrhage. The page 1 *Globe* bannered: "Murnane Drops Dead in Theatre—Baseball Editor at Globe for 30 Years—Notables of Game Pay Tributes of Esteem." His memorial service, Jack Kavanagh wrote, "would top them all," and to many did, packing suburban Brookline's St. Aidan's Church.

That September, a crowd of 17,119 at Fenway raised $14,000 for Murnane's widow and four children. Fanny Bryce and other Ziegfeld Follies sold programs before an All-Star team–Sox exhibition: Townies, 2-0. Contests included throwing, won by Cleveland's "Shoeless" Joe Jackson's 396⅔ feet; "bunt and run," Boston's Mike McNally, 3½ seconds from home plate to first base; fungo hitting, Ruth, 402⅔ feet; and around the bases, the Tribe's Ray Chapman, 14 seconds. Will Rogers lassoed team members. Boxing champion John L. Sullivan coached first. Next month the AL donated a monument at Murnane's suburban Roslindale gravesite. His Hall plaque hails a "tireless and enthusiastic worker. Authority on Baseball and one of game's best friends," the past still whispering. As Cole Porter wrote, "So good-bye, dear, and amen."

In June 1917, Ruth walked the first batter, argued, got bounced, and was relieved by Ernie Shore, who retired the next 27 Senators. Jack Barry entered the service, replaced by Ed Barrow, who asked, "Babe, how would you like to play left field?"—and pitch. In 1918, Ruth batted .300, finished 13-7, and helped take another pennant. The World Series ended early, America at war. Boston beat the Cubs for its fifth world title—four since 1912. Babe's then Series record climbed to 29⅔ straight scoreless innings. At the time, it seemed a portent. In fact, the Sox had depleted providence.

In seven years, Boston twice had led in league attendance, twice won more than a hundred games, and beat the Yankees 18 straight times—in New York. "Dynasty," Ned Martin said. "It's the only word that applies." History is said to repeat itself. The Sox may have tired of repeating themselves.

In November 1916, Broadway financier and former bellhop Harry Frazee bought Lannin out. Later, writer Fred Lieb called Frazee "the evil genie." At first, he mimicked Father Christmas. The new owner was said to have bid $60,000 for Walter Johnson, chiming "nothing is too good for the Boston fans." Oh, say, Harry could even see: the first to play "The Star-Spangled Banner" before a baseball game— September 9, 1918. His real song was greed.

Next year, Ruth's 29 home runs *v.* the rest of his team's *four* broke the NL and AL home run record of 24 and 16, respectively—also, Ned Williamson's 27 in 1884, making Babe wonder if "they pitched him underhanded." Ruth led in RBI and slugging percentage, hit a then record four grand slams, and became, George Will wrote, "the man who gave us the category . . . superstar." Unmoved, Frazee sold Babe in January 1920 to New York for $125,000 and a $300,000 loan for such would-be Broadway hits as *My Lady Friends*—aptly, farce. Barrow soon became Yanks general manager, warning him, "You're going to ruin the Red Sox in Boston for a long time."

In late 1919, Frazee had held Babe Ruth Day. "I had to buy my wife's ticket to the game," the honored said. "Fifteen thousand fans show up and all I got was a cigar." A truckload of sold or dealt Townies helped the Yankees win their first Series in 1923: of 24 players, *11* former Red Sox. The 1924 *Reach Guide* rued, "Last season Boston reaped the fruits of four years desolation by the New York club. And for the second time in [AL] history, this once-great Boston team . . . fell into last place, with every prospect of remaining in that undesirable position indefinitely." Nine times the 1920–1933 Sox finished last. A Politburo member asks about the Kremlin's latest five-year plan. The bureaucrat replies, "Ask me in the thirteenth year."

In 1923, Frazee sold the more Dead than Red Sox to ex-Browns general manager Bob Quinn. The Victorians called a cloudless spell "Queen's Weather." Quinn lamented, "Every time *we* get ready for a big crowd, it rains. They even have an expression here when it does: 'Here comes *Quinn's* weather.'" It was especially dark one day when Yankees scout Paul Krichell saw Lou Gehrig, 19, play for Columbia against Rutgers. Back at The Stadium, Krichell told Barrow that he had seen another—ouch—Ruth.

Frazee died in 1929, New York mayor Jimmy "Beau James" Walker at his side, the pinstripes exteriorizing baseball. The Sox hoped only to avoid miming the Atlantis of the American League. In 1925, 18 BBWAA writers covered Hubball for nine daily papers, including the new *Transcript* and *Christian Science Monitor*. Among them: *Globe* cartoonist Gene Mack and the *Post*'s Fred Hoey, the latter soon to change one day job for another.

LONG, COLD WINTER (1920–1938)

Tennessee Williams called the 1930s "that quaint period . . . when the huge middle class of America was matriculating in a school for the blind." Baseball matriculated in a 1920s school for the ear, public address (PA) announcing—"sound in the round"—joining print, portrait, and photograph. Cleveland's Tom Manning stood behind home plate, using a megaphone to voice each battery. Later PA men divulged starters, scoring rules, and substitutions. New York's Bob Sheppard seemed existential, not merely excellent. Ebbets Field's Tex Rickard sired Texisms. "A little boy has been found lost." Leaving, "the pitcher don't feel good." Coats draped the left-field wall. "Will the people along the railing please remove their clothes?" The Senators' Phil Hochberg called baseball "bigger than all of us, including people you hear but seldom see." Radio was as big, long before the Red Sox first full-time PA, Jay McMaster, began in 1958.

In 1895, Guglielmo Marconi had sent and received his first radio signal in Italy. 1909: Explorer Robert Peary messaged, "I have [found] the pole." 1912: The RMS *Olympic* telegraphed a wireless operator: "S.S. *Titanic* ran into iceberg. Sinking fast." For three days and nights that operator, David Sarnoff, sent "updates to reporters and friends," later founding the National Broadcasting Company. On Election Night 1920, commercial radio debuted on Westinghouse Co.–owned fifty-thousand-watt KDKA Pittsburgh. Going back to the future: Losing vice-presidential nominee Franklin Delano Roosevelt boasted a born-for-wireless tenor, language-made-literate, and ability to make the complex simple.

Needing programming, "We thought sports a natural," said Westinghouse foreman Harold Arlin, 26, who bought a seat at Forbes Field, used a telephone as microphone, and spawned baseball play-by-play August 5, 1921. What did Arlin sound like? None live to tell. How many sets heard him in Western Pennsylvania? No one knows. Often the transmitter failed, or crowd noise squelched him: "We didn't know if we were talking in a vacuum." Also vague: "If we'd do more ball. Everything was so primitive."

In October, writer Grantland Rice aired radio's first World Series: KDKA feeding WJZ (later WABC) Newark and WBZ Springfield, Massachusetts. In 1923, a 25-year-old piano player on lunch break from jury duty entered New York's AT&T Building, won a WEAF audition, and called the World Series, ending Monday. By Saturday he got seventeen hundred letters: said a later peer, "like a zillion now." Ten percent of Americans owned a radio. Sixty-three percent did by 1933. "How do you do, ladies and gentlemen of the radio audience?" said its first leading man, ending, "This is Graham McNamee speaking. Good night all"—less waif of a moon than bright noon sun.

McNamee aired foreign visits, coronations, presidential inaugurals, political conventions, and 10 sports including boxing, track, marbles, the first Rose Bowl, and 1923–1934 Series, conceding "being an entertainer first and a broadcaster second." Ring Lardner typed, "I don't know which game to write about, the one I saw or heard Graham McNamee announce." A reporter could be heard saying, "McNamee, will you pipe *down*?" Such bile evinced fear: Why pay to read about a game if you could hear for free?

Baseball had meant books and guides, periodicals like *Vanity Fair* and *Liberty*, and above all, daily papers. "All sports'd been in print," said McNamee. "Now, increasingly they meant a box." Network radio aired just the Series, then All-Star Game, so local teams filled the void. Arlin voiced the Pirates through 1924, sporadically and laconically. St. Louis's France Laux spoke with a soft tone and clipped precision. In Detroit, wrote Bob Latshaw, "there wasn't an afternoon . . . that anyone could escape Ty Tyson." The first *daily* Voice, Hal Totten, called the first game (April 23, 1924) of the first station (WMAQ) to air an entire home schedule (Cubs').

"Notice the cities with regular-season coverage," said the great *Boston Globe* radio/TV sports critic, 1968–1996's Jack Craig. "They were in the Northeast quadrant, since that's where the majors were," radio knitting Baker Bowl, Death Valley at Yankee Stadium, League Park's sole two-flagpole site, and Griffith Stadium acreage grown heavy with base hits. "Everyone else just got the Series," said future Voice Ernie Harwell, raised in Georgia with the wireless on his mind. Picture America as a clock: the bigs ran from 12 to 3. The Hub could be found around 1:15 on your dial.

Contrary to urban myth, Ben Alexander and Charles Donelan, not Fred Hoey, called Boston's first baseball—the 1925 Braves randomly on WNAC 1230, later 1260 and 680, AM. Next year Gus Rooney covered the Red Sox Opening Day. By 1927, Hoey aired each Sox and Braves home game live, Gerry Harrison on "color." Print could be still life, deadened by monotony. Radio was a sonata, falling lightly on the ear. In a house, bar, or office, "say a guy hit to left-center," said Harwell. "Mentally, you saw it all—runners, ball in play, relay, catcher bracing." Nothing happened till the announcer spoke.

Born in Boston, raised in suburban Saxonville, near Framingham, Hoey saw his first game at 12—the 1897 Beaneaters v. Baltimore Orioles Temple Cup Series. Later he played amateur and semipro baseball; ushered at Huntington Avenue Grounds; aired the Yankee and later Colonial Network; officiated high school and college football; was a Boston Garden executive and New England's Mr. Hockey as player, coach, manager, referee, and announcer; and wrote 1909–1946 schoolboy and big-league sports for three of the Hub's then six daily papers: the *Journal*, *Herald*, and *American*.

Si Burick spent 54 years "without a promotion" as *Dayton Daily News* sports editor, covering, among other things, the 1975 Boston-Cincinnati Fall Classic. About that time the lover of puns said, "I may be shy, but I am not retiring."

Each day the rabbi's son drove 50 miles to see his Reds. A friend asked why.

"When you walk in the press room," answered Burick, "just listen."

"Listen for what?"

Si: "The noise of the typewriters"—and Western Union's ticker tape. "It either mesmerizes, or it doesn't."

It mesmerized Hoey, hired in 1926 by WNAC's John Shepard III. "No one can tell how this man will sound," a colleague said. "But *we* can tell that *this* man knows his sports."

Most must prove themselves in a new career. At 41, Hoey was spared. In 1930, Shepard officially formed a baseball-high 22-affiliate Yankee Network, "issuing the ultimatum that no major sporting event in New England should be neglected in the broadcasting schedule of that network," said *The Sporting News*, "and that each event must be broadcast only by a recognized authority in those sports. As a result, the Yankee Network boasts a staff of sporting announcers second to none in the country." Hoey became its poster boy: wintry, curt, and credible.

Til Ferdenzi, of suburban Walpole, later worked at the *New York Journal American* and NBC Sports. "Fred was a part of the sporting scene," he said, "not trained, with a dry, biting voice." Pro: local boy made good. Con: his subjects of discussion bombed. Thomas Wolfe called presidents between Lincoln and TR "the lost Americans: their gravely vacant and bewhiskered faces mixed, melted, swam together. . . . Which had the whiskers, which the burnsides, which was which?" Like their one-size-fit-all, you tried in Hoey's first decade on the air to tell one team from another.

In 1928, the Braves owner, judge Emil Fuchs, built an eight-foot inner fence—"a wall within a wall"—from left- to right-center field. Behind it sat six thousand new bleacher seats: "the idea," said Jim Britt, "less to swell capacity than to hit." One game Les Bell thrice homered—and barely missed another. By mid-June, 47 balls once in play had cleared the fence, "the problem *who* hit them!" said Leo Egan—the visitors, not Braves. Upset, the team moved the wall in and out. Would Braves Field be an Ebbets bandbox? A Comiskey Park–like canyon? "They should have made the inner fence portable. It'd have saved a lot of work." Fence height varied, too: right field, 10 feet; left, at a scoreboard, 64; right-center, 20, 25, then 19. Ibid., climate. The Braves planted trees behind the wall to hide railroad smoke. In New England's 1938 hurricane, a Cardinal drove to center—and catcher Al Lopez caught it behind the plate.

Six times the 1925–1938 Nationals placed seventh or eighth in an eight-team league, once drawing three thousand per date. In 1929, Fuchs added managing. "A manager must no longer chew tobacco and talk out of the side of his mouth," he said. "The club can't do any worse with me as manager than it has done the last few years." Naturally, the Braves placed last for the first time since 1924.

Once, loading the bases with none out, Fuchs beseeched the help. "What shall we try for now, boys?"

"How about a squeeze play?" one player said.

The judge's face reddened. "No," he said, "let's score in an honorable way."

In 1930, rookie Wally Berger hit 38 homers. In 1935, Ruth ended his career as a Braves scrub and suit. Ninety-five watched a July game there, salary preferred to commission. Next year, hosting its first All-Star Game, NL Boston was hurt by bungling—a frequent guest. "The team said that all *reserved* seats had been sold out," read the *Globe*, "which led many to believe the game was sold out," creating 12,000 empty seats. Voicing on the Mutual Radio Network, Hoey forgot to mention them. "A big crowd," he misled, "which is why there's so much noise."

The age's Red Sox were as losable. 1926: Fenway bleachers beyond third base burned and were not rebuilt. 1927: Ruth outhomered AL Boston, 60 to 28. 1929: The Hub OK'd Sunday ball, a nearby church excluding Fenway. Braves Field became the Sox Sabbath kirk. 1930: The Yankees dealt Cedric Durst, who hit .245 and retired, for Red Ruffing, Cooperstown '67. 1931: Boston put numbers on its uniform. 1932: The Fens staged its first Sunday game. "I was seven," Ken Coleman said. "The Yanks romped, 13-2." Tip O'Neill called baseball "Boston's real religion," affirmed when Marty McManus was named Sox skipper while still at Mass. His Townies won 95, lost 153, and became the unquick and the dead.

In 1931, each team honored Hoey's river of handclapping through New England: "the first to work on a network [Yankee, also Colonial, simulcasting on flagship WAAB] covering the game, giving the play-by-play of the home games of both Boston clubs," said *TSN*. "He has one of the biggest daily followings of any announcer in the country because of the large number of stations served." Baseball's first Radio Appreciation Day gave Hoey a special gift from Fuchs; gold, Braves players; purse and pipe, Sox management and players, respectively; and $3,000 certificate of deposit, listeners.

The honoree noted his two "main" principles—"to describe exactly what he saw, without embellishments, and never to criticize a player or umpire," said *TSN*—ignoring conflict between the first (report) and second (minimize a muffed play). Few challenged the man whose mail "keeps the mailman loaded down." By now, Fred *meant* Boston's two-headed baseball Janus.

By the end of 1931, Hoey had aired a record number of broadcast hours: 1,920, including that year's 320, "drawing word pictures of the major league games at Boston and [ferrying] them to countless thousands of baseball fans," said *TSN*. The only fly in Fred's ointment was "a double-header on a hot day," the booth temperature hitting 95 degrees. Hoey never complained on air, only about how "in articles on broadcasting, he has yet to read where concentration is a vital part of the work." Ads were easy, but extempore material "requires concentration on the subject, which is severe strain not only on the eyes, but on the nerves." For a long time Fred had tried to ease the latter.

"Yes, he liked the sauce, or so I've heard," said Coleman. In 1929, Rabbit Maranville said, "There is much less drinking now than there was in 1927. I know because I quit drinking on May 24, 1927," unlike Fred. In 1933, CBS Radio awarded his first network gig—the Giants-Senators Series. Grateful, Hoey reached the booth before Game One, gassed. "By the fourth inning," Ferdenzi said, "garbled, incoherent, he was yanked off the air." Fred blamed "a bad cold," vowing never to work again without a tin of throat lozenges.

Unhorsed, he came home a conqueror. "In Boston, where people knew about his drinking, all was forgiven," said Coleman. "There'd been thousands of letters to papers saying, 'How dare you hurt our Fred?' No criticism, just total acceptance, because he was looked on as 'The Man Who Does the Games.' That was *something* then," criticism subtler. "I literally never heard *anybody* say—and I grew up, like we all did, listening to Fred—'Gee, I think he's lousy.'"

Raised in Holyoke, 90 miles west of Boston, Jack Buck didn't. Hearing Hoey, the future Redbirds royalty wondered how green the Green Monster was. Ned Martin "never met or read much about Fred, but I feel like I *know* him," he said in 1986, "because people still swear *by* him. In love or anything else, the first, you don't forget." Coleman hadn't, even before losing an eye at age 12 to a BB gun. The accident replaced one hero, Jimmie Foxx, with another. "I wanted to *be* Hoey, had to fight not to talk *like* him. We were both so desperate to succeed," Coleman said, later learning balance, "laughing at yourself because the sun doesn't rise and set on an individual." Fred never learned.

Like a centerfold, TV dims imagination. The wireless brightened it. Amid satellite, YouTube, iPod, and Twitter, it is hard to re-create radio's effect. A garage owner in Ferdenzi's Walpole upped volume "to blast it around town." Stores put long-legged speakers on the sidewalk, Hoey bursting from a box. Cars fender-bended one another, stopping to hear The Man. Ferdenzi paused a long moment. "Sound coming from a box was all we had"—buoying even a franchise about which he said, "There was a running joke that the Red Sox had three teams—one there, one coming, and one going—*always* a lot of broken-down players bought from other clubs."

The 1932 Red Sox finished 64 games behind New York: home attendance 182,150, topped by 2011's first five *games*. Fenway was a joke, Til added. "Many chairs lacked bottom parts. There were bird turds on the seats. The structure was beautiful—just pathetically kept up. And if you wanted a long nap—boy, this was the place to go." Late that year the AL went looking for relief.

Bob Quinn owed it $150,000, cash to concessionaire Harry Stevens, and a mortgage to Yankees owner Jacob "Colonel" Ruppert. Thomas Austin Yawkey's uncle had owned the 1904–1907 Tigers. "They've got money. I don't think the league should be a bank," Detroit successor Walter Briggs told other owners, who asked A's coach and former White Sox second baseman Eddie Collins to contact his ex-prep schoolmate. As Eugene O'Neill might say, he soon asked Yawkey to make a humble thing his own.

"Why don't you look into the Red Sox?" Collins said. "I know Quinn will sell it to the right man." Intrigued, Yawkey, nearing 30, said he "had already laid out a great deal of cash, and wondered if he could carry the mortgage into the following year." Ruppert agreed, "Glad to have you in the league." Boston then swept a five-game home series from New York, the Colonel's lawyer calling Yawkey's to demand mortgage payment—"Jake doesn't like to lose five straight." The new Sox owner sent "that SOB" a check.

Yawkey, T. A. to intimates, was shy, kind, courteous, and used to getting his way. He named Collins vice president and general manager, then eyed Washington's seven-time All-Star, 1930 AL MVP, and 1933 pennant-winning shortstop-skipper. At a meeting, Yawkey cornered Senators don Clark Griffith: "What will you take for Cronin [Joe, to play and manage]?"

"Why," Griffith said, "he's just married Mildred [Griffith's niece]."

Puzzled, Yawkey asked matrimony's relationship to making a 6-4-3. Griffith dodged: "Oh, I couldn't sell Joe. I'd want too much money for him anyway."

"Put your figure down on the back of the envelope and see," T. A. said. Griffith wrote, "Of course, I won't have anybody to play shortstop, so you'll have to throw in Lyn Lary." A postage stamp cost three cents, scotch $2.50 a quart, rooms at a Boston luxury hotel $3 nightly. Cronin cost a record $250,000, which Yawkey gladly paid.

"As much as he saw himself as the man who owned the team, to most he *became* the team," Bart Giamatti said later. Red Sox offices open onto Yawkey Way—Jersey Street before 1977. A plaque reads: "THOMAS AUSTIN YAWKEY / 1903–1976 / IN MEMORY / FROM THOSE WHO KNEW HIM BEST / HIS RED SOX EMPLOYEES."

Another plaque hails: "EDWARD TROWBRIDGE COLLINS / 1887–1951 / HIS ABILITY, LOYALTY AND INTEGRITY / AS A PLAYER AND AN EX-ECUTIVE IN / THE GAME OF BASEBALL WILL FOREVER / BE REMEM-BERED AND CHERISHED / ERECTED BY THE BOSTON RED SOX 1951." Finally: "NEW FENWAY PARK BUILT—1912 / RECONSTRUCTED—1934 / BOSTON AMERICAN LEAGUE BASEBALL COMPANY / THOMAS A. YAWKEY PRESIDENT."

T. A. renovated until a four-alarm blaze virtually wrecked construction on January 5, 1934. Another $750,000 then painted fences, cleaned aisles, reinforced supports, and heightened the Wall: to pitchers, still too close. "If you were a right-handed pitcher and threw sidearm, your knuckles would scrape it," said Yankees left-handed Lefty Gomez. Advertisements appeared: "Be wise. Clear heads choose Calvert [whiskey]"; "Lifebuoy stops B.O." Nothing stopped Fenway's April 17, 1934, rebirth—or August 12 and 19 and September 22, 1935, double-header 46,766, 46,995, and record 47,627, respectively—"never-to-be-equaled crowds from fire laws and league rules," Curt Gowdy said, "tightened after World War II."

Collins said, "We'll get you [Cronin] players. You work with them." Yawkey secured pitcher Wes Ferrell and his brother Rick, a catcher. In 1934, 1938, and 1940, émigrés Bill Werber, Joe Vosmik, and Doc Cramer rapped two hundred or more hits, respectively. As a boy, Lefty Grove taught himself pitching by throwing rocks. The student went 31-4 in 1931, left the A's in 1934, was named the Red Sox all-time best left-handed hurler in 1969, and holds Fenway Park's highest winning percentage: .764.

Foxx also joined Boston from Philadelphia, hitting 222 of 534 career dingers. In 1938, a then Townie record 50 (35 at Fenway) made him sole AL righty to twice hit that many. Double-X led in average (.349, .405 at home), slugging (.704), total bases (398), and RBI (175, including a Hub lunar 104). On April 18, the Sox opened *v.* the Yanks at home, Hoey saying that Foxx, "in great condition," would "have a terrific year"; Rudy Vallee had just cut a record; New York's Red Rolfe and umpire Bill Summers were "the two best cribbage players in the American League"; and Sox pitcher Jim Bagby—"B-A-G-B-Y"—had "good physical equipment. And he can hit that apple, too."

Audio preserves Hoey's staccato pace, informality, and detail. Cramer's *vitae* took twenty seconds. The pinstripes' Frank Crosetti was 27, "stands 5-10, weighs 165, lives in San Francisco," and had missed spring training with a "very bad charley horse." George Selkirk was one of two ALers born in Canada. Lou Gehrig, in his 1,966th straight game, had batted .345 in Florida; started "his wonderful run" June 1, 1925; and presently hit a drive that curved foul—"fortunately." A Yanks sleeve insignia "advertised the 1939 New York World's Fair." Boston's Ben Chapman hit the Screen. "There's one! It may be a home run! It may be in there! It may be in there! It is a home run! Well, well, well!" said Fred. "The ol' ball game is tied up!"—final, Sox, 8-4.

A safety was "a beautiful single," "dandy hit," or "sweet" double. A foul stirred "some very lively ducking." New York's Charlie Ruffing became "Ruff"; skipper Joe McCarthy "McCardy"; Fenway Park "pahk"; last season "lahst." The hitter stayed in the batter's box; pitcher, didn't dillydally; game, *moved.* Hoey still had time to reference "birthdays and births today"; the minor leagues, more frequently than now; and telegrams from Florida, Long Island, Manchester, Bangor, Bar Harbor, Cambridge, Newton Center, and Worcester, "and the boys at the vets"—a veterans hospital.

In one break, he pimped for Socony Oil's "drain out winter service." In another, Fred said "to appreciate baseball, you have to see it. To get Kellogg's Corn Flakes, you have to taste it." A year earlier he malapropped, "Homer Hit a Foxx!" Tomorrow meant a 10:30 a.m. and 3:30 p.m. Patriot's Day twin-bill. Since 1919, Boston only twice had placed even fourth. In 1938, it finished second. "They were getting better, people actually thinking, 'Hey, we might *win* something,'" Hoey said. Yawkey felt so, endorsing a 1936 poster: "After waiting eighteen years," it read, "Boston now has pennant hopes." Not to hurry: Deferred, the Red Sox were seldom dull.

Ordered to sacrifice bunt, Chapman swung, hit into a double play, and told Hoey, "I don't sacrifice." Cronin lined a bases-full ball off Indians third baseman Odell Hale's head to shortstop Billy Knickerbocker, who tossed to second baseman Roy Hughes, who threw to first: triple play. A popular film showed an actor trying to sleep in an upper berth by humming "[Senators outfielder] Heinie Manush, Heinie Manush . . ." Traded to Boston, Manush was serenaded on the train, recalling, "I never got much sleep."

In 1937, Bobby Doerr had joined the Sox, later regretting "Mr. Yawkey's trying to buy a pennant." Failing, T. A. eventually built it from within. By then The Man Who Does the Games no longer did.

"Take Bob Costas, add Al Michaels, and stir in Vin Scully," Ken Coleman said. "That's how big Fred was in 1920s and '30s New England." Fancy them being axed, abruptly and unexpectedly, after a decade where a bystander could walk down the street, windows open, and not miss a pitch. Boston's First couldn't believe he was gone, until he was.

Hoey knew his region, with its small shops and cobblestones and Indian names. He knew how and what to shill—"When you mention Fred," said Ken, "people remember Kentucky Club pipe tobacco and Mobil's Flying Red Horse, like Curt Gowdy later with Narragansett beer"—and how to instill Euripidean concern.

He was old-shoe, thus wearable. "Fred's phrase was, 'He throws to first and gets his man,' which he used constantly," said Coleman, "and I think I subconsciously picked it up because I'd listen to past tapes and *I've* used it." He had "an electricity—a feeling Fred conveyed that baseball was special"—which survived early radio's cuckoo land. Most games began at 3 p.m. At 6, the score might be tied: ninth inning, bases full. The Yankee Network still broke for news.

Above all, Hoey forged a New England style followed by Gowdy via Coleman and Martin to Dave O'Brien and Castiglione: respect and understatement over schlock, kitsch, and shtick. "Because of a general attitude toward sports and listening habits developed from certain announcers, different regions are receptive to varying styles," said Jack Craig. If forced to choose, just the facts, ma'am, trumped a wild and crazy guy. None of this mattered to The Men Who *Sold* the Games.

In late 1937, John Shepard III sacked Hoey. Earlier that year Franklin Roosevelt had used his unorthodox, overhand lob to throw out the first ball at the All-Star Game. Under "all politics is local," FDR now said that Hoey should remain. "Letters, telegrams, phone threats, and pickets forced Shepard's hand," said Leo Egan. "All of it went to his head." Fred got a raise.

A year later he sought another, Shepard replying, "Oh, by the way, you're fired." Again rallying, the public "hooted and threatened a boycott." Socony Oil and General Mills ignored it, wanting *their* Voice, not Kentucky Club's and the Flying Red Horse's. "Radio was changing," Coleman said. "Fred paused a lot," lacking gloss. "Plus, the booze affected him over time."

Newly fired as Cardinals manager, Frank Frisch joined Sox announcer Tom Hussey. Childless, unmarried, Hoey began a decade of last things and final bows:

pee-wee hockey, emcee, and journalism—again. "On the air he *was* Boston base-ball," mused Coleman, "and it was not the same without him." In *Death of a Salesman*, Willie Loman says, "And that's the wonder of this country, that a man can end [up] with diamonds on the basis of being liked." Liked, Hoey ended up alone.

He died November 17, 1949, at 64, having recently retired from the *Boston American*, in his gas-filled home in suburban Winthrop, of "accidental . . . asphyxiation," reported the *Boston Daily Globe*. "He was generally credited with building up baseball broadcasting to the lofty spot it holds in the American sports scene today."

5 A MOST ERUDITE REBIRTH (1939–1950)

Between 1939 and 1950, 10 major league teams won at least a single pennant. The other six made the first division. Hailing the last decade to have a .400 hitter or a pitcher complete more than 35 games in a season or the Indians take a World Series; first with a black major leaguer (Jack Roosevelt Robinson), one-armed outfielder (Pete Gray), and playoff (1946 and 1948); first/last to have a 56-game hitting streak and a "Subway [strictly, Streetcar] Series" west of the Mississippi, respectively, you recall Matthew Arnold saying of the playwright Sophocles that he "saw life steadily, and saw it whole."

In 1939, Jack Benny and Fred Allen anchored NBC Radio. In more than fifteen thousand cinemas, Hope and Crosby dueled Rogers and Astaire. Clark Gable said, "Frankly, my dear, I don't give a damn." Fox Movietone Newsreels was film's website of the time. NBC presented baseball's first telecast: Columbia *v.* Princeton at Manhattan's Baker Field. Lou Gehrig left the Yankees lineup after 2,130 straight games. In Boston, rookie Frank Frisch ad nauseam uttered, "Oh, those bases on balls." Each walk brought a perfectionist turned fussbudget closer to the Hub.

Chemistry fuses molecules. The Red Sox' and Braves' Jim Britt fused nouns and verbs and terms. "No broadcaster better used the English language," Ken Coleman felt. Many thought Britt savvy. Some found him snooty, panning the average Joe.

"There are twenty-seven thousand *persons* here today," Jim observed.

"Jim, you always say *persons*," Ken replied. "Is there a reason you don't say *people* or *fans*?"

"Yes, *people* is correct," he stiffened. "And *fans* is correct. But *persons* is *more* correct." English is taught in public school. Britt taught much about public life.

By 1921, the 11-year-old son of the Burroughs Adding Machine Co. board chairman and chief executive officer had lived in San Francisco, Erie, Baltimore, and Denver. In 1933, the English and philosophy major and speech and history minor graduated from the University of Detroit. Britt père made computers and calculators. Calculating, fils got married and earned a USC law degree, but he never took the bar.

"Why not?" a writer said.

"Because I'm an idiot," Jim barbed, his term not apt till the 1950s.

Returning to Detroit, Britt taught high school debate, public speaking, and dramatics, telling Detroit's college football coach its announcer was a dud. "Show me you're better," the coach dared him. Soon Jim cracked Notre Dame football radio, heard of a job at WKBW Buffalo, and aired the Triple-A Bisons: home games live; line charges making road coverage iffy. Solution: wireless telegraphy "[enabling] play-by-play," wrote *TSN*, "within three seconds of the time it occurs."

A park operator in, say, Syracuse sent Morse code to 'KBW. *B1L* meant ball one, low; *S2C*, strike two, called. In studio, Britt *re-created* a game he never saw. A pencil tapping wood simulated bat hitting ball. The soundtrack featured background murmur. Infielder: "Come *on!*" Skipper: "Don't give *in!*" Fan: "You couldn't hit my *house!*" WBEN's Roger Baker re-created the same game, Leo Egan, a native Buffalonian, said, "but stayed a half-inning behind in case the wire broke. Not Jim." The young man in a hurry finished 20 minutes ahead.

Egan was, if not Oscar Madison, more carefree than Britt's Felix Unger. "Jim could be icy," said Leo, "hard to work with, and he didn't take kindly to criticism. But why should he? To a neutral observer, he didn't do much wrong." In February 1939, Egan came to Boston to write for the *Herald*, work at WHDH Radio, and call football from the roof of Harvard Stadium. "One day [in 1931] Ted Husing had been fired after calling Harvard's quarterback 'putrid' in a game there," he said. Another Voice left eight years later.

Save "bases on balls," Frisch's favorite mot was "take two and hit to right." By mid-1939, many wanted to take the "Fordham Flash" and raft him down the Charles. That October, Pittsburgh named Frisch manager, saving John Shepard from canning him. "I'd got Frank his job," said Egan. "Now I called Jim," still in Buffalo, "and said, 'Get down here for an audition, fast.'"

On November 10, WNAC made Britt, 29, sports director, a seeming pitch-perfect fit: baseball's grammarian, in the Athens of America, airing the 1940–1942 and 1946–1950 Red Sox and 1940–1942 and 1946–1952 Braves, each day signing off, "Remember, if you can't take part in a sport, be one anyway, will ya?" The National League deserted Boston in early 1953. Until then, Britt rued not what he called but a year he had not.

After Double X's record 50 homers in 1938, Bobby Doerr next spring told a rookie, "Wait till you see Foxx hit." Ted Williams replied, "Wait till Foxx sees *me* hit." Like Hoey, Jim missed 1939's debut of John Wayne in baseball woolies: ultimately baseball's greatest magnet since the Babe—at bat, quick, loose, and striking. Britt later said of the then rail-thin Splendid Splinter (aka Toothpick Ted), "He less *made* than *became* Red Sox history."

Williams first played ball in the second grade in San Diego. "I didn't even consider playing baseball practice. The most fun I ever had in my life was if I was hitting a baseball and if I could hit one—pow!—gee, that felt good to me." The Kid often carried a bat from class to class: "a school bat," Teddy Ballgame said. "I got there early enough so I could be there to get the bat and ball and wait for the kids to play."

At Herbert Hoover High School, Ted averaged .430, banging so many balls onto an adjacent lot that his team had to change fields. The Thumper—he had as many names as AL batting titles: six—signed with the hometown Padres, homered in each 1937 Pacific Coast League (PCL) park, and next year hit .366 at Triple-A Minneapolis. He awoke at night (to rehearse the Swing), wouldn't watch a movie (protecting vision), and still walked around with a bat (for feel). In batting practice, The Kid screamed at himself for missing a pitch or grounding out.

In 1939, Williams homered off lefthander Thornton Lee. In 1960, he dinged Lee's son, righty Don. Born 13 days before the Sox' then last title, Ted fanned *v.* an ex-Townie in his first two bigs at-bat. "Ruffing was sneaky fast. He threw with a little oomph and, boy, there it was! If you didn't realize this guy could throw and do so with less motion and effort and excitement, then it was by you." Already the Splinter knew how "as you get better at something you tend to like it a little more." Next up he ripped a double off Red.

Fiorello La Guardia said, "When I make a mistake, it's a beaut!" The 1939 AL Rookie of the Year hit .327, had 31 homers and 145 RBI, and tipped his cap.

"Yep, Ted waved it," said 10-year teammate Doerr. "But next year they started to boo him for hitting fewer home runs, and Ted got mad. To him, they were fair-weather"—"politicians," spit Williams, never doffing it again.

In 1939, a future politician, 15, memorized box scores, as he had since age seven. "My favorite park was Fenway," said George H. W. Bush. "It's nice to know that some things don't change," including awe for anyone who could *hit*, "something I never mastered at Yale." Batting eighth—"*second* cleanup"—Bush tried to teach it after packing up his red Studebaker in 1948 and leaving Connecticut for Texas. Wife Barbara carpooled players to Little League, giving umpires her mind. Eldest son George W. became Texas Rangers general managing partner. Leaving office in 1993, père gave speeches to help build his presidential library. Gratis was 1994's keynote opening the sadly short-lived Ted Williams Museum and Hitters Hall of Fame: "a dear friend," Bush said, "and the greatest hitter who ever lived."

By then, having seen his first Sox game in 1938, Bush's 1988 presidential foe was professor of political science at Northeastern University. Michael Dukakis still recalls his introduction to the Fens: "I was four and a half, Lefty Grove pitched, and my mother took me and my brother." Inspired by a grade-school principal—"like her second father," said Massachusetts's 1975–1979 and 1983–1991 governor—Euterpe Dukakis (née Boukis) is thought to be the first Greek American woman to graduate from an American university—Maine's Bates College. Baseball was not an elective. "I've never been so bored in my life," she told her sons at Fenway. "*You* come back—not me." They did.

Dukakis's father, Panos, immigrated to Lowell, Massachusetts, in 1912; graduated from Harvard Medical School; and became an obstetrician. Michael was born in 1933. At three, "I began swinging a bat." Later, he caught for Brookline's Baker School team in its "very well-organized system of eight-school league baseball competition in the sixth, seventh, and eighth grades. We'd play all the time"—listen, too. Dukakis recalls "as a kid working around the house and cutting grass with Jim Britt's voice on the radio loud enough so I could hear it above the sound of the push lawn mower wherever I was."

In Waterville, Maine, George Mitchell, also born in 1933, "knew the batting average and power stats of every Sox starter long before I knew the names of my state's senators." Like Bush and Dukakis, the future Bowdoin College graduate,

U.S. senator, and presidential emissary to Northern Ireland and the Middle East checked box scores each morning. "Then I'd look at the standings. If the Red Sox were in first place, I knew it was going to be a good day all around." In 1999, he missed the League Championship Series to remain in Belfast. "But after the Red Sox were beaten by the Yankees, I was glad to have been in Ireland."

Britt missed Boston's three best days of the 1930s: a July 7–9, 1939, five-game series in the Bronx. By coincidence, Yankee Stadium would host the July 11 All-Star Game, AL manager Joe McCarthy staying in his hotel room July 7 to prepare. Nine pinstripes studded the 25-man league roster. New York baked in hundred-degree heat. What, me, worry? The Yanks led the Townies by 11½ games. Friday the Sox won, 4-3, Marse Joe laughing, "It's a 10½ game lead. This is too close for comfort." Next day he left his room, Boston winning a 3-1 and 3-2 double-header. "Who the hell are supposed to be the [1936–1938] world champions, us or the Red Sox?" McCarthy yelped, no longer the Good Humor Man.

On Sunday, nearly fifty thousand "cheer[ed] mainly for the Red Sox at every turn," read the *New York Times*. Added skipper Cronin, "We didn't dream of a [five-game] sweep—just, 'Let's win one and keep off the floor.'" Tripling and homering, Foxx helped hit the ceiling, 4-3 and 5-3, few knowing that Boston had never swept even *four* straight at The Stadium. That fall McCarthy won another Series. Next April 16 Britt's time in the Hub began: Brooklyn 5, Bees 0, at once—and future—Braves Field.

Emil Fuchs had left managing in 1930, replaced by Bill McKechnie, who preceded a comedian. Later, Casey Stengel told a U.S. Senate Committee, "I became the manager of several big-league teams and was discharged. We call it discharged because there was no question I had to leave." When a taxi struck him, putting Casey in the hospital, *Boston Daily Record* columnist Dave (the Colonel) Egan named the cabbie Hub "Man of the Year." After the 1939–1942 Braves placed seventh, "there was no question": Stengel "had to leave." Williams was more piqued by the 1940 Sox putting bull pens in front of the bleachers, shrinking right-center field. Said Britt, "Ted already loved Fenway's tiny foul ground [voiding would-be outs], center-field backdrop [no ads], and not selling seats above it [no white shirts to hide a pitch]." The 23-foot bull pen diminution—"Williamsburg"—made getting that was good even better. Williams hit .403 at Fenway in 1951 and 1957—and .428 in 1941. That did not assuage the Colonel.

To Dave Egan, Ted always pulled, walked too often, and was a pain in the patootie. He felt Yawkey another problem, said to drink, hire hangers-on, and treat the workforce too gently. "I can be hard," T. A. said, "but I'd rather not. I'd rather trade a man than cut his pay." Even Fenway took a hit, slow built-for-the-Wall batters like Rudy York putting the road Sox at sea. "Although he was with the team less than two seasons," wrote Martin Nolan, "York became the prototype of Fenway sluggerdom. Instead of first basemen, the Sox . . . for decades built a row of condominiums down the right-field line—Foxx, Walt Dropo, Vic Wertz, Dick Gernert, Mickey Vernon, Norm Zauchin, Dick Stuart, Lee Thomas, George Scott, Tony Perez [later Mo Vaughn and David Ortiz]." Yawkey succumbed, though the Monster was not his Great Wall of Boston.

Originally, he "wanted to hit and run," T. A. told writer Jack Mann. "Steal a base. That's the way I like to play the game. I say the hell with the fence and play as if you were in Comiskey Park." The Wall wouldn't let him, aides advised, so Yawkey built a team to fit its park. "We've done very well at home," he said, much later. "If we'd been able to play .500 ball on the road we'd have been a lot higher. But damn it, that Wall hurts; it has an effect on the organization from top to bottom. We have to go after players who have that Fenway stroke," then tried to pull on the road. "Hitters' habits are hard to break." T. A. smiled. "Williams is one guy we never tried to change."

The Kid's three-run ninth-inning homer won the 1941 All-Star Game, 7-5, Ted kangarooing around the bases. The Yanks clinched September 4, the early terminus making pressure interior: become the bigs' first .400 hitter since 1930. On September 27, the Splinter had a .3995 average—.400 in the record book—prior to next day's year-ending twin-bill in Philadelphia. "You got .400. Sit it out," said Cronin, who could have been talking Sanskrit. "I don't want it that way, I'll play," said No. 9, walking miles that night with clubhouse attendant Johnny Orlando. Ted whacked a homer, hit the loudspeaker horn, and went 6-for-8 to finish at .406, Britt and Tom Hussey re-creating in studio. "That day," Jim later said, "the Prodigy became the Legend." How to top the topper? In 1942, T. Ballgame took a .356, 36 home run, and 137 RBI Triple Crown.

Trained as a pilot, Williams joined the service like teammates Doerr, Dom DiMaggio, and Johnny Pesky. The farm showed Boston no longer trying to buy a pennant. If not enough—save 1946, it wasn't—"the Yankees' experience, defense, pitching, and finesse, but certainly not hitting, was the reason," said Ted. Doerr six times had more than 100 RBI, five years led the league in double plays, and handled an AL-record 414 chances sans error, but had a headache—literally. The Kid could be a chatterbox, especially with the "Silent Captain of the Red Sox," his name for the migrained second baseman. Finally Doerr demanded a 90/10 rule, getting to talk at least 10 percent of the time. In 1940, Joe DiMag's younger brother—bespectacled: thus "The Little Professor"—joined them. A song hyped, "He's better than his brother Joe! Dom-in-ic DiMaggio!" Nolan said, but "we didn't believe it," even when Dom earned the fielding kudo "Jesse James without the horse."

In 1942, the Oregonian who shined Doerr's shoes as a PCL Portland club-house boy became Sox shortstop—to Cronin, "our table setter"—leading the AL with 205 hits. John Michael Paveskovich batted as high as .335, hit 8 of his life-time 17 homers off Fenway's right-field—aka "Pesky"—pole, and faced *one* 3-0 count in 4,085 at-bats, pitchers loathe to walk him ahead of Williams. "Each home game I'd see 'em swing," said Britt, "baseball arranging the schedule so Boston's two teams were never home simultaneously. Whoever was, I did live"—also WNAC's daily 6:15–6:30 *Jim Britt's Sports Roundup*, "a mix of straight report-ing, commentary, and in-studio interviews with newsmakers," wrote the Society for American Baseball Research's Mort Bloomberg: the Hub's highest-rated radio show till its host went to war.

Before 1976, the commissioner and sponsor, usually the Gillette Company, chose All-Star Game mikemen. On July 6, 1942, Britt aired his first Summer Clas-sic, with Mel Allen and Bob Elson—later partners: Allen 1946–1950, Bill Corum 1946, and France Laux 1948—noting the Polo Grounds' would aid Army-Navy relief. Leadoffer Lou Boudreau spanked Mort Cooper's second pitch: "There goes a long drive towards left field! That ball is given a real ride! And it is up in the stands for a home run!" Jim said. Four batters later a close pitch "very nearly shaved the letters *Detroit* right off Rudy's [future Red Sox York's] chest." Next pitch: "A drive goes towards right field! A long drive! And that ball is going in for another home run!"—Americans, 3-0.

The AL had "exploded like gun powder, pounding Cooper savagely." One pitch was "buckle-high." In time, the Cardinals righty "buckled down"—a "jinxi-fying hurler for wearing numeral 13 on his back." He might "be another Jerome—Dizzy—Dean." The Kid was already "thumping Theodore Williams." Catcher Birdie Tebbetts was "a fire-eater"; Jimmy Brown, "hit in the small of the back";

Spud Chandler, the "American League twirler." John Mize "stepped back almost imperceptively" to avoid a pitch. Mel Ott "cocks that right foot well up in the air." Art Fletcher was "a celebrated sign-stealer and Yankees third-base coach par excellence." Prose shone, neither bogus nor offensive: final, 3-1.

That week the future Navy intelligence officer taped a Yankee ad tweaking his "take part in a sport" slogan: "If you can't take part in a war, be one [a good sport] anyway, will ya?" Stationed in the South Pacific, Britt attacked enemy-held Nauru Island, hit another U.S. plane in mid-air, and barely made his base in the Ellice Islands, only eight surviving. Meanwhile, General Tires and Atlantic Refining carried Hubball over 20 stations: flagships WNAC and WAAB and 8 other Bay State outlets; 3, Maine and New Hampshire; 2, Connecticut; 1, Rhode Island and Vermont. In 1945, George Hartrick joined Hussey, Narragansett Brewing replacing General Tires: "each re-created," said Leo Egan, "no crowd noise, a ticker tape heard. 'Ball one, ball two,' very staid."

Like Hoey, the pinch-speakers faced a quirk. "Didn't matter if it were Babe Ruth hitting," said Hussey. "From 5:15–5:30 daily the show *Superman* pre-empted our description" of wartime castoffs, rookies, 4-F and/or Triple-A. Britt's martini mixed twist and bite. Hussey's and Hartrick's resembled a glass of milk. In March 1945, a platoon from the Ninth Armored Division crossed the Rhine, a half-globe from Britt. On September 2, Douglas MacArthur signed Japan's surrender decree. "We have had our chance," he said. "If we do not now devise some greater and more equitable system, Armageddon will be at our door." Nirvana briefly stood at Fenway's.

In 1946, Britt returned to WNAC, a year later moving to the Sox' new flagship: WHDH 850 AM and its smaller-than-Yankee's 11-outlet network of Chicopee, Pittsfield, and Worcester, Massachusetts; New Britain and New Haven, Connecticut; Augusta, Bangor, and Lewiston, Maine; Concord and Manchester, New Hampshire; and Providence, Rhode Island. "Money," he explained the change. On any station, most were pleased to have Jim back. Future *TSN* columnist Wells Twombly heard Britt when he was thirteen: "He [made] baseball sound better than red-haired girls with freckles." Coleman listened "growing up, then to the other fill-ins in the war. Returning, Jim seemed so erudite—of all the broadcasters I've heard, with the greatest command of language." Others felt patronized: "He was used to being top dog," said Ken. "Some thought him spoiled."

For 28 years, the Sox had been a hero of every dog that was under. The '46ers made up for lost time. Tex Hughson won 20 games for the second year. Dave (Boo) Ferriss was 25-6 and said to be ambidextrous—"amphibious," said Yogi Berra. York helped at bat (119 runs batted in) and in the dugout (telling Williams to hustle). Chastened—"Rudy knew about that little game you play with the pitcher"—The Kid wed .342, 38 homers, and 123 RBI. "By the time [the press] has completed its daily treatment of Theodore S. Williams," John Lardner wrote, "there is no room in the papers for anything but two sticks of agate type about Truman and housing, and one column for the last Greater Boston girl to be murdered on a beach."

Number 9 dinged Opening Day at Washington. On June 9, he hit Fenway's longest blast—502 feet, to right field—off the straw hat of Joseph A. Boucher, 56, a construction engineer from Albany in right-field bleacher section 42, row 37, seat 21. "The sun was in his eyes," laughed Britt. "It bounced a dozen rows higher, but after it hit [Boucher] in the head he said he wasn't interested," even when the seat was painted red. Next month Fenway finally hosted the born-in-1933 All-Star Game, eight Townies on the roster. The Kid's "treatment" touted two homers, one off Rip Sewell's blooper, or "Eephus," pitch, four of 14 AL hits, and five RBI: final, 12-0. Sewell threw the Eephus like a softballer "but could get it called for a strike," said Williams. "And I swung as hard as I could and the wind was blowing out." On Mutual, Britt chimed, "I can't believe it—but it's *gone!*"

Five days later Cleveland shortstop/skipper Lou Boudreau shifted all but his left-fielder to the right-field side of second base, trying to make Ted pay for thinking it unconstitutional not to pull. New England paid, too, 1,614,944 doubling the prior Sox attendance record. On September 13, Williams poked his only inside-the-park homer to clinch the pennant, 1-0, in Cleveland: "looking back, our last peak moment," said Britt, who, like his team, would reel. Since World War II, Nolan later wrote, "the Red Sox have brought their disciples to the foothills of glory a half-dozen times," notably:

> *October 15, 1946*—Enos ["Country"] Slaughter scores from first on a single [*sic* double] in the seventh game and St. Louis wins the game and the Series. In his only World Series, Ted Williams is outhit by a rookie catcher for the Cardinals, Joe Garagiola.
>
> *October 4, 1948*—The first American League playoff ends early as the Cleveland Indians pummel starter (at 8-7) Denny Galehouse and win the pennant, 8-3.

October 2, 1949—A team bulging with .300 hitters and two 20-game winners heads into Yankee Stadium needing one victory out of two. They
lose twice, 5-4 and 5-3.

September 26, 1950—Again with steady hitters and two 144-RBI sluggers,
the Sox challenge, but the Yankees eliminate them a week early.

By then, Britt knew the drill.

"A year ago, I'm in a war," he said in 1946, "and now I'm on the World Series,"
with Mutual's Arch McDonald and Bill Corum, picked by Gillette, the commissioner, and participating teams. York's tenth-inning belt won the opener. Next day
The Kid, elbow hit and swollen by a pre-Series exhibition pitch, didn't get out of
the infield: Cardinals, 3-0. "We'll handle this thing back at Fenway," Cronin said,
and did, 4-0, skipper Eddie Dyer emulating the Boudreau Shift. A Hub paper
screamed: "WILLIAMS BUNTS!" Game Four's laugher wasn't funny: Redbirds,
12-3. Boston took the next set, 6-3: Fenway's last Series till 1967.

At Sportsman's Park, St. Louis tied the Classic, 4-1, then led Game Seven,
3-1, until the eighth. Dom D. doubled to score the three-all run but jammed an
ankle sliding and was replaced by weak-armed Leon Culberson. What happened
next, to quote *The Impossible Dream*'s Coleman, became a "Red Sox tale of old."
Slaughter singled, headed for second base on a 2-1 pitch, and raced to third on
Harry Walker's hit to left-center field. Culberson relayed to Pesky, who turned
toward the plate and a) was or was not stunned to see Enos still running and b)
did or did not hesitate before throwing up the third-base line, Country scoring
the winning (4-3) run.

Returning East, Williams wept in his locked train compartment. Raised near
Philadelphia, the wretched A's and Phillies creating a "vacuum into which my irrational ardor for the Red Sox flowed," John Updike, 14, heard the final in the
family car in his high school parking lot. More than half a century later he recalled
how like 1903, 1912, 1915–1916, and 1918, the 7-20 favored Sox had expected
to win. Instead, losing bred habit. Ted won the 1947 Triple Crown; Joe D. became
MVP. That year paint—ergo, *Green* Monster—replaced tin ads on the Wall. On
June 3, Ferriss won Fenway's night debut. Cronin replaced Collins as VP/general
manager, "not firing a scout" in the next 11 years, said a writer. Replacing *him* in
1948: a manager who never played in the majors but played them like a bass.

"Twenty-four years managing, never in the second division," wrote Harold
Rosenthal of Joe McCarthy. "A .614 percentage—all-time best." The Yankees'

1931–1946 skipper won eight pennants and a record seven Series. Williams "couldn't wait to play for him," though Marse Joe had made the stripes wear ties, which Ted likened to a noose. McCarthy was a pragmatist, eating breakfast at 1948 spring training in a bright open-necked sports shirt and saying, "Anyone who can't get along with a .400 hitter is crazy." That is presumably how Joe felt June 12, trailing his old club by 11 games.

The Sporting News 1948 preview issue called Braves and Red Sox "television plans indefinite pending installation of equipment by the station." In late April, Channels 4 and 7—aka WBZ and WNAC, respectively—agreed to show each club. On May 12, Channel 4 "tried out [experimental] cameras for the first time at Fenway," said author Ed Walton, "few homes equipped yet with the expensive sets." Added *TSN*, "Two $10,000 television cameras were pointed down on the infield"—from behind home plate and along the first-base line.

On June 9, WBZ aired Massachusetts's TV debut—a 15-minute report from Braves Field. Six days later Britt, Hussey, and former Yanks pitcher Bump Hadley voiced Boston's first bigs telecast—Braves 6, Cubs 3. Fenway's late-June debut followed a 14-game road trip: "What a zoo," sniped Britt. "Ad spots didn't work, the camera missed the ball, but no one complained because coverage was novel." Egan became first to call an away TV game live, in Cleveland. Hadley, of suburban Lynn, foretold the Mets' Ralph Kiner, who named Howard Johnson Walter Johnson, Cary Carter Gary Cooper, and Milt May Mel Ott. Bump called one "ball going, going . . . and caught by Sam Jethroe in short center field," his regular Channel 4 show ending "heads up and keep pitching." Irregular was how Hub teams briefly achieved rough equivalence.

The 1947 Braves and Red Sox had drawn 1,277,361 and 1,427,315, respectively. The Nationals' Bob Elliott batted .317, had 113 RBI, and was MVP. Warren Spahn led in shutouts (7) and ERA (2.33). A year later pitching meant "Spahn and [24-15 Johnny] Sain and two days of rain." Eddie Stanky couldn't run, said Leo Durocher, "he can't hit, he can't throw, all he can do is beat you." The Troubadours—aka the Three Earaches—prowled the grandstand, a poor man's Dodger Sym-phony Band. SABR's Mort Bloomberg recalls "hiding my portable radio underneath the covers at night listening to Britt describe yet another 1948 heroic comeback staged by the Braves during their victorious pennant chase," drawing a record 1,455,439.

WHDH's now 19-outlet network included Gardner, North Adams, and Fall River, Massachusetts; Portland, Maine; Rochester and Claremont, New Hampshire; and St. Albans and Waterbury, Vermont—each alight about an all-Boston Series. On Saturday, October 2, the Sox downed New York, 5-1, moving a game behind Cleveland with one game left. Next day Detroit's Hal Newhouser beat the Indians' Bob Feller. Boston again won, 10-5, to force the first AL playoff—last till Bucky Dent. Boudreau started league-best ERA Gene Bearden, Marse Joe's criteria seemed more suspect: "You saw the bull pen today. I had everybody out there. Maybe I'll get the word tonight in a dream. Or better still, just find some nice little man and rub his curly head." In June, journeyman Denny Galehouse had beaten Cleveland. McCarthy now chose him over Ellis Kinder and Mel Parnell.

The Sox, 55-23 at home, won a coin toss to host the game. "A playoff there was like throwing the Christians to the lions," said Cleveland Voice Jimmy Dudley. The Christians won, 8-3, Boudreau homering twice to "keep Beantowners from a baseball bash," wrote Mets radio's Howie Rose, "that might still be talked about had both teams . . . squared off in the Series." Airing it was radio's immovable object, on 37 million receivers, and television's emerging irresistible force, quintupling in 1948 to 940,000 sets. Before videotape a camera had to tape a screen or monitor to record—a process called kinescope: "fuzzy, tube bulky," added Curt Gowdy, "so people threw 'em out." Little Britt TV endures. Radio does—Jim lyrical, musical, unpredictable, but not hyperbolic: as Huston Horn wrote of Mel Allen, an "indefatigable hinged-in-the-middle tongue."

Britt aired the DuMont Network National Football League (NFL); radio or TV Notre Dame; East-West and Blue-Gray Game; Rose, Sugar, and Cotton Bowl football; the All-Star Game; and Mutual 1948 and 1950 and NBC TV 1949 and 1951 Series, evoking Howard Cosell, once told "You're like shit. You're everywhere." In 2011, Rose found "a [radio] jewel waiting to be unearthed on [Internet] archives": 1948 Classic Games One and Five. "Chipper and hyper-professional," Allen set "[the opener's] scene amid . . . pre-game fanfare." *Queen for a Day* would air on the last out. *Gillette Cavalcade* sponsored "boxing, turf, gridiron, and this greatest of all sports spectacles." Names fill a psychic attic: Spahn, Earl Torgeson, Satchel Paige. A "Wigwam perched on the Charles." Braves Field looked out onto "Fair Harvard, Somerville, and downtown Boston." Introducing Britt, Mel termed him "full of verbal pyrotechnics." Said Howie, "If you never heard of [Jim] . . . neither had I. But this guy was a monster."

To Rose, "tapping Britt was a stroke of genius on [Mutual's] part, familiar" with each big-league team. His play-by-play "tour-de-force" had a "logical and hallucinatory stream-of-consciousness and . . . unique phrasings, baseball lore," and basso voice. Each batter had a hometown, even college, closed or open stance. Gene Bearden seldom "went a' cropper." Sain "dusted [Ken] Keltner's whiskers." Torgeson "wears eye glasses"—a rarity. The scoreless first 4½ innings took 48 minutes—now even rarer. Game One pivoted in the eighth. When Feller picked Phil Masi off second base, Bill Stewart wrongly ruled *safe*! Boudreau argued "with the umpire, who says, 'no, he's back in,'" said Allen. Tommy Holmes then "hit one down the third base line for a base hit—Masi heading home for the plate": Braves, 1-0. A day later Bob Lemon beat Spahn, 4-1. Next Cleveland won, 2-0 and 2-1, at its huge lakeside bowl.

Game Five wooed a then record 86,288, including "eight or nine thousand standees behind the portable fence," said Britt. Elliott's first-inning belt matched Boston's prior Series output. "A long drive to right field. [Wally] Judnich's going back! And it is a [three-run] home run!" Dale Mitchell replied in the bottom half: "And *that* one is a home run!" Braves win, 11-5. Back East, Sibby Sisti's ninth-inning bunt double play killed Boston's last-game rally: Cleveland, 4-3. "Take away one game," said Braves skipper Billy Southworth, "and we scored six runs all Series." *Ten* times Williams had at least that many RBI in a *game*—not surprisingly, Boston taking each.

In 1946, hitting got the Sox to the Series—.271 from April through September—and failed them in October (.240). In 1948, Britt reported the Braves' 34 runners left on base, Nelson Potter's batting, and the courses of Feller's pitch curricula. Paige "throws the ball every possible way but left-handed." Southworth was "a believer in the two-platoon system." Left to right forged the Braves' "outfield disposition." An incoming breeze was "an East Wind, we call it in Boston"—Britt "synonymous with ball," said Rose.

He was sure that "Britt could now pretty much pick up where he left off a half-century ago and not only be pretty much right at home but accepted by the entirety of Red Sox Nation." Much of it would still be cursing 1949.

That year Egan and Hadley joined daily radio/TV, the Sox added "more road radio games [said *TSN*] when no Braves game," and WBZ and WNAC telecast each home game—"coverage increasing," said Britt, "because interest was." Williams led the league in ten categories, including career-high RBI (159, with Vern Stephens) and homers (43). Dom D. styled a still–Sox record 34-game hitting streak. The infield swanked Billy Goodman (.298), Doerr (.309), Stephens (.290), and now third baseman Pesky (.306). Parnell won 25 games—a team lefty record. Kinder added 23, "drinking more bourbon and pitching more clutch baseball than anyone I knew," said a mate. The Sox averaged .282. No Yankees regular topped .287. How could Boston lose?

One way, Nolan wrote, was "pinstriped paranoia. When Joe Page lumbered out of the Yankee bull pen in the late '40s, he resembled King Kong and the Red Sox performed like Fay Wray. Tommy Henrich always made the clutch hit, or Gene Woodling did, or Yogi Berra." Another: fate. "If that old man [McCarthy] didn't lose those three pitchers [Ferriss, Hughson, and Mickey Harris to injury]," said stripes skipper Casey Stengel, "he'd a won a ton of pennants." Finally, as Santiago says to Manolin in *The Old Man and the Sea*, "Think of the great DiMaggio." On April 10, 1949, Joe limped off an exhibition—"a heel spur," Gowdy said, "could barely walk"—missing the first 65 games. On June 28, a Fenway night record 36,228 welcomed him. Hearing Britt, Bart Giamatti thought Yanks-Sox "one of those great American events, like the coming of snow or the end of school."

Not facing real pitching since September 1948, DiMaggio hit "a drive on the first pitch for a single!" said Britt. Later, he crashed a homer: Yanks, 5-4. A day later Boston led, 7-1, when Joe went deep. In the eighth, he "went over the Wall, Screen, and everything," Pesky said. "It might have gone to the Hotel Kenmore, for all I know": stripes, 9-7. Next afternoon DiMag hit a light standard. Number 5 made *Life* magazine's cover, America loving the geometry of the diamond. "When they referred to the Giants, it was the New York Giants," said HBO TV. "There was an American League team in St. Louis, and a National League team in Boston." The 1949 Americans drew 1,596,650 fans—more than they had, or would until 1967, from Kittery, Maine, and Mystic, Connecticut, and Montpelier, Vermont. Behind by 11 games July 4, the Sox climbed within a game and a half of New York by Labor Day. On September 27, Boston took a one-game lead. The famous old contenders then each won two of a three-game series. Still to play, October 1–2: the Townies in the Bronx.

As we shall see, Gowdy was then Allen's pinstriped aide: "As long as I live, I'll never forget the dueling volleys of that weekend's Yankee and Red Sox fans."

Their denouement began Saturday—Joe DiMaggio Day—before 69,551, Boston shaping bloops and walks into a 4-0 lead. The Bombers rallied one run at a time. In the eighth, Johnny Lindell, homerless since July 31, knifed Joe Dobson. "Into the right-field seats!" roared Allen, Britt's audio unpreserved: Yanks, 5-4. "What noise!" New York infielder Jerry Coleman still remembers, "You could hear it in *Ashtabula*."

In the final, Phil Rizzuto's leadoff drive *v.* Kinder bounced like silly putty. "The ball gets away from Ted!" said Allen. "It's a three-base hit for the Scooter!" Tommy Henrich's grounder scored a run. In the eighth, behind, 1-0, McCarthy vainly pinch-hit for Kinder. Henrich promptly homered off Parnell, used earlier that week. Coleman batted: 3-2 count, two out, bases full. "A little blooper into short right field. Zarilla comes fast and he can't get it! Here comes [Hank] Bauer! Here comes Johnson! Here comes Mapes digging for the plate . . . and Mapes scores!"—5-0. A Sox tease scored thrice in the ninth. "When it was over," Ted said, "I just wanted to go and hide somewhere." Kinder died in 1968, still blaming "the old man. If he leaves me in, we win."

A half-century later, the sore rubbed raw. "Williams hated us," said close friend Coleman. "'Christ, I wanted to beat the Yankees!' He never forgot that eighth—two [*sic* three] guys get on and I knock 'em in. No. 9 was so pissed. 'What a rinky dink, that little Texas Leaguer.'" Jerry: "Ted, you just saw the cover of the baseball. Its core is still in orbit." The Yankees won their sixteenth pennant. "Ted never did stop fuming. What got him were all their superstars, and little Phil and I beat him. I said, 'Scooter, we're carrying this club, it's just that nobody knows it.'"

After the 1975 World Series, Gowdy malapropped, "The Red Sox future is ahead of them." In early 1950, few envisioned Boston's or Britt's future behind. Seven .300 or above regulars lit a 34-station network: "Each year," Jim said, "more outlets." Goodman's .354 led the league. Walt Dropo became Rookie of the Year. On June 8, the Townies bombed the Browns, *29*-4. Pitchpoor Boston hit *.302* yet placed four games behind New York. At least Stengel spared McCarthy more last-week pain, Marse Joe retiring to his farm near Buffalo in June. Some still hoist a brew, hail the postwar Sox, and rue the dynasty that never was.

"With our team, we should have won three World Series in four [1946–1949] years," said Britt, who aired three, anyway, the 1949 stripes beating Brooklyn in the latest chapter of their serialized novel. The Fall Occasion was broadcast in its entirety east of the Mississippi River over each ABC, CBS, DuMont, and NBC outlet, Jim wisecracking over "safety in numbers." 1950: He and Jack Brickhouse televised west to Omaha; 38 million watched. 1951: Britt and Russ Hodges covered TV's first coast-to-coast Series, NBC touting its "network, now up to 64 stations, including the first foreign affiliate in Matamoros, Mexico." Britt's last postseason plot, like prose, was choice.

On August 11, NL New York trailed Brooklyn by 13½ games. In the best-of-three playoff final, the Dodgers led, 4-2, in the ninth inning: one out, two Jints on base. Bobby Thomson homered, Hodges five times baying, "The Giants win the pennant!" To Stengel, Thy Series will was rain. Down, 2 games to 1, Casey rested his tired staff after Game Four was postponed, won twice, and led the sixth set, 4-3. "Will history [Thomson] repeat itself?" Britt said as Sal Yvars lined to right-fielder Bauer, making a ninth-inning catch on the lush Bronx grass. "The Yankees win again!" Tomorrow seemed to lay ahead of Jim, the *Globe*'s Ray Fitzgerald noted, "his situation ideal."

Britt "was the biggest name in Boston radio at a time when Boston meant the game," Fitzgerald said. He won the Brotherhood and the Great Heart Award, joined the Massachusetts Committee of Catholics, Protestants, and Jews, and was the first Voice to help the Jimmy Fund. A listener was unaware of "Jim's drinking and marital problems," said Leo Egan. "All he heard was Britt doing Dartmouth football and painting a classic description of the New England fall." Power is said to corrupt. It made Jim more prickly.

One blast toward the Wall inherited an ill wind. "Jim yells, 'That ball is smashed and it's gone!'" said Egan. "But no—it's an out."

Next inning a second hitter went long. "Britt yells, 'It's gone!' Same thing: The Northeasterly U-turned it. Oh, was he peeved."

Later Boston again buzzed the fence. "It's really smashed and I don't care what *anybody* says—it's gone!" Britt said. "*Another* out," Leo shook his head, "and now Jim's berserk."

At Braves Field, a ball cleared the inner wall. "It's way outta here!" Britt said. "It's gone *under* the fence!" Laughing, Egan left the booth "to regain my composure." Off-air, Jim asked why.

Egan hesitated. Persisting, Britt said, "What's wrong?"

Finally, Leo said, "You said 'under the fence.'"

"I did not, did not."

Forty years later Egan reworked the dialogue. "Like a little kid, Jim wouldn't admit he made a mistake." Britt's greatest "mistake" was not preserving what he had.

Narragansett Brewery—"the beer," ads bayed, "with the seedless hops"—had sponsored each Hub team since V-E Day. In late 1950, P. Ballantine & Sons, inking a Braves contract, made Britt pick one club or the other. "Leaving WHDH," Ken Coleman said, "Braves owner Lou Perini returned to the [WNAC AM/FM 24-station] Yankee Network, going head-to-head with the Red Sox: a terrible misjudgment as to the relative popularity of the teams." Britt felt the younger Braves—Eddie Mathews, soon Billy Bruton, then Hank Aaron—a better bet than the Red Sox. Yawkey countered—"He wanted to do this anyway," said Ken— by making *all*, not just home, coverage *live*. Unavailable to succeed Britt was a 22-year-old wunderkind whose career had begun at Fenway.

In mid-1949, Fordham University senior and WTOP Washington announcer Vin Scully met CBS Radio news director Ted Church in New York. He also was introduced to Dodgers Voice and CBS sports director Red Barber, who "didn't have much time to talk." Barber told him to "leave your name, address, and number," Vin thinking he would never again see the network. That Saturday Scully tuned to *College Football Roundup*, airing four games simultaneously, bouncing "from place to place for an update on each game."

In October, a spot opened on *Roundup*'s Boston University–Maryland in the Fens. "I got bumped up to a bigger game, Notre Dame–North Carolina in New York," said Ernie Harwell. BU-Maryland reeled: Who to replace him? Barber thought of Vin, asked WTOP for references, then phoned Scully's home, getting mother Bridget, who that night waited at the door.

"Vinny, you'll never guess who called you. It's such a great thing that he called here, such a busy man. It's so exciting. He wants you to call him."

"Who was it?" said Scully.

"Red Skelton," mama said.

On Friday, Vin stayed at the same Kenmore Hotel where Pesky imagined DiMag's homer landing. Assuming a Fenway booth, next day he shed coat, gloves, and hat. "I made a dumb kid's move, because what I really cared about was Saturday night's [Fordham, playing Boston College] alumni dance. I was 21 years old," finding no booth, just a roof site between home plate and right field. "My engineer got an old card table strong enough to hold my equipment, and a cord letting me walk the full length of the field." BU's star was Harry Agganis, "the Golden Greek. Every time he threw a pass, I'd run down the roof to see what happened."

Depending on the game, *Roundup*'s Voice called a play, drive, or quarter. Vin had a watch, microphone, 50 yards of cable, 60-watt bulb for light, and lineup card. By the third quarter, "wind up, sun down, I'm fighting frostbite" as Red warmed in studio. Scully's game was close—Maryland, 14-13—so coverage shifted there. By game end, "I was sure I'd blown the greatest opportunity I'd ever had in my life." Instead, he aired *Roundup* through 1955.

Fenway higher-ups apologized to Red for lacking a booth. "I guess that impressed him," Scully said, Barber feeling a protectiveness for "the son I never had." Again he called Vin's residence: "You'll have a booth next week—Harvard-Yale." In early 1950, Red hired him at Brooklyn. What if Britt had left the Sox in November 1949, Scully just off the roof? Word had already impressed Tom Yawkey. Would T. A. have signed him? Given Vin's and Gowdy's later struggle to peacefully coexist, the possibility intrigues.

In 1951, Curt left Yankee Stadium to relocate in New England. Updike followed, adding teaching (Harvard fellow) to writing (the *New Yorker*); "lying in back yards or on the beach, driving in the car or squinting into a book, I listened to the games and internalized Curt Gowdy." A lesser writer had tagged the balding Britt "Tuft," "Meathead," or "a radio Rollo." Now Dave Egan wrote, "The beer salesman who for years has been trying to sell the beer that *doesn't* have seeds in it is going to try to sell us beer that *does*." He failed.

"Curt had the top product going for him," said the *Globe*. "Britt had the Braves when they were cracking up." In 1945, Lou Perini, Guido Rugo, and Joe Maney—The Three Steam Shovels—had bought the team, spending $500,000 to fix plumbing, brace supports, and paint seats for Opening Day, only to find some wet. "Clothes were damaged," Britt recalled, "so the Braves apologized, told fans to go to the dry cleaners," and opened a "Paint Account" at the local bank. Perini paid $6,000 to more than 18,000 claims. By 1951, the Braves telecast "all home day and 14 selected nights," said *The Sporting News*, on Channels 4, 7, and Providence WJAR 11. It didn't help attendance, one-third of 1948's.

Tommy Holmes replaced Billy Southworth. Charlie Grimm then replaced *him*, "drawing so poorly we were playing to the grounds help." *TSN*'s 1952 preview issue presaged trouble: "Radio and TV sponsor not yet named." Boston played its last home game September 21, before 8,822. "What's sad is that in a couple years the Braves had something," said Britt—winning or losing a final-day 1956–1959 pennant. "It's the Sox who might have moved." Instead, the Braves drew an NL postwar low 281,278, Jim grasping hope like a cigarette before execution.

Players dispersed to homes in Charlotte and Marion, Wisconsin, and Oil City, Pennsylvania, shuffling blankly to 1953 spring training. On March 18, the Braves of Boston since 1876 decamped for Milwaukee, leaving the radio Rollo behind. "They wanted somebody local for their radio," Britt said: Earl Gillespie and Bob Kelly over flagships WTMJ and WEMP AM/FM. At Braves Field, tickets dropped from windows into waiting trucks on Gaffney Street. Boston University later bought the site, renamed it Nickerson Field, and peddled seats to a soft-ball park.

1953: The second-place Braves' attendance more than sextupled to a league record 1,826,397. 1955: Milwaukee hosted the All-Star Game. 1956: "Rush for tickets to Braves' games," said *Sports Illustrated*, "rivaled only by *My Fair Lady*." The ex-Bostons approximated an All-Star team. Del Crandall caught. Aaron, Bruton, and Wes Covington outfielded. The infield tied Joe Adcock, Red Schoendienst, Johnny Logan, and Mathews. Burghers gave players free beer, milk, and cars. "We'd go into Forbes Field—Pittsburgh was lousy—and there'd be 30,000," said Gillespie. "Baseball's smallest town became its capital."

One night Walter O'Malley flew to Brewtown. "Look at this," Brooklyn's owner said, pop-eyed, of County Stadium's full house. "They're outdrawing us a million. We can't afford this—not even a couple years." Britt had vocalized a region. Allen meant the Big Ballpark in the Bronx. Harry Caray packed the Church of Cardinals Baseball. "None had what we did," Gillespie crowed, Milwaukee topping 2 million year after year.

The Braves were the first big-league franchise to change sites in half a century. Their success made others follow. The Los Angeles Dodgers likely would not exist had the Braves not owned Wisconsin, Upper Michigan, and parts of Minnesota, Illinois, and Iowa. Other homesteaders included the San Francisco Giants, Milwaukee Brewers, Texas Rangers, and *Atlanta* Braves.

In Boston's last NL training camp, pitcher Vern Bickford retired Williams his first at-bat. "Ted's up this inning," he told mates later. "I'm gonna see how far that big donkey can hit one."

"What are you gonna do?" said Braves 1950–1958 starter and reliever Ernie Johnson.

Bickford said, "Lay it in there about three-quarters speed and see what happens."

Williams hit the right-center field light tower. "We're roaring as the inning ends," said Johnson. "Bickford comes back, shakes his head, and says 'Well at least I got my answer.'"

Today few know much ex-Bees history. Gone: grass transplanted from South End Grounds, replaced by Astroturf at BU. Remaining: fixtures, photos—first-base grandstand, right- and center-field outer wall, and Gaffney Street ticket entrance— and plaque, dedicated in 1988. Britt is unmentioned, "never recovering from what he'd done to himself," said Coleman. "When the Braves left, there was *nothing* left. He stumbled around a year, then came to Cleveland, where we did [1954–1957] TV baseball for Carling Brewery"—Jim still refusing to go along to get along.

Local dialect pronounced 1950s Indians All-Star second baseman Bobby *Ah-VEE-la*. Britt preferred *AH-vee-la*. "We got every kind of calls and letters," said Ken. "People didn't like it."

Carling's chairman said, "You know, Jim, in view of the local colloquialism, we should probably call him *Ah-VEE-la*, like most fans want."

The chairman's name was Ian Bowie, as in *bow-ee*. Britt said, "All right with me, Mr. Bowie," as in *boo-ee*.

In 1958, he returned to WHDH "haunted by the Red Sox' 'what if,'" said Egan: televising the popular candlepin *Bowling* and magazine-style *Dateline Boston* and watching his station air the Townies. Axed, Britt moved to Detroit, St. Petersburg, and Sarasota, braving a divorce, unemployment, and arrests for drunkenness.

He died December 28, 1980, less tragic than forgotten, at home in Monterey, California. "In truth," wrote Ray Fitzgerald, "life had turned its back on him a long time ago."

6
THE COWBOY AT THE MIKE (1951–1965)

A song by Bob Smith proclaims, "I Saw It on the Radio." I first saw Fenway Park on a 1960 family trip from Western New York to Nova Scotia. For a time, Allen showed why a writer said, "If Mel sold fish, he would make it sound as if Puccini wrote the score." East of Albany I turned to Gowdy, who seemed fair, did his homework, and ferried me to the coast of Maine. My first bigs game in person was that August 30 in the Fens: T. Ballgame's 42nd birthday, last as a player. I took home a wonder as to his effect on the crowd. As dizzying were several days spent in the Boston area. Curt was everywhere: at the office, in the backyard, in a convertible, in your den.

By then, sponsors helped distill baseball's radio and TV essence. I liked Byrum Saam hyping Phillies cigars and Jimmy Dudley's "Mabel, Black Label." Bob Prince hailed Iron City beer; Harry Caray, Busch Bavarian; and Allen, Ballantine's Three-Ring Circle. Vin Scully sold Farmer John's sausage. "It's 3:30 a.m.," said announcer Jon Miller. "The lights are off. Vin wakes up, puts his robe on, and wanders toward the refrigerator. Does he always talk this way? 'Good evening, wherever I am. Can't wait for some Farmer John's.'"

In New England, a brewery had become as synonymous with the Red Sox as any of the above, hawking Narragansett on the Cape, at Bar Harbor, in the Berkshires, on Mt. Katahdin—"Hi ya, neighbor! Grab a 'Gansett!"—its mot in print and on the air. "A perfect slogan," Gowdy said. "It meant approachability: Fenway to the fans, Mr. Yawkey to the players," even the Jimmy Fund, Curt its post-Britt spokesman. "New England was our neighbor, and we wanted them to visit." The Cowboy visited, thus:

"Have you noticed the swing in Narragansett Lager Beer? Well, there's a reason. Today's Narragansett Lager Beer is lighter, drier, finer flavored than any beer that Narragansett has ever served," touting a "thrifty big-sized bottle that gives you 33⅓ percent more beer"—a long drinking record—"than 12-ounce bottles—two long drinks of good cool 'Gansett." Inevitably, many used the product to forget the product on the field.

From 1951 to 1965, Gowdy posed questions to which we already knew the answer. Could the Sox break .500 on the road? From the hole, could shortstop Don Buddin manage not to heave the ball into boxes beyond first base? Could the skipper of the month—Mike Higgins or Billy Jurges or Billy Herman—find a decent stopper? Was this the biblical year when Sox regulars got a cast? As Roseanne Roseannadanna later said, "If it's not one thing, it's another."

Why did Felix Mantilla greet grounders like leprosy? (Practice.) When would the bull pen not self-immolate? (Dick Radatz, briefly.) Could Dick Stuart pick up a hot dog wrapper without dropping it? (Yes, to applause.) Some ask the South's, Midwest's, or California's core. In New England, such doubt would be as rare as a J. D. Drew Fan Club: *Fenway* is the cynosure. In the evaluating and rubbing together of the American century, the Red Sox own their diocese.

Even now, something remains, if but a vague recollection, of the Cowboy's time in Boston: work, fondness for the familiar, and Fred MacMurray–type affability. Like Ike, baseball seemed middle-brow and -class. Then-novel color highlight films—*Baseball in Boston, The Red Sox at Home, Pride of New England, Play Ball with the Red Sox*, and *Forward with the Red Sox*—conjure the age's feel. Boats floated on the Charles. Men in suits and suited ladies approached "one of the country's best-kept and cleanest" parks, said Curt, voice-overing. Vendors hawked. Ushers tipped their cap. Towheads collided for a foul.

Opening Day meant "the State Dome gleams a welcome and magnolias bloom on Beacon Hill." Conductor Arthur Fiedler led "The Star-Spangled Banner"—to Gowdy, "nothing better typifying America than the sight of Old Glory waving." A decade after D-Day, Curt addressed "all you ex-GIs," noting the Sox "farm system has 138 players now in the uniform of Uncle Sam." Mel Parnell threw the first Sox no-hitter at the Fens in 39 years. Headlined the *Boston Herald*, "I Was Just Lucky—Mel." In the Hub, said Gowdy, "They do it [baseball] up big"—Maine Day, Shriners Night, Rhode Island Day—a game for every outpost.

A sign deemed The Kid "The Greatest American Since George Washington." Players drove their white-walled Thunderbird, Impala, Cadillac. "Solidity, community, Curt fit the era perfectly," said Martin Nolan, the style home-style—less Jon Stewart than Jimmy Stewart. Later the Cowboy called Fenway "New England's night club." By any name, both were ours.

Williams's exit divided Curt's Red Sox timeline into 1951–1960 and 1961–1965. The first drew between 931,127 and 1,312,282, contending only in 1955. Post-Ted was worse, Boston losing a hundred games in 1965 for the first time since 1932. One season the Townies lured fewer people than in *1909*. By five-year intervals Gowdy's Sox were 400–369, 385–385, and 362–445. "The longer I stayed," laughed the Rocky Mountaineer, "the more they were unintentionally funny." One spring training a press steward asked Curt about a drink as the local mayor readied an exhibition's first pitch. "The attendant was too far away to answer, so he wrote down a suggestion—a *milkshake*—and handed it to me." Gowdy misinterpreted, saying, "Here is the Mayor, Mike Shane." Somehow—*this* is the mystery—curiosity survived.

By 1953, read *TSN*, Boston had five TV outlets: "all home games except night against the Browns," presaging their trek to Baltimore. WNAC/WBZ coverage mixed "Saturday, Sunday, holidays, and selected weekday nights"—50 to 55 games yearly. In 1958, WHDH (channel 5) became network flagship, tying Hartford, Connecticut; Greenfield and Springfield, Massachusetts; Bangor and Presque Isle, Maine; Mt. Washington, New Hampshire; and Providence, Rhode Island. Meanwhile, radio's network reached 40 stations in 1954, behind only the Cardinals and ironically Braves; rose to 48 in 1958; then fell to 1965's 41. For the Cowboy, as we shall see, it was time to mosey on.

"Mostly lousy teams, yet what personalities!" he said. "The Peskys, Doerrs, Williams. That's why the Red Sox are *like* baseball. It's not really a team game, like football. It's a game of individuals." Actor Art Carney said of TV's *The Honeymooners*, "I started at the bottom in this business and worked my way right into the sewer." Gowdy started with individuals haunted by recent memory. "Doerr still asks me, 'Why didn't we win?'" Tommy Henrich said of the late 1940s. "Jeez, it was something special. Red Sox and the Yankees," and rivalries within—The Kid and DiMag, Doerr and Joe Gordon, McCarthy and Stengel. "You think you're not gonna fear those birds?"

"Didn't we have a good ballclub?" the Silent Captain asked.

Henrich said, "You scared us to death. Sure, you had a good ballclub."

"Then why didn't we win?"

"I don't know," said Henrich, dubbed "Old Reliable" by Allen. "I think the owner over there liked you better than our owners did us." Each year new cars jammed the Red Sox parking lot. "We had to bear down more for ours."

Some fixated on 1948–1949 to their future detriment. Others treated it like a locked room in a deserted house. Slowly, players left, were hurt, or faded. In the 1950 All-Star Game, Williams caught Ralph Kiner's drive, hit the wall at Comiskey Park, and hurt his elbow. "It took me until I came back from Korea [in 1953] to really get over that one." Doerr retired with a bad back. In 1952, Pesky, Dropo, and three other Townies were traded for four Tigers, including George Kell. By 1954, Pesky and Dom D. retired. The team was breaking up.

The 1946–1949 Red Sox flaunted four 20-win pitchers. The 1950–1966ers boasted two—Parnell and Bill Monbouquette, 21-8 and 20-10 in 1953 and 1963, respectively. In 1979, columnist Erma Bombeck wrote, "It hasn't happened yet, but it's inevitable. One night [an actress] will lean over the footlights of a Broadway theatre and in the childlike voice of Peter Pan ask, 'Will anyone who believes in Tinker Bell clap your hands?' And the theatre will resound in silence. The silence will record the [end of] faith in America."

In 1951, Boston clapped for the Olde Towne Team, losing faith a decade later. Its common denominator was the Cowboy.

Britt roused response to language; Allen, personality; Mel's ex-aide, perspective. "The game is the important thing," Gowdy said. "A Voice is no better than his script." Curt's listed the Series (13), All-Star Game (16), Final Four (24), Rose (14) and Super (9) Bowls, Olympics (11), Pan-American Games, PBS's *The Way It Was*, ABC's 1964–1985 *The American Sportsman*, and a decade of *Game of the Week*, airing virtually baseball's entire network schedule. Gowdy was a 13-time Emmy Award recipient, sportscasting's first George Foster Peabody grandee for "broadcast excellence," and inductee in 22 Halls of Fame, including Cooperstown, basketball's in Springfield, Massachusetts, and the Hall he was proudest of: the International Game Fishing Association. "Putting a town into a piece about [him]," a writer said, "is like trying to establish residence for a migratory duck."

Born in Green River, Wyoming, Gowdy moved to Cheyenne at age six. Dad Edward, a Union Pacific Railroad dispatcher, "said, 'Curtis, there's a big world out there. Someday I'd like to see a big-league game.'" Mother Ruth, a housewife, insisted he study typing and elocution and read one book a week. Basketball was an early swain till coach Jack Powell said, "Curtis, you're off the team."

"What'd I do?" yelped the senior. As Powell explained, Mom had seen the principal, been distressed by Curt's low English grade, and ordered him not to play.

"How can you *do* this?" said the livid five-foot-nine guard. "Basketball's my life."

"Get your English up!" Mom said. The state high-school scoring leader did.

Gowdy entered the University of Wyoming, won six basketball and tennis letters, majored in business statistics, and joined the Army Air Force, hoping to become a pilot. Instead, surgery failed for a hoops-bred ruptured disk in his spine. Curt sulked ten months in a hospital, doctors discharging him in 1943: "More rest, no sports, and with luck you won't be a cripple." The Cowboy eyeballed ghosts: pals had joined the service. "It was as low as I've ever been," he said, before a phone call swished a high.

Bill Grove managed Cheyenne's sole radio station, KFBC. "There's nobody else," he told the Cowboy. "I need you to call [tiny Pine Bluff–St. Mary's six-man] football." That Saturday, Curt "stood on a soap box, guessed where the ball was, and made up the name of every player" without yard lines, sidelines, goal posts, or player numbers. He liked it, writing for the *Wyoming Eagle* newspaper and airing basketball, football, Western Union baseball, and what passed for "big events. At Christmas we made a big to-do over Santa Claus's arrival." In March 1945, chance made his life over.

Driving through Wyoming, Ken Brown, owner, fifty-thousand-watt KOMA Oklahoma City, heard Curt announce hoops. Soon Gowdy called Oklahoma A&M roundball, Oklahoma football, and CBS's *College Football Roundup*, one week Barber switching to the Cowboy. "Red," Curt said, "the Oklahoma Aggies can make or break their season against the mighty Texas juggernaut this Saturday." CBS journalist Edward R. Murrow sent a telegram saying, "I'd [Gowdy] done a great job with the game. I wish I'd kept it." The Cowboy also covered the Triple-A Oklahoma City Indians—"the biggest break of my career"—later terming the minors "a bigs workshop: all the demands of the sports broadcast business—ads, production, play-by-play—in one."

In 1948, Curt's business became General Mills, sponsoring 13 bigs teams, and account executive Frank Slocum, seeking "talent to sell its products"—Wheaties, above all. That fall Allen aide Russ Hodges crossed the Harlem River to the Polo Grounds, leaving a vacancy. Hearing Gowdy, Slocum "asked for a brochure with tapes." Mel already knew the Cheyenne émigré. "Curt would come to New York for basketball at the [Madison Square] Garden, and had his biography with pictures. I'd say, 'You should have gone into Hollywood.'" Gowdy signed for $10,000: "I'd have settled for nothing. Fortunately, I didn't have to."

Later, Curt conceded "a tense first year," disliking, among other things, Allen's propensity to pun. "The rain's coming down helter skelter," he said. "Hi, helter." Gowdy, pained: "Hi, skelter." A future peer thought him cowed. "Mel wanted things precisely done," said Ned Martin. "For a while Gowdy thought he'd toss it." Instead, Curt abided it: "Mel could lose his temper in a game and ride you, but he was loyal and generous to the people who worked for him," including Hodges, Jim Woods, and Brooklyn's Connie Desmond: "Alumni of Allen Tech," wrote the *New York Daily News*' Pete Coutros, "having shared hours of joy and anguished with him at the mike."

In 1950, Gowdy married Jerre Dawkins, a University of Oklahoma graduate student. The best man made him better. "My other sports had come along. But Allen showed me how far from a baseball hot shot I was." Gowdy thought Mel, like Jerre, a perfectionist. "They can be a pain in the ass, all the ashtrays have to be cleaned just right. Mel had attention to timing, reading an ad, weaving it in, then done all the time." That winter Britt guessed wrong about the Braves. The Sox, in turn, considered the Giants' Ernie Harwell. "It never got too serious," said the first Voice traded for a player, baptized in the Jordan River, and to telecast coast to coast. "I'd done the Dodgers in 1949, Giants in '50, and didn't want to jump again—a bad reputation." Curt got the offer, later saying, "I can't believe I was torn."

On one hand, Gowdy pined to be lead announcer: "I knew Mel would never leave, and the Sox meant Fenway, six states, great fans." On the other, he loved the stripes, New York meant baseball, and he was doing ads, Garden donkey basketball, "trying to make my name." Allen vowed—"*threatened* a better word," Gowdy laughed—to piggy-back him to the Fens. Yankees don Dan Topping—"close to Yawkey"—helped, voiding his contract. In 2003, Curt looked past NBC to "the greatest fifteen years of my life."

They began with two losses in the Bronx, Boston scoring once in 18 innings. Curt got telegrams—"Go back to New York, Yankee lover"—blaming him for the start. Worse, he mispronounced area towns with an English accent—Worcester, Swampscott, Ipswich—Yawkey hiring a speech tutor. "Here it is, my first week in 1951, and I'm thinking I should have stayed at The Stadium."

Back at Fenway, Curt learned that T. A. wished to see him. Terrified, he walked from the field up the stairs. "I'd never met him," Gowdy said. "I open the office and, well, here's this multimillionaire, dressed in khaki pants and faded shirt, looks like he doesn't have a dime."

Yawkey stood. "Curt, I just want to welcome you to the Red Sox. I followed you in New York and liked it." No scent of Swampscott: expecting a sentence, Gowdy felt reborn.

"Mr. Yawkey, what kind of broadcast do you want?" he said.

"Look, they've had major league baseball here since the 1876 Braves," Yawkey said. "The Red Sox came into the American League in 1901. No line drives made into pop-ups or excuses for errors. New England knows the game. Tell it straight."

Gowdy exhaled, knowing then that Yawkey loved the sport. At 18, Bob Feller had signed an Indians contract that Commissioner Kenesaw Mountain Landis deemed illegal, putting Feller on the market and getting Yawkey not to bid: "Tom, don't let your wealth dominate the market." Old-line money, T. A. even liked the help. In 1957, Curt reinjured his back, missed the entire year, and was replaced by Don Gillis and Bill Crowley. "I don't care how long this kid misses," Yawkey told a neurosurgeon, "one year, five years, he's got a job here."

Gowdy's job was contradictory from the start.

In July 1951, Allie Reynolds no-noed the Indians. That September the Yanks righty neared another. In a two-out ninth inning, Williams fouled to the catcher: "incredibly," said Gowdy, "Berra dropping it." Ted then popped to the same spot, Yogi catching it. Frank Sullivan once had a 2.91 earned run average, his puzzle Boston's: Sully couldn't beat (0-5) the stripes. Twice Willard Nixon had a plus-six ERA. Another year he batted .293 to lead AL pitchers. A twi-night double-header lasted 26 innings: Sox sweep. Next night's game went 19: Sox lose. Fenway's hit-and-run scoreboard placards include numbers 0 through 19: the highest used, 17, in June 18, 1953's seventh inning. In 1955, Cleveland's Herb Score won, 19-0, after a black plastic cat, failing as a lucky rabbit's foot, was buried below a headstone in the Boston pen. "In football, you remember entire games," the Cowboy said. "In baseball, you remember *stories!*" Many helped him avoid anything germane to score.

In Curt's early tenure, Kinder—"Ollld Rubber Arm," Gowdy said, elongating the syllable—became Boston's first true reliever. "Ellis liked to stay out all night—*night* after night," future Voice Bob Murphy said. "One [1953] morning they picked him up off the sidewalk at five o'clock. So much for using him in today's double-header. All he did was save both games"—the two-fisted hurler setting then single-year team marks in saves (27) and games (69). Antipodal was a Boston University quarterback–turned–Townie who as a 1954 rookie hit four homers in a home stand. To Curt, Harry Agganis meant the hypothetical.

"Agganis grew up in [nearby] Lynn, of Greek descent," he began. "[Cleveland Browns coach] Paul Brown wanted him to succeed Otto Graham at quarterback." Instead, Agganis was hitting .313 when he caught pneumonia in 1955. In and out of the hospital, the Golden Greek visited the clubhouse, sweating. Seeing him, Curt popped a cork.

"What the hell are you doing?" Gowdy said.

"Working out," said Agganis.

"You're crazy. You just got out of the hospital."

Agganis boarded a team flight to Chicago, where Curt saw him next day with a suitcase in the hotel elevator. "What's the matter?" Gowdy asked trainer Jack Fadden, who didn't know. Back in Boston, Harry was checked by doctors who found a blood clot in his leg. It entered Agganis's lungs, killing him at 25.

Frank Sinatra wrote "The Sunshine of Your Smile." Gowdy's eulogy etched the Greek's. Later Curt recalled Yawkey's "awful luck, nothing worse than this." Bonus baby scouting also hurt long before the 1965 free-agent draft. T. A. bought pitchers Ted Bowsfield, Ted Wills, Tom Borland, and Nels Chittum and infielders like Billy Consolo, Gene Mauch, and Ken Aspromonte. All flopped. Boston opened 1950–1957 with a different shortstop each year: Vern Stephens, Lou Boudreau, Jim Piersall, Milt Bolling, Ted Lepcio, Eddie Joost, Don Buddin, and Billy Klaus. The *Globe's* Clif Keane said Buddin's license plate should read "E-6." Others said he had no license to play.

"Stories!" Curt reminded you. Billy Goodman was "Sox handyman," playing five positions in a season. Catcher Sammy White stole "more strikes from umpires than anyone else," said Stengel. "I'm not being critical. I'm just bowing to his skill."

Washington lefty Pete Runnels regularly made out to deep left field. Dealt to Boston, he sprayed the Wall, batted .300 in 1958–1962, and won two batting titles: as Senators Voice Bob Wolff said, "Clark Kent became Superman on the train to Fenway from D.C." Runnels played at first and second base. At third Frank Malzone "won a position on the [1957] All-Star team and a place in Boston's heart," said *Sports Illustrated*, "and in 1957–1958 drove in more runs (190) than the other M and Ms"—Willie Mays, Eddie Mathews, Roger Maris, or Mickey Mantle. "He can hit, he can field, and he's the best in the league at his position. Boston just wishes he were triplets."

In *Forward with the Red Sox*, Gowdy said, "It doesn't matter where they hit. Malzone will catch the ball." Malzone didn't catch the 1958 World Series. NBC's Cowboy did. That week Movietone Newsreels headlined, "Mel Allen Relives Series Thrills." His protégé was thrilled to speak. "Allen is a professional but too obviously so, talking too much for TV," a critic wrote. "Gowdy is our type of announcer. Just enough chatter, newsy," literally "restrained," wearing a steel brace with a painkiller for his back. It let Curt do pro basketball, college football, first 1959 All-Star Game (Forbes Field), and second 1961 (Fens)—if not help the Sox. Ball and chains were defense and speed. "When Boston pitchers are being judged, it must be remembered that the burden they bear is heavy," wrote *SI*'s Robert Creamer. They were not alone.

"No one has spent more money for more disappointment than [Yawkey]," Creamer mused. "Ten years ago he had the team everyone wanted: Williams, Doerr, Stephens, Pesky, and DiMaggio. But it won no pennant," at least obeying the age's code. In 1940, a holdout wired Chattanooga Lookouts owner Joe Engel: "Double my salary or count me out." Joe answered by telegram: "1-2-3-4-5-6-7-8-9-10." In 1959 an injured Williams hit .254, then demanded that Yawkey *cut* his pay.

Each fall Curt chose a game to sum up and say good-bye. In 1953, he began with the Jimmy Fund, wishing to thank the world. *Selahs* accented bread and butter: "The Narragansett Brewing Company, Atlantic Richfield, and Chesterfield—three great firms, with many wonderful people." Next: "The Variety Club of New England. Tom Yawkey, Joe Cronin, Lou Boudreau, all the personnel of the Red Sox," including those "helping with all the mail that Ted Williams receives." The "small fry" had "put on a play, sold lemonade, took collection" at a Little League game. "Personnel at drive-in theaters—and you housewives and countless other patrons" helped. Finally, the "motion picture industry, baseball, the chiefs of police all aided this wonderful cause." More than "two hundred kids are now under treatment," Curt said. "God bless you all."

The game commenced: Athens *v.* Sparta. "McDermott, then Flowers, then Sullivan, then Ike Delock faced New York—Delock pitched good ball, by the way," Gowdy said. By the ninth inning, "on the Narragansett scoreboard, it's the Yankees 10, the Red Sox 8." Looking "ahead for all you Red Sox fans," Boston would bat the bottom of the order. Tom Umphlett led off by arcing "into deep left field. And it's off the Wall. And there goes Umphlett going for two—and he goes in with a stand*ing*"—not usual stand-*up*—"double."

Earlier Williams had left for Karl Olson, the now-tying batter. "There's one into deep right-center field!" Curt said. "Bauer runs over and holds the ball to end the ball game. At the last moment he reached across his body, going away from the plate on the dead run, to rob . . . Olson of an extra-base hit!" The crowd "had got its money's worth." Ahead: "the total, scoreboard, and old wrapper-upper." In 1946, Updike heard Slaughter in a Chevrolet. Boston's '50s shock-jock outfield was a mercurial Ferrari. "In right, we got Jackie Jensen, who's afraid to fly and hires a hypnotist for road trips," Gowdy ribbed No. 9. "In left, you're not the sanest guy who ever lived. Add Piersall in center, and we got the kookiest outfield that ever played in the major leagues." Laughing, Ted agreed.

By position:

In 2000, Gowdy wrote a foreword to the book *The Golden Boy*, terming Jensen "maybe the best athlete I ever covered": baseball's first real two-sport All-American since Jackie Robinson, another West Coast running back. His Golden Year was 1958: .286, 35 homers, league-high 122 RBI, and first Sox MVP since 1949. "Jensen drives home a hundred runs every summer [*sic*, five times]," a writer said, "the way other men mow their lawns." The problem lay above. Until 1955, the AL's farthest posts were Boston and St. Louis. The A's move to Kansas City made rail kaput. "I can see him now," said a mate. "Jackie'd travel all night by train to get to a game on time. We'd gone by plane and got in the night before." Worn, he retired in 1960, returned next year, and left again—for good.

"My most memorable character was Piersall," 1980s Cubs outfielder Darrin Jackson said of his then minor-league instructor. "Everyone knew from his 1950s problems that he was certifiably nuts." Piersall joined the Townies as a 1950 short-stop: fast, lithe, and antic. He struggled, dropped to Class AA Birmingham, and panicked the front office. One night its GM called Yawkey, saying, "You better come get this kid. I think he's sick."

"What's the matter?" T. A. said.

"He's squirting water pistols at home plate, and goes out and hangs numbers on the scoreboard and runs the bases backwards. There's something wrong with him. The fans love it, but I don't. If you saw it, you wouldn't, either."

Film's 1957 *Fear Strikes Out* etches Piersall's mental breakdown, prognosis, shock treatment, isolation, and resilience, if not recovery. In 1956, he batted .293, "making Waterbury, Connecticut," said Gowdy, "proud of its hometown boy." In 1958, he won the new Gold Glove award—fielding's Oscar—after "making three of the five greatest catches I saw in baseball," including Mantle's almost inside-the-parker. Once Joe Collins drove to Fenway's home-team pen. "Way back! Way back!" Curt said. "Piersall leaping up—oh, he robs him of a home run!—going high in the air out there! Another sensational catch by Piersall!" Collins shook his head "as if to say, 'I wouldn't have believed it if I saw it.'" Gowdy confessed to having "stopped using adjectives, Piersall . . . making catch after catch like that all season!" He "had to have saved a hundred runs this year with his arm and with his fielding"—already "one of the greatest outfielders of all time."

Praise didn't cure manic depression. Leading off first base, Piersall so unnerved Satchel Paige by imitating a pig that the pitcher loaded the bases and yielded Sammy White's slam. On Opening Day 1958, he watched President Eisenhower throw out the first ball, then gave him another as players fought for the original: "Mr. President, would you sign *this* ball while those idiots scramble for *that* one?" By 1963, leaving Fenway via Cleveland and Washington for the Metropolitan Baseball Club of New York, Inc.—the Mets—Jim ran the bases *backward*, as in Birmingham, to celebrate his hundredth homer.

"Usually, you can't get away with [my] language or what I do," he told Darrin Jackson. Piersall could, "because I'm crazy."

This left the man of whom Gowdy said, "His batting stroke and swing [were] copied by kids all over the world."

In 1957, Williams, 39, was intentionally walked a franchise record 33 times, had a monumental .731 slugging percentage, and batted a big-league high .388. Slowing, he had 12 infield hits *v.* Mantle's 48, Mick sitting on the dugout step when the Thumper hit, "studying him," terming Ted better than DiMag. Next year Williams hit a final batting title .328. To paraphrase rocker Rod Stewart, he wore age well.

Writer Murray Kempton told Martin Nolan, "I don't think of myself as a Democrat as much as I am a fan of Adlai Stevenson." Nolan nodded, knowing that he had been first a fan of Williams, then baseball. "Teddy Ballgame was not likely madly for Adlai," he wrote, "but Ted's politics were not germane." In *My Favorite Year*, a character says of Peter O'Toole, as actor Alan Swann, "With Swannie, you forgive a lot, you know." Nolan did, his "boyhood admiration of the graceful swing of number 9 not much upset by revelations that he cussed and fussed." Once he saw Ted give boo-birds what papers primly called "a French salute."

Williams was loyal, profane, and drop-dead handsome—Gowdy's ultimate inner-directed man. In 1966, entering Cooperstown, he wrote a night-before longhand acceptance speech that resonates even now, hoping "that someday the names of Satchel Paige and Josh Gibson in some way can be added as a symbol of the great Negro players that are not here only because they were not given a chance." Curt noted that there "was nothing in there for Ted, just him doing what he thought right." Later, jostled for autographs, he roared, "I'm not signing—you pushy kids, learn some manners." The part-child and part-Gibraltar moved to the crowd's periphery, booming, "I'll sign *theirs*—kids who aren't rude."

Something about Ted lured contempt and adulation, capable of bullying but also feeling pain. Williams's mother—"the Angel of Tijuana," preferring volunteering to parenting—left his boyhood home a sty. Hurt, he helped those who felt alone. In town for *Game*, announcer Bud Blattner told of a 10-year-old with leukemia who made his Midwest hospital room a shrine to Ted. Each day nurses sat him on the floor with a little bat, got on their hands and knees, and rolled a ball down the corridor. "He'd hit it," Blattner said, "and as it rolled they yelled, 'Oh, that's a double. That's a triple.' If it was a homer, it was hit by Ted!" Listening, The Kid insisted on seeing him—Williams flew his plane—on two conditions: that there be no media and that Bud wouldn't mention it. "The boy died but met his hero," said Gowdy. "This happened all the time."

Later, Ted became what *SI* termed "the patron saint of Cooperstown"—an opinion on everything, less mellowed than matured. At a charity event, meeting Nolan, he growled, "'Ah, a knight of the keyboard!' inquired about Clif Keane, the needling *Globe* sportswriter he respected, and cheerfully told stories about Willie Tasby and others." Playing, he was less serene. One Opening Day in Washington, announcer Chuck Thompson asked a Hub reporter, "What kind of spring did Ted have?"

Fantastic, the writer said. "Must have hit over .400, but the unusual thing is that he didn't hit a homer."

Ted's first up Chuck told the story on Senators TV: "Great average in the spring, but no power." Ted hit the next pitch over the apple tree behind deepest center field.

Next day, Williams left his dugout ripping "this big-nosed, loud-mouthed, bald-headed broadcaster that doesn't know his something from something," said Chuck. In batting practice, Ted still mocking "'no power' this and that," Thompson had no choice but to man up and approach the cage. Baseball's Diogenes stopped, turned, and eyed his prey. "Kid," the Splinter said, "it's the first bleepin' ball I've hit all spring."

Williams was as passionate about fly casting bait, buying the best gun, knowing which stream oozed with bass. "That was our tie," said Gowdy. "We talked hunting and fishing, then baseball." His friend Bush 41 twitted the "vision thing." Ted's vision was perfect in the Air Force, brass disbelieving what he saw.

"There!" Williams boomed, hunting. "Watch two ducks coming at 3 o'clock."

Curt: "Where?"

"*There!*" In two minutes, ducks appeared.

To Gowdy, he was "the most competent man I ever knew. Best hitter. Best fisherman. Best hunter." In 1988, the Jimmy Fund hailed No. 9 at a seventieth birthday dinner, actor David Hartman emceeing. Spotting astronaut and U.S. senator John Glenn, the Cowboy introduced himself: "I used to broadcast Red Sox games. What's your connection with Ted?"

"I was his flight commander in Korea," Glenn said, "and that's how I became an astronaut. It was my Air Force background. Williams was my wingman."

Gowdy: "What kind of a pilot was he?"

Glenn: "Best I ever had."

Curt's "most competent man" was not stingy with what he knew.

Williams regularly advised what Yawkey termed "the enemy"—Ted too selfless for the Townies' good. "Look, T. A.," he bayed, "when you're a block away from a park and hear the crowd roar, somebody's just hit the baseball! Fans love a home run or double or triple or rundown play or a cutoff. It's all action because it's hitting."

The Kid once bombed a bases-loaded ninth-inning pitch off Herb Score, later saying, "Herbie, do me a favor. Don't ever throw me a fastball on a count of three and two"—less selfless than prioritized. "That little game between the pitcher and hitter" meant more than the final score. Each day Williams halted batting practice: "The only player I ever saw where both dugouts paused to watch him: a mesmerizing one-man show," said Bob Wolff. "Ted could be convivial stepping into the cage. If he didn't do well, he'd come out storming, 'Get out of my way!'" By and by Bob approached Vesuvius—if not inactive, cooled.

On August 7, 1956, in a scoreless game at Fenway, the crowd jeered Ted for misplaying a fly. Two batters later he made a third-out diving catch. Nearing the dugout, Williams spit toward the boxes, sat down, came out, and spit again. Next night he went long, crossed home plate, and put his hand over his mouth. "Ted Spits at Fans!" screamed the *Globe*. Yawkey fined him $5,000: "in *front* pages across the country," said Wolff, "everybody talking about 'Williams, there he goes again.'" In 1958, he threw a bat that accidently struck Gladys Heffernan, Cronin's housekeeper, in the face. That Christmas the Splinter sent her a peace offering—a $500 diamond watch.

"You haven't lived till you've seen Williams," Gowdy told each new Sox sidekick: his first, an Elmira, New York, native; Syracuse University graduate; and WFBL Syracuse announcer. "I happened to be standing on the corner. The hook picked me up," said Bob Delaney, joining Curt in 1951. Jim Woods thought Bob "one of the strangest damn ducks to ever work in studio," disliking baseball and putting doggerel in his scorebook. Antipodally, Joe Castiglione liked his vocabulary and "terrific pipes—easy to listen to." The pipe organ agreed: "If there's one thing I know how to do well, it's sell."

In 1954, he went to the Polo Grounds, succeeding Harwell, off to Baltimore, not the Fens. In 1957, the Giants and Dodgers left New York, leaving the ex-Navy man at sea. Delaney became John F. Kennedy's PA Voice in the 1960 presidential campaign, introduced him at one rally after another, and hosted the 1960s Yankees six-state radio network, feting "Red Ball Service" and how, as in a grease-spot intellection, "Atlantic [Richfield] keeps your car on the go." Later he did Ivy League football, narrated the *NFL Game of the Week*, and became a disc jockey, dying of a stroke in 2008, pipes intact.

A 1991 film asked *What About Bob?* By the late 1940s Okie Bob Murphy was an ex-Marine master technical sergeant and University of Tulsa graduate: like

Delaney, unsure of his postwar career. "You like sports. Why don't you try radio?" Jack Murphy, later San Diego *Union* sports editor, told his brother, who soon did Oklahoma football's record 47-game winning streak, basketball, and even hockey, having never seen a game. Like Gowdy, Bob found the minors at Class C Muskogee and Oklahoma City one-stop rote: "ads, play-by-play, set equipment up." In 1954, hiring Murphy, Curt began tutoring—"demanding. Get it right, or else"—as Allen had mentored him.

Once Mel razzed Gowdy's sports coat on the air. "A few buckets of paint," Curt replied, "you dip an old T-shirt, and you really got yourself a nice sports shirt." Murphy now took the heat: "You're wearing a cardigan sweater, cowboy boots, and a cowboy hat," said the Cowboy. "We got a lot of work." In 1952, Ted briefly returned from Korea. The Sox held a "Day," the diva homering. In 1954, he broke his collarbone diving for a ball, missed five weeks, and returned in a double-header, going eight for nine. One day Williams fanned twice, telling mates, "Next time I'm up, [Cal McLish's] gonna throw me that sidearm slow curve and I'll hit it in the upper deck." He did. "His drama was uncanny," said Murphy, who till now hadn't lived.

Ultimately, baseball, as opposed to hitting one, became a chore. "The Red Sox are young and full of ginger," a late-1950s writer said, prematurely. "But Ted Williams is their big man, and he is old and full of bitterness" at age, near-misses, glad-handing phonies, and more than five years lost to service (1943–1945 World War II and 1952–1953 Korea). "He wanted to go to World War II, but Korea?" said a friend. "Younger players weren't drafted. He thought politicians singled him out." Some saw a defense-shirking, Sox-harming, draft-dodging (!) brat. The charges stung, not stuck.

What did were Williams's .344 average, franchise-high 521 home runs, and as many as 43 single-season dingers, 86 extra-base hits, 368 total bases, and 162 bases on balls, walking more overall than anyone, save Babe Ruth and Rickey Henderson. He led six times in batting: 1941–1942, 1947–1948, and 1957–1958 (.406, .356, .343, .369, .388, and .328, respectively); four, homers: 1941–1942, 1947, and 1949 (37, 36, 32, and 43); four, RBI: 1939, 1942, 1947, and 1949 (145, 137, 114, and 159, with Stephens); and twice won the MVP and Triple Crown. "Take away his military time," Curt said, "and Ted'd own the record books." Number 9 "wanted people to say, 'There goes the greatest hitter who ever lived.'" They do.

In 1960, Williams hit his five hundredth home run, batted .316, and helped his team draw more than 1.1 million, the last time they passed 1 million till 1967. Most came to bid an affectionate farewell. "For so long," said Gowdy, "he'd been too stubborn to meet Red Sox fans halfway." Only as Ted graced *Sportfolio* to *Sport*, touted baseball buttons, Ted's Root Beer, Moxie soda, and the Jimmy Fund—and New England eyed a future without, to cite a 2001 poll, its leading person of the century except for JFK—did a white-hot affair become old-shoe love.

In 1960, Boston played the Cubs in spring training in Arizona. An hour before the game, Williams, taking batting practice, hit the first five pitches over the right-field wall. The Cubs watched in silence. Finally, one said, "I'll be darned if that guy doesn't play this park like a pitch-and-putt." Let us retrieve a Final Swing greater than any Hole in One.

On Wednesday, September 28, 1960, Gowdy cut ads in downtown Boston, had a tape recorder break, and arrived only 30 minutes before the year's last game at Fenway Park. Johnny Orlando, the equipment manager with whom Williams walked Philadelphia the night before hitting .406, revealed that Ted had a chest cold: thus, would miss that weekend's final series in New York. "Listen, this is The Kid's last game," he said. "He's gonna retire after today."

Gowdy approached the Splinter: "Are you?"

"Ted said, 'Yeah, don't mention it till the game starts.' Nobody knew."

In a pre-game salaam, the Sox retired No. 9 and gave Ted a silver bowl, plaque, and $4,000 check for the Jimmy Fund. Gowdy emceed, Sox Voice–turning–publicity director Bill Crowley warning, "You don't have a note!" Curt replied, "I don't need any about Williams," ad-libbing:

"Today we honor a man who in my opinion and many of yours was the greatest hitter who ever lived." Applause. "I didn't get to see Ty Cobb, Paul Waner, or Rogers Hornsby, who hit .400 four or five times, but I don't see how they could be better than Ted Williams."

The Cowboy referenced "pages of batting records [he could have had] up here, but what really made Ted was pride. He had an intense pride that every time up he wanted to produce a hit. Not only for himself but for the fans at Fenway whom he secretly loved, who stood behind him amid ups and downs. Pride is what made him go and why he's here. The greatest hitter of all time, Ted Williams."

Moved, The Kid whispered, "I want a copy. That's one of the nicest tributes to me ever."

"I don't *have* a copy," Curt said.

"Oh, shit," Ted said, walking to home plate.

To the last, as Ned Martin might have said, the Big Guy was himself. He pricked reporters: "Despite some of the terrible things written about me by the knights of the keyboard up there, and they were terrible things—I'd like to forget them but I can't." He lauded T. A., Joe Cronin, and past and present mates, then addressed the Nation. "My stay in Boston has been the most wonderful part of my life. If someone should ask me what one place I'd want to play if I had it to do all over again, I would say Boston, for it has the greatest owner in baseball and the greatest fans in America." Gowdy understood. "Ted wanted to thank the New England fans who cherished him—and they did. You had to know Ted—he got mad at himself more than anybody. I think New England forgave him more than he did himself."

The game *v.* Baltimore followed—meaningless and all-meaning. Williams walked, flied to center, then hit to Orioles right-fielder Al Pilarcik, who caught the ball against the bull pen. "If that one didn't go out," Ted told Vic Wertz, "none of them will today." In the eighth inning, The Kid, 42, batted against Jack Fisher, 21, born in his 1939 rookie year. It was raining. The lights were on. The ball wasn't carrying. Fisher threw a ball, then "laid a ball right there," Ted said. "I don't think I ever missed like I missed that one but I did. I'm there trying to figure what happened"—luck. "I could see Fisher out there with his glove up to get the ball back quickly, as much as saying, 'I threw that one by him. I'll throw another by him.'" Fisher "practically gave it [the pitch] away."

Gowdy's WHDH radio call was thought lost for several decades. Re-creating, Curt said, "The count one and one here on Williams. Everybody quiet here at Fenway Park after they gave him a standing ovation of two minutes knowing that this is probably his last time at bat. One out, nobody on, last of the eighth inning. Jack Fisher into his windup." Some say Fisher grooved the pitch. Gowdy noted it wasn't even a strike. "Williams never swung at a bad pitch. His thesis was, get a good pitch to hit, and you'll be a better hitter." Ted swung anyway. "There's a long drive to right field! That ball is going—and it is gone! A home run for Ted Williams in his last time at bat in the major leagues!"

In 2000, ESPN TV's *SportsCentury* broadcast the original coverage. "Good afternoon, everybody, Curt Gowdy, Fenway Park, Boston, Ted Williams's last game in a Red Sox uniform," it began. Later: "And there's a long drive to deep right-center! It could be! It could be! It is!" said the Cowboy—joyous, incredulous, tone rising, voice breaking. "It's a home run! Ted Williams has homered in his last time at bat in a Red Sox uniform! . . . At home plate, they're waiting for him!" Curt remembered being "choked up. My heart was pounding—unbelievably emotional." A crowd of 10,454 had tonsils redder than Red Sox hose.

In 1986, NBC TV recalled The Swing. "How did you know it was Williams's last at-bat?" said Bob Costas. "Ted told me," Gowdy said. The Kid refused to tip his cap, Updike observing that "God does not answer letters." In 1958, a writer said, "Williams is the greatest hitter since Babe Ruth, and last year was in many ways his finest. Because of him, Boston finished third. Without him, it is hard to say how far they could sink." The Athens of America was about to learn, wrote Ed Linn, "how England felt when it lost India."

In 1951, Allen made Gowdy join the Townies. In 1960, Curt made Murphy leave Boston for the Orioles' lead job—"I know you love it here, but you can't *not* go." Next year Jack Fisher faced Roger Maris, as he had Williams in the rain. "It's [home run] number 60! He's tied the Babe!" Murphy said on WBAL Baltimore. In late 1961, the O's ditched sponsor Hamm Brewery, Bob "getting lost in the shuffle." He approached expansion Mets general manager George Weiss, who already had hired Lindsey Nelson, a network paladin, and ex-jock Ralph Kiner, for cachet. The third man should leaven them, Weiss said: "be a steady professional." Hearing the Maris tape, George found his man.

"Bob's distinctive voice filled the air," Nelson later said. "Calling baseball, guys now sound the same." Like Allen, Curt was a conversationalist. Lindsey "was a straight-ahead announcer, eyes on baseball," said Murphy. Adjusting, Bob found the water fine. The 1962–1978 Mets forged the bigs' longest broadcast triad. In 1979, Nelson resigned, Murphy increasingly "the first sign of spring," the *New York Post's* Jay Greenberg wrote. *Newsday's* Marty Noble called his "the voice of all things Met"—at a deli, aboard the Staten Island Ferry, rabbit ears ferrying the Apple's Channel 9—summer's soundtrack, dog-eared and beloved.

As in 1955, Murphy's baritone swooped. He liked the word "marvelous," coined *The Happy Recap* after a Mets victory, and rejoiced at the epic 1986 Sox

World Series collapse. "Heee struck heeem out!" A batter flew to left. "Deep . . .
it may go . . . let's watch." Then: "Here's the throw. *Out* at the plate!" In 1969,
Jerry Koosman was "wonderful"; 1973, Tug McGraw "unbelievable"; 1985, Dar-
ryl Strawberry's "the most amazing homer I've ever seen," striking the Busch Stadium clock. The patriarch outlasted 112 Mets third basemen, at 79 received an
American flag that flew over Iwo Jima, and loved baseball's "redeeming features."
Sox redemption meant musical chairs in the wake of Bob's vamoose.

In 1951, two future Townies replaced Curt in New York. Later Crowley did
Holy Cross football and basketball, taught economics there, and economically
called 1957–1960 Boston. Art Gleeson had been a California League announcer,
World War II submariner, and 1946–1949 Voice of the PCL California Oaks. He
aired Mutual's 1953–1959 *Game of the Day* before succeeding Murphy in 1960 at
the Fens: "a gentleman, kind, courteous, never wed, loved baseball," said Gowdy.
Crowley's leaving radio for publicity still left the Sox one 1961 Voice short. Curt
responded by hiring a 37-year-old rookie.

Hoey taught New England baseball. Britt played English like a harp. Coleman never really left Fenway. Gowdy anchored an entire network. Ned Martin
became the Sox most beloved Voice. That view is personal, not parochial. I think
much of Red Sox Nation would agree.

Raised in suburban Upper Merion Township, Pennsylvania, Ned saw his first
game at Shibe Park at nine. Dad, a former semipro pitcher, liked the A's, one
night bringing home cocktail coasters autographed by Johnny Marcum and Jimmie Foxx. "Foxx!" Martin gaped, seeing the coasters next morning. "He was like
God to me because the Philadelphia Athletics were my team!" Pop got the autographs in a lounge. Later Ned got Skeeter Newsome's outside Shibe—"What a
thrill"—loving columnist Red Smith's idiom, "the music of the game." In 1941, he
entered Duke University, then the Fourth Marine Division, where a darker score
played maim and gore. Its effect, Norman Mailer wrote in another context, bred
"an attentiveness in his eyes which gave offer of some knowledge of the abyss."

For a long time Martin spurned talk of courage. "I'm not one of the guys that
you see raising the flag [on Iwo Jima]," he said, having grown up fast. Hub TV's
Clark Booth noted, "It is always that way with the guys who saw the real bitter
action. He never bragged, needed praise, and hated shtick and self-promotion."
In 1990, Ned finally recalled the isle. "I don't think we were there thirty minutes

before we came upon a shell-hole," he told the *Herald*'s Joe Fitzgerald. "I looked in and saw it was filled with dead Marines; I mean blown-up Marines, with entrails and . . . oh, God, I'd never seen anything like that before. Then I started looking around and pretty soon death got so common." He spoke during Desert Storm—a distant made-for-TV epic. "This was different, people being blown apart."

American brass foresaw a nine-day operation. On Day 26, "word spread that the flag was flying on Mount Suribachi—our flag! What a feeling!" Ned returned to major in English, read Wolfe and Hemingway, and do—what? Inchoate, he didn't know. At war, then publicist Nelson met the French Foreign Legion, served Dwight Eisenhower, and helped reporter Ernie Pyle. Back home, he wrote for a paper: "after Europe, not excited about a drunk in city court." By 1950, Martin worked on the Pennsylvania Turnpike, hearing the Phils win a pennant, then brave a Yanks' Series sweep. He tried advertising and publishing—"fabulously unsuccessful"—before conjuring college wireless. "I'd worked at the same station where [Duke '42] Bob Wolff'd started. Now he critiqued my tapes," helping Ned crack Rockville, Maryland's country music—"then 'hillbilluh'"—WINX. Finally he was on his way.

In 1955, Martin began play-by-play at Athens, Georgia, including Fran Tarkenton's minor-league no-hitter. Next year Ned leapt to Triple-A Charleston: the next five, he said, as mentally hard as Iwo. "I kept sending tapes to big-league teams, but nothing happened." Then, in September 1960, Boston visited Baltimore, Martin doing an inning and a half. "We didn't call it an audition," said Curt, "but it was." Next January Ned visited Fenway to accompany players like Bill Monbouquette on the Red Sox Caravan—"a ticket-selling type of thing"— having only seen it in 1948 playoff film. He left the Kenmore Hotel, crossed the bridge and railroad tracks, and saw "what looked like a brickyard from the outside, not at all like a baseball park."

A week later Martin met Gleeson, Crowley, and Helen Robinson, the team's beloved 1941–2001 switchboard operator—"one of those classic institutions in the park," Ned said in 1980. "An Art Moscato [1947–1989 ticket salesman, then director] or Lib Dooley [seeing more than four thousand straight home games between 1944 and 1998] or Joe Mooney [1971–2000 head groundskeeper, dubbed "a cross between General Patton and Tom Thumb"] or [press steward] Tommy McCarthy or John Kiley," Fenway's 1953–1989 and Boston Garden's full-time organist, scored by a writer for "not psyching up the fans." Kiley's response: "Mr.

Yawkey wouldn't permit it, and now it's become a tradition." Pause: "Anyway, the fans can psych themselves up," and did. Each grasped Fenway's strategy and continuity: Like each classic park, it shaped the game within.

A single off the Monster was a dinger in the Bronx. A pop fly elsewhere found the Screen. Jack Mann wrote, "Hitters love . . . and pitchers hate [the Wall], and it drives managers crazy." Dick Radatz felt it "an equalizer," encouraging lefties to swat outside pitches. "People come to see what it's like," said Ned. "'You mean it's that close? Damn right.'" (Yankees pitcher Ralph Terry likened the Wall "to spending three hours in a phone booth.") Unpredictability was key. "Get behind by four runs, no problem. Ahead by four in the eighth, delay champagne," mused Martin. Missing: security. "A little hit, an error, can open a door. A walk, triple to right, maybe down the line, poof," smooth sailing gone. "Spellbound by the big leagues," Ned recalled "certain plays."

Dick Williams once drove toward the bull pen. "Crack of the bat—there went Al Luplow, right-fielder of the Indians, who leapt at the ball and fell into the pen," said Martin. Several Red Sox raised their hands, hoping to deke the umpire. "Instead, he said, 'You're out!'—the greatest catch I saw at Fenway." Another Tribe outfielder fell down, giving Gary Geiger an inside-the-park grand slam. Dick Stuart arrived to hit baseballs over tall buildings in a single bound. Dr. Strangeglove "was ten years too soon with Boston," said Pesky, his 1963–1964 manager. "He would have been a great designated hitter. Just no interest in being a real player. Nobody could hit well enough to make up for what that jokester cost us in the field." The joke was not always on the Sox.

One day Stuart—"no Jesse Owens," said Ned—lined "a shot off the Wall that hit the center-fielder in his Adam's apple and knocked him down, the ball ricocheting to the corner." Stuart "kept running—uphill—and got what may be the shortest inside-the-parker ever hit! Fair or unfair park, people argue." Unarguable: Yawkey's and wife Jean's initials in Morse code (TAY and JRY) spliced two vertical stripes on the scoreboard. Gowdy's booth was just above the first home-plate screen, built to shade a visitor and roll fouls on the field: "the closest spot in the league, so near what Cronin called the 'lousy'—to me, terrific—geometrics: the Monster, vast center field, big right." Fenway was "a Japanese garden," pristine and tended; to *SI* writer Robert Creamer, "oddly shaped but most attractive, great in which to view a game. It is hard to find a really bad seat in the rambling one-level stands."

Sit "along the left-field line and listen to the more pungent comments," he urged. "Special 'skyline' boxes swing out from either side of rooftop press box." Ushers were "plentiful, courteous, and helpful, and may not accept tips. The refreshment stands are easily accessible from most seats for a quick snack." Hot dogs (not-yet Fenway Franks) and beer ('Gansett only) were "staples, plus 'tonic' [New England term for soda pop]. . . . Subway from nearby Kenmore Square station connects with all parts of Greater Boston, as well as to all New England via railroad, bus, or airplane. It's easy to drive to Fenway, and there's supposed to be parking space for 8,500 cars in vicinity, but don't rely on it; parking ranges from 25 cents to $1. Leaving park area after game can be difficult." Dicier was replacing Williams, though Creamer had a candidate. "Boston fans may find [Carl Yastrzemski's] name hard to pronounce, but they will not find him hard to take."

In 1959, the Phillies had expected the then 20-year-old second baseman to take to baseball's first steel-and-concrete plant—Connie Mack Stadium (née Shibe Park). "I had a lot of batting practice there, a much better park for a left-handed hitter," said Yastrzemski, who then reconsidered. The Sox had a near-cellar team and deep-pocket owner: Yaz could play, and get a $100,000 bonus. He topped that year's Carolina League at .377, then hit .339 in 1960 Triple-A. One day Boston played an exhibition *v.* his Minneapolis Millers. "We were all curious," said Gowdy, "so I ask a guy, 'Which one's Yastrzemski?' He pointed to a figure swinging a couple of bats, and I said, '*That* little guy?' Not really, but I expected a giant after seeing Williams."

April 11, 1961: One rookie, Martin, called another's first of 3,419 hits. In early June, Yaz averaged .213. The son of a Long Island potato farmer straightened up, tried to pull, and climbed to .266. "Without patience," he said, "[skipper Mike] Higgins would not have stuck with me. He was great with young players but not the kind who make big things happen. Remember, he had lousy teams." We do. "My rookie year was very difficult. I was playing left field, where Williams played, and there was that pressure." Martin felt it, too. "We were on the downside, and only the Yankees drew." The Sox brooked a 19-day road trip. Jackie Jensen "jumped the club and went home." On the other hand, Ned liked the booth arrangement: He did innings 1-3 and 7-9 on radio and 4-6 video; Gowdy, the inverse; Art Gleeson, TV.

First-year Chuck Schilling fielded like Bobby Doerr. Rookie of the Year Don Schwall pitched in the All-Star Game, before 31,851 at Fenway, rain forcing a

1-1 regulation tie. Monbo set a then Sox K mark—17, at Washington. Carroll Hardy became the only man to pinch-hit for Williams *and* Yastrzemski. Martin's year began with No. 8, ending with non-Sox No. 9. The Yankees' Roger Maris needed a last-game home run to beat Ruth's regular-season 60. In pre-game, Ned asked "something that announcers aren't supposed to: 'How you feel about No. 61?'" Starter Tracy Stallard said, "I got one good fastball. I don't want to walk him, and I'll throw him the fastball. More power to him if he hits it." In the fourth, he did.

"Most people have only heard Phil's [Yankees' Rizzuto's] call," Martin said. "It's in the Hall of Fame." Incredibly, Ned's wasn't taped. Maris worked a 2-0 count. "Fastball, hit deep to right!" said Rizzuto. "This could be it! Way back there! Holy Cow, he did it! Sixty-one for Maris! Look at 'em fight for that ball out there! Holy Cow!" Ned looked on, conflicted. "I was a kid when Ruth played and sad to see the record fall. I also remember Stallard following every footstep as Maris toured the bases. What a climax for an amazing rookie year." How to surpass it? Six years later he found a way.

In 1953, Martin saw Satchel Paige throw in Washington, "his hesitation pitch still getting people out." In 1965, Ned aired his childhood hero's last bigs game: one Sox hit in three innings at Kansas City. Later hero and hero-worshipper retrieved that night at a baseball dinner, Paige saying, "If you think I'm gonna throw any place but the letters, shame on ya!" If Martin wanted shame, he need only eye the field.

The 1961–1965 Sox placed sixth, seventh, eighth twice, and ninth. Each summer our family left Upstate New York to visit my Grandma's home in Worcester, 45 miles west of Boston. At 11 a.m., Dad would say, "Let's go to Fenway." By 1:30, we arrived for a 2 p.m. game, found a ticket window, and got a seat—a *box* seat. A writer had wailed on The Kid's good-bye, "What are we going to write about now?" As 1960 skippers Billy Jurges, Mike Higgins, and Del Baker fell to Higgins (again), Pesky, Billy Herman, and Runnels; 1947–1958 general manager Cronin became AL president, replaced by Bucky Harris, Dick O'Connell, Higgins, and O'Connell (again); and T. A. played pepper, won at bridge, shuffled the cabinet, and confessed, "The trouble is, I like to think of my people as associates, not employees"—they wrote about what was wrong.

An old dirge played a new refrain: The franchise was country club. "They told me when I came here," Schilling said of 1961, "that there were a lot of guys who didn't care much whether they won or lost as long as they had fun." *SI* knew who to blame: "When Yawkey liked a player—and Yawkey falls in love with players—he wanted to keep him on the payroll, so scouting . . . became a sort of pension pool." This starved the farm, money spent on bonus babies buying "only a pauper's return." Increasingly, brass merited being returned to sender. After Harris dealt Sammy White for Russ Nixon, White retired, Indians GM Frank Lane got Commissioner Ford Frick to let him keep Nixon, and Boston was left with untried catchers 6-foot-6 Don Gile, six four Haywood Sullivan, six three Jim Pagliaroni, and five eleven Ed Sadowski. T. A. would have traded all for 5-foot-7 Yogi Berra.

Some even imputed bigotry. Jackie Robinson broke the color line in 1947. The '50s Cubs inked shortstop Ernie Banks, who could beat Buddin with a whiffle bat. In 1956, according to one report, the Townies vainly tried to buy Al Smith and Charlie Neal, each black. In 1959, infielder Pumpsie Green ended their stain as baseball's last all-white team. Later signed were Reggie Smith, George Scott, Cecil Cooper, Jim Rice, Mo Vaughn, David Ortiz, and Manny being Manny—belatedly, not begrudgingly. "Other clubs get an Aaron," said a friend. "Our first black player hits a career .246," Green not worth the wait. Racism can be real (Jim Crow, red-lining) or faux (Duke lacrosse, Al Sharpton, and Crown Heights). Boston was an equal opportunity bungler, muffing Willie Mays *and* Pee Wee Reese. Yawkey conceded "a lot of mistakes. It could have been managed better, and it's my fault it wasn't." Tellingly, The Kid and Gowdy both called him "the greatest man I ever met."

About this time, a photo showed President Kennedy and aide David Powers perusing *TSN* at a Senators home opener. Powers, later JFK library director, was unofficial "Undersecretary of Baseball," keeping "Jack briefed on the Sox." 1961: Philly's 6-foot-8 Gene Conley, "in the twilight of my mediocre career," and Boston's six seven Frank Sullivan begot baseball's still-biggest two-man trade. 1962: The Sox bus stopped in Manhattan traffic. Conley and Green got off, sought a restroom, and resurfaced three days later trying to board a plane for Israel. "I'm going to fine you $1,500," said T. A. "But if you stay in line for the rest of the year, I'll give it back." Each did. "Good thing," said Conley. "We really needed the money." 1963: Stuart led the league with 42 home runs, Yaz won his first batting crown, and Boston vied till June. 1964: Rookie Tony Conigliaro hit 24 dingers. Radatz won 16 games, saving 29.

Lindsey Nelson said of the original Mets: "They played for fun. They weren't capable of playing for anything else." The Sox could be Metsian. Gleeson rued "a home run for [Baltimore's] Jerry Adair" and "a bunt. Radatz throws it away!" Martin said: "Ground ball, nice stop by [the O's Luis] Aparicio"; "the White Sox are howling now"; and "[Al] Kaline scores, and the Tigers win it, 9 to 8!" Gowdy knew feast: "One of Stuart's longest drives of the year"; "[Eddie] Bressoud scores, there goes Lenny Green to third!"; "a double! Monbouquette will talk about that for a month!" Also famine: "There's a blast by [Brooks] Robinson!"; "We'll have a new pitcher, Arnold Earley"; and "[Yankees' Phil] Linz is in there! The ball game's over!"

In 1961, a shy, quick-wristed 18-year-old pull hitter narrowed signing to the Sox or stripes. Like Yaz, Rico Petrocelli frothed over Boston's lineup. Batting practice convinced scout Bots Nekola that he had "the perfect swing for Fenway." In turn, Rico was "so impressed by how well they treated us"—key in baseball's pre-draft early '60s—that he said, "This is it," inked as Yawkey retilled the farm. Dick O'Connell became executive vice president, making career scout Neil Mahoney director. Aide Ed Kenney said, "We didn't fire many [scouts], but we called them all in and reindoctrinated them. We wanted a complete player, not just slow but strong, but one who could run and field and throw."

Petrocelli's first full Sox year, 1965, was Gowdy's last. In Florida, 27 of 39 roster players were in-house, mostly young. The season commenced in the presidential opener at D.C. Stadium, Lyndon Johnson "throwing out not one baseball but two," said Curt. "The Red Sox lost [missed] each." It was a trailer for their year.

"It's Red Sox baseball!" Curt began, partly brought to you by the General Cigar Co. "Things go right when you have a White Owl!" Would they for Petrocelli? Doubt was in the saddle. "There's no question about his fielding ability. There is . . . about his bat," said Gowdy. "A marvelous fielder, with great range, a good pair of hands, a strong arm. If he can hit even a little"—.251 career average, 773 RBI, and still tenth Sox all-time in homers (210)—"he could be a coming big-league star." Rico, "deep in the box, slight crouch," struck out to start the game. Batting second and fifth were new center-fielder Green and Lee Thomas, moving to first base, respectively. "Outside of that," said the Cowboy, "it's"—sadly—"about the same."

In November 1964, Gleeson, 58, died. Replacing him: Mel Parnell. "We've got him back in a sense," Curt mused. "If you're half as good a broadcaster as you were a pitcher [1947–1956 Boston: 1949 league 25-win leader: lefty franchise-best 123-75 record; relying on guile, not control], you're going to be a smash hit." He wasn't. Gowdy's stories were. Armed Forces Radio meant that "in Germany, they're listening at night, and Japan and Far East, in the morning." In the presidential box "sat Joe Cronin and Mike Higgins, Red Sox vice president, an old friend of Lyndon Johnson"—their coda four innings later. Vice President Hubert Humphrey, Speaker of the House John McCormack, Congressman Gerald Ford, and Senators Mike Mansfield and Everett Dirksen gathered, the Illinoisan's "curly gray hair flying in the wind."

Monbouquette, "a lad of French-Canadian descent," pitched his "fifth opening-day assignment." Despite losing 27 pounds, D.C.'s Frank Howard, "with Radatz is one of the [bigs] two most monstrous men." Parnell quoted Ron Santo calling Conigliaro, 20, "the most aggressive young hitter he'd seen." A .368 spring average, Curt said, suggested "the blossoming of a star." (That year Tony C. became the youngest AL home run titlist.) Below, Conig, then Yaz, stole second. Gowdy: "Billy Herman really has 'em running." (Everything is relative.) Thomas hit a three-run dinger. Green followed: "a fair ball bouncing in the corner—no, it just cleared the fence!" Final: 7-2.

Martin hyped the Red Sox yearbook, "on sale now throughout newsstands and outlets all over New England." By mail, send 50 cents, "plus a dime for postage," to "Fenway Park, Boston 15." Gowdy read telegrams, including, "On your fifteenth year with the Red Sox, hope that you have happiness and the gladness we had together. Your pal, Johnny Orlando." Invoking that "Red Sox clubhouse boy" brought Lyndon Johnson back to life.

The then Senate majority leader and Speaker of the House Sam Rayburn entered the 1950s Sox clubhouse after a game, Curt recalled. "We'd like to see Pinky [Mike] Higgins," LBJ said of their fellow Texan. Orlando knew his etiquette: "*Nobody's* allowed in the clubhouse." Johnson calmly explained who he and Rayburn were. "I don't care *who* you are—[President] Eisenhower, whoever—*out!*" said Orlando, banishing a *future* President.

Gowdy relived the story whenever he saw Johnny—also how Thomas's 1965 ground-rule Fenway double was grabbed by a Labrador retriever, making Baltimore's Chuck Thompson pun, "Well, that was a dog-goned double." On September 16, 1,247 in the Fens saw Dave Morehead face Cleveland. By the eighth inning, a no-hitter was in the works. Listening in his office, Curt rushed to the booth, bumping Ned off radio. "Grounder back to the mound. The throw to first. That's it!" he said of Vic Davalillo's pinch-hit final out. "A no-hitter for Dave Morehead!" That winter the Cowboy moved full-time to NBC.

Nothing lasted, Ned observed in 1997. "You think Schilling's set, and he loses it. Same thing, Schwall and Radatz. Morehead reverts to form. Tony C. seems set for Cooperstown"—till the Angels' Jack Hamilton began his wind. In 1963, Conley hurt his arm, was released, and pratfalled to the minors. Noting a service near the team hotel, he entered the church, found a pew, and began to cry.

A kind man sat next to him, whispering, "What's the matter, son? Did you lose your dad or your mom?"

Still sobbing, Conley said, "Neither, sir. I lost my fastball."

7 THE RUBICON (1966–1973)

In 1962, ABC gave Gowdy the nascent American—some said Almost—Football League. In 1964, NBC bought it, and Curt. A year later the New York Jets signed quarterback Joe Namath. "Suddenly," said the Cowboy, "the league didn't mean Upper Slobovia anymore." Meanwhile, in 1953–1965 Mel Allen, Bud Blattner, Jack Buck, Dizzy Dean, Joe Garagiola, Merle Harmon, Lindsey Nelson, and Bob Wolff, among others, did network baseball. In 1966, NBC asked Gowdy to replace them all.

Entering the Hall of Fame in 1953, ex-Cardinals pitcher Dean thanked God for "a strong body, a good right arm, and a weak mind." That June his Saturday *Game of the Week*—TV sport's first network series—debuted on ABC, moving to posher CBS in 1955. Ol' Diz made baseball a regular-season *national*, not just *local*, product. If *Game* failed, "maybe TV sports has a different future," said then CBS Sports head Bill MacPhail. Instead, it added Sunday in 1957, luring an amazing two in three sets in use.

Diz sang "The Wabash Cannonball" and called the viewer *pod-nuh* and trashed English like no one had, or will. Runners *slud*. Fielders returned to their *respectable* positions. A hitter stood *confidentially* at the plate. CBS offered Dean a prime-time series. (He declined: too much work.) Diz cracked the Gallup Poll's Ten Most Admired List (the only broadcaster, ever). Middle America loved the three hundred pounds, string tie, and Stetson—the whole rustic goods.

In 1965, ABC bought exclusivity, inanely dumping Diz. Next year NBC became baseball's sole network, expecting Curt to match what critic Ron Powers called Dean's "James Fenimore Cooper by way of Uncle Remus." It kept the Series and All-Star Game. Better, *Game* would air everywhere, not, like CBS, in just non–big league cities—raising rights, thus stakes. "We'd liked Gowdy with the Sox and AFL," said NBC sports head Carl Lindemann. "He gave us two sports for the price of one."

Curt's second Series was 1964's. "There's a high drive to deep right! And forget about it! It is gone!" said Gowdy of Mickey Mantle. "The ball game's over! [2-1] Mantle has just broken a World Series record [Ruth's 15 home runs]." Just axed by the Yankees, Allen had done each 1947–1963 Classic, Curt now replacing *him*. Needing help, Gowdy convinced The Kid to join him: "outspoken, would have been a terrific analyst." Williams bit "because I trust Curt implicitly, and on the condition I don't have to wear a tie."

Their March 1966 deal soon came undone. Sears spokesman Williams was pictured putting gear into the back of a Ford truck, irking *Game* sponsor Chrysler Corp. Another client, Falstaff Beer, yelped when Gowdy KO'd its Falstaffian face. "I'm not Dean, I can't sing 'The Wabash Cannonball,'" Curt protested. Falstaff's Pee Wee Reese had been Diz's 1960–1965 *pod-nuh*. "I liked Pee Wee, I figured we'd get along, and Falstaff'd have their boy," said Gowdy.

NBC said OK—but would a generation to which *Game* bespoke Dean?

"As spectacle, baseball suffers on [TV]," Harry Caray later wrote. "The fan at the park rarely notices the time span between pitches. The same fan at home . . . finds things dull." Gowdy frowned on spectacle. The late 1960s and early '70s smiled. "The good news is that Curt was thorough," said Blattner. Bad: "He may not have many downs," said Associated Press, "[but also] not many ups." Just the facts, ma'am, worked in a Republic umbilically attached to baseball. They felt Paleozoic in an anything-but-bore-me age. The Cowboy seemed too bland for a hip "place, environment, relations," to quote Thornton Wilder. By contrast, the two men who *meant* the Sox for the next quarter century fit New England fine.

After high school, Ken Coleman had joined the army, served in Burma, and aired Indian rugby, cricket, and soccer on Armed Forces Radio, saying, "Try performing with twelve thousand troops listening." Released, he studied Oratory at Curry College, voiced a 250-watt Worcester affiliate, Vermont's Northern Baseball League, and later Boston University, Ohio State, and Harvard football, and golf, hoops, and bowling. *On the Waterfront*'s Marlon Brando mourned, "I could'a been a contender." In 1952, contending with Ken for Cleveland Browns radio, Lindsey

Nelson suddenly joined NBC. Coleman inherited the team's huge network, disliking the bogus and seeing humor in reverse.

In 1954, Ken added Indians TV. "Ten years I did them," he said. "My first year they win 111 games, get swept in the Series, then not much to tell." The exception was Rocky Colavito, tall, dark, and their primo pin-up since Boudreau. In 1959, No. 6 led the AL with 42 homers, Coleman not yet coining, "They usually show movies on a flight like that." That winter Cleveland dealt Rocky for Harvey Kuenn, Ken trying to ease the shock. One day now-Tiger Colavito retreated to the fence. "Back goes Wally against the rock," Coleman said, then red-faced: "For those of you interested in statistics, that was my eleventh fluff of the year. It puts me in third place in the American League."

For 14 years, his Browns were at or near first place in the NFL. Coleman aired seven champions, did eight network title and two College All-Star games, and called each pro touchdown (126) by Jim Brown, who ran the ball better than anyone has, or is ever likely to. One Sunday: "He is gone for the score! Eighty yards and the place is going crazy!" Another: "Jim Brown trying the left side! And Jim Brown is running! Getting his blockers and coming down the *right* side!" Of a screen pass, "At the 20, 30, 40, 45, still going, Jim Brown, one of the greatest runs we've ever seen him make! It's a touchdown: an 83-yard play!" A rival said, "Brown says he isn't Superman. What he means is that Superman isn't Brown." Jack Buck liked Jim's Boswell: "People [came to] identify Coleman with baseball, but he's the best football announcer I ever heard."

Ken's last Brownscast was Brown's farewell: Green Bay 23, Cleveland 12, in January 1966's NFL title game. Number 32 retired to Hollywood. At his peak as an institution, Coleman revisited the points of his past. Replacing Gowdy, the Townies spurned Martin, the natural heir: first, contacting Bob Murphy, who declined; then Coleman. You lucky stiff, Ken told himself, "taking Britt's and Hoey's job." He was introduced at a Red Sox press conference, silken and restrained: "a beautiful horn," said Boston Bruins Voice Bob Wilson, "and, oh, Ken played it well." Few then knew of EST, Zen, "If it feels good, do it," or "Honk if you want peace." Increasingly, the Nation *did* sense how the mid-1960s Sox could make you turn off, drop out, or give up baseball.

"The atmosphere was awful," said Ned, applying for Curt's No. 1 job "by sending a telegram to WHDH," later saying of ad men and higher-ups, "I'm just not a commercial person. I don't have the gift for gab." Some expected friction,

Ken's hiring "a deep disappointment" to Martin, Jon Miller said. Improbably, their friendship bloomed, Martin too busy grieving to resent. In 1955, his father's A's had moved to Kansas City, loyalty defaulting to the Phils. In September 1964, Philadelphia led the league by 6½ games. "With the Red Sox kaput, it looked like my other team'd make the Series," Ned said, on an off-day visiting dad. "He'd had several heart attacks, was thin, seemed tired. I was worried, but said good-bye." That week wife Barbara phoned him in Detroit: "Your Dad has died." Returning home, he found a letter from the crypt.

"Baseball had been our bond," said Martin. "By the time I saw him, the Phillies' fold had begun," losing 10 straight games and, ultimately, the pennant. In the letter, his dad predicted it: "'They're pitching [Chris] Short and [Jim] Bunning on panic and no one else. I'm afraid they're going to crash.'" Distraught, Ned rejoined a team that long ago had. "That fall," he said, "could have been wonderful. But the Phils' collapse and Dad's death brought a resounding nothing to its end." New England grasped his pain. Baseball, the *Globe*'s Mike Barnicle wrote, was not a matter of life and death. The Red Sox, he said, *were*.

Pain: Each 1966 Sox pitcher had a .500 or worse record. Progress: Boston drew 158,971 more than 1965, ending 14 games nearer first. Six-foot-five Jim Lonborg, soon aka Gentleman Jim, led in strikeouts and innings. Jose Santiago won 12 games. Joe Foy, Mike Andrews, and George Scott debuted at third, second, and first base, respectively, the farm overhaul kicking in. Tony C. led in five team-high categories, including homers (28) and RBI (93). Once he hit "the hardest ball off me ever," said Ralph Terry, striking the Screen near the top. "There was this crash, like a car accident, and the ball dropped straight down." Such Townies might be good. *As* good, they were young.

"We were getting better. The pitching just wasn't there," said Petrocelli. The 1965–1966 Sox lost 190 games. On September 27, 1966, Carl Yastrzemski lost game 535: a seemingly above-average player on a forever below-average club. Number 8 did not make next month's World Series. Coleman's Sox predecessor did.

As noted, local-team announcers aired the Series before 1966. "Our new pact changed everything," said NBC's Carl Lindemann. "Getting exclusivity, we intended to showcase our boy." Gowdy telecast half of every Dodgers-Orioles game. Vin Scully and Chuck Thompson did 4½ innings in Los Angeles and Baltimore, respectively, not *each* game like before. Ernie Harwell, Bill O'Donnell, and Miller had or would air the Orioles. Only Thompson defined Charm City, his voice somehow evoking a "guy sipping a cold beer on his back porch," said Bob Costas, "keeping up with his team."

Scully had already televised the 1953, 1955–1956, 1959, 1963, and 1965 Series. Before Game One NBC mandarins explained the change. "My fans [in California] won't be able to hear me," Vin replied.

"Yes, they will," said Lindemann. "In Baltimore you'll be on NBC *Radio*."

"What about *TV*?" Scully countered, not televising daily. Carl never forgot the chill.

Game One bred tit for tat. Scully did the first half: "Just wonderful," said Lindemann, "with Gowdy supplying color." Curt then completed a 15-strikeout 5-2 Orioles clunker made duller by Vin's reluctance to speak. "He sat there, wouldn't say a word, getting back at us." Only the Dodgers were as cold, not scoring for 33 straight innings. Four years later the Cowboy and Scully cohosted a CBS TV late-night awards dinner from L.A. "We kept 'em apart," said Lindemann, "practically did handstands to make sure they got the same amount of airtime."

By this time, baseball had been invaded by pro football body snatchers. D.C. (later RFK) Stadium rivaled a warehouse without the charm. The Braves moved—*again*—to antiseptic Atlanta–Fulton County Stadium. The Cardinals traded cozy-as-a-kitchen Busch Stadium for a same-name oval. Some felt Fenway Park a dinosaur, not realizing what they had. "About 20 times" Yawkey had tried to close Lansdowne Street and "move the Wall back," he said. Repeatedly, the city balked. T. A. also backed Governor John Volpe's three-man commission's $87-million retractable roof stadium: Give *us* a cookie-cutter! The state legislature refused. Leonard Bernstein said, "Music . . . doesn't have to pass the censor of the brain before it can reach the heart." Out of nowhere, '67 reached the heart, unforgettably reviving baseball in the Fens.

The season began with new skipper Dick Williams vowing to: a) "have only one chief [him]. All the rest are Indians"; and b) win more than he lost. "This might seem modest for some clubs," Petrocelli laughed, "but to us he was nuts. What Dick knew was the talent he'd had managing at [Triple-A] Toronto." That winter Carl Yastrzemski had begun a conditioning program: to Rico, "maybe the first player ever." Boston didn't get the program, the home opener drawing 8,324. "In terms of interest," Coleman added, "the bottom had fallen out." On April 14, a rookie began his bigs career at Yankee Stadium. "A kid pitcher from Toronto," Ken said later, like liturgy. "That's where this story starts."

In a one-out ninth, "Billy Rohr [was] on the threshold," Ken said on WHDH radio. "Eight hits in the game—all of them belong to Boston . . . Fly ball to left field! Yastrzemski is going hard—way back—way back! And he dives—and makes a tremendous catch! One of the greatest catches we've ever seen by Yastrzemski in left field! . . . Everybody [14,375] in Yankee Stadium on their feet roaring as Yastr-zemski went back and came down with that ball!" Two batters later Elston Howard singled, Tony C. catching "it on the first hop. No chance." The rook won only two more games, became a Garden Grove, California, attorney, and wrote Coleman a letter on the Sox twentieth reunion that "was lovely, about the closeness of that club." In 1967, Fleetwood Records repackaged WHDH's *The Impossible Dream*, from Broadway's *Man of La Mancha*, as a must-have Christmas gift—Ken voicing beautifully, as if his "past life," Churchill said in another context, "had been but a preparation for this hour."

Of Rohr, Coleman said, "The fans began to sense it. This year was not quite the same." That year riot seared Detroit—43 died—and an estimated 125 other cities. Protestors fought police. Viet Nam was a horror house. Said Martin: "The Red Sox were, if not an oasis, a sanctuary, if you will." Lonborg checked a losing streak the last day before the All-Star break, Boston six games back. On July 23, the Sox returned post-break to Logan Airport after a 10-game winning streak. "There are ten thousand people waiting for you," the pilot said. "They seem happy with what you've done." Usually, "after a road trip you want to sleep," said Rico. "Not tonight. They let the fans meet us, and we shared a special thing." As special were pilots from the Hub to Novia Scotia, tracing a late-season West Coast game by light in homes below.

"It is late on a late-summer night in 1967," wrote the *Herald*'s Kevin Convey. "The house is dark except for the flashlight beside my bed. It is quiet except for my transistor, in a whisper. Ken Coleman didn't just call baseball games. He called my summers"—spring and autumn, too.

In April, Jose Tartabull lined a fifteenth-inning "base hit to right! Here comes Tony! Here comes George! And the Red Sox have won it, 11-10!" said Coleman. One day Joe Foy "lined toward left field deep—and it's up there for a home run!" Another, "Line drive to Foy! Over to second! And on to first! A triple play!" When rookie Reggie Smith hit a scoreless tenth-inning triple, a listener "refused to enter the Sumner Tunnel until he heard the outcome," Ken said. Hundreds of drivers backed up, also listening. By late summer 2½ games divided five teams, at which point a gentle sport forgot its core.

On August 18, Conigliaro batted against Jack Hamilton. "He threw inside, and I moved my head back so quickly that the helmet came off." The ball grotesquely wounded the area around Tony's left eye. A week later ABC's Howard Cosell interviewed him on *Wide World of Sports*. "I felt the ball hit my temple, my knees crumbled, and my nose and mouth were bleeding," said Conigliaro, teeth on the left side "still numb. I can't see too much. I see only images," unable to read Samaritans' five hundred telegrams and six thousand letters. The Cowboy had seen it before—"Just broke your heart, like Harry Agganis"—his *Game of the Week* now often visiting Fenway. The day after the beaning showed why.

The Angels took a 4-3 lead as NBC scrawled, "Here one of baseball's best outfields once played—Tris Speaker, Harry Hooper, and Duffy Lewis." Curt began a history lesson from 1912 via "a fine young left-hander known for hitting ability" through Williams "moaning about the east wind that would blow off" the Charles to Mel Parnell, "a left-hander who liked Fenway" better than the road. In the fourth, "Here's Andrews, a line drive toward left!" said Gowdy. "It's off the Wall! Ball game's tied!" The lead kept changing, Boston winning on last-out ballet: "A chopper. Over the mound. May be tough," Sox radio's Martin said. "Charged by Petrocelli. Throws to first. He's out! The ball game is over! A clutch play by Rico Petrocelli ends it all as Jerry Stephenson gets a save in a wild and woolly ball game in a 12 to 11 win by the Red Sox!"

Next day the Townies trailed, 8-0, the bottom falling out, prompting Yaz to navigate the dugout. "'We're going to *win* this game!' he told each of us," said Petrocelli. "Man, by now we *believed*!" Smith homered: 8-1. Number 8 scorched a three-run shot. In the eighth, tied at eight, a Boston infielder smacked a "fly ball deep into left-center field and it is . . . a *home run!*" Coleman cried. "Jerry Adair has hit his second home run of the 1967 season and the Red Sox, who trailed, 8 to 0, are now leading in the eighth inning, *9 to 8!*" Four miles away, Adair's poke sired "a sound wave—one crescendo after another"—from a hundred thousand at Revere Beach, most listening to Sox radio. "Ken's attitude was beautiful," said Rico. "To his death, he thought that reaction symbolized the year."

A week later Boston led, 4-3, in the ninth inning at Chicago: Duane Joseph-son one-out batting. "[Ken] Berry, a fast man on third," Martin said. "[Townie reliever John] Wyatt looks at him and throws. And there's a little looper to right field. Tartabull coming on, has a weak arm. Here comes the throw to the plate. It is—out at home! He is out! Tartabull has thrown the runner out at the plate, and the ball game is over!" On TV, Coleman said, "Caught by Tartabull! Runner tags! Here's the throw home! And he is *out* at home plate!" Before 1967, Jose would not have nabbed Aunt Maude.

In mid-September, a blanket shrouded the Red and White Sox, Twins, and Tigers. The Townies trailed, 5-4, in the ninth inning at Detroit. "There's a drive to deep right field," blared Coleman, "and it's tied up!"—Yastrzemski again, five-all. Next inning the ultimate reserve, Dalton Jones, "raps one deep toward right, and it's up, and it is gone!" Ned said. "The Red Sox take the lead!" winning, 6-5. The blast meant a two-game swing: few believed what they were seeing. Faith fell back on the man with, as Gowdy said, "that unbelievable last name."

Dick Williams had played on the 1950s Dodgers of Furillo, Hodges, Robinson, and Campanella. "Great players," he said, "but I never saw a year like" Yaz's 1967 MVP Triple Crown. One game he beat Cleveland with a third of seven Gold Gloves: "Hit toward left," said Martin. "But Yastrzemski is back, still back, he runs, he's got it!" Later, Ned etched another weapon of mass destruction: "A base hit to left field. Charged by Yastrzemski. Runner is being held. He runs past the sign. The throw—he's out at the plate!" Eddie Stanky called No. 8 "a great ballplayer from the neck down." Yaz replied with six hits, including two dingers, in a twin-bill at Chicago. Rounding third, he tipped his cap to the White Sox manager.

Yastrzemski led in five AL batting categories: "tough, in a tougher era," said Rico. "If you were a rookie and hitting everything, they'd see if you could hit on your back. Show you're not intimidated, and they'd try something else. They tried everything against Yaz. Look at *what* he hit [.326, 44 homers, 121 RBI] and *when*": 23 hits in his last 44 at-bats. "One week left!" Williams said. "Four teams within 1½ games." By Thursday, September 28, advantage Twins: a game lead with Saturday and Sunday left at Fenway. "We were nervous, particularly Thurs-day and Friday when we were waiting," said Yaz, "but it'd been like this for three months." Stores closed. Churches opened. Truth and consequence: Boston must sweep to win or force a playoff.

In Saturday's two-all sixth inning, "Scott hits one deep into center field!" said radio's Coleman. "This one is back! This one is gone!"—3-2. Next inning he let TV's camera talk: "Deep to right field! [off Jim Merritt] Number 44!"— Yastrzemski's last regular-season homer. On wireless, Martin piloted Yaz's slip to port: "Hit deep toward right field! This may be gone! It's outta here!" Girders throbbed. The receiver seemed to quiver. Seconds later Ned tied precision, disbelief, and 1967's frame of reference: Why should *this* surprise? "If you've just turned your radio on"—pause—"*it's happened again*. Yastrzemski's hit a three-run homer, and it's now 6-2, Red Sox." Final, 6-4.

On Sunday, Detroit had to twice beat California to tie the Sox or Twins. Minnesota led, 2-0, as the Gentleman led off the sixth. "The applause is for Jim Lonborg," Coleman said, "who's pitched tremendous baseball today." An older-than-Fenway play ensued. "Lonborg bunts it down third! Tovar in, no play!" After two hits filled the bases, Yaz "lines a base hit to center field! One run in, Adair's around third, he will score. Going to third is Jones. It's tied, 2-2!" The Twins mirrored the late 1940s Townies. Each could club you, deeming defense a frill. Recently acquired Ken Harrelson hit to shortstop Zoilo Versalles, who hesitated and was lost: "No chance at a throw to the plate. Safe! Jones scores! The Red Sox lead, 3-2!" Two wild pitches and a muff scored two more runs. "The Red Sox are out in the sixth," said Coleman. "But what a sixth inning it was!"

In Detroit, Ernie Harwell's "Tiges" won the opener. Meantime, Minnesota's Bob Allison lined to the corner with two out in the eighth, Tony Oliva on first, and Harmon Killebrew on second. Number 8 threw to second base, nabbing Allison: rally over, Sox, 5-3. Next inning Rich Rollins batted with two out. "The pitch . . . is *looped*"—softly arced: the perfect word, as author Shaun L. Kelly wrote of Ned—"toward shortstop. Petrocelli's back, he's got it! The Red Sox win!"—but what? Martin couldn't say: Detroit had to lose. "And there's pandemonium on the field!" he continued—arguably the greatest line ever spoken by a Sox announcer. Finally: "Listen!" We still are.

At third base, Jones started jumping up and down: "Roomie, we won!"

Stunned, Rico could only say, "You're right!"

As the ball settled in his glove, students and workingmen and housewives on the field became a wave, hundreds of bodies rocking, collectively and ecstatically. "I was terrified," said Lonborg: Petrocelli, too. "It's a miracle I'm even here," the

1963 and 1965–1976 Townie, two-time All-Star, and 1979 Red Sox analyst said in 2009, joining MLB Network radio, where '67 seldom wanders far away.

"[Afterward] the players came in from the field," said Coleman. "Some were crying, some yelling, and I was trying to interview." A radio lit the background: "no ESPN, iPod, or Internet, just Harwell in the nightcap from Tiger Stadium." The Angels led, 8-5, in a two-on and one-out ninth. "[Dick] McAuliffe at bat," mused Tigers skipper Mayo Smith. "Hasn't hit into a double play all year. All of a sudden it's 4-6-3, game over"—uncorking Wakefield and Woonsocket and Blue Hill and Brattleboro.

In the clubhouse, Bobby Doerr, now a coach, conceded, "I was sure we'd have a playoff." Dick Williams said, "I'd like to thank God." Rico saw tears in Yawkey's eyes: "spent so much money, loved the Sox so much, all those near-misses, drinking champagne, more fan than owner." The next-day Boston *Record American* cover blared "CHAMPS!" above a drawing of two red socks. It was crewel, not cruel.

In Cambridge, Updike and some neighbors interrupted a touch football game to listen to a transistor radio. In Brookline, Michael Dukakis feared for Lonborg's post-game safety. "To me, he's what stands out about '67, even more than Yaz," said the then State House of Representatives member. "Went to Stanford, later became a dentist." In California, businessman Joel Fox thought of his father, Harry, in the Hub: "like all relatives dating to my grandparents' generation, a die-hard fan." Dad died in 1998, the funeral back East, where Joel eulogized his Bronze Star under General Patton at the Battle of the Bulge. Brother Mitch feted other priorities: "I know for certain my father lived a long time because he was alive the last time the Red Sox won the Series."

Fred Barnes was three when the Sox made the *1946* Series. At five, the future journalist got a baseball autographed "by the players on a team Dad once coached as an army lieutenant in Monterey, California," including then 17-year-old private Dom DiMaggio, who, Fred's father said, "grew up to become the center-fielder for the Boston Red Sox. And so I became a Red Sox fan. It's a passion that has never died." Married on Labor Day 1967, Fred and his new wife honeymooned on Florida's Gulf Coast. Nightly he went outside, tuned to fifty-thousand-watt Sox outlet WTIC Hartford, and fiddled with the dial. Barbara didn't understand what Barnes was doing. "Then I explained—and she still didn't understand." On October 1, "she understood."

In Fall River, outside Boston, Emeril Lagasse, 8, played in Maplewood Park across from Sox rookie catcher Russ Gibson's house. "I'd come home from school and practice pitching, then play stickball, Little League, city league," made a local all-star team. He liked school, music, and working in a Portuguese bakery at age 12. "But always there was baseball." Lagasse preferred "ballpark food: Fenway Franks, french fries, a hamburger." Some parks—"sushi," he sniffed—later tried "to be hip": as *verboten* as the Yanks. In 1967, "my dad and uncles drank beer at the park. Today so do I." To the "baseball junkie," Yastrzemski was "the guy. I took pride in knowing every position and player, especially Number 8." Cooking, Lagasse still utters *Bam*! "Know what it means? My secret code for Yaz going deep."

Each spring the young son of *Globe* reporter Will McDonough spent a month at the Sox then Winter Haven, Florida, training site. Teachers gave mother lesson plans. Sean did homework, practiced on a tape recorder, and watched Coleman and Martin fill a scorebook: "good training," said Boston's 1988–2004 TV Voice. "To me, the '67 pennant meant friends." To Joe Castiglione, it meant leaving his 1950s and early '60s Hamden, Connecticut, childhood: "all Yankees," little Sox feeling west of the Naugatuck River. "Later, the area swung Boston's way, but back then Mel Allen was the world," termed by *Variety* magazine among "its 25 most recognizable voices." Once Mel hailed a taxi at night, the driver not seeing who he was. "Sheraton, please," Allen said, simply. The cabbie swiveled his head, almost driving off the road.

Yogi Berra said, "If you can't imitate him, don't copy him." Emulating, if not fixating, Joe called backyard fungos like Mel, asked Santa for a beer glass to pour sponsor Ballantine beer, and fifty years later confessed that "Allen's the reason I'm in broadcasting." A "great vocabulary" sustained rout and rain. "He'd weave stories, so tough to master, never caught short" on a two-strike tale. "A Gowdy was great on nuts, bolts, and action." Mel was a thespian, not technician, whose 1964 stripes firing stunned. "Allen was almost bigger than the product," said Castiglione. "I wonder how he'd have handled the Yankees' fall"—no 1965–1975 titles after 14 in the prior 16 years. "As it was, they lost their identity," harder to accept than the Sox having none.

At Colgate University, Joe aired football and basketball, was a campus disc jockey, hitchhiked 23 miles each Sunday to a commercial outlet to "spin records and read news," and called the best part of college "Cooperstown being down the road." In 1967, he interned at Yanks affiliate WDEW Westfield, Massachusetts, for the first time visiting Fenway. "Thank God for no new stadium! Fenway knocked me out," said Colgate '68, changing loyalty. No Evil Empire could match The Impossible Dream. In the last-day clubhouse, garbed in champagne, Coleman told a listener, "This is, if I may add a personal note, the greatest thrill of my life." Other upsets became "child's play, believe me, compared to 1967." Forty years later Petrocelli said, "Not a day goes by that somebody doesn't thank me."

It was unthinkable then to call a World Series anticlimactic. It was also true. Yaz had transcended myth, Scott hit .303, and Santiago gone 12-4. Lonborg was a Cy Young 22-9, had a 3.16 ERA, and led the AL in starts (39) and strikeouts (246). Frank Capra would have had Boston face the Washington Generals. Instead, the Cardinals were an All-Star team. NBC's Gowdy, Reese, and Sandy Koufax had aired the last regular-season Saturday and Sunday from the Fens. Now, in pitch-perfect symmetry, Curt and Coleman did each Hub Series telecast.

Bob Gibson beat Santiago, 2-1. Game Two retrieved late-season: Lonborg one-hit St. Louis, No. 8 going yard. El Birdos won Games Three and Four behind Nelson Briles and Gibson, respectively. The Gentleman took Set Five, 3-1. The Fall Occasion returned to Boston, where rookie Gary Waslewski left up, 4-2, St. Louis tied the score, and Yaz, Smith, and Petrocelli homered in the seventh: Sox, 8-4. Headlined the *Herald Traveler*: "It's All Even now." In Game Seven, Gibby and Julian Javier homered, Lonborg working with two days' rest. No win for the weary: Cards, 7-2. Said Coleman, "One sportswriter called it 'the Series nobody lost.'"

St. Louis relived Lou Brock's seven steals and Gibson's three victories. T. A. tabulated an all-time attendance record: 1,727,832. Except for Yaz and Lonborg, Coleman became the person most affixed to 1967. It was *his*, like Britt's 1948–1949, Martin's 1975 and 1978, and Castiglione's 2004 and 2007. Ruth's 1920 sale to New York almost destroyed the franchise. As Martin said, 1967's "garrison finish" spectacularly revived it. In a eulogy, the *Herald*'s Kevin Convey recalled the flashlight beside his bed. "There will be other summers. And I will listen to other announcers. But I will never stop hearing Ken Coleman."

If no one could replace Yaz, a Hawk might succeed him. The Athletics' Dick Howser gave Ken Harrelson his *alter idem*: "It wasn't hard, my nose broken in six places." Later it turned *alter ego*: "Inside, I was quiet, cautious. Hawk was my public self. I'd be in the on-deck circle, saying, 'Kenny, get out of the way and let Hawk take charge.'" Hawkspeak began at first base and right field: batter up, Catfish Hunter

K-ing him, and Ken crowing "He gone" or "grab some bench" or "Get that next SOB up there." The 1960s Natural Man later became a Natural Voice. "Talking as often as we do, you better be yourself, 'cause people spot a phony fast."

In 1951, Harrelson, 10, born in Woodruff, South Carolina, moved to Savannah. Mother Jesse, a single parent, "didn't make much in a week. We had an itty-bitty house: no air-conditioning, holes in screens." The high school All-American fancied "a [basketball] scholarship with Kentucky," playing four sports at Benedictine College. "Mama thought I'd make more money with baseball. We compromised. I played baseball." In 1959, the "mama's boy, still am" got a $30,000 bonus to sign with Kansas City; 1961, Charles O. Finley bought the A's; 1963, Ken joined them, soon calling Finley "Cheap! Italicize it!" That year he acquired Rocky Colavito, mama's favorite player.

In August 1967, the A's flew commercial from Boston to Kansas City, Finley "such a skinflint he spread us three across in coach." Pitcher Lew Krausse began boozing, after which skipper Alvin Dark refused to suspend him, whereupon Finley axed the former Boston Brave. Hawk termed Charlie "detrimental to baseball." The A's could have dealt Harrelson, or claimed a $50,000 waiver. Instead, they asked if he wanted an unconditional release. Hawk said no, "making and needing my $12,000 salary." Incredibly, Finley had Mike Hershberger phone his roommate: "Hawk, as of this moment, you're no longer a member of the green and gold." The release made Ken baseball's first free agent. Each AL Sox team phoned, Chicago's warning of "a bidding war" turning on his light.

"Whoever gets you will win the pennant," Dark said, "and you're going to get at least $150,000. Play the field." Heeding him and mama, Hawk "got exactly that," signing with Boston and hitting .173 with the Sox. "We won the pennant *despite*, not *because* of, me," he laughed, popularizing the one-handed catch. "Don't drop one!" Dick Williams pled. Mama's boy said he was being smart: "With bad hands like mine, one hand is better than two." Another light had gone off earlier. Expecting a Yanks right-handed starter, the righty Hawk played golf, got a blister, discovered lefty Whitey Ford pitching, and said, "Guess who's in the lineup? *Me*." Ken found his golf glove, made it a *batting* glove, and homered twice. Next day each stripe wore one, Mickey Mantle having the clubhouse manager buy in bulk.

In 1964, Harrelson nearly quit due to fear. "Once Al Kaline, spotting it, walked past me, saying, 'We all have fear at the plate,' and kept on walking," Ken told ESPN's Tim Kurkjian. "That helped." So did watching Tony C., the "only totally fearless batter I ever saw."

"Before or after his beaning?" said Kurkjian.

"Both," Hawk said.

In 1967, Yaz had seemed as fearless. Strangely, he became Hawk's fixation. "A lot of athletes pick out one guy for motivation. All winter I worked my butt off to beat Yaz and in '68 had the best year of my life," as Martin and Coleman said: "It's a home run—high, wide, and handsome"; "The Hawk has a stand-up double"; "Harrelson jumps on a McDowell fastball"; "Kenny Harrelson, who is really on a tear."

That fall Nos. 8 and 40 had dinner. "You've had a hell of a year [35 homers and 109 RBI]," Yastrzemski said.

Ken: "It's your fault."

Yaz: "What are you talking about?"

"I was obsessed with you, so I tried to stick it up your ass."

Carl started laughing, Harrelson later said, "because that's what teammates do: egg each other on."

The Nation egged Hawk on, too. "Fans wanted a character, so I gave 'em flair, bigger than life, the clothes"—love beads, bell bottoms, a cowboy hat—"the *Hawk.* A gentleman meets a lady. Suddenly, sparks fly—'68." At one point, he had 150 pairs of pants. A cedar chest housed 70 sweaters. "Remember the Nehru suit?" Harrelson bought 15. "Before I wore five, they were out of style."

In 1969, he was dealt to Cleveland. "We loved the garb and RBI," said Martin, "but we needed pitching more." In Christmas week 1967, Lonborg tore his left knee skiing. Next year Santiago hurt his arm. "For Ken we got [Vicente Romo and] Sonny Siebert, a darn good pitcher." Harrelson broke down, got hurt, moved to Hub, Chicago, and New York TV, even became White Sox GM in 1986.

"Why'd I try it? Mama said, 'Son, you're a good kid and I love you, but you ain't the smartest thing I ever saw.'" The exception, he said, "is when I went after Yaz."

On Election Eve 1960, John F. Kennedy spoke to a packed throng at Boston Garden. Weary, he did poorly. Aide Richard Donahue eyed envious politicians. "You know, they can't understand this," he said. "They think he has a trick. They're listening to him because they think if they can learn it they can be president, too." It is no trick to say that baseball's radio/TV late 1960s had a Red Sox tilt. For one thing, Gowdy almost exclusively aired the 1966–1975 bigs. Inevitably, the viewer tired. A. C. Nielsen's 1966–1968 *Game* and Series ratings fell 10 and 19 percent, respectively. Only the All-Star Game nixed the view of a pastime *past* its time. In a 1964 Harris poll, 48 percent named baseball their favorite sport. Just 17 percent did in 1975. *The Sporting News* got so many letters—"atrocity . . . a pallbearer . . . baseball is not dead, no thanks to Curt"—that it routed them to NBC. Not responsible, Gowdy was made accountable.

Each Series starred the Cowboy and Company. 1967: Reese and Caray joined Curt and Coleman. 1968: Detroit's George Kell joined Pee Wee and Holy Cow! 1969: An old *New Yorker* cover showed several downcast Mets, a bystander saying, "Cheer up. You can't lose them all." Curt, Nelson, Bill O'Donnell, and Tony Kubek described it all. "Waiting is Jones!" said Gowdy. "The Mets are the world champions! Jerry Koosman is being mobbed!" Later Curt regretted wearing out his welcome. Then, a brigade at Utah Beach would not have made him recede. 1970 Series: Brooks Robinson auditioned for *Biography*: "Look at that grab! He's playing in another world!" 1971 All-Star Game: "That one is going—way up! It is—off the roof! That hit the transformer up there! A tremendous smash!" by Reggie Jackson. 1974: "The Oakland A's are the first team since the New York Yankees to win three world championships in a row!"

Writer Jerry Lister likened "a week in Gowdy's life [to] a chapter in Jules Verne's *Around the World in 80 Days*": 22 papers read a day, fifty thousand miles trekked a year, trips memorizing names, dates, and numbers. Each January 1, Curt did the Granddaddy of Them All; fall, pro football; March, tourney basketball; always revering the cathedral of the outdoors. On March 27, 1972—"my greatest day"—Wyoming opened the Curt Gowdy State Park between Cheyenne and Laramie. "It has two beautiful lakes, hiking trails, camping, boating, fishing, and beauty—everything I love. What greater honor can a man receive?" Other days honored a man "born with a fly-rod in one hand."

November 17, 1968: NBC showed a movie instead of the Jets–Oakland Raiders' final minute. Only the West Coast saw Oakland, scoring twice, win. "I'm leaving when our assistant starts yelling, 'Gowdy! Gowdy! Here are earphones to the truck.' The guys there say, 'Uh, uh, phone calls are blowing lines up.' I have to re-create the last-second scores" for next morning's NBC *The Today Show*. The *Heidi* Game buoyed a sport once akin to wrestling—except that wrestling had a niche.

January 12, 1969: "I guarantee a [Super Bowl III] victory," said Joe Namath. Baltimore was a 19-point lock. Joe Willie had the key, throwing as nimbly as Robin Hood used a bow. Christmas 1971: Miami's second-overtime field goal beat

Kansas City, 27-24. December 23, 1972: Oakland led, 7-6, with 22 seconds left. "I'd better congratulate the boys," says Steelers' owner Art Rooney, leaving for the locker room. Pittsburgh won, 13-7, on a deflected pass. "The Immaculate Reception" joined The Kid's Final Swing as Curt's first-in-the-class call.

Each week Gowdy and Reese, then successor Kubek, attended a pre-*Game* meeting in New York. As others haggled, the star raised a hand. "Yes, Gowdy," they sighed.

"What about the ball game?"

"Hell with the ball game. We have to have the opening and the close."

"Yes," said Curt, "but, fellahs, we're here for the game."

In 1972, NBC began a 10-game prime-time schedule, hoping "*Monday* [*Game of the Week*] will take off like football," wrote *Broadcasting Magazine*. Next year it aired 15 straight. For a man who lived on numbers, the Cowboy's stalled: Saturday down; Monday slightly up. Even the All-Star Game, Series, and 1969– Classic prelude, the League Championship Series—"our crown jewels," said Bowie Kuhn—seemed on autopilot. As fall guy, another NBCer had a thought.

"I'm not Joe Show Biz," said Joe Garagiola, "just a sweat shirt guy running at top speed to stay even. Those guys on the bubble gum cards, they're mine." Joe's TV card already listed *Memory Game, Sale of the Century, The Today Show, Major League Baseball,* and Monday pre-game *Baseball World of Joe Garagiola*. In 1974, he aired the All-Star Game with Gowdy, then collared Lindemann: "[Curt] kept cutting me off. I couldn't say a word."

Garagiola was "one of the most likeable voices in broadcasting," said the *New York Times*: also pitchman for *Game of the Week* sponsor Chrysler. Joe wanted balls and strikes. Baseball wanted cash. In 1975, he got Saturday, Monday, LCS, and Classic play-by-play, Chrysler "maneuvering," Lindemann said, "to get Gowdy off baseball altogether." Ironically, even as the Red Sox flagged, interest in his old club rose.

In 1968–1971, third- or fourth-place Boston made *Game* a big-league-high 38 times. By a new century, the Sox appeared on network free/cable TV—Fox, ESPN, and TBS—the single-team maximum 27 games a year. In 2011, Harrelson told Castiglione that "Yastrzemski is the most important figure in Sox history."

"Over *Williams*?" Joe said.

"Ted *was* the franchise. Carl *resurrected* it," Hawk said. "Without him there's no '67—and without '67 Fenway's gone." In a 1980s Mason-Dixon poll, Boston trailed only Atlanta as Dixie's favorite club. "It's TV," said NBC's Harry Coyle of the jammed stands and jai alai walls and coffee klatsch of coverage. After 1967, the Nation dispersed to buy Sox piggy banks, bobby dolls, pennants, popcorn megaphones, and old ink pens shaped like bats. "A great offseason," said Martin. Greater was '67's glow.

"The Sox gave the lie to baseball's supposed '60s death," he mused, first in 1967–1971 AL attendance every year but one, including 1968's record 1,940,778—73 percent capacity. On July 20, 1969, the Red Sox hosted Baltimore as PA announcer Sherm Feller announced Neil Armstrong's moonwalk. Applause began. Umpire Marty Springstead called time. Due to hit, Brooks Robinson asked what Feller said. Told by the man in blue, he dropped *his* bat to clap.

Out of nowhere, a leather-lung in the left-field corner began singing "God Bless America," the entire park soon caroling. Chuck Thompson had learned baseball in his grandmother's Palmer, Massachusetts, home that boarded Connie Mack. Said the former big-band singer, "That sound would have made Tommy Dorsey proud."

In 1968–1971, ex-Cub Ray Culp led yearly in Sox Ks and innings. Rico hit a league record 40 homers by a shortstop. Smith topped the club at least once in 11 categories, including batting average, home runs, RBI, hits, runs, and steals. On June 25, 1969, a hip, engaging, and/or crazy as a loon lefty relieved Romo *v.* Cleveland: "young [Bill] Lee," Ned noted, "pitching in his first big-league game." Yastrzemski twice crashed 40 homers, played 350 straight games, and won a third batting title—and almost a fourth, losing on his last 1970 at-bat. George Scott aka the Boomer—to Dick Williams, "old cement head"—wore second baseman's "teeth" (beads and shells) around his neck. Williams was canned, replaced by a less martinet-than-minister. "I loved [Eddie] Kasko," said Yaz. "No controversy. He would have been a great manager with a great team." Neither was.

Play-by-play stirred time, tone, and name: "A home run in the net for Boog Powell!" Coleman said. Next week "[Eddie] Brinkman scores the winning run," a Senators ninth-inning three-spot beating Sparky Lyle. At Tiger Stadium, "the ball is in the corner—and Kaline has it!" Martin described the A's "Danny Cater [a future Townie] coming up with his third hit." In the Bronx, "Bobby Murcer hits this a long way. Over to third base and holding." Replied No. 8: "Well-hit to right field. Boy, that's deep! A tremendous shot by Yastrzemski—that ball is outta sight!" Fans "chanted, 'We want a hit'"; camera placement was tight and personal; the only graphics were a player's name.

On May 16, 1970, nostalgia had a fling. Once-regular Leo Egan subbed for Coleman. "The center-field bleachers are well-populated." Below, "a constant chatter among the youngsters." Tribe coach Johnny Lipon "played [1950s] short-stop for the Red Sox." Egan was less sure about today: Ray Fosse became *Foss*. In May 1971, Siebert faced Oakland's phantasmagoric rookie Vida Blue. "At Fenway [35,714] people are hanging from the rafters, and Boston wins [4-3] when Dave Duncan's drive that looked like it would tie the game went foul," said Ned. Before cable, "each of the [Hub's] four local professional franchises was prominently featured on fifty-thousand-watt stations," read Shaun L. Kelly's website, Boston Dirt Dogs. "The team's announcers were as identifiable as [their] squads," especially, said Keith Olbermann, the "subtle, controlled, educated man from Duke to Iwo Jima."

In 2002, the *Globe*'s Bill Griffith called "today's broadcasters slicker and technically superior, but [Martin's] bygone days were a wonderful time to be a [Boston] baseball fan." In a sentence, Kelly wrote, Ned might use "rocket, balloon, soar, sail, glide, dart, float, sputter, plummet, plunge, bound, skip, hop, spring, or dribble"—a "living and breathing thesaurus." To Craig, he was "the East Coast's answer to Vin Scully." Castiglione called him "the most literate of all broadcasters." In *SI*, Jonathan Schwartz praised "as articulate and creative a sportscaster as there is in the country." The ex-Marine read poetry by Allen Ginsberg, had politics similar to John Wayne's, and loved Richard M. Nixon. Milhous thrice lost Massachusetts: It revered Ned, anyway.

As Kelly said, a swing might stir "a crosswind in the box seats"; fielder, "coax the ball down to his glove as if by supplication"; pitcher, exult "after settling down a gaggle of Yankees!" A dank night prompted Carl Sandburg's "Fog comes/on little cat feet." When a Sox skipper overstrategized, Martin quoted Hemingway's "Never confuse movement with action." Inverting habit, the Townies won a match they should have lost. Post-game Ned cited Shakespeare's "'Fortune brings in some boats that are not steered.' Good night from Fenway Park." Listening was an exercise in self-improvement.

Martin closed bars, haunted bookshops, and had disdain for jack, sham, and fools. Mercy! After a 1971 double-header loss at Cleveland, he said, "We'll be back in a moment." Just then, traveling secretary Jack Rogers said, "Be on the bus in 40 minutes." Not in "good humor," Martin blurted, "Bullshit," unaware of an open mike. In that gentler age, the phone rang off the hook. WHDH told him to "recap the incident, seal your letter," he might be fired. "It was outrageous to happen then," said Ned. "Now it'd be a nursery rhyme." That August a station suit knocked Martin's working on TV sans necktie—in hundred-degree heat. "I'd finish radio, then post-game interview the TV star," he said. "I didn't have on a jacket, tie, and shirt outside. What sane person *would*?" Another memo told Coleman to find a post-game substitute if Ned was "not attired in accordance with company rules." Vowing to wear a tuxedo, he felt himself a long shot for the best-dressed list. Wrote Clark Booth, "Given how many clowns Ned offended, it's a wonder he lasted 30 years."

Succeeding Gleeson, Parnell had lasted four, coining the "Pesky Pole." In 1969, Pesky replaced *him*: like Mel, might confuse adverb and adjective, had a tart voice, but told a better tale. By turn, No. 6 hit safely in 26 straight games, became Dick Stuart's bête noire, and raised two Series flags—said Castiglione, "an institution" like Fenway. "For years '67 buoyed ratings," said Martin, "but not our [WHDH] network": 45 radio and six to seven television stations. "We'd got as many as we could." In 1972, WBZ TV bought exclusivity when WHDH lost its license—Coleman the new big guy, knowing the medium's shorthand. After a decade as understudy, Ned became *radio's*, doing Patriots pro and Dartmouth, Harvard, and Yale college football, but baseball his milieu. Pesky joined Coleman. Ned hired 1956–1960 Mutual *Game*, 1961–1968 D.C., and 51-year-old Voice John MacLean. "I liked his style but couldn't foresee John's illness": a June 1972 stroke, hospitalizing, then killing, him.

The season-opening walkout cost 13 days, equity (Boston lost seven games, Detroit six), and interest (pre-August drew sparsely). A year earlier Luis Aparicio arrived from Chicago to go 0 for 44. Cater forgot how to hit after leaving New York for Lyle. Catcher Bob Montgomery—aka Monty or the Hammer—averaged .258 lifetime, was the last bigs player to bat without a helmet, and was sacked for 1972 Rookie of the Year Carlton Fisk. Balding, bulging, English-breaking, cigar-smoking, back-from-the-bushes Luis Tiant—El Tiante—saw more of a crowd than anyone, pirouetting on every pitch. Newcomer Tommy Harper and Petro-celli led with 141 hits and 75 RBI, respectively. "We weren't that powerful," said Yaz. "But we still should have won." Joe McCarthy couldn't have said it better.

Dave (no relation) Martin succeeded MacLean. I knew Ned Martin. Ned Martin was a friend of mine. Dave was no Ned Martin. On October 2, the Sox readied for a year-ending series—three games at Detroit. "That schedule!" said Coleman. "The strike made us play one fewer game than the Tigers." Boston led the AL East by a meaningless one-half game, needing two of three to win. Kaline took John Curtis deep in the opener. Next inning, Harper and Aparicio one-out singled. Yaz lashed to deep center field, Harper scoring easily. Luis lost his balance nearing third base, turned it, fell down, and retreated, finding Yastrzemski on the bag. "He had at least a triple," Eddie Kasko said, "maybe an inside-the-parker." Boston would have led at least 2-1 with Yaz on third. Instead, he was out, Smith fanned, and the score stayed tied.

Splengarian burlesque towers. Little Looie! Losing a pennant on a running botch by the best runner of his time! "If we had that one, and we should have, we would have been certain to win one of the next two," said Yastrzemski. "We lost it right there"—the game, 4-1, then division, 3-1, next night. Even before Aparicio's slip-slide away, brass had decided to go younger, sooner. Veterans led in most 1973 categories: Yaz, Smith, Harper, and Orlando Cepeda, Boston's first designated hitter. "Their last hurrah," Ned said. "The old order passeth."

Placing second, Kasko was canned. The Sox won their final game, 3-2, scoring twice when Milwaukee's catcher, arguing a call, forgot to ask time. Bill Lee, "flaky to the end," said Martin, "applauded to the crowd." That same day Yankee Stadium closed, "torn up" for 1974–1975 renovation. "Fenway Park will stay here, though, and we'll be back next April 9."

8 MARTIN AND WOODS (1974–1978)

By the end of 1974, said Martin, most of the more oldie-than-goodie Red Sox "were gone," like Boston's late-August seven-game East lead. Never had it lost a title after leading by so much, so late in the season. New skipper Darrell Johnson's team stopped hitting, Reggie Jackson asking, "Who are all these Mario Andretti [infielder Mario Guerrero] guys?" The *Globe*'s Leigh Montville wrote, "The Red Sox fan, of course, is mad mostly at himself. He had forgotten his inbred pessimism, his rooting heritage. He had stuffed it in a drawer." Out it came, the Townies placing third. By now, Yastrzemski, 35, was the regular first baseman. He led in average (.301), RBI (79), total bases (229), slugging percentage (.445), and home runs (15, with Petrocelli): each a club worst for any 1960s and '70s year.

As they would again, the Sox eyed Triple-A Pawtucket. Jim Rice, 21, became International League MVP. Fred Lynn, 22, promoted in September, was 18 for 43. Dwight Evans was 22; Fisk, 26; shortstop Rick Burleson, 23; Tiant, circa 33. Only Yaz, Rico, Martin, and Coleman remained from 1967. That spring ageless 58-year-old Jim Woods joined Ned to become, Mike Barnicle wrote, a "Tracy-Hepburn of radio, the Gable-Lombard, Lunt-Fontanne, Redford-Newman, Fiedler and The Pops kind of combo that lend class and style to the phrases that describe the perils of our Olde Towne Team." The *Boston Phoenix*'s Michael Gee jibed, "Anyone who'd tell [them] how to announce baseball would give Jack Nicklaus golf tips at a cocktail party."

A 1960s' Avis ad blared, "We're number two. We try harder." Woods was number two to Allen, Barber, Russ Hodges, Bob Prince, Jack Buck, Monte Moore, and Martin: "baseball's peripatetic 'second' announcer," wrote William Leggett, "who has worked for a quarter of the clubs in the majors." Being top gun seldom crossed his mind. "Having fun, Jim wanted *not* to try harder," Ned laughed. As we have seen, Enos Slaughter once likened Woods's buzz cut to a possum. Were 1958–1969's Poss and Prince as good as Woods and Martin? Did any trio top the Yanks' 1950s Jim, Mel, and Red? "It's no coincidence," said Allen. The common tie was Woods.

Possum's patchwork start rivaled Martin's: Kansas City Blues mascot at four; team batboy at eight; local radio score reader in high school; University of Missouri freshman dropout.

Dad: "Son, I hate you leaving school."

Jim: "You won't when I get to Yankee Stadium."

In 1935, the ex–journalism major joined KGLO Mason City, Iowa—*The Music Man*'s "River City." By 1937, he replaced Ronald Reagan, dealing Big Ten football for Hollywood. Later Poss crowed, "Nothing like topping a prez!" Reagan's voice soothed, like a compress. Woods's slapped you in the face. In 1942–1945, he rode the Navy War Bond circuit. Back home, Poss succeeded Ernie Harwell at Triple-A Atlanta when the Georgian left for Brooklyn. Ernie's dad was an invalid. One day Mom phoned: "Our son's broadcasts were our life. Jim, you've made us forget our worries."

In 1949, Poss's Crackers became the first team to air an entire home year of television. Four years later a voice phoned surpassing even Woods's. "Mel asks me to New York. I walk into his suite, and he's on the phone talking to Joe DiMaggio about Marilyn Monroe." Poss knew then he was in the bigs. Actor Joe E. Brown was to have succeeded DiMag on Yanks pre-/post-game TV and air several innings. "Guess Brown should have stuck to film," Allen said. Replacing him, Woods stuck to balls and strikes.

One day Possum was at Toots Shor's Restaurant, several bar stools from Yanks and Dodgers owner Dan Topping and Walter O'Malley, respectively, when Brooklyn's boss began ripping his announcer. "I hate the son of a bitch," he termed Barber. Just as gassed, Topping reciprocated: "I can't stand him [Mel]." Amazed, Woods heard "the heads of baseball's biggest teams trashing sportscasting's then biggest names." O'Malley raised his glass. "I'll trade you the SOB." Dan flushed. "I'll give you Allen." Poss laughed: "Talk about a shock—Mel for Red, at the top of each career." Next day, sober, they reneged.

The 1953 pinstripes drew 1,537,811, down half a million since 1950. One cause was TV's growing ubiquity, another the Bombers' broadcast sheen. Like Gowdy, Woods respected, but feared, Allen, especially Mel's habit of snapping his fingers when something popped a cork. Poss described Mickey Mantle's "foul ball on top." Fingers snapped. "What'd I do?" Jim said. Allen: "On top of what?" Woods: "The roof." Mel: "Then say the roof and complete your sentence." Jim never forgot the tutorial. "I learned to take nothing for granted and not to fear dead air, surprising for a guy famed for talking."

Woods's first-year team won a fifth straight World Series. Stranger than fiction: The sole Yankee to play every pre-1956 Series *v.* Brooklyn was born in Flatbush. That August Phil Rizzuto was told by GM George Weiss, "We've got a chance to get Slaughter. What do you think?" Taking cyanide, Scooter said, "Boy, getting him would be a help." At 39, Phil became unemployed, Enos replacing him on the roster. Allen let Rizzuto call a half-inning here or there. As Richard Reeves writes of politics, broadcasting "magnifies charm and institutionalizes seduction." By late 1956, Phil had charmed Ballantine Beer sponsor Carl Badenhausen, who told Weiss to hire him.

Poss entered George's office to find him staring at the floor. "Jim," Weiss groped, "I have to do something I hate doing, something I've never done—fire someone without cause." Stunned—"It's a funny business. Things happen."—Woods joined the Giants and NBC's *Major League Baseball*. In 1957, he did that network's first weekly baseball: a Brooklyn-Milwaukee exhibition. The Jints' exit led to Pittsburgh. "People said, 'Prince is out of control, you'll never get along,' but I decided to try him on for size." The "Ringling Brothers" gilded KDKA with a pencil and scorecard. "That was it," said Bob. "We'd do play-by-play—or tap dance if the game stunk." On the last out Jim turned off his mike. "Enough of that! *Booze!*"

One rainy Friday, Coleman, in Pittsburgh for NBC, heard Prince confess, "'Poss, I wish they'd call the game so I could get home and watch that John Wayne Western.' So different than what I knew." Another night Prince—aka the Gunner after the husband of a woman Bob was talking to in a bar pointed a gun at him—spied "a broad" roaming an aisle. "Poss, check that one out in black!" he howled. You're on the air, Woods cautioned. "Geez," Bob replied, "when I think what I *coulda* said!" Once Prince ribbed some Bucs about baseball being sedentary. Mocking the former college swimmer, Gene Freese said, "Here's $20 you can't dive into this pool." Racing to his third-floor hotel room, Bob cleared 12 feet of concrete. Later Poss recalled the dive: "How'd your act check out here?" Gunner: "One way to find out," knifing from the ledge.

In 1960, NBC's Prince voicing, Pittsburgh won its first World Series since 1925. Eventually, Westinghouse's KDKA bought Pirates rights from Atlantic-Richfield Company, "began to hem us in, said we wandered." Woods had "never got enough money. So when a bigger offer came, I jumped": in 1970, to St. Louis, "where the front office was paranoid"; then Oakland, the A's winning two straight Series. Owner Charles O. Finley fired him in late 1973. "I was loyal to the man, but Finley loved the Midwest style where you scream at a foul ball. 'Jim, you're a great announcer when something's happening, but when nothing is going on you're not.'"

Weiss, St. Louis, Finley: Woods pined for Pittsburgh. Instead, the Red Sox hired him, ditching Dave Martin, in early 1974. That same day the phone rang. "Jim, I've thought this over," said Charlie, "and I'd like you to come back."

"Look," Poss said, "I've just obligated myself to do the Red Sox for the next two years."

"Shit," Finley snapped, "everybody knows those contracts aren't worth the paper they're written on."

"I'm tied up!" Jim huffed, *hanging* up. He thought of Boston, knowing that "Sox fans like it toned down. If I did a Prince I'd have been run out of town." Before long he *won* the town, noting "a couple of fans down below waving a Yankees' banner—their parents must have raised some pretty foolish children." That Closing Day Ned said, "Jim Woods came from Oakland. I knew about him. I knew what he could do, and I was fortunate to have a hand in getting him to come here."

Martin hailed "an easy guy to work with." Poss reciprocated by recalling his "37 years in the business, the bunch of mail this week just to say thank you," never "treated better than by this group here." Each knew the game, played off the other, and refused to toot his own horn, as instantly recognizable as John Kiley's chords. "Martin reminded us that baseball is a game of wit and intelligence. Woods kept alive our sense of wonder," wrote novelist Robert B. Parker. "Between them they were perfect."

Woods's first Red Sox game was April 5, 1974. Three days later three men scaled the decade's baseball summit, Henry Aaron crossing a most Ruthian line. "Sitting on 714," the Braves' Milo Hamilton said, and then, "That ball is gonna be—outta here! It's gone! It's 715!" Said the Dodgers' Scully, context, like din, all around: "A black man is getting a standing ovation in the Deep South for breaking a record of an all-time baseball idol." NBC's Gowdy was more matter-of-fact. "That ball's hit deep . . . deep . . . it is gone! He did it! He did it! Hank Aaron is the all-time home run leader now!"

That fall, Curt and Vin did a vapid All-California Classic. An exception was Oakland's Reggie Jackson's first-game fly. "[Joe] Ferguson took it [from Jimmy Wynn], with the better arm," said Scully. "Here comes the throw! They got him [A's Sal Bando]!" Next day "the Dodgers with a [ninth-inning] one-run lead," said Gowdy. Scully: "Screwball!" Curt: "That's it, getting him [Angel Mangual]." In Game Five, L.A.'s Mike Marshall stopped warming up to watch the crowd hurl trash at teammate Bill Buckner. Homering, Joe Rudi made him pay: A's, 3-2, their third straight title.

Before the opener, rebroadcast in 2010 by MLB Network, Gowdy and Scully faced the camera: evoking 1966 and 1970, each ill at ease. Ultimately, Vin "made [Curt, the A's Monte Moore, and Kubek] sound like college radio rejects," said the *New York Post*'s Henry Hecht. For a time, 1975– Red Sox television was, if not rejected, similarly unrespected—a reason, the wireless. Later, Clark Booth asked, "Was it ever better than when Ned and Possum did a game on an August night when the pennant race was just beginning to simmer and the mood was evocative of the fifties?" The poet and peripatetic inherited WHDH radio's six-state network as Sox TV tried to reinvent its wheel.

For years, the club had "been stuck at 55 to 60 games," said VP/emeritus and team historian Dick Bresciani. "It's all the programming our TV flagship could handle." In late 1974, ultra-high frequency (UHF) WSBK Channel 38 bought exclusivity for a team-record $1.6 million a year, starting in 1975. "[38 GM] Bill Flynn told me he wanted to go with a new cast," Ken Coleman said, returning to Ohio to televise the Reds. At age 10, his Sox successor had been introduced to baseball in 1951. Dick Stockton's dad had season tickets at the Polo Grounds. He also bought the son's first Bowman baseball cards: five in a pack. Fils' favorite player, Al (Red) Schoendienst, was shown horizontally close-up, bat over shoulder, wearing a blue cap with red peak and intertwined *STL*. Stockton remembers "each team's pennant floating in the breeze, walking from the Speedway on Coogan's Bluff," and light towers atop the upper deck, like corn stalks in a field.

Through the runway Dick eyed roofed bull-pen shacks, a Chesterfield ciga-
rettes sign, and batting practice, the visiting Cardinals in the cage. Each wore the
road uniform: gray with red numbers trimmed in blue, red stockings with blue
and white stripes, and the familiar cap. Two had "one foot on a tire supporting
the cage": Number 6, Stan Musial; and 2, Schoendienst, bats switch, throws right,
born Germantown, Illinois. "My card came alive," Stockton said, especially on the
road, studying the Giants yearbook's aerial shot of each NL park as Hodges noted
Braves Field's right-field "Jury Box" or Crosley Field's "laundry" behind left field's
wall. Forbes Field meant Schenley Park; Wrigley Field, ivy; Ebbets Field, the high
wall in right. "If radio was *my* friend," said Stockton, "*creativity* was radio's."

Reality preceded Syracuse '64's first baseball telecast. In 1969, KDKA named
Dick sports director on its 6, 7, and 11 p.m. *Eyewitness News*, "a first-of-its-kind
idea, anchors and reporters speaking amid live news room chaos. When film or
commercial ran, our police radio was turned on full." That fall Pittsburgh skipper
Larry Shepard was fired, his successor expected to be Don Hoak or Bill Virdon of
the annus mirabilis 1960 Pirates. On the eve of "Decision Day," Stockton repeated
his on-air view that "Don's personality was needed after Shepard's quiet manner."
The next day at 5 p.m. retired 1960 manager Danny Murtaugh was surprisingly
rehired. Dick spoke to him, raced to the office, and took a call from Hoak: "hurt,
furious, wanting to come on and blast the Pirates." Dissuading him, Stockton
went live at 6.

Minutes later police radio reported that Hoak had been found dead in suburban Shadyside. Numb, Stockton said, "We have just found out a shocking and incredibly sad development. Don Hoak, who had been a prime candidate to become
new manager of the Pirates, has died of a heart attack. Details to come on the 7
p.m. newscast." After the 30-minute network news, he told how someone had
tried to steal the car of Don's brother-in-law. Hoak started his own auto, chased
but never caught the other car, and was found slumped over the steering wheel
at the bottom of a hill. "To this day, Hoak's wife believes that Don, who so badly
wanted to manage the Pirates, died of a broken heart," Stockton mused. "Before
broadcasting baseball, I endured a baseball tragedy."

In 1971, Stockton moved to WBZ radio/TV, covering basketball's Celtics.
In 1974, he got a call from Gene Kirby, Dizzy Dean's *Game of the Week* producer.
"Gene had some hilarious stories," said Dick, "since Dean was awful at pronounc-
ing surnames." A batter hit to left-center field, bases full of Italian and Polish

runners. "There's a line drive," Diz said, "and here's Gene Kirby to tell you all about it." The recently hired Red Sox VP, administration, told Stockton about WSBK—"not a network affiliate, so they've got more room for games"—95 by 1977. Send a tape, Kirby said. Dick didn't have one, having never done the sport. "So?" Gene said. "Go out to Shea Stadium"—the Yanks' home while The Stadium was renovated—"record a game, and send me what you do."

Dick thought Kirby would recommend him or say "I wasn't what Gene was looking for." Instead, Dean's ex-*podnuh* phoned, starting: "Got a pad?" Stockton took notes—"seven pages, back and front"—as Kirby lectured him "from the starting lineup to final out, the little I'd done right, the more I'd done wrong." Go to Shea, Gene ordered, and tape again, which *six* times Dick did, Kirby demanding that he "phrase correctly—baseball's 'patter'—and properly inject things and describe plays." After the *seventh* tape Kirby called to say "Eureka!"—he could finally recommend Stockton to the Sox. In October 1975, Dick called Carlton Fisk's Rock of Ages blast. "Who could have predicted when I was enduring the grueling exercise of taping and being harshly but honestly critiqued that one year later I would call such a play?" He wouldn't have, without Gene.

In 1979, Stockton left for a Klondike of baseball, the NFL, NBA, Pan American Games, Winter Olympics, and Fox, CBS, and TBS baseball, saying "my time in Boston pivoted my career." Such a trope seemed equally applicable to his Red Sox analyst who later called the White Sox "good guys" and urged them to "put it [a run] on the board." Some claim Ken Harrelson beats his own drum. It is fairer to say he follows his own drummer, saying upon his 1969 trade to Cleveland, "Where else in the league is the lake brown and the river a fire hazard?" People picketed. Hub switchboards jammed. Said the Hawk, "Baseball was never fun again."

In 1970, he broke a leg, took up golf, and found *it* his handicap. By November 1974, "I'd thought about golf for months and that night decided to give it up. Golf ain't cutting it." At 3 a.m., panicked, Harrelson awoke: "What am I gonna *do*?" By quirk, the Townies called that morning. "A year before, [GM] Dick O'Connell'd offered me TV color. How amazing was it to offer again when he didn't know I was shucking golf?" In WSBK's first exhibition, Ken neatly navigated till Montreal's Tim Foli hit. "Feisty little guy," Hawk ad-libbed. "Lot of balls." Stockton's jaw dropped. Suddenly even golf looked good. Harrelson discovered that Red Sox Nation is a forgiving, if not forgetting, lot, as long as you don't refer on-air to gonads. He also learned what worked.

"Some guys, especially ex-jocks, coast on their names. Others numb you with statistics." Ken spurned each, having long ago inhaled "mama's" love of baseball. From Stockton he learned to "do your homework, be professional, a perfectionist," finding that in New England that might not be enough. Before 1975, neither Dick nor Hawk had called a pitch. UHF penetration was erratic: as Michael Gee tweaked, "hit or miss, to put it kindly." Most of all, "Red Sox fans, perhaps more than any other team's, are dependent on radio. The stations in their chain stretch from Woonsocket to Presque Isle, and there are uncounted Red Sox rooters for whom a trip to Fenway Park is an annual adventure."

The wireless fed backcountry, small towns, and burnt-orange hills. Harrelson knew the pecking order. "So much of the region is isolated," he said, years later. "No matter the announcer, radio's usually top banana." This did not stop television from trying to climb Boston's tree.

By 1975, baseball's best teams like Oakland, Pittsburgh, and Baltimore drew poorly, played far from New York's video colony, and/or had a K-Mart–like park. In the next 13 years, the Red Sox played three of arguably the six best games of our video age: Game Six of the 1975 World Series; 1978's playoff against the Yankees; and Game Six of the 1986 Classic. (The others: Bobby Thomson's Shot, Bill Mazeroski's whopper, and David Freese icing Texas in 2011.) Never before had the Republic been so affixed to the Boston American League Baseball Company. "The Red Sox by themselves didn't save the game," said Bowie Kuhn. "They did, however, help."

The '75ers began in a northeaster—and before a then record 35,343 first-day home crowd. "They're all up as the groundswell continues for Tony C. in his comeback in a Red Sox uniform," said Martin. "There's a line drive, base hit to right field! Tony's got a base hit!" On April 19, Poss turned gently manic: "From here the Sox will go to Baltimore to play Brooksie-Baby and his merry mates . . . Then it's on to New York where Bobby Bonds and 'The Fish' [Catfish Hunter] await." In May, Conigliaro hit his final homer, later enduring a heart attack, coma, and death at 45. By Memorial Day the Sox were only 21-17.

The stripes arrived three weeks later, Fisk overcoming a broken wrist to ultimately hit .331. "Deep left field! Way back! Way back!" growled Woods of Pudge's return. "It is gone! . . . his first home run of the year. And look at him jump and dance! He's the happiest guy in Massachusetts!" The Sox took the series, three games to one, and first place, to stay. Cecil Cooper batted .311, Denny Doyle hit in 22 straight games, and sophomore Burleson steadied shortstop. Petrocelli slowed, retiring a year later. Boston had only 134 homers but led the league in batting average, slugging percentage, and on-base percentage: "not a typical Sox club," said Bobby Doerr.

Regularly Fenway said a rosary. "People screaming, '*Loo-ie*! *Loo-ie*!'" said Ned, "Luis Tiant, scheduled to pitch every fourth day, leaving the bull pen before games and waddling across the field. Folks coming into the ballpark, or even passing by on Boylston Street, heard it, and that gave you an idea of something big going on." Tiant's 18-14 record hinged the staff. Rick Wise was 19-12, Roger Moret 14-3, Bill Lee 17-9. Jim Willoughby and Dick Drago moored the pen. "The Sox always need pitching," mused then *Globe*ster Peter Gammons. "In '75, they had youth, too."

By June, Martin referenced "another Fred Lynn spectacular." He "played center field like Frank Sinatra sang Cole Porter, beautifully. Fred had a gangling kind of lope toward the ball and always got there." Next month Boston led New York, 1-0, at Shea. "Drive to left-center field. May be a gapper! Lynn is running! Lynn is going! He's got it in a great catch!" said Martin. "Oh, mercy, what a catch by Lynn! . . . Red Sox fans are going ape out here! This is World Series time!" Earlier he knit a month in six at-bats. "And there goes a shot deep to right field!" Ned cried at Tiger Stadium. "High in the air, and we watch this go into the upper deck! His third home run of the night . . . [with] ten runs batted in!"—.331, 21 homers, and 105 runs batted to earn the first same-year MVP and Rookie of the Year award.

Left-fielder Jim Rice, Lynn's "Gold Dust Twin," was so strong he broke his bat checking a swing. In July, he became the sixth player to clear Fenway's center-field back wall. "Long drive, way, way back, out of sight!" Poss bayed. "Over the American flag and outta here! Man alive, did he get all of that one! . . . It disappeared in the folds of the American flag." Hailed by "*Dewey*! *Dewey*!" Dwight Evans completed the best Sox outfield since Lewis, Speaker, and Hooper. Martin felt Boston's "right field the toughest in the league, the afternoon sun bad, and the low wall a problem because the ball got to you so fast you didn't have time to see how close it was." Tougher was Evans's arm: as Bugs Baer described Lefty Grove, able to "throw a lamb past a wolf."

Poss loved another outfielder's name—"Wilver Dornel Stargell"—dividing syllables like a fraction. Understatedly, Ned said, "They're playing between the raindrops" as a storm soaked the Fens. Once he interviewed the *Times'* Red Smith, who famously said of writing, "All you do is sit down at a typewriter and open a vein." For an hour, wrote the *South Middlesex News*, "the best baseball broadcaster alive and the best sportswriter of our time talked" ball—the "bartender in Philadelphia who said the most beautiful sight on earth was the bases loaded, two out, 3-2 count, tie score. Perpetual motion, suspense, anticipation, hope, fear." New England's most beautiful sight was whenever the Sox pursued a pennant.

In August 1975, Boston began to lose. Worse, the runner-up Orioles began to win. A columnist dubbed the team "Great Boston Chokers" after Albert DeSalvo, the "Boston Strangler." A disc jockey for WFBR Baltimore flew to Nairobi to ask a witch doctor to apply a hex, the shaman getting $200 and two cases of beer. On September 3, a two-all road game entered the tenth inning, Poss telling Ned at break, "I've got a hunch on Coop." Cecil hit Jim Palmer's first pitch "to right field! It's deep! It's deep! It's deep!" Woods boomed. "And it is off the wall, bouncing away . . . Cooper's at second, on his way to third! . . . He's in with a triple! Cecil Cooper just narrowly missed a home run! Now they rule it home run! They rule it home run! That ball hit over the wall and bounced back into play!"

On September 16, El Tiante faced Jim Palmer at 24 Jersey Street. Fisk and Petrocelli homered. Ken Singleton hit in a two-out ninth. "And you might think the pennant's here right now," Ned said. "Tiant pouring it on in the atmosphere he loves best—when it means something." The "arm around! The pitch! Right-center field! Freddie Lynn's under it! He has got it! Ball game over, and the Red Sox win it, 2-0—5½ in front!" Kiley played "Stout-Hearted Men" for Tiant—"the master of all he surveys," said Martin. *Looie*! *Looie*! filled the yard. "We've crawled out of more coffins than Bela Lugosi," blustered Orioles manager Earl Weaver, his door closing September 26, Baltimore losing twice.

The season ended two days later, WSBK's Stockton and Harrelson noting how the last-month roster of 40, not the usual 25, made rookies as much as results the thing. Butch Hobson and Ted Cox were "two fine-looking third base prospects," Dick observed. Hobson got "a base hit to right"—his first—but also Kd on a curve. "That old Uncle Charlie has given a lot of youngsters problems," said Hawk. (A writer accused Harrelson of "doing for instant replays what the . . . Strangler did for door-to-door salesmen.") Indians first baseman Joe Lis homered: to Stockton, "rammed it out of here!" Hawk: Dick Pole's fastball "was right in his wheelhouse . . . shot up into the twine." Few cared that Alan Ashby homered, Sox freshman Steve Dillard got two hits, or the Tribe romped, 11-4. The best-of-five LCS, then World Series, were already in the public mind.

That day Woods passed an eighth-inning baton: "Now Ned Martin will steer our ship with all colors flying safely into port."

"What *are* our colors, Mr. [Fletcher] Christian?" Ned said, referencing *Mutiny on the Bounty*.

"Well, they ain't [Finley's] green and gold, I'll tell you," Poss said.

"Probably red, white, and blue," said Iwo Jima '45.

A minute later Ned announced 1975's attendance—1,748,587—saying a larger Fenway would have made 2 million "a mere bagatelle."

"Whatever that is," said Poss.

Martin: "I'm not going to tell you."

Relaxed, Ned mimicked Dr. Seuss: "[Two] strikes to [Charlie] Spikes"— pause—"as in a pitch to [Bobby] Grich." Pause. "We go on the road October 15." Finally: "Dance, pit pat, party chatter."

At this point we must introduce the Sox then new radio flagship: not caring that "they were not Martin or Lewis, nor even Rowan and Martin," said *SI*. "Just Martin and Woods, the best day-in, day-out announcers covering the American League."

The year had begun with Martin fusing Rousseau and Reggie Cleveland. Woods regularly called Ned "Nedley." Martin ribbed Poss about his and Prince's booth as bar. "Did Budweiser sponsor you, or did you sponsor Budweiser?" The Dodgers' Charley Steiner defines a sufficient voice as "not having to be Charlton Heston's, just cut through background sound." Woods's baritone was "gravelly, literally whiskeyed," said Ned, *his* Scotch-Irish tenor as old-shoe as a slipper. Clark Booth recalls thinking that "the best play-by-play combination in the history of American sport would continue forever." Silly us.

In 1974, Boston had tapped Kirby to make over the on-air Red Sox: Mutual '50s *Game of the Day* announcer, Phillies broadcast director, and Expos traveling secretary; later, ESPN consultant, *The Natural* film adviser, and friend of future Sox skipper Don Zimmer. Stockton credits Kirby for "making me an announcer." How could anyone so instructive be so destructive of the Townies? On September 18, 1975, WMEX—later, WITS—succeeded WHDH as flagship, Kirby hiking new fees so high that "only those two stations bid," said Joe Castiglione. WMEX general manager Paul Kelley refused to say Ned and Poss would return, saying, "We should give consideration to getting the best men that are available." He excluded the Sox booth, where "the best" already worked.

To pay a record $450,000 pact, WMEX began a pre-game show, launched a *during*-inning ad blitz, and commenced a home run inning. "It prostituted the product," Ned said, "hurt our rhythm, thus the game." More cash demanded VIP schmoozing, which Woods and Martin loathed. WHDH had fifty thousand watts. WMEX fell to five thousand after dark: so weak, wrote Barnicle, that your hairdryer would provide more current. "A Coast Guard ensign sends a better signal. Rub two sticks together and you come up with more power." A mental short was Kirby's "objecting to Martin's description of muddy conditions at home plate at Fenway," wrote Jack Craig, as if a listener wouldn't note the rain. "He believed that *bad* news was *no* news, a policy put into effect by Stockton under Kirby's tutelage." The perceived tilt, Jack felt, hurt Dick's credibility.

A day after WMEX's rights announcement, the *Globe*'s Bob Ryan said that Kirby, "without whom the Red Sox somehow struggled through their first 75 years of existence, is behind the obvious move to dump Martin." He wondered if Gene knew that "Boston is unique in its sports sophistication"; "the NFL players' strike end was obliterated by the subject of Martin and Woods"; and "thousands of people are listening to the radio while they're watching games on television." A confidential 1978 Kelley memo showed a shocking *21* percent of Channel 38 viewers muting TV sound for Poss and Ned. Said Ryan, "Fans know what they have in Martin and Woods and they are not going to accept losing them graciously."

Signing off, Ned issued a last-day "personal injection," waving a "fond good-bye" to WHDH producers and engineers. Then, "tossing bouquets," he "tossed one" to the Nation. Like 1974, Poss replied, "I've never seen such backing."

Martin: "Mr. Possum, you've been unforgettable. I hope we'll be together for five hundred more games."

Eerily, including 1978's playoff, they were "together" for 487.

Stunned by the blowback, WMEX rehired *broadcasting's* Gold Dust Twins, economic Darwinists still mocking "The Voice," Gee wrote. "Every baseball fan grew up with one. It was a simple equation: the voice was the team. Mel Allen meant the Yankees, Bob Prince the Pirates, By Saam the Phillies, and so on. Here in New England there are two voices—Ned Martin's and Jim Woods's—and the equation holds better here than it does anywhere else."

Later, when Fenway seemed old-timey, Gowdy warned, "Don't change a thing." A Soxaphile didn't want to in late 1975. Reggie Jackson, Sal Bando, and Joe Rudi had spurred the A's fifth straight Western Division title. They were favored in the LCS, Boston twitted for its Ancient Mariners (Yaz and El Tiante) and Kiddie Corps (Rice and Lynn). Tiant opened, winning, 7-1: to Jackson, "the Fred Astaire of baseball." Next day No. 8 launched a fourth-inning net-detector—an out anywhere but Fenway. In the seventh, Poss roared, "Fly ball, left field! Don't know if it's deep enough or not. And Rudi will watch it go into the Screen for a home run! Rico Petrocelli has homered into the Screen. Boston leads, 5-3, and Fenway Park is an absolute madhouse!"

Fenway was scene and actor: It *mattered* where a game occurred. The two homers swung the series. In Oakland, Yastrzemski, playing left, nabbed one third-game runner and kept another from the plate. An eighth-inning 6-4-3 toppled the A's reign. "Bando on third, Jackson on at first," said Woods. "Drago is set. Here's the pitch. Ground ball hit down at Burleson, on to Doyle for one, on to first. They've got two!" Townies sweep, 5-3. Yaz hit an LCS-team-high .455. The calendar must have read 1967.

WHDH's pact had elapsed after the last regular-season game. "For that reason they couldn't do the playoffs," said Ned. Again the switchboard jammed, lighting "a firestorm of fan protest," read the *Globe*, leading WMEX to cover the LCS, the Sox paying Poss's and Ned's fee. Next fall began a two-network four-year plan: NBC, Saturday's *Game*; ABC, *Monday Night Baseball*; shared, postseason and the All-Star Game. The pact also dumped local-team for network mikemen. "Prior to the networks taking over, I snuck in under the wire," Ned rejoiced, making the World Series at age 51. The 1975 Classic walked a *high* wire. Seldom have so many aired so much to such effect.

NBC had done Series TV and radio since 1947 and 1957, respectively. Aiding Martin: Garagiola, Gowdy, Kubek, Stockton, and Reds radio's Marty Brennaman. Had Cincinnati added TV's Coleman, four of seven would have had Townies DNA. As it was, three of six did, the Sox refusing to drop Ned or Dick. "Talk about luck," said Martin. "This Series was maybe the greatest ever. I'd waited a long time to do one." Before Game One at Fenway, Stockton evoked a Series opener in another surreal park: September 29, 1954, at the Polo Grounds, "immortalized by Willie Mays's over-the-shoulder catch off Vic Wertz and Dusty Rhodes's game-winning tenth-inning homer," Dad and Dick "playing hooky from job and school, respectively," to sit eight rows behind the Cleveland dugout.

The Series lured scribes, celebs, and baseball royalty: bigger than Ike, brassier than Milton Berle, more boffo than *Our Miss Brooks*. America "stopped and paid attention," wrote Heywood Broun, to Gillette's "Blue Blades March" ("Da-*da*-da, da-da-da-da-da," sang Bob Costas), Sharpie the Parrot ("Mister, how ya fixed for blades?"), and voice-over ("Look sharp. Feel sharp. Be sharp."). Connie Mack wore his high-starched collar. Yankees skipper Casey Stengel finally had a Classic to watch, not win. Tallulah Bankhead and George Raft held court. In infield practice, photographers snap a picture. "Do you know who that gentleman is sitting right behind you?" Stockton Sr. asked Dick. "Douglas MacArthur. Those photographers think you're his *son*." Only later did *fils* grasp how the game "proved baseball's unpredictability. Rhodes hit a 257-foot homer; Wertz, a 460-plus-foot out."

Cincinnati's All-Star team included Hall of Famers Sparky Anderson, Johnny Bench, Joe Morgan, and Tony Perez, should-be Dave Concepcion, and once-was Pete Rose. None helped: Tiant, 6-0. Next day Boston led, 2-1, when a rain delay broke Lee's seventh-inning rhythm: Reds, 3-2. For a while Game Three was as drab as Cincy's Riverfront Stadium, Sox down, 5-1. In the ninth, Evans drove "to left field! Back near the wall goes Foster!" said Martin. "At the wall! He can't get it! The game is tied up [at five]!" An inning later, Cesar Geronimo reached first, then third, base when Fisk threw away Ed Armbrister's bunt. "Armbrister interfered [with a force-out]!" screamed Darrell Johnson. "Forget it!" cried plate umpire Larry Barnett, unlikely when Morgan's hit won the game. Boston's best big-game hurler since Ruth then tied the Classic: El Tiante, 5-4. Game Five was Don Gullett's, pitching, and Perez's, dinging twice: Reds, 5-2.

Ending there, the Series might be as dimly recalled as, say, 1945's Tigers-Cubs. Instead, play returned to Boston, where for three days it rained. Some felt the delay would starve interest. In fact, it fed pressure—e.g., Tuesday, October 21. Behind, 6-3, in the eighth, Lynn singled, Petrocelli walked, and pinch-hitter Bernie Carbo arced a parabola. Later Giamatti caressed "the evening, late and cold, in 1975, the sixth game of the World Series, perhaps the greatest baseball game played in the last 50 years, when Carbo, loose and easy, uncoiled." Said Curt, "Carbo hits a high drive! Deep center! Home run! [bedlam for 15 seconds] Bernie Carbo has hit his second pinch-hit home run of this Series! That was a blast up in the center-field bleachers. It came with two out . . . And the Red Sox have tied it, 6 to 6!"

Inning by inning, narrative unwound. In the ninth, Lynn hit a none-out bases-full pop to left field. Then–third base coach Zimmer told the runner, "No, no!" Doyle thought Zim cried, "Go, go!" Gowdy, who had seen it all, hadn't: "Here's the tag. Here's the throw! He's out! A double play! Foster throws him out!" In the eleventh, Morgan pulled a one-out and -on drive to right—a sure triple or home run. "Back goes Evans—back, back! And . . . what a grab! Evans made a grab and saved a home run on that one!" Curt said. Ned found the seesaw "indescribable. Carbo. Doyle. Add to Dewey's great catch his presence of mind to throw to [first baseman] Yaz for a double play." Martin *had* seen it before: "With Fenway's low seats in right, Evans was always diving toward the stands."

Midnight came, and left. At 12:34 a.m., Fisk drove Pat Darcy's twelfth-inning pitch toward the Monster. "NBC had opened a wonderful door for me when it named me on TV to the Series," Stockton later said. Now: "There it goes! A long drive! If it stays fair! . . . *home run!*" In Game Two, Ned had likened Curt, Tony, and himself to "Winkin', Blinkin', and Nod." *Un*blinkingly, he referenced "numerous heroics tonight, both sides," then Darcy's "one-oh delivery to Fisk. He swings. Long drive, left field!" Fisk employed hand signs and body English to push or prod or pray the ball fair. It caromed off the foul pole. "Home run!" Martin said on radio. "The Red Sox win! And the Series is tied, three games apiece!"

Gowdy followed, "Carlton Fisk has hit a one-nothing pitch. They're jamming out on the field! His teammates are waiting for him! And the Red Sox send the World Series into Game Seven with a dramatic 7 to 6 victory. What a game! This is one of the greatest World Series games of all time!"—the Fens alive with music. Plainly, as we shall see, NBC felt there was nothing left for Curt to sing.

Recently elected governor, Michael Dukakis had sat with wife Kitty along the third-base line. "Things looked terribly bleak," he said. "Then, out of nowhere, Carbo, sort of a daffy guy, hits that blast." They left Fenway thinking that "win or lose Game Seven, we'd seen one of the greatest games ever." In Beijing, nearly eleven thousand miles away, it was noon Wednesday. George H. W. Bush, then envoy to China, and the embassy staff "cheered almost as soon as Fisk's homer cleared the wall." Ted Williams said he was glad Fisk had hit a strike. Reds skipper Anderson sleepwalked to his Hub hotel. "I got there," he said, "and I was stunned."

Being the Sox, Boston led Game Seven, 3-0, till Rose upended Doyle on a potential sixth-inning double play. Fisk then ordered a curve. Named Spaceman for a reason, Lee threw a blooper that Tony Perez deposited on Lansdowne Street: 3-2. In the three-all ninth, Johnson inexplicably relieved Jim Willoughby for rookie Jim Burton, who built a winning run more redolent of Dead Ball than the Big Red Machine. Ken Griffey walked, was sacrificed to second base, moved to third on a ground out, and scored on Morgan's 4-3 Series-winning lob. Burton pitched one more bigs game.

Anderson called Game Six "a keeper," luring 62 million viewers. It was a changer, too. Next night a then record 75,890,000 watched, presaging the first all prime-time Series (1985). Nationally, Martin became "a comer, a quality announcer of pure gold," wrote Craig. The sport left TV's critical list, Fisk topping *TV Guide*'s 1998 "Fifty Greatest Moments": "Every little boy who has ever played on a sandlot has dreamed of winning a World Series game with a last at-bat home run. Even better: do it in front of the rabid fans of the team you grew up rooting for. In short, do what . . . Fisk did. As if in a trance"—it remains—"the catcher bounced up and down near home plate, waving at the ball, willing it to stay fair. And when the ball obeyed, he leaped into the air and began his trot around the bases, both fists raised—just like a kid on the sandlot."

Fisk's haymaker "remained the ultimate moment in TV sports, not for its drama (the Red Sox lost the seventh game) but because of its sheer beauty—an American dream come true," *TV Guide* continued. The reaction shot—"Since then," said Harry Coyle, "everything's up-close, including people's response to the play"—echoed the Hippocratic Oath. Lou Gerard's camera had been inside the Wall, "my task, no matter what—follow the ball. As Fisk swung I saw a rat four feet away. *I didn't dare cause harm* by moving, which is what I [would have] had to do to shift the viewfinder." The lens stayed on Fisk. Months later, the *New Yorker* wrote, "The Series was replayed everywhere in memory and conversation through the ensuing winter, and even now its colors still light up the sky."

In 1947, green paint had replaced Wall signage. Fenway's interior now changed almost as vividly as then. "In the Series Lynn hit the center-field concrete wall and crumpled to the grass," said Gammons. "He went down, the whole park quieting." In 1976, Yawkey padded the outfield fence base, replaced the Wall's tin facade with plastic, shrunk the board by dropping NL scores, and moved it 20 feet to the right. An enclosed press box rose. Up went a new center-field ad message board.

A quarter century later the group Save Fenway Park felt redeemed. "Money," huffed John Valianti of Marshfield, Massachusetts. "The board, [1982–1983 private] suites built atop the left- and right-field stands. When Fenway started playing by other's rules, it began not being Fenway."

At the time, "the change was seen as meteorological," not commercial, Gammons said. Fenway's wind had blown mostly in and out. The new press box and message board made it cross. "Fouls used to find the seats," added Nolan. "Now they can catch the wind and end up fair." Castiglione found the debate cultural: "On one hand, New England is progressive socially. On the other, when it comes to baseball fans like things exactly like they were, including numbers." The distance to the left-field pole—315 feet—had been immutable, like the rock at Plymouth Point. In 1997, the Sox revised it to 310, like saying that the Pilgrims landed at Bayone.

Post-Fisk, *Gowdy's* number came up. "Garagiola loved to throw elbows," mused Coyle. "For all Curt's success [owning four homes and seven radio stations in Florida, Massachusetts, New Hampshire, and Wyoming], he was a small-town kid." Carl Lindemann wanted to forget being odd man out. Chrysler "kept pushing for Joe to get all play-by-play. It was brutal," he said. "I was the only guy behind the Cowboy." In November 1975, NBC made Carl fly to Maine, where Gowdy was filming *The American Sportsman*, and tell baseball's foremost Voice— "Curt was stunned"—that he was through.

"Mr. Garagiola will do our [1976] play-by-play [Kubek, keeping color]," said NBC, hoping that his unorthodox charm and wit would halt *Game's* hemorrhage. When ratings slid, Joe moved to analysis, Scully getting 1983 balls and strikes. By then, Gowdy had become "a roving [Series] reporter"—to Coyle, "humiliation"—done a last Rose and Super Bowl, and been replaced by Dick Enberg, who kept even more balls in the air than Curt. One hoops Saturday the Cowboy misidentified each starter. His spotter had blundered: Gowdy got the blame.

In 1981, CBS TV put Curt, 62, out to pasture. "It was an ugly end," said Lindemann. "Neither Curt nor I know why." Having met Gowdy on 1960 Sox wireless, I heard him on 1980s' CBS Radio baseball, Patriots local football, and HBO's *Inside the NFL*: the game, the important thing; the voice, still as sturdy as a post. In 1998, he recited "Casey at the Bat," with the Boston Pops Orchestra, at Tanglewood. "The music, my family there, the summer breeze. Yes, that had to be the greatest." The crowd went daft: to many, *the* Red Sox Voice, coming home.

What a conundrum wrapped in hard to get a handle on: genuine, in a bogus age; nice guy, good at business; loyal friend, in a disloyal field. His legend towered, then and now. "You look at McNamee, Husing, Allen," said Lindemann. "With networks dividing sports, nobody ever did what Gowdy did"—or will.

Like 1947 and 1968, the 1976 Sox found defending a title harder than winning it. El Tiante was 21-12. Only Rice had as many as 25 homers. "With the talent we have on this club," said Yaz, "playing .500 is a disgrace." A brawl between Fisk and the stripes' Lou Piniella broke Lee's left arm but awoke a dormant rivalry. Woods and Martin didn't ignore losing's 800-pound gorilla. "You can't fool anybody. The same players who won last year are losing this year," said Ned, back aching, *SI* wrote, due to "years of leaning over a desk to do play-by-play." He had to announce an 11-game road trip standing up. Once the Sox led, 12-0, then braved a 51-minute rain delay, radio's Twins soldiering on.

Woods: "Ned, you have to love this game."

Martin: "I do. I really do."

Woods: "When we finish up this home stand, we go to Cleveland for a twi-night double-header on Saturday."

Martin: "I can't wait to get there."

Woods: "Will you ever quit?"

Martin: "They'll have to tear the uniform off my back."

On July 9—to Poss, "a gray, dreary day"—Yawkey, 73, died of cancer, tearing the heart out of ownership. "Good evening," Woods began. "Welcome to Fenway Park—a very subdued Fenway Park—or it will be as the news echoes through the stands." At 4:20 p.m., "the owner of the Boston Red Sox some 42, 43 years, passed away. The mood here is still a state of shock." Even players who didn't know him "were walking around, like, on eggshells," said Martin, noting that Yaz "considered Mr. Yawkey like a father. There was nothing you could say to him, really, because he seemed to want to be alone with his thoughts." Pre-iPod and -Twitter, Woods doubted that the crowd, "for the most part, know what has happened." Upstairs, press steward Tommy McCarthy wept.

The Sox asked a moment of silent prayer before playing Minnesota. Poss suggested Boston had lost "an awfully fine man." To Ned, "the Patriots, Celtics, and Bruins [had gone] by the light of Yawkey's Sox," preserving "the class of a baseball field being a baseball field—no phony stuff, gimmicks." He helped New England remain "more Red Sox territory than the Braves, and the Braves were here a long and honorable time, fans who died when they left"—Martin still had A's scar tissue. Woods cited Cardinals owner August Busch: "There are three giants left in baseball—[Philip] Wrigley in Chicago, Yawkey in Boston, and"—modestly— "me." Coleman's classic record resonated: "Owner, sportsman, fan. Baseball lives in Boston through the efforts of this man."

The Sox stranded six runners in the first three innings: a longtime Yawkey bugaboo. Behind, 8-3, Yaz batted in the seventh. "There's a long drive—right field!" Poss said. "Way back! Way back! It's gone—a three-run homer," as if T. A. were in his rooftop box. Waxing: the Bicentennial's Tall Ships—"more than 50 of the world's greatest sailing vessels," a *Globe* ad went—arriving in Boston Harbor next day from New York—"frigates, full-rigged ships, schooners, clippers." Waning: ownership. Yawkey's successor, wife Jean, sold a large interest of their estate in 1978 to a group—JRY Corporation—led by ex-catcher Haywood Sullivan and longtime team trainer Edward (Buddy) LeRoux. "Since then," the *Globe* wrote in the '90s, "it has displayed the smarts and stability of a banana republic"—Sox radio/TV making the republic look sane.

An exception was Martin's CBS 1976–1978 LCS. "It's the first time anyone has ever phoned me and asked me to work for them," he said, "and it's a nice feeling." Nicer—teaming with Ernie Harwell, a fetching and inspired choice. Each knew how a 10-year-old would spurn the pitchout and hit and run for the long ball, the soul-crushing poke—the homer. We were all 10 in the first full post-Yawkey year. The 1977 "Crunch Bunch" belted a Sox-record 213 dingers, five with more than 25, including ninth-place hitter Hobson's 30. Rice, with 39, led in eight team categories. For the first time Boston drew more than 2 million customers, one having moved to Harvard University for a year-long Nieman Fellowship, another teaching there.

Raised in suburban Washington, Fred Barnes had seen The Kid homer off Camilo Pascual, Reggie "Smith make one of the greatest catches ever, reaching over the fence to rob the Senators' Hank Allen of a homer and holding up his glove with the ball sticking out like an ice cream cone as he ran back to the dugout," and the Sox play at Griffith Stadium, RFK Stadium, then Memorial Stadium "after the Senators moved away." In 1977, he saw 35 to 40 games on renamed Yawkey Way, "often in the bleachers, often alone, since my wife and daughters weren't always interested in going." That year the first woman journalist to enter the Red Sox locker room, Doris Kearns Goodwin, a future Pulitzer Prize–winning biographer, wrote her first book, the best-selling *Lyndon Johnson and the American Dream.*

Born in Brooklyn, Doris had listened to the afternoon Dodgers game for her father, still at work, not imagining loving the Boston Red Sox. At night, they sat together on the porch and relived the game, "which I had so carefully preserved in the large, red scorebook I'd been given for my seventh birthday," she later wrote in the *Globe.* "I can still remember how proud I was to have mastered all those strange and wonderful symbols that permitted me to recapture, in miniature form," their Bums. Dad already knew the score yet let Doris think that, without her work, "he would be unable to follow our team in the only proper way a team should be followed, day by day, inning by inning. In other words, without me, his love for baseball would be forever incomplete."

In 1958, "the unforgivable O'Malley" broke the heart of a borough forever in baseball bloom. Many went underground. Others forswore baseball for a time, or life. Doris went to school, the Johnson White House, and Harvard to teach. Once burned, the professor of government finally agreed "half reluctantly" to go to Fenway. "There it was again: the cozy ballfield scaled to human dimensions so that every word of encouragement and every scornful yell could be heard on the field; the fervent crowd that could, with equal passion, curse a player for today's failures after cheering his heroics the day before; the team that always seemed to break your heart in the last week of the season. It took only a matter of minutes before I found myself directing all my old intensities toward my new team"—the Sox. Like Gowdy at Tanglewood, she was home.

"Pitching! We need pitching!" Yaz bayed in 1977. (Brooklyn had, too.) Reliever Bill Campbell's 13 victories and starter Ferguson Jenkins's 3.68 ERA led the staff. Lyle won the Cy Young Award, helping New York edge Boston by 2½ games. Meanwhile, Giamatti wrote a classic essay: "The Green Fields of the Mind." Since 1983, Castiglione has recited it at the end of each season. "It breaks your heart," he begins. "It is designed to break your heart. The game begins in the spring, when everything else begins again, and it blossoms in the summer, filling the afternoons and evenings, and then as soon as the chill rains come, it stops and leaves you to face the fall alone. You count on it, rely on it to buff the passage of time, to keep the memory of sunshine and high skies alive, and then just when the days are all twilight, when you need it most, it stops."

In 1977, it stopped October 2: "a Sunday of rain and broken branches and leaf-clogged drains and slick streets, [after which] summer was gone. Somehow," Giamatti wrote, "the summer seemed to slip by faster this time. . . . The real activity was done with the radio—not the all-seeing, all-falsifying television—and was the playing of the game in the only place it will last, the enclosed green field of the mind"—Ned and Poss completing each other's sentences, communing on-air by "a hand gesture, shrug, raised eyebrow," wrote Bill Griffith. After a game, "broadcasters, writers, and the coaching staff [gathered] during which Martin and Woods would be spellbinding with their baseball tales."

A day earlier the Sox, one loss from elimination, had played their final game, bowing to Baltimore, 8-7. Giamatti wrote, "Summer died in New England and like rain sliding off a roof, the crowd slipped out of Fenway." Sunday's game was rained out. Ahead: "the apocalyptic Red Sox collapse," said the *Globe*'s Dan Shaughnessy, "against which all others must be measured." In every way, 1978 broke your heart.

Early that year WMEX owner Dick Richmond sold the station to Cincinnati-based Mariner Communications, which changed the name to WITS and suggested it might drop a shoe. A January press release about the Sox exhibition schedule omitted Woods and Martin. General manager Kelley declined comment. Mariner president Joe Scallan was, as they say, unavailable: an Andover Academy graduate and Harvard MBA who had forgotten *The Music Man*'s "But you gotta know the territory."

Arriving in New England, the midwestern Scallan, 50, panted to transform it. "I'm going to change listening habits," he informed Woods, incredulous. "What you don't know is that I could replace you and Ned with King Kong and Donald Duck and not lose one listener."

"Well, Joe," said Possum, "I don't know about King Kong, but I do believe that Donald is under contract [to Walt Disney–owned theme parks] in Anaheim and Orlando."

Ned told the *Globe*, "I'm thinking positive"—like Woods, soon retained for 1978. (It was too late to fire them.) Norman Vincent Peale would have found it hard to think positively about their boss. For one thing, WITS stayed at five thousand watts at night: Gene Kirby, fired, had paid the price. "Haywood [Sullivan, 1977–1984 Sox GM] can't hear it [at his Canton home 20 miles from

Fenway],"said Poss. "I've seen stronger college stations." For another, paraphrasing "I went to a fight, and a hockey game broke out," Woods and Martin, hoping to do baseball, brooked a blizzard of "reading beer [ads] between strikes," Barnicle jibed.

"This marked the first commercial encroachment *into* innings," said then WITS sports reporter and talk host Tom Shaer. Out of nowhere Ned segued to Crimson Travel: "So you're taking a trip this winter." New England Chrysler-Plymouth Dealers' home run inning gave some lucky lottery listener a car if a Townie dinged. One night W. E. Sanborn of Concord, New Hampshire, was picked, Poss roaring, "We're trying to put a new Volare in his driveway." The rule changed after listeners won more cars than expected: Only the first got keys. Hating the ad clutter, Ned and Poss tried manfully to salute. "Woodsie was especially wonderful: 'It's deep! It's deep! Mrs. Shakespeare, you've got a car!'" Shaer laughed. Scallan didn't notice: Poss could have been talking French.

Had the Nation fretted, it might again have saved the Twins. By 1978, however, "rumors of their depature from the booth [were] as much a part of Sox Septembers as slumps," said Gee. Beside, who could fret about what the *Globe* termed "SuperTeam"? In 1976, Johnson had yielded to his fine third-base coach. As manager, Don Zimmer remained a fine third-base coach. "We remember '78's close," said Martin. "But for a long time it meant hitting." Pitcher–turned–Angels Voice Don Drysdale helped the Dodgers win the 1959, 1963, and 1965 Series. He told Ned, "'You guys can't lose. I haven't seen a team this great in a long time.' And Drysdale saw some good teams." Ironically, Martin's "best team in my time there" still spurs a pursed lip or plaintive sigh. That was not true before the fall.

Boston took first place in May, was 62-28 on July 20, and led New York by 14 games and "a thousand games over everybody else," said Ned. (*Sic* Milwaukee and Baltimore also topped the Yankees.) To Reggie Jackson, "if the Sox keep playing like this, even Affirmed couldn't catch them." Seven Townies made the All-Star team. Dennis Eckersley left Cleveland to go a Sox-best 20-8. Mike Torrez took $2.5 million to leave New York. Starter/reliever Bob Stanley was 15-2. "Super-Team" starred Pudge and Rooster (Burleson) and Rice's 139 RBI, 406 total bases, and 46 homers, 28 at Fenway, and "Hobson with all those homers" and Eck, "a favorite then and years later when he came back as a relief pitcher." The Yankees resembled Alydar.

It was '49 again: How could the Red Sox *lose*? "You wish the story could end there," Martin mused. It didn't. Some breaks were physical. Burleson hurt his ankle. Second baseman Jerry Remy cracked his wrist. A beaning dizzied Evans. In 1977, Hobson had begun rearranging elbow bone chips between pitches. "What a gamer!" Zimmer said, refusing to rest Butch or rib-cracked Fisk. "He wouldn't bench the regulars," Remy said. "It was always build that lead." Other cracks were mental. Zim led by instinct, shelved pitchers he disliked, and drove home listening to talk radio trash him. Spaceman thought his manager fat, bald, and dumb—"The Gerbil."

The Sox went 2-8 on a road trip, losing six games in eight days. On Thursday, September 7, a four-game series in the Fens began. By Sunday, New York had romped 15-3, 13-2, 7-0, and 7-4, tying for the lead. The stripes led the Boston Massacre, 12-0, 13-0, 7-0, and 6-0, the last rookie Bobby Sprowl's debut—Zimmer refusing to start Lee. The Townies went 3-14, hit .192, made 31 errors, and fell 3½ games behind, then perversely won their final eight: "our last chance," Remy mused, "not to have this over our heads for the rest of our life."

In Toronto, Ned noted how "the Yankee score is up," briefly lighting the message board. "Soon it too will be gone. It will flash away like a lightning bug into the chilly Canadian night." On September 28, a game behind New York, Boston played Detroit. The Twins began with humor: in Seattle, attendance lagged.

Woods: "A lot of people were spending their money to see [a] King Tut [exhibit]."

Martin: "And the club ended up in about the same position as he was."

It was "a windy, cold night at Fenway," Ned said, "Sox infielders with their meat hands in their back pockets." Possum, airing innings three, four, and seven, inherited a scoreless game. Fisk "gets one [pitch] right over the coconut." Woods spelled a fractured name. Martin: "Nice going." Jim: "I did my best." In the fourth, Rice's topped four hundred feet. "Fly ball! Deep center field! Back goes Stanley!" Poss roared. "And this one is gone—number 45 for Rice! Wind or not, a tremendous shot halfway up into the Triangle!"

Martin resumed, frozen bleachers showing "all sorts of alarms and excursions." Torrez walked seven, but got four double plays. That day Pope John Paul I died. Hub TV teased a newscast: "Pope Dies, Sox Still Alive [1-0]." The regular season ended October 1. Cleveland beat New York, 9-2. In the Fens, Tiant blanked Toronto, 5-0, to tie the Yankees: his last Townies game. Boston won a coin toss to host next day's AL East playoff—the league's first since 1948, Sox losing each—"maybe the most exciting and crushing game I ever broadcast at Fenway," Ned allowed, "and also the most difficult."

Earlier that week Scallan had dropped the shoe. "Not all fans knew it," said Martin, "but this was Jim's and my last Sox game. What a way to leave—with a game to be treasured as long as baseball lives." Poss began at 2:30 p.m. on Monday, October 2: "This is one for the money. All of it. The big bag of marbles." Ned referenced "a playoff before the playoff. And maybe after that"—pause; crowd roar—"here come the Red Sox." Woods listed each lineup, Ned saying, "I can't hear you!"

In the second inning, Dorian Gray faced Yanks starter Ron Guidry: "It's a long drive, right field, this may be outta here! It is a . . . fair ball! Home run! Red Sox lead, 1-0! Carl Yastrzemski!" cried Martin. In the sixth, "there's a [Rice] base hit to center field," said Woods. "And here comes Burleson with the second run!" The stripes then began to turn the screw. With two on base, Lynn, a spray hitter, pulled Guidry: sure to score them, except that catcher Thurman Munson had told Lou Piniella that "[Guidry's] slider was slowing up, acting like a curveball," Sweet Lou moving near the right-field corner. "He's got it at the railing!" Poss marveled. "A saving catch!"

Next inning, down, 2-0, Bucky Dent, hitting with two out and on, fouled Torrez's second pitch off his foot. Limping, he asked for time: "a lull," said Woods, "in the day's occupation." On-deck, Mickey Rivers saw a crack, giving Dent another bat. Bucky swung, Fisk thinking, "We got away with a mistake pitch." Earlier Jackson's drive had dropped off a cliff into Yaz's glove. Another turn: The wind now blew *out*. "A drive toward left!" said Poss. "Yaz will watch it go into the Screen and the Yankees lead, 3 to 2! . . . Suddenly, the whole thing is turned around!" Seeing, Ned disbelieved: "Dent, a borrowed bat, and a little fly ball into the net, and the silence was deafening. Maybe Fenway's greatest silence ever—unless you were honoring someone who had passed away."

Each team scored twice, including Jackson's eighth-inning belt. "Fly ball, deep center field!" Martin stated. "Pretty high! It is up! It is away! It is gone!" Many forget, he later said, that "Reggie's was the winning run off Stanley. They never, ever forget Fisk or Dent: the losses as big as the wins of this crazy, antiquated little park." The final turn of "the Red Sox–Yankee competition," wrote Peter Gammons, "reached a peak of intensity rare even in that legendary rivalry." In the ninth, behind, 5-4, Burleson drew a one-out walk: "Piniella, in right field, in a semicircle of sun," Ned foreshadowed. Remy then lined to right—"Piniella can't find it!" Somehow Lou blocked the sun to spear the one-bounce drive, preventing an inside-the-park pennant-winning homer.

Two men roosted. Rice flied out, Burleson taking third. In the on-deck circle, Fisk eyed the 32,925 standing. Yastrzemski's fly had ended the 1975 World Series. Number 8 now lofted Goose Gossage's second pitch. "A high pop-up to the left side!" said Martin. "In fair ground is Graig Nettles! In foul ground is Nettles! He's got it! And the Yankees win the pennant!" Yaz wept. The Yankees had inherited the wind. The congregation remained, standing.

In the clubhouse, two 1961 rookies mourned. "I tried, Ned," Yaz said, voice breaking, reported bystander Craig.

"I wanted you up there, captain," Martin almost whispered.

"I wanted to be up there, too," said Yaz: as the reader knows, his last chance for a World Series ring.

"Nothing to be ashamed of here at all," Ned said post-game. "No such words as 'choke' should ever be said to a Red Sox player on this team. If they are, he'll get himself belted in the mouth, and with reason."

Reason did not describe the asylum ahead.

That winter, a New Haven bar owner mourned, "They [Townies] killed our fathers and now the sons of bitches are coming to get us." Rice played 163 games, missed only one at-bat, had a third straight year of more than two hundred hits, and was named MVP. Boston won its most games since 1946, drew a record 2,320,643, and helped forge "baseball's Golden Age," said *Sports Illustrated*. "There is impressive evidence to suggest that the old game . . . is now enjoying unsurpassed popularity and prosperity . . . The latest [post–Fisk and Dent] polls show baseball to be *the* sport these days." Boston's sky housed a constellation of stars.

Brightest was "still the ballpark," wrote Martin Nolan. "In the age of Tris Speaker and Babe Ruth, the era of Jimmie Foxx and Ted Williams, through the empty-seats epoch of Don Buddin and Willie Tasby and unto the decades of Yastrzemski and Rice, the ballpark is the star. A crazy-quilt violation of city planning principles, an irregular pile of architecture, a menace to marketing consultants, Fenway Park works." It worked as a "symbol of New England's pride, as a repository of evergreen hopes, as a tabernacle of lost innocence. It works as a place to watch baseball"—especially true, he said, "of the poetically inclined. It is old, it is idiosyncratic, and a frequent citadel of dashed hopes—all enduring themes of literature."

In late 1978, John Cheever proclaimed that "all literary men are Red Sox fans—to be a Yankee fan in literary society is to endanger your life." He saw "the Yankees–Red Sox rivalry as the Trojan War," Nolan mused, "with the Red Sox as the tragic Trojans"—its birth Ruth's sale to New York, "the symbol of capitalist crassness, that day los[ing] future generations of poets." Nolan had been a *Globe* reporter, Washington and West Coast bureau chief, editorial page and associate editor; fellow at Harvard, Duke, and the Hoover Institution; and Pulitzer Prize finalist for editorial writing and commentary. He felt that Fenway, "the vestibule of approach-avoidance, would win any literary plebiscite over Yankee Stadium, a self-confident garage for a juggernaut. The arrogance of easy winners against the charm of the underdog? New York neon vs. New England pewter? Trendy vulgarity vs. traditional serenity? No contest." At first base, he said, "playing for William Dean Howells, [was] David Halberstam. In right, John Updike would spell Nathaniel Hawthorne."

On October 2, Updike and his wife heard the final out, parked on a Boston street, on their way to dinner—"Slaughter rounding third all over again," he said. Next came more last things and farewell twists. Stockton went to CBS to host *Sports Spectacular*, having tutored Harrelson and learned baseball's "patter." Released from a final year of Reds TV, Coleman retook the Logan shuffle to his boyhood park, many expecting him to man 1979 Sox video. As we have seen, WITS wanted company men, not good listening company—"Hit parties, ooze oil," Poss said. "I couldn't, nor would Ned." The flagship now told each to hit the road, creating "such an uproar," wrote Shaughnessy, "that the fellow who fired them [Scallan] was soon gone as well."

According to Craig, Woods, 62, disliked the clubhouse post-game show, forced to "almost plead for the star of the game's attention." Martin's alleged sin was "a failure to improve in his broadcasting." Ned's reply: "After 18 years, it's difficult to improve." Baseball mocked their exit for "lacking the right kind of attitude for dealing with clients in the VIP lounge for the constant marketing exposure," said Scallan. Even Kelley finally grasped the madness: "Ned and I have walked commercially together since 1967," his November 6, 1978, memo said. "I wonder whether change for a few on-air errors [Lou Whitaker became "Steve," "two men left on base, one man left on base, actually nobody," "trailing by three runs, 8 to 6"] will be worth the risk of a major change." His conclusion: "The pluses for Ned outweigh the minuses."

Scallan differed, ending what Shaun L. Kelly called "a radio duo, unmatched, before or since, by anybody." Seventeen years later Bob Ryan was still amazed. "You know what's sad? Sad and scary, actually. . . . The people who ruled over them and signed their paychecks had no idea how good and how special Martin and Woods were—none." This is not unusual, baseball often clueless how to even sell a poet. In 1995, Bob Wolff won Cooperstown's annual Ford C. Frick Award for broadcast excellence, Gene Kirby and I renting the same Induction Weekend bed and breakfast. For years I had scored his trying to fire Ned. Still angry, Gene found another inn on learning of my presence. The coffee tasted fine.

Woods moved to USA Network's 1979–1982 Thursday *Game of the Week*, dying February 20, 1988, at 71, of cancer. "He had to go to Heaven," said a friend, "to find a better boss than Ned or Prince." Over a quarter century, Coleman had mastered the kinetic tube's picture plus caption. Since Martin "thought TV too glitzy," Ken mused, "worse, that it frowned on his kind of beautiful word-picture," why did the late-1978 Sox give Coleman radio and Ned TV—especially, said Craig, "since his [Martin's] popularity in the past had been a source of irritation" to WSBK?

"Easy. The answer's Scallan," Tom Shaer said. "He didn't want Ned on radio. Otherwise, Ken could have possibly returned to television," where literacy was a luxury *v.* radio's job one. Privately, Martin preferred the wireless. In public, he greeted TV as gracefully as Astaire: "With Dick going to CBS, why not try it?" If the Sox had been a scorecard, they would have merited Phil Rizzuto's "WW"— wasn't watching.

As it was, many recall 1974–1978 like the British soldier who, on the eve of D-Day, called his last glimpse of England "exhilarating, glorious, and heartbreaking." He could have been portending Martin and Woods.

9 SEEING BUT NOT BELIEVING (1979–1989)

WITS's Paul Kelley had warned against a "major change" in radio. In 1979, Joe Scallan, oblivious, tried to hire the Reds' Marty Brennaman—"he just threw money at me"—who declined: 1) liking Cincinnati, 2) deeming the Sox booth not exactly stable, and 3) fearing New England might soon think the edgy Marty too big for his britches. Scallan "knew what he liked, but not what New England wanted," said Jon Miller, shortly to enter our narrative. By contrast, Coleman might ease the uproar: as a writer said, "admired, if not worshipped." In November 1978, Rico Petrocelli, still revered for 1967 but having never aired a game, was named Ken's sidekick. None of this immediately hurt the bottom line.

In 1979, a then best 136,364 jammed Fenway for a four-game series, 2,353,114 attendance broke a one-year record, and Lynn won a batting title (.333) and Gold Glove (like Evans and Burleson) and hit 39 homers (like Rice). On July 24, WSBK interrupted regular coverage for each Yaz at-bat. Ned: "Long drive, right field! Way back! Near the wall! And there it is!" into the bull pen. "Home run number 400—Carl Yastrzemski! Now listen and watch!" Signing off, Martin said, "We now return to our film, *Battle Hymn*." Ken Harrelson, classically: "Man, what a letdown." Closed circuit caught off-camera talk. "He [the first-base cameraman] did a hell of a job," Hawk told WSBK producer/director Tommy Todisco. Ned: "That was fun. Now we'll go for three thousand."

In September, after 12 straight hitless ups, Yaz pricked Jim Beattie for "a base hit! Number 3000 . . . Yastrzemski's got it!" said Martin. "And all hell breaks loose at Fenway Park!" WITS's Rico deferred to Coleman—"even if I'm behind the mike, *you* should call it"—Ken saying: "A ground ball base hit into right field! . . .

127

Just out of reach of Willie Randolph!" Yaz praised two "people who aren't here, and should be—probably my two biggest boosters, my mother and Mr. Yawkey." Clark Booth said, "So ends the Yaz Watch. Sentimentalists will keep it well," re-calling "being relentless for its own sake." The man of action deferred to thought: "There's something inside [me]," said No. 8, "that never gives up."

Even to Yastrzemski, the Sox scent of post-high tide. "You couldn't help but understand what was going on, and it hurt." Jackie Gleason coined "a little travel-ing music." El Tiante joined the Yankees: still top 10 all-time in, among things, Boston AL innings (1,774), starts (238), 10-strikeout games (9), and wins (122). Zimmer shipped Bill Lee to Montreal, Spaceman going 16-10: 1979 Hub lefty starters won a single game. Bob Stanley was 16-12: still Townies top 10 in games (637), saves (132), relief wins (85), wins (115), and losses (97). A year later Zim was axed, succeeded by Pesky, Ralph Houk, then John McNamara. Boston's most glorious team since Speaker and Smoky Joe and Rough Bill was breaking up.

Woods and Martin reunited October 3, 1980, at Montreal's Olympic Sta-dium: Phils 2, Expos 1, on USA television—"magical," stated Jack Craig, like a next-year three-game WSBK reunion, Hawk off golfing. Ned wrote and voiced that year's highlight film: "The summer of their discontent." Dick Drago "started in relief, then found relief as a starter." The Townies "charted their course through the narrows of the season." On November 12, it reached a port half 1960s celebrity wedding—"Nobody was invited," said a wag, "except the immediate country"—and half 1970s *The Waltons* TV—"Good night, Ted," "Good night, Yaz"—a "Jim-my Fund Tribute to Thomas A. Yawkey."

The gala was televised by WNAC and emceed by Gowdy—to one speaker, "the world's most famous sportscaster" but aka locally "as the guy who did the Sox." From Fenway, Hawk introduced members of the Yawkey "family." Club-house attendant Vince Orlando evoked T. A. playing pepper with "bat boys and clubhouse boys"; Frank Malzone, "getting into things with you deeper than other owners"; Jim Lonborg, giving him the game ball after 1967's final. Joe Cronin was "tickled to death that there weren't any agents then," making it "tough to sign those birds." Mel Parnell, Petrocelli, Haywood Sullivan, and Buddy LeRoux draped the dais. Teary, No. 8 saw a video ending with hit three thousand. "Oh, boy," he said, introduced, telling how Yawkey daily visited Yaz's ill mother in 1975.

The top-this was Williams, in *tie*, still electric at 62: wading through the crowd like Caesar taking Gaul, giving a plaque to Mrs. Yawkey—"just as shy," he said, "as T. A."—recalling how "dumb I was [in the 1940s] saying, 'Jesus, I want 'em to trade me the hell out of here.'" Carol Channing sang, "Hello, Teddy." Gowdy noted, "Yawkey never saying, 'You work *for* me,' but '*with* me'" and felt "the vast popularity of the Red Sox came from the integrity of their owner." At that instant the Sox as *en famille* seemed as irrefutable as the tide. By January 1981 the clan appeared dysfunctional. Sullivan traded Burleson and Sinatra in center field to Anaheim, then mailed Fisk's contract after the deadline, making Pudge a free agent.

The Red Sox were "in disarray, confused, and chaotic," said Hawk, trying to be nice. Number 27 bolted to Comiskey Park, becoming No. 72. In 1982, Harrelson joined Fisk, salary more than doubled, replaced by—whom? "Many wanted Woods back with Ned," mused Craig, Poss replying, "One [USA] game a week is fine." Instead, Townies TV tapped 1970–1979 catcher Bob Montgomery—Monty—Ken succeeding the White Sox' Harry Caray: ironically, the only Voice he could hear in 1950s Savannah over KMOX St. Louis.

"I learned from listening," Hawk said, "like every guy I've worked with. You take A from one, B another. I learned the most from Don Drysdale, arguing on and off the air." Harrelson once stopped his car, yelling, "Let's do it, man." Later he sweated what-might-have-been. "Big D would'a drilled me."

Howard Cosell—"Coach"—often called, asking Hawk to join him on ABC.

"No," said Harrelson.

"Why not?" said Cosell.

"Because you don't know what the hell you're talking about."

Cosell, laughing: "Don't tell anybody."

Hawk has aired the White Sox for all but three of the last 31 years: a five-time Illinois Sportscaster of the Year "whose Southern charm," a writer said, "could have swept Scarlett O'Hara off her feet." A harsher Hub brogue made him. "Ken was close to Yaz and Williams, studied their strokes," said analyst Steve Stone. "Thirty seconds into a conversation about Civil War in China, Hawk's quoting 'Teddy'!" His 1983 Pale Hose won the AL West. Tom Seaver won game three hundred in 1985. "Two outs! Fans come to their feet . . . The biggest media representation in Yankee Stadium in years!" said Harrelson. "So it'll be two veterans—Seaver and Don Baylor, who represents the tying run . . . High to left, playable! Reid Nichols camps underneath it! History!"

Southern Man spent a trying 1986 as Chicago general manager. In 1987–1988, he did Yanks SportsChannel, warming to the Big Apple. "I hated New York before I arrived full-time," he said. "Too big-city for a small-town boy. I'd tell [then GM] Dick O'Connell, 'Subtract my pay for the next three away Yankees games.'" In 1973, George Steinbrenner bought the club for $10 million, it and TV's YES Network worth $4.6 billion at his 2010 death. "George and I argued constantly, but he changed my view of New York's people, inner workings."

Its view of him was dicier, Hawk "rejoining White Sox superstation WGN-TV after negative reaction from viewers and executives," cited the *New York Post*. As mama might say, she hadn't raised a fool.

Fenway turned 78 in 1990. Comiskey Park, White Sox founder Charles Comiskey's 1910– Baseball Palace of the World, closed at 80 that September 30. Next year a namesake copied the original's exploding scoreboard and rose exterior, lacking its charm and open arches. New Comiskey solidified the cross-town Cubs' prepotency. The Sox had Harrelson: reading notes, citing birthdays, and wooing viewers one by one. Later, owners Eddie Einhorn and Jerry Reinsdorf began a New Comiskey facelift: green seats, an ivied scoreboard, a less vertigo-inducing upper deck. The Big Guy didn't need a lift. "Let the home team win!" boomed Hawk, discussing a 3-2 curve or *Three Faces of Eve*. The last third of a century has been as good to another early '80s Red Sox Voice. "A broadcaster has to have personality, especially on TV," Ken said. "I love listening to Jon Miller: humor, mimicry, draws word pictures, so natural."

Bob Prince, an army brat, was raised on baseball at six boyhood posts and 14 or 15 schools. Orphaned, Harry Caray saved money from selling papers to borrow a book at the library. Bob Costas played Little League near Hartford, Connecticut. "I was good field, no hit, and you know about guys who can't even hit their weight. That was true of me, and I weighed 118 pounds." Like them, Miller absorbed baseball young. In Hayward, a small town east of San Francisco, Jon played the board game Baseball Strat-O-Matic, miming the PA Voice, organist ("dum-dum-dum"), crowd (blowing, like the wind), and home team's Russ Hodges or Vin Scully from Dodger Stadium. "Friends'd say, 'Let's hit the wave.' I'd say, 'I got a big series coming up—first place for grabs.'"

To Miller, Strat-O-Matic was "like life, only more important." Today's has a computer version. Jon's game relied on prior-year statistics, every player represented with a card, involving dice and chart. The idea was simple: "If we played the entire season, everything would end like life." Since Willie Mays hit 52 homers in 1965, Jon's card said he would belt as many on Strat-O-Matic '66. "Actually, at 35, he hit 37, meaning he was still Willie Mays." (At 38, Yastrzemski hit .296, meaning he was still Yaz.) Hearing Jon through the door, a friend of his mother's asked who it was. Mom pled ignorance, adding, "It sounds like he has a little bronchial condition."

April 16, 1962: Jon, 10, sees his first big-league game, at Candlestick Park. Go figure. Los Angeles outhit San Francisco, 15-12, but lost, 19-8. Billy O'Dell threw a 15-hit complete game. Mays, Felipe Alou, and Jim Davenport homered. Attendance was 32,189. "Other than that," he laughed, "I don't recall a thing." In section 19, upper deck, Miller used binoculars to eye Mays, then Hodges, to whom he was listening by radio. What happened next was "almost like being backstage." Inhaling french fries, Russ called a curve: to Jon, multitasking. "I *see* him do it—and *hear* him chew!" Next pitch: "Fastball, outside, ball 3," Hodges said, drinking. Watching, Miller had an epiphany: "*This is the life for me!*"

By 15, Jon became basketball Voice of Hayward High School, "which is, you must admit, an honor." Next day he heard his voice—"highlights, from a reel-to-reel recorder"—fill the school intercom. At 19, the College of San Mateo sophomore became a new area TV station's sports director. "The pay was awful, hours worse, and experience spectacular." He loved every word, even offering to televise owner Charlie Finley's hockey California Golden Seals, treated locally like castor oil. "You sound like you've done this for years," a producer gawked till Miller accidentally began puck with *f.* "In baseball, you call a ball *fall* and nobody notices," Jon said, thereafter dubbing the puck *it*.

The National Hockey League acquired the Seals in early 1974. Straightaway Miller targeted Finley's A's. "Charlie owned them for 13 years and had more broadcasters than managers—and more managers than any team." Monte Moore outlasted each to announce a 3,001-game streak, 1972–1974 World Series, 1962–1977, 1987, and 1989–1992 A's, and 1980s NBC and USA *Game of the Week*. Con: Finley's designated runner, mechanical rabbit, and orange baseball. Pro: Jim Hunter's perfect game, Billy Martin's Billy Ball, and the Bash Brothers. Their common chord was Moore's Gary Cooper twang. In March 1974, Finley, spurned by Woods, had Monte hire a new No. 2. Balding, Miller, 22, looked 32. The resume read 26.

Nervous, "not wanting to screw up," Miller soon worried he wasn't exciting enough, once practicing off-air. "Ground ball, *right at the shortstop! Unbelievable!*

Oh-boy! He could have hit the ball anywhere! But right to him!" Antsy about Jon's sanity, Monte turned off the mike, saying, "What the hell are you *doing?"* Miller confessed his fear. "That's ridiculous," Moore said. "We hired you because you're the best guy for the job. You sound great. Just do it." Jon then exhaled.

Thirty years later, Miller as faux Scully recorded a phone message for American Sports Association head Lou Schwartz, calling himself "the best announcer—*in his price range."* In 1974, Miller's "young and cheap" range got him hired. That fall it didn't keep him from being canned. "Charlie had previously axed guys like Caray, Bob Elson, and Woods," said Jon. "My stock immediately went up—what company!" In 1978, he joined Texas Rangers radio. Later that year WITS's Kelley wrote, "Certainly nobody can be upset with Rico's hiring. The fans in New England love him." What wowed Scallan was age.

"Our demographic studies have shown that the age of our radio listeners is going up while the age of the ticket buyer at the park is going down," he said. "Petrocelli [35] should help," though by that criterion less than the Jackson Five. Rico began dismally—"as nervous as a school girl on her first date," wrote Joe Fitzgerald—to Gowdy, "lacking diction, couldn't paint a picture." Management defended, then fired, him after a year as Coleman's analyst, Petrocelli having worked hard, improved, and in a speech accused the Sox of "accepting losing and mediocrity" (e.g., 1979–1985).

In hindsight, Scallan was clearing the deck for Miller. Replacing Rico, Jon was soon hailed by Sox literati, in a way he could not have expected, or hoped.

"Ken's the reason I went to Boston," said Miller, then 28. "In late '79 he said Sox radio was going to make a change—and he thought we'd team well. He explained the region, its landscape, how to pronounce towns"—Gowdy in 1951. "Ken helped me navigate every step of the way." Miller had done imitations since the early 1960s: "Scully, Chuck Thompson, Caray, PA's Sherm Feller and Bob Sheppard," said Coleman, "but as watercooler material." Even in 1980, Boston aired almost each spring training exhibition, so Ken and Jon drove to Florida's western Gulf Coast, Midwest interior, or southeast Gold Coast—"travel takes forever." One day Miller began mimicking in the car: more hobby than future gig.

Next month an Opening Day rain delay hit Fenway in the seventh inning. Out of the blue, Coleman said, "Jon, in Florida you did this great Vin Scully impression. Do that!"

Miller was shocked, having never mimicked on air. "Our network had 53 stations, and I knew that everyone was listening to the *Sawx* and now waiting to hear me speak. Ultimately, I conclude this is an offer I probably can't refuse."

The rain delay lasts an hour: Miller's birth as baseball's Rich Little. Later, at his hotel, he finds a cache of telegrams. WBZ TV sends a limousine for its 6 p.m. news, the sportscaster saying, "I'm sitting on the Southeast Expressway, at 4:30 a parking lot, and I hear your bit and even though I'm not moving I almost drove off the road." Pause. "Do Scully."

"Thank you very much," said Miller, who does.

Next day Craig wrote, "Boston Welcomes New Voice[s]," a niche Jon never changed. "Here I am, goofing around," he said, "and soon I'm invited to banquets and luncheons because of Ken. He was patrician but incredibly giving, saying go beyond the statistical, be expressive, do mimicry: 'I think you have something not many people have, and you should do it on the air.'"

That August 12, Detroit's sore-armed Mark Fidrych, "The Bird," named after TV's *Sesame Street* character, started at Tiger Stadium, patting the mound and talking to the ball: "trying to come back," Miller said, "but keeping his routine. A huge crowd"—48,361—Jon and Ken cramming like an exam. Later, hearing a tape, Miller cringed. "I had a ton of facts and figures. Meanwhile, Ken drew a picture: 'Fidrych landscaping the mound.'" It was, he said, an "eye-opener. It changed my style"—pause—"really, life."

Miller did the Townies though 1982, their network adding 27 stations for a then record 80. In the 1981 split-season layoff, he and Coleman called the end of professional baseball's longest game. April 18 at 8:25 p.m.: Pawtucket's Bruce Hurst starts at home *v.* Rochester. Things adjourn two-all at 4:07 a.m. next (Easter) morning before 19 of the original 1,740 paid crowd. They resume June 23— "Dave Koza—line drive, base hit, left field, [Marty] Barrett scores, and Pawtucket wins it, 3 to 2, in *33* innings!" said Ken. Game time: *8* hours and 25 minutes! "It took 8:07 [in April]," added Miller, "not to accomplish what we did in 18 minutes tonight."

The Red Sox finished second in the season's second half, the early 1980s otherwise as dim as pitcher Dennis "Oil Can" Boyd, explaining why fog off Lake Erie postponed a game in Cleveland: "That's what you get when you build a stadium on the ocean." Banality, said Gowdy, "tests a broadcaster. You don't even get the romance of a team being bad." On Boston's May 1, 1982, first Old-Timers' Day, a romantic's outfield reunited Williams, Piersall, and Jensen, 63, 53, and 55, respectively. To Martin, "the Day was always a little more fun in Boston than elsewhere. Williams made one catch in left field that brought down the house."

Jon loved that house, especially as '80s baseball endured one new multisport lookalike after another. "Football's field is rectangular," Michael Gershman wrote, "baseball's diamond-shaped. No place can serve both." Computers and steel design let concrete cantilever, build multiple tiers, hang loge seats under a deck, and make the site column-free—thus, distant—at the Kingdome, Metrodome, and Riverfront, Three Rivers, Veterans, and Olympic Stadium, the Big O, as in zero. In relief was Boston's "grand place to see a game," *SI* said. "Most seats are on sprawling grandstand level . . . a short drive from downtown." Why only *later* did baseball think to emulate the Fens?

In 1982, Seattle's Joe Simpson played center field at Fenway. Out of nowhere a bleacher creature yelled, "Okie Joe!"—the Oklahoma-born Simpson thinking, "This guy had done his homework." Chanting "Ok-ie Joe!" the "guy" then sang the title song of Broadway's *Oklahoma!* Simpson turned and began conducting: "The guy's pals join in, and we converse." Next night, "the same fellah passes copies of the words around and the *bleachers* join in song!" A year later the now Royal returned. "This game I'm not even playing, and from the stands I hear 'Where the wind comes sweepin' down the plain.' Amazing." The musical ends, "Oklahoma! OK!"—a good word, said Joe, for Boston.

That October Baltimore announcer Bill O'Donnell died of cancer. "Broadcasters spend seven months, every day, with the same person," added colleague Thompson. "Without this dear, sweet man, I knew radio wouldn't be the same." In 1983, Chuck moved exclusively to Orioles TV, Miller applying for his and O'Donnell's post. Like Hawk, following his own drummer, Jon's riff soon beat the band.

"Part of it was money," Miller said of rafting from Boston Harbor. Other parts counted, too. Jon wanted to be a primary Voice. O's owner and Hartford-born trial lawyer Edward Bennett Williams was a closet Soxaphile, telling protégé Larry Lucchino, "If I could buy one team, it would be them." The Townies still swam in catatonia and disarray. In 1981, Mrs. Yawkey had formed the Jean R. Yawkey Trust, named John Harrington co-trustee, and tried to preserve control. "One partner [Yawkey] got the team by default, another [Sullivan] was in it for fun, and the third [LeRoux] was in it for profit," observed the TV show *Power Play*. Two years later, on "Tony Conigliaro Night," LeRoux and limited partners tried to seize the team—"Today," Buddy announced, "I was named managing general partner"—a macabre coup d'état. By then, Boston had KOd 1983's last year of WITS's pact for non-fee payment. "Place your radio upright again," said Craig. "Take down that coat hanger antenna." The rub was falling Sox leverage: some stations changing format, others not liking what they saw.

Before a trip to Europe, Mrs. Yawkey told LeRoux she wanted a fifty-thousand-watt WBZ-like flagship. Returning, she learned his pick: *Plymouth's* same-strength WPLM-AM/FM. (Hub outlet WRKO became de facto head.) Not trusting LeRoux, Miller left—an artist if not yet institution fleeing Dodge. In Baltimore, he became "The Franchise, with great broadcast instincts and sensibilities," said *The National*. Would that have happened in the Fens? We don't know—only that radio/TV is regional. Certain areas prefer Voices larger than a franchise. To some, the Pirates' Prince was a maniac. More hailed how he was maniacally a gas. The Cubs were glad God broke the mold *before* He made Caray. Allen not as much aired as became the Yanks. Twice Scully was voted all-time Most Memorable Dodger. Other teams feel unease. The Red Sox are that kind.

In 1916, New Hampshire's Robert Frost wrote his four-stanza, twenty-line poem "The Road Not Taken": "Two roads diverged in the yellow wood," one "less traveled by." Boston's road less traveled is broadcasters who transcend. One was Hoey: Coleman's "The Man Who Does the Games." Another, Gowdy, brandished longevity and wearability. Woods was less loony toons with Martin than Prince—still a larger-than-life Sox exception to the rule. Caray said, "You have to know when the game can speak for itself, and you have to speak for the game." Contrast the Cowboy, as *Dragnet*'s Sergeant Friday: "'Just the facts, ma'am.' It's what the Red Sox fan expects."

Remaining, would Jon have ruled radio? Coleman, rejoined TV? Hawk, eclipsed the wireless? Craig remembers Harrelson "talking a wonderful game while he was here, inside phrases tumbling out of that sweet, Southern drawl." Shaer recalls "his commercials for the Yellow Pages and Colonial Provisions, among others—hugely popular." Hawk left when Chicago laid gifts at his feet to start a new pay cable channel. Later, he and Jon thrived nationally—"maybe too Falstaffian for New England," said Curt. On Opening Day 1983 Miller hosted a rally at the Inner Harbor, fifty thousand cheering O-R-I-O-L-E-S. In Boston, "even if the Sox lost the Series, everybody'd say, 'They just break my heart,'" he said, hymning a Hub accent. "Sox fans are demanding, Baltimore's more forgiving."

Miller inherited a seven-state O's network. His rookie year enlarged it, the LCS *v.* Hawk's Hose pivoting in Game Three. "There's a high fly ball to deep right-center field! And, baby, way back! It's long gone!" said Jon. "Three-nothing, Orioles! And Eddie Murray's first hit is a monster shot at Comiskey Park!" Baltimore's first post-1970 title completed a monster year. "The [World Series] cheering you hear is from Orioles fans," Miller said in Philadelphia. "Everybody else is in muted silence. The pitch! Line drive! Ripken catches it at shortstop! And the Orioles are champions of the world!"

Strat-O-Matic. Mimicry. A rookie title. Everything came early for Mrs. Miller's son. To him, TV baseball was film: "You see what the producer shows you." Radio was a novel, to be absorbed. "Before ESPN, you never knew anything until the radio announcer said it," said Bob Costas. "This romantic figure sat in a booth, very personal, mostly gone except for Jon as the Harry Kalases and Harwells and Jack Bucks die." The dinosaur tethered the banquet circuit, NBC's backup *Game*, and ESPN *Sunday Night Baseball*. In 1990, he began a 21-year suzerainty as baseball's prime-time network Voice.

Each March, wife Janine said, "Have a good day, honey. Listen, any time you're in town, stop by."

He nodded. "I'm Jon Miller, your husband. See you in October."

In 1983, New England was introduced to a Voice whose first year would have tested him had the Red Sox been Murderers' Row.

After Colgate, Joe Castiglione was a part-time salesman—"I hated it"—before getting an MA at Syracuse. To pay tuition, he moonlit at NBC TV's WSYR—"at student wages, naturally"—as voiceover, *Hollywood Matinee* fill-in, and *The Today Show* cut-in: "best of all, something to put on the resume." It swelled in 1970, Joe's "one-man band" in Youngstown, Ohio, playing football, hoops, sports at 6 and 11 p.m., and "six radio shows a day. And for very little money." Perry Como was crooning's "Mr. C." Baseball's future Mr. C. spent the next decade in Cleveland news and sports, covered the 1975 sinking of the SS *Edmund Fitzgerald*, and aired another wreck, the 1979 Indians. In 1981, Castig, miming Russ Hodges, called the Milwaukee Brewers' first division clinching. "The Brewers win the second half! The Brewers win the second half!" Cheeseheads still chant it among bowling, brats, and beer.

Next year Joe returned to Cleveland's struggling the Sports Exchange, TV's first regional network, headed by Ted Stepien: to talk host Pete Franklin, "T. S." for "Too Stupid." By January 1983, all staff but Castiglione had been canned. One day, announcer Casey Coleman, Ken's son, sent Joe's tape to WPLM, looking to replace Miller. Brewers broadcast guru Bill Haig gave a thumbs-up: "especially good on word-pictures." What wasn't good was timing. Castiglione was scheduled to meet Monday with Stepien—"my assignment, to bring donuts." Instead, he flew to Boston four days earlier to interview, meet WPLM head Jack Campbell, and visit Coleman Friday night.

Next morning Campbell cautioned, "You've got the job, but don't tell anybody. We'll announce you Monday." In Ohio, neither donuts nor Mr. C. arrived, Stepien refusing later to speak to him on the phone. The ex-college DJ—"Give me the Rolling Stones, the Kinks, the Animals, and my favorite, Motown Sounds"— soon found Coleman caught between Bing Crosby and Patti Page. "Sort of like the Red Sox fan, Ken liked things as they were," said Joe. On the field, sixth-place things were dismal. "People ask, 'How do you sound excited going to work when your team is down twenty games?' They don't understand that no two games are the same. It's like a lousy long-playing record. You look for a good song to play."

Rice had a league-high 39 homers and 126 RBI, dinging three times six years to the day after homering thrice at Fenway. Another "song" was Boston's purest post-Kid hitter. Wade Boggs was superstitious, "eating chicken at all his meals," said Marty Barrett, "and running sprints at the same time each night." He was experimental, as girlfriend Margo Adams showed, and a Merlin, seven times with two hundred or more hits, leading the 1983–1989 Sox in batting and taking the 1983 and 1985–1988 AL title (.361, .368, .357, .363, and .366, respectively), his team often numbing. In 1983, Cleveland scored twice in the eighth to lead, 3-2, Ken saying, "Here comes the tying run and the winning run, and the Indians win!" Coleman then saw Bob Stanley pumping. "It was then that I realized baseball is a nine-, not eight-, inning game."

Two years earlier, Steinbrenner and Ted Turner offered to pay Yaz "three times what I could make here. But I didn't want to leave. I liked it here. I liked . . . what the Red Sox are." Number 8 ranks second lifetime in big-league games (3,308), third in total at-bats (11,988) and walks (1,845), eighth in total bases (5,539), and thirteenth in RBI (1,844). He even inspired "Yastrzemski Song," by Hub radio/ TV's Jess Cain, to the melody of "The Hallelujah Chorus," lyrics tying "The state of Maine is going quite insane," "In Vermont, it's only Yaz they want," and "He's [still] the idol of Boston, Mass." The idol retired October 2, 1983, running around the field, handshaking everywhere, then playing left field for the first time since cracking his ribs in 1980: "the love-in complete," said Ned. To Gammons, it "passionately explain[ed] that he understood what makes the Olde Towne Team what it is."

In the seventh inning, Cleveland's Toby Harrah lined off the Monster. Yastrzemski retrieved the ball, whirled, and held him to a single. "This great superstar from the heart made some noise," Martin continued. In the Sox half, Yaz batted. "The crowd is on its feet, everyone aware that very possibly this will be the last time he will ever step into that batting box," mused Coleman. He looked at the first-base side, behind the plate, "and now toward the folks along third and into the left-field area where he patrolled for so many years." The din was insupportable. "Waving to them all, and they're all on their feet. Clearly one of the great moments in the history of this great little ballpark."

Yaz exhaled, "stands in the dirt . . . again [took off] the batting helmet and again the response." Umpire Rich Garcia had told Tribe pitchers, "Fellows, if he doesn't swing it's a ball." Aiming, Dan Spillner went to 3-0. "You think he's got the light?" Coleman said. "You better believe it!" Trying "to jerk it out," Yaz confessed, he popped up, went to left, was replaced by Chico Walker—on TV, Martin referenced "his own little acreage"—and "walked over to a little boy and tossed him his cap," said Ken. Afterward, hundreds on Van Ness Street chanted "Yaz, Yaz, Yaz"— No. 8 a day earlier having addressed Fenway's crowd: insurance v. Sunday rain.

"I saw the sign that read, 'Say It Ain't So, Yaz,' and I wish it wasn't," he had said, thanking the Nation, Yawkeys, and third-year manager Ralph Houk: "I wish we could have been together for [all] 23 years, 'cause I know we'd have won more pennants." Kiley played "Auld Lang Syne." Many would read his plaque at Cooperstown: "YAZ. Boston, AL 1961–83. Succeeded Ted Williams in Fenway's left field in 1961 and retired . . . as all-time Red Sox leader in 8 categories. Played with graceful intensity in record 3,308 AL games. Only AL player with 3,000 hits and 400 homers. Three-time batting champion, won MVP and Triple Crown in 1967 as he led Red Sox to 'Impossible Dream' pennant."

For most of 1983, none of this reassured Castiglione—"part of Jack Campbell's cost-cutting program," he joked—living the entire season at Boston's Susse Chalet, family in Cleveland because it couldn't sell the house. "Twenty-six dollars a night. But the worst part was packing my trunk and taking it to the basement each time we went on a road trip so I wouldn't be charged for the room while I was away." Meanwhile, Hub print treated him, as Ring Lardner said, like a side dish it declined to order. Where was Jon Miller? Why wasn't Martin on the wireless? The *Herald*'s Jim Baker had Joe fired. "I got ripped a lot that first year," he said, "and it hurt."

By 2000, Bob Ryan wrote, "It's time someone finally said it: Joe Castiglione is the official 'Voice of the Boston Red Sox.'" Typically, he demurred. "It's different today, with the proliferation of media. There's [cable], there's over-the-air TV, and there's radio—not like the good old days. To call one person that would be misleading." Ryan, in turn, cried tommyrot: "The No. 1 radio man will always be the essential link between a . . . team and its fans." In New England, "that voice belongs to Joe Castiglione." Ryan conceded Joe's "voice ripe for parody— comparatively thin and reedy and nasally." Offsetting it were traits undervalued in 1983, including decency, wearability, credibility, precision—Jack Craig said that if a ground ball took three hops, Castiglione would say three, not two or four—and encyclopedic baseball knowledge.

"I've always been blessed with good recall," he told Ryan. "But I do have a system. I start a file card on every player the first time around. I still do them all in longhand because it helps the recall process." In his freshman year, Joe recalled how, growing up, he watched the Mantle-Maris Yankees on New York Channel 11, their manager the Major, decorated in the Battle of the Bulge.

Ralph Houk's stripes made the 1961–1963 World Series. "You just assumed that the Yankees'd make it every year," said Joe. In late 1983, the now Sox skipper asked how he was. "I don't know, Ralph," said Mr. C. "I'm not sure I'm coming back."

Castiglione's boyhood manager put an arm around the rookie. "Everybody's happy," Houk said. "You're doing a hell of a job." At that moment, Joe rued being too young to have served the Major at Bastogne.

In 1984, "a good song," in Joe's phrase, was Tony Armas's Americans-best 43 homers and 123 RBI. At the Fens, Channel 38 showed an Opening Day sign: "Hey, Where's the Yaz?" Acquired for Eck, first baseman Bill Buckner hit 46 doubles in 1985, John McNamara, a baseball lifer who succeeded the retired Houk, becoming Sox manager after stops in Oakland, San Diego, Cincinnati, and Anaheim.

Next March *Sport* magazine wrote, "The Red Sox are the most boring team in baseball." Gammons had termed Yaz's farewell "a two-day Easter celebration." On Good Friday 1986, the parish team traded Mike "The Hit Man" Easler for 1979 AL MVP Don Baylor—the first Sox-Yankees trade since Lyle. "When he came into the clubhouse," said Castiglione, "you knew who the team leader was going to be."

On April 7, Evans banged the year's first pitch for a homer at Detroit. Told no one had done it before, he jousted, "Big deal. We lost." That April 29, a Tom Seaver pitch-alike, college All-American, and Boston's best mound prospect since World War II faced Seattle at Fenway on "a chilly, misty night," noted Joe. "The kind of game that brings out only the diehards—and the announcers." In 1984, Roger Clemens went 9-4; 1985, had shoulder surgery; 1986, neared Joe Woods's 1912. "This night the basketball Celtics played a playoff set at Boston Garden—a big game," said Martin. "So our TV audience was limited, and so was the crowd"—13,414.

Before the game, catcher-turned-analyst Montgomery said, "This Seattle club has been striking out a lot. The way Clemens is throwing, we may see a few Ks." Castig also had a premonition. "I knew Roger was on his game that night, because batters usually hit a lot of foul balls off him." Tonight the Mariners swung and missed. "Something's going to happen," Joe said. What did: "the most memorable game of the most memorable season of my life." (He said this *before* 2004.) Clemens had 12 strikeouts by the fifth inning. Word wafted to the Garden, which began emptying: the Rocket was on a roll. Steve Carlton, Nolan Ryan, and Seaver held the bigs' nine-inning 19 mark. "Whenever Clemens pitched," said Ned, "this guy in right field posted a *K* for every strikeout," arriving in the fourth from the Garden to record each Special K.

The Rocket struck out each batter in the seventh and eighth inning. In the ninth, the first two Mariners whiffed. Coleman then gushed "Strike three!" of Phil Bradley. "Roger Clemens has broken the major league record for strikeouts in one game! He has struck out 20 Mariners!"—incredibly, walking none. Martin spoke as if still on radio: "And here they come up at Fenway! A new record! Clemens has set a major-league record for strikeouts in a game! Twenty! What a performance by the kid from the University of Texas!"—eight straight Ks tying the AL record. "One after another," Joe gulped, "and I felt a thrill like I've never known in baseball." Clemens added, "The strikeouts just came on coming." He finished 24-4, had a league-low 2.48 ERA, and won the 1986 Cy Young and MVP.

On May 15, the Sox took first place for good. Rocket began 14-0, not losing till July. "We weren't a powerful club, not a lot of homers, but fate seemed to like us," said Joe, ironically, given that October. One ninth inning Boston trailed Texas, 1-0, as Barrett and Steve Lyons each slid into second base—"me from one direction," Lyons said, "Marty the other." Outfielder George Wright's throw took a wrong turn into the Rangers dugout. Both scored: Sox win. Another day, down, 7-6, in the twelfth, Baylor popped between home plate and third base to Rick Burleson, "of all people," laughed Castiglione, "playing for the Angels at the end of his career." His dropped pop and a balk scored the tying, then 8-7 winning, run.

The Sox slumped in July, one journal asking, "Poised for another El Foldo?" Instead, the damndest, not damnation, happened: Boston won 11 straight, traded for outfielder Dave Henderson and shortstop Spike Owen, and rebuilt its lead. A Hub TV *Chronicle* special said that "Pennant Fever Grips Hub": Clemens was baseball's "version of the Terminator"; "Sox fans," knowing better, "have put their skepticism on hold." Contributor Mike Barnicle called Fenway "a place where time is frozen," first seeing it in 1950, with dad, and having been in a left-field seat for the Final Swing; Section 16, Lonborg's ride; and press box, Carbo's homer. Baylor clubbed 31 homers. Buckner had 102 RBI—more irony: "fans," Owen said, "loving how he gutted it out"—ankles hurt, taped, and gouged again.

Clemens started the All-Star Game. "Oil Can" Boyd and Bruce Hurst finished 16-10 and 13-8, respectively. Boston drew four of the decade's top 10 three-game series—2,147,641 for the year. "My house, my house, though thou art small," George Herbert might have said of Fenway, "though art to me the Escurial." It was on September 28, Boston taking its first title since 1975. "A high pop-up! This may do it! Buckner is there! It's all over! [Sox 12, Blue Jays 3]!" said Martin. "The Red Sox are the new divisional champions." The still station-to-station Townies hugged the man with the gimpy gait and high-topped shoes.

For a decade, Tribe Voices Jimmy Dudley and Bob Neal didn't speak on or off the air. At Wrigley Field, Caray once kept a TV colleague from the mike by locking him out. "It's a long season in a short booth," Gowdy told Martin. By contrast, Ned, Castiglione, and Coleman largely avoided spite or strife. The night of

Rocket's launch, the Sox had just released their yearbook, listing players' favorite musicians. Reading, Joe marveled at Ken thinking that music ended in 1953.

"This is interesting. Roger's favorite singer is Steve Nicks," said Coleman.

"Ken, I believe that's Stevie Nicks," said Joe.

"Well, I know him well. I call him Steve."

"Uh, Ken, Stevie is a girl."

Next day Clemens sent to the booth a wall-sized Nicks poster. Till his death "Ken could break me up," said Joe, "by saying, 'Stevie is a girl.'"

In 1967, Dick Williams introduced Coleman and Martin to California's Crescent—aka Hard Bellies—Beach, surf up, seals sunning. Later the Voices acquainted Joe, going daily when the Sox visited Anaheim: Ken snorkeling, Castiglione swimming, and Ned diving and taking pictures. A clubhouse manager said, "There they go—two 60-year-olds and a 40-year-old playing in the sand."

On a flight, Ken read a biography, planned a Jimmy Fund event, or heard pre–Bill Haley & His Comets. Ned put his Walkman on, used a headset plug, and channeled the chairman of the board. "He loved Sinatra," said Joe. "Ken did, too, so he'd use the other plug—each listening to Ol' Blue Eyes and breaking into song." It was, he laughed, "not broadcast quality."

"My Way" might describe Ned's would-be memoir. "Summer Wind" took a lofter toward the Wall. If "Luck Be a Lady," "Bewitched" was the Sox' card. "It Was a Very Good Year" could mean 1912; "Fly Me to the Moon," 1978. "Nothing But the Best" meant The Kid, coiling. "Drinking Again" recalled the Townies' once front office. Liking "The Best Is Yet to Come," Martin couldn't know 1986's worst lay just ahead. "That's Life" was a favorite, the Sox having been a puppet, a pauper, a pirate, a poet, a pawn, but not since 1918, king.

That fall, several friends in the Secret Service arranged lunch at the White House for a Red Sox party. "Their instructions were very specific. We're told no photos, above all, recordings," Joe smiled. "Someone forgot to tell Ken." Vice president George H. W. Bush entered the Roosevelt Room to recount his good-field, no-hit time at Yale. President Reagan then entered "at his theatrical best," evoking the 1930s Cubs, re-creation, and film, especially 1952's The Winning Team.

Reagan had played the great epileptic and alcoholic pitcher Grover Cleveland Alexander; Doris Day, his wife; Frank Lovejoy, Rogers Hornsby. "Knowing the script by heart," said Castiglione, Coleman "had a recorder, determined to tape the Gipper." At lunch questions start, and "Ken's is a doozie. Like most Red Sox fans, he liked a time-warp fine."

In *The Winning Team*, Coleman noted, "[St. Louis's] Alex in relief strikes out the Yankees' Tony Lazzeri to save Game Seven" of the 1926 Series.

"Right," says the president.

"How did Doris Day take a cab all the way from mid-Manhattan to Yankee Stadium"—even then, a lengthy ride—"while Alex trudges from the pen?"

"Well, uh," Reagan says. Next question. Lunch soon adjourns.

"It was amazing," said Joe. "The Secret Service must have seen the recorder but didn't say anything." That night the taped president guested on Ken's pre-game show. "With security, it could never happen today." What did makes you wonder, even now.

The 1986 Red Sox, Angels, Mets, and Astros easily won their division, then began a month as the game had rarely been played before—"at its summit," *Newsweek*'s Pete Axthelm wrote later. "Millions are still savoring their rendezvous with baseball at its pinnacle. It leaves you breathless." The now-best-of-seven LCS began at Fenway, Clemens losing, 8-1. A day later Rice homered and Angels pitcher Kirk McCaskill lost a grounder in the sun: Sox, 9-2. Game Three: California took a 2-1 playoff lead. Four: Clemens led, 3-0—till Doug DeCinces homered and two batters singled to start the ninth inning. Reliever Calvin Schiraldi got Gary Pettis on a fly till Rice lost it in the lights, Dick Schofield scoring. Schiraldi went 1-2 to Brian Downing. Future reference: One strike would win the game. Instead, the next pitch hit the batter, tying the score: Halos win, 4-3, in eleven. Enthused ABC's Al Michaels: "This series is getting interesting."

Next day Boston led, 2-1—until Bobby Grich drove to center. Dave Henderson egressed, leapt, and, said Michaels, "knocks the ball over the wall for a two-run homer!" In the ninth, despite Baylor's two-run dinger, one out would win Game Five, 5-4—and first Angels pennant. Manager Gene Mauch inserted reliever Gary Lucas, his last hit batter 1982. Lucas plunked Rich Gedman, yielding to Donnie Moore, who worked Henderson to a 2-2 count—Boston one strike from elimination. At "2:47 Pacific Coast time," said Coleman, Moore threw a forkball. "There's a fly ball to left field! Downing is going back . . . back . . . back! It's gone! It is gone! Dave Henderson has homered! And the Boston Red Sox have taken the lead! Boston has come up with"—Ken's exact language from 1967's last-day sixth-inning fivespot—"four runs and has a 6 to 5 lead in the ninth!" Michaels: "Anaheim Stadium was one strike away from turning into Fantasyland!"

In *their* ninth, the future Los Angeles Angels of Anaheim tied the score. After DeCinces and Grich failed with the bases full, Boston, reprieved, scored an eleventh-inning run. In the bottom half, "Schiraldi throws, and it's popped up down the first-base side!" said Coleman. "[Dave] Stapleton in—he's got it! And the Red Sox have won it! One of the most incredible victories in the history of the Boston Red Sox, 7 to 6!" Then: "Joseph [Castiglione], two days ago I became a grandfather. This was her gift—truly an incredible baseball game." Back in Boston, the Townies took Game Six, 10-4, over and out behind Boyd. Next evening Clemens led, 4-0, when Rice skied to left. "There it goes! It's looong gone!" said CBS's Harwell. Boston won, 8-1: its first triumph in a winner-take-all game with a division title, pennant, or World Series at stake since 1912, and first seventh-game postseason victory since 1903.

The Sox were a 2½ to 1 underdog *v*. the 108-54 regular-season Mets, but won the first two Shuttle Series games, 1-0 and 9-3. Boston flew home "sitting pretty," said Joe. Tip O'Neill threw out Game Three's first ball, having said all politics is local. Dinging Boyd's third pitch, Len Dykstra showed some hits are crucial: Mets, 7-1. A day later New York evened a heretofore more Dull than Grand Event, 6-2. The Kid first-pitched before Game Five: to Henry Berry, "still the overwhelmingly dominant player of Red Sox history." Hurst then took his second victory, 4-2. Ahead: a game proving the aphorism, "If you want to make God laugh, tell Him your plans."

At Shea Stadium, behind, 2-0, in Saturday's Game Six, the Mets tied on a single and run-scoring double play. Barrett scored on a ground out force attempt: 3-2. As omen, Rice was thrown out trying to score on a single, a blister on Clemens's pitching hand forced Schiraldi to relieve, and Buckner stranded eight runners. Gary Carter's eighth-inning sacrifice fly retied the score: "Everything to decide," said Ken, "and nothing decided." In the top half of the tenth, Henderson hit a drive at 11:59 that struck *Newsday's* billboard, reaching the dugout as the clock struck midnight. Boston scored again: 5-3 insurance, having paid a 68-year premium. Due to air the bottom half, Joe deferred to the senior partner, "since Ken had been there so long."

With two Mets out, the scoreboard read, "Congratulations Boston Red Sox." In the runway, Castiglione watched the Series trophy and 20 cases of Great Western champagne enter the visiting clubhouse. *Again* one out would win—the Classic. All year Stapleton had replaced Buckner with Boston ahead. Inexplicably, McNamara now kept Billy Bucks at first. After Carter and Kevin Mitchell singled, Ray Knight went to 0-2. A *strike* would end the famine. Knight singled, Carter scored, and Mitchell took third: 5-4. "They're going to do it," a friend told Peter Gammons. "Just when we thought that we had been freed at last, they're going to create a way to again break our hearts that goes beyond our wildest imagination."

Sans wild pitch all year, Stanley, relieving Schiraldi, threw six pitches to Mookie Wilson. "He throws the [seventh] pitch inside, it gets away from [catcher] Gedman!" Coleman said: the inning's thirteenth pitch that could have won the Series. "And the tying run is home! The tying run scores! And down to second base goes Knight—55,078 fans go wild, as the Mets, with two outs and the bases empty, in the last of the tenth, have tied it up!" Wilson fouled off two more pitches. "Knight at second. Three and two," Ken resumed. "The pitch, ground ball to first base! Buckner—*it goes by him*! And here comes the winning run! The Mets have won it, 6 to 5, on a ground ball to Buckner that went through him!" Coleman refused to hear his broadcast until 1988.

Waiting, a clubhouse security agent had turned on his radio. Finding the score tied, Joe heard a roar as he ran toward the booth. "I never saw the play, but my heart sank. I knew it was over." In one moment, Gammons wrote, "41 years of Red Sox baseball flashed in front of my eyes." O'Neill "didn't sleep for three months. I'd wake up every night seeing that ball go through Buckner's legs." The wild pitch completed Stanley's fall from late-'70s comer to hard-luck oaf. One driver rammed his car. Billy Bucks was threatened, Boston's Zakim Bunker Hill Bridge aka Buckner Bridge because cars passed through its Y-shaped "legs." At his Wellesley home, Martin rued baseball's local-TV Series ban. Buckner was released next year: "Things were good for me up here until after the sixth game. After that, it just went down." Finally, he moved to Idaho.

Game Seven was postponed Sunday, the Nation sensing what lay ahead. Monday night the Sox again led, 3-0. In the sixth inning, Keith Hernandez batted with the bases loaded. Joe told himself, "If Hurst retires Hernandez, the Red Sox win. If Keith gets a hit, the Mets will win." He singled, plating two. As New York tied the score, reliever Sid Fernandez gleamed, and Knight hit in the seventh, the Sox faced a fourth straight seven-game Series loss. "The pitch!" said CBS Radio's

Jack Buck. "Swing and a fly ball, left-center field, well-hit! May not be caught! It's gone! It's gone! Over the fence in left-center! A home run by Ray Knight to give the Mets their first lead of the evening, 4-3!" Final: 8-5.

We had been this way before.

For the first time, the World Series final opposed ABC's *Monday Night Football*, routing it in audience share (55 to 14 percent) and Nielsen ratings (*38.9* to 8.8). In Los Angeles, New York, and Boston, the Series swaggered, 4-, 7-, and 19-to-1, respectively: "fourth-highest rating of all time for a World Series game," said NBC sports research's Greg Seamans, "and most-watched World Series game of all time, with 34 million households." The Classic averaged a 28.6 rating—about 25 million households per minute. The *Washington Post*'s Shirley Povich hailed "baseball as Americans know and love it—a throbbing, good-God-what's-next World Series that had Americans' hearts pumping in every time zone."

Future CBS Radio correspondent Peter King recalled NBC's Vin Scully's "*a little roller up along first . . . behind the bag . . . It gets through Buckner! Here comes Knight and the Mets win it!*" then hushing, letting pictures rule: "Exhilarated fans and Met players, dejected Red Sox, game-ending play replays, a sign 'Now Boston Chokes'—NBC. Get it?" Before trying to sleep, King replayed the inning on his VCR "to ensure it wasn't a dream." Later, meeting Scully at Dodgertown, Peter persuaded him to record a new version of his call for a friend, ending "and Buckner catches the ball and the Red Sox go on to win!" Others recalled the Series differently, like a car crash or a storm.

On CBS Radio's "Home Town Inning," Castiglione called Henderson the fastest Sox runner. Analyst Sparky Anderson was amazed: "If you think he's fast, that shows how slow your team is." Michael Dukakis had just finished a gubernatorial debate with GOP opponent George Kariotis at Faneuil Hall: "We had about 40,000 watching on TV, and 2 million watching the Sox." He remembers receiving a note, telling the audience the Townies were ahead, and getting home in time to see "the ball go through Buckner's legs. Poor guy, practically crippled, I'll never understand why McNamara left him in." In 2001, George Mitchell, hoping life "lasts long enough to see the Red Sox win a World Series," said that 1986 still made him ask if he were dreaming, "kidding himself once more?"

In California, Joel Fox had champagne on ice, hoping to modestly hail the Red Sox "first world title in nearly 70 years" before a KABC Radio midnight debate. The game ended about 10 o'clock Pacific Time, Fox gathering notes and leaving home "with a vacant gaze saying nothing to my family," including puzzled in-laws from Indiana. He got in a car, drove away, but didn't know to where. "I didn't turn on the radio. I was in a daze. I didn't even swear," just drove the coast road, finally heading for Los Angeles. "I get to the station just in time for the show," his wife forcing herself to stay up and listen, worried that "I had driven into the ocean in despair."

Nearby, a Bostonian named by the *Wall Street Journal* "America's greatest thinker on crime, punishment, and historical order" had been at a meeting "at the worst possible time," he said. Adjourning, James Q. Wilson raced to his L.A. hotel. "No longer would Red Sox fans have to bear the crushing hex put on them by the sale of Babe Ruth to the Yankees, a sale that seemed to end forever any chance of the Sox owning the baseball world." In his room, the Harvard professor watched "the most famous, agonizing, gut-wrenching [tenth] inning of baseball that I ever watched." One more out and "the Sox would own the world. I would be ecstatic, emotionally young forever."

After the tying run, "all was [still] not lost. If Mookie was put away, the Sox could score again in the eleventh. *One more strike* and Red Sox fans could breathe." *Their* Wilson picked up the telephone, dialed the area code of his home and first six digits of his number, and readied to press the last digit on Mookie's out: "My wife and I could celebrate at least staying alive." Instead, he put the phone back in its cradle. "My youth was over. I was now, at least for baseball, an old man. [Wilson died in 2012 of leukemia, at 80.] The Curse lived on."

Back east, a friend asked if he knew that Buckner, so depressed at missing the ground ball, had leapt before an onrushing bus.

"Oh, no," Wilson said.

"Not to worry," the friend replied. "It went between his legs."

Half a million graced a Sox post-Buckner parade through Boston. "For me it took away some sting," said Castiglione. "Not for McNamara." Entering skip's office to say good-bye, Joe found Mac disconsolate. "Why me, why me?" he said. "I go to church, have my whole life. I don't understand why this had to happen."

Neither did Wilson, after Harvard, UCLA, and Pepperdine teaching at Boston College near children and grandchildren. Said The Wiser but Sadder Man, "They have a legal obligation to be within 30 minutes of Fenway Park."

American dramatist and humorist George Ade said, "The time to enjoy a European tour is about three weeks after you unpack." It took a long time to unpack 1986's baggage. In early 1987, Joel Krakow of the Newton, Massachusetts, Captain Video Store put the Series highlight film in the horror/science fiction section. That October, McNamara sat in the dugout before the last regular-season game: "You know, I sit here thinking and I *still* can't believe we lost the sixth game of the World Series. There's a part of me that just doesn't believe it: one f---ing out. That's all we needed was one f---ing out."

Again the Townies folded after a prior-year pennant. Clemens left training camp when his salary was renewed at $400,000—half of Stanley's. Unvexed, general manager Lou Gorman said, "The sun will rise, the sun will set, and I'll have lunch." At one time or another, Gorman said, "That burns gas like it's eating peanuts," "I'll keep my ears posted," and "I vaguely and vividly remember in my own mind." A pitcher "looked like he threw real good listening on the radio." "We are face to face with the face" of a prospect. "The toe nail on the top toe is growing into the nail." Perhaps Lou was growing into Yogi Berra, whom Gorman could have used.

In 1987, Gedman hit .205, McNamara sticking left-fielder Mike Greenwell behind the plate. Evans had a career-high 34 homers, 123 RBI, and .305 average. Youth should be served and was, Greenwell's first hit a dinger. Sam Horn became Boston's first freshman to homer in his first two games. Ellis Burks seemed a righty Lynn, vacuuming center and tattooing the Wall. "There's a fly ball to left field! Deep! It is going—it is gone!" said Castig. "Ellis Burks, high in the light standard above the Screen!" Nothing helped: the Sox finished 20 games behind.

That June Coleman asked, "If you were paying your way today, who would you pay to see?"

Teddy Ballgame didn't hesitate. "Reggie!" he boomed.

The Sox announcer informed the object of Williams's praise. "'The man said that about me?' Jackson beamed—beside himself, like a kid at Christmas." Later Reggie did a Jimmy Fund public service announcement, also giving "a considerable amount," Ken said. "'I know what the Jimmy Fund is about,' he said, 'and I want to put money where my mouth is.'"

In July, Jackson, retiring, batted a last time at Fenway. Sherm Feller, 69, had been Sox PA announcer since 1967, mixing soulful understatement and exacting prose. Each game began, "Ladies and gentlemen, boys and girls, welcome to Fen-

Present at the Creation: In 1903, Huntington Avenue Grounds helped host the first World Series. The Red Sox' initial home had an in-play tool shed, pop gun rightfield, and 11,500 capacity. (National Baseball Hall of Fame Library)

Fenway Park construction, 1911. Build it, and they came. The Grounds' $650,000 successor opened in April 1912. "It's in the Fenway section, isn't it?" said Red Sox owner John I. Taylor. "Then name it Fenway Park." (National Baseball Hall of Fame Library)

You can look it up: The Sox were an early dynasty. Boston won the 1903, 1912, 1915–1916, and 1918 World Series. On Opening Day 1924, an American, not title, flag was hoisted after 1923's last-place finish. (National Baseball Hall of Fame Library)

Fred Hoey aired the 1927–1938 Red Sox and Braves: New England radio's baseball original. Raised in nearby North Quincy, Ken Coleman felt him "The Man Who Does the Games." (Courtesy of the Boston Public Library, Print Department)

1940–1950 Voice Jim Britt. A then-teenager said, "Britt made baseball sound better than red-haired girls with freckles." [Right] Radio's *Roget's* 1950 Sox exit aborted his career. (Courtesy of the Boston Public Library, Print Department) [Top] A sponsor's dream. (Courtesy of the Collection of Richard A. Johnson)

Ted Williams was baseball's Roy Hobbs—the greatest hitter who ever lived. *Look* magazine was among many to profile The Kid's swing: to Donald Hall, "coiling on itself like a barber pole turning around." (National Baseball Hall of Fame Library)

A .344 average, six batting titles, and Red Sox–high 521 home runs made Ted Cooperstown Class of '66. Jim Britt called him "the hub around which the Hub revolves." (National Baseball Hall of Fame Library)

In 1946, the big-bopping Red Sox won their first flag in 28 years. Helping: future announcer Johnny Pesky, Williams, and Bobby Doerr (second to fourth from L) and Dom DiMaggio (fourth from R, on skipper Joe Cronin's L).
(National Baseball Hall of Fame Library)

Curt Gowdy, "that ever-so-soothing and sensible voice, with its guileless hint of Wyoming twang," said John Updike, was the Townies' 1951–1965 Cowboy at the Mike. Curt, R, and '50s aide Bob Murphy each made the Hall of Fame.
(National Baseball Hall of Fame Library)

[Left] A 1960 "Red Sox on the Air" WHDH guide featured Curt and aides Art Gleeson and Bill Crowley. "Hi ya, neighbor!" Gowdy caroled for sponsor Narragansett Beer: never more neighborly than on Williams's homer "in his last time at bat in a Red Sox uniform!" (National Baseball Hall of Fame Library)

[Bottom] Boston entered 2012 with a big-league record 712-game home sellout streak. It was not always so. A sparse mid-century crowd enjoys a day in the Fens. One year the Red Sox drew fewer people than in 1909. (National Baseball Hall of Fame Library)

[Top] To pique interest, Gowdy, analyst Mel Parnell, and ball-and-striker Ned Martin, R to L, this day broadcast from the bleachers. It didn't help. In 1965, Dave Morehead no-hit Cleveland at Fenway before 1,247. (National Baseball Hall of Fame Library)

[Left] Succeeding Gowdy in 1966, Ken Coleman never split an infinitive, dangled a participle, or misplaced a preposition. "He had a beautiful horn," said Boston Bruins Voice Bob Wilson, "and, oh, Ken played it well." (National Baseball Hall of Fame Library)

Someday someone may have a better year than Carl Yastrzemski's 1967, but it is hard to see how. The AL MVP won the Triple Crown, helping Boston script a last-day Impossible Dream—first Sox flag since 1946. (Courtesy of the Boston Red Sox)

"This is, if I may add a personal note, the greatest thrill of my life," Coleman said after Jim Lonborg's 1967 final-day 5-3 victory. The Gentleman then one-hit St. Louis in World Series Game Two. Infielder Jerry Adair, R. (National Baseball Hall of Fame Library)

Before 1967, Fenway Park increasingly seemed passé, many wanting a trendy multi-sport clone. Afterward, New England again knew what it had—a basilica of varying distance and wall height and nonpareil intimacy. (National Baseball Hall of Fame Library)

"As much as he saw himself as the man who owned the [1933–1976] team," wrote Bart Giamatti, "to most he *became* the team." Tom Yawkey rebuilt Fenway, buoyed the Jimmy Fund, and was called by Gowdy and Williams "the greatest man I ever knew." (National Baseball Hall of Fame Library)

1961–1992's Ned Martin likely became the Sox all-time most beloved Voice. One night he called The Kid "Big Guy." The next might invoke Thoreau. Ned stormed Iwo Jima, read Allen Ginsberg, and uttered 1967's timeless "And there's pandemonium on the field!" (Courtesy of the Boston Red Sox)

THE VOICES OF THE RED SOX

RADIO

Ned Martin and Jim Woods

Ned Martin and Jim Woods teamed up for the first time in 1974 and became an instant hit with Red Sox fans throughout New England with a smooth, compatible delivery style.

This will be Ned's 15th year as a Red Sox play-by-play broadcaster, since joining Curt Gowdy in 1961, and his fourth season as leader of the radio team. A graduate of Duke and a native of Philadelphia, Ned is a World War II Marine veteran who came to the Red Sox after extensive broadcasting experience of all sports in Charleston, West Virginia.

Jim Woods is one of the real veterans of radio sports, entering his 23rd major league season in 1975. Since 1953, when he came up with the Yankees, he has broadcast play by play for the New York Giants, the Pirates, Cardinals and the Oakland A's before coming to Boston. Through the years he has teamed with such radio names as Mel Allen, Russ Hodges, Bob Prince and Jack Buck.

Al Walker

Engineer Al Walker returns for his 23rd season handling Red Sox radio play by play. In all that time, Al has rarely missed a game, home or away, and has worked with 12 different announcers through the years on crews headed by Curt Gowdy, Ken Coleman and Ned Martin.

An artifact of the age: 1975's Red Sox Yearbook. By then Dick Stockton and Ken Harrelson forged Olde Towne Team TV. A year earlier Jim Woods joined Martin on radio: to critic Clark Booth, "the best play-by-play combination in the history of American sport." Unbelievably, both were fired in 1978. (Courtesy of the Boston Red Sox)

TELEVISION Ken Harrelson and Dick Stockton

A new television arrangement with Channel 38 in Boston as the anchor station has brought the introduction of a new television play-by-play team of Dick Stockton and Ken "The Hawk" Harrelson. Stockton, a 1964 graduate of Syracuse University, is well known in New England as sports director of WBZ-TV, Boston from February, 1971 to March, 1973, and more recently as play-by-play man for the Boston Celtics telecasts. Since 1967, he has been seen frequently on the CBS-TV network. Before coming to Boston in 1971, he had been sports director of KDKA-TV, Pittsburgh and KYW-TV, Philadelphia.

Ken Harrelson returns to baseball, where he had 12 years playing experience, after an unsuccessful attempt to make the national professional golf tour. "The Hawk" came to the Red Sox in late 1967, after being granted his unconditional release following a famous feud with Charles O. Finley.

He became an overnight favorite of Red Sox fans in 1968 when he hit 35 homeruns and drove in 109 runs, and became the center of attraction with his colorful clothing and unconventional hairdo.

In 1983, Red Sox Nation and Yastrzemski bid an affectionate farewell. In Yaz's final game Ken Coleman said, "[He's] waving to them all, and they're all on their feet." Earlier No. 8 spurned a huge Yankees and Braves offer, saying, "I liked what the Red Sox are." (National Baseball Hall of Fame Library)

New England's most recognizable Voice. Twenty twelve was Joe Castiglione's thirtieth season on the Townies' vast radio network— Fenway "still my office." His Everest was 2004's first Red Sox world title since 1918, Castig immortalizing "Can you believe it?" (Courtesy of the Boston Red Sox)

"Red Sox fans like things as they are," said Castiglione. In one form or another, Fenway's hand-operated scoreboard has entranced since 1934. Yawkey's and wife Jean's initials in Morse code are spliced on two vertical stripes. (Cindy Loo)

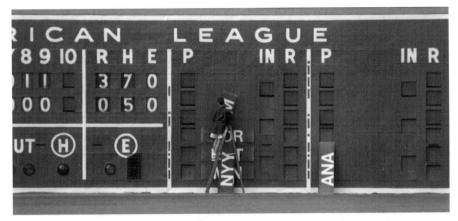

[Middle] Inside, Fenway has no bad seats except behind a post. Outside, visitors flank the park's brick facade. To generations, going to the Fens has been like coming home. (National Baseball Hall of Fame Library)

[Right] An announcer who left: Jon Miller, for Baltimore in 1983. By 2010, baseball's master mimic became the third Sox Voice to make Cooperstown, thanking 1980–1982 partner Coleman. (National Baseball Hall of Fame Library)

Two who stayed. [Left] Jim Rice, 1978 MVP, Hall Class '09, now New England Sports Network analyst. [Bottom] 1978–1984 Boston infielder Jerry Remy joined NESN in 1988—ultimately, wrote Gordon Edes, achieving "cult status . . . where does it all end?" (Courtesy of the Boston Red Sox)

Other Voices, clockwise from upper L:
Sean McDonough (1988–2004 television),
Jerry Trupiano (1993–2006 wireless),
Uri Berenguer (2003– Hispanic radio,
succeeding deceased J. P. Villaman),
and Don Orsillo and Dave O'Brien
(2001– television and 2007– radio,
respectively). (Courtesy of the
Boston Red Sox)

[Top] By the 1990s, scoreboards and club suites had been added, an enclosed press box built, the Wall padded, and 25-foot Coca-Cola bottle affixed to the left-field light tower. (Dr. Kevin Penird Photo Collection, National Baseball Hall of Fame Library)

[Left-Bottom] Boston's primo 1-2 punch. In one year or another, Manny Ramirez forged 45 dingers, 144 RBI, and a .349 average. David Ortiz's 54 homers broke the Sox single-year mark: "legendary blasts to win unforgettable games," said Dave O'Brien, "always smiling, mobbed everywhere"—*Big Papi.* (National Baseball Hall of Fame Library)

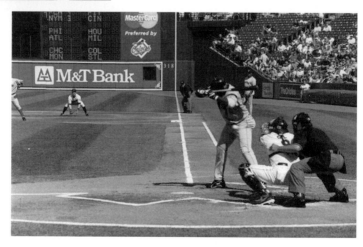

In 2001, hedge-funds manager John Henry, film/TV producer Tom Werner, San Diego Padres head Larry Lucchino, L to R, and partners bought Fenway, the Sox, and 80 percent of NESN, winning two World Series in their first six years. The triumvirate celebrates 2004's. (Courtesy of the Boston Red Sox)

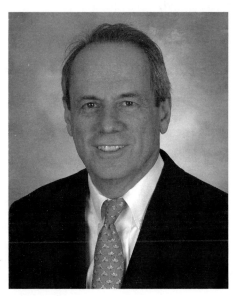

Pittsburgh-born Lucchino loved "Forbes Field as a kid and saw the damage done by [successor] Three Rivers Stadium." His concept, Oriole Park at Camden Yards, has begot 21 new old parks since 1992. It also saved Fenway from the wrecking ball. (Courtesy of the Boston Red Sox)

In 2001, Michael Dukakis said, "Anyone who wants to tear down Fenway Park should be criminally indicted." Instead, Boston spent $285 million to renovate and enlarge. [Top] In 2003, Green Monster seats replaced the Screen. The Sox enhanced the sound system, concourses, scoreboards, luxury suites, seating bowl, and capacity. [Middle] By 2010, Fenway sat nearly 38,000—to *USA Today,* "a cathedral" rebuilt pew by pew. (Courtesy of the Boston Red Sox)

Fenway's most famous sign lies near a statue of The Kid, another based on David Halberstam's book *The Teammates*, pilgrims baying "I need tickets!" and the carnival of Yawkey Way. (Cindy Loo)

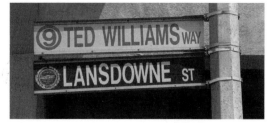

way Park." Feller's drip-drop cadence kept it simple—"Number 23, Luis Tiant. Pitching, Tiant"—ostensibly due to calling a game without his dentures. Sherm hosted WEEI's *Club Midnight*, was likely the first Hub call-in talker, and wrote a *Boston American* music column. He composed orchestral songs including "Ode to JFK," played by Arthur Fiedler and the Boston Pops, and more than a thousand pop tunes like "Summertime, Summertime," sung by The Jamies.

On Jackson's adieu, Feller, who died in 1994, said memorably, "Number 44, Mr. October." CBS Radio's Ted Robinson remembers a "great player, great PA announcer, great park." Reggie's pending absence was not Fenway's sole change.

In 1976, Ted Turner bought the Braves, renamed Atlanta WTCG superstation WTBS, and began to use satellite to "sell us a world from Georgia." Soon other superstations included WOR, WPIX, and WGN, flinging Harry Caray into every corner of the land. The problem was access: Cable systems varied from one block to another. As penetration grew, more clubs began pay-for-play. In 1983, the Red Sox, hockey Bruins, and Gillett Communications formed the regional New England Sports Network, "hoping to lure subscribers fees," said TV's *Power Play*, "but they don't know yet, because they're not on the air." Next year NESN was, joining Channel 38 and radio to earn $9.5 million, 43 percent of team revenue, the Sox worth $40 million *v.* 1978's $20.5 million. Mike Andrews and Kent Der Divanis voiced, Petrocelli and Radatz guesting. The network aired 80 games *v.* WSBK's 75. (It still uses Feller's "boys and girls" soundclip.) "[Random] exposure," said Andrews, "depended on where you lived." Another change: Gowdy, retrieving radio on CBS's 1985–1986 *Game of the Week*, working in his old Fens booth. "I missed baseball," he said. "I'm glad to be back."

The poet Goethe said, "I am the Spirit that denies." Undeniable: the status quo's eclipse. In 1988, Hector Martinez and Bobby Serano began Spanish-language coverage on Boston's WRCA. By then, Martin had done CBS's 1981 Intra-Division Series, aired up to 159 cable/free TV games a year with Montgomery, and was increasingly felt to muff fact and phrase. On radio, Ned quoted *Macbeth* to paint two battered bull pens: "If you can look into the seeds of time, And say which grain will grow and which will not, Speak then to me." Poss's brush-cut stood on end. On TV, Ned confessed to "lapses, but never on the big plays." Even as "mistakes increased," said the *Globe*, "the public seemed not to mind." We forgive those whom we love.

"Similar to other sports announcers bred for so long on radio, Martin never fully adapted to television," Jack Craig wrote. Radio focuses concentration, TV diffusing it. Sinatra's 1998 funeral service, Shaun L. Kelly wrote, included the Latin dictum—*Ars longa, vita brevis*: "Art is long, life is short." Ned's art was using language that let you grasp, view, *feel*. On December 7, 1987—Pearl Harbor Day—WSBK head Dan Berkery fired the ex-Marine, NESN retaining him. "Martin Out at Channel 38," headlined the *Globe*. "No Mercy! 38 Cans Ned," the *Herald* added. Martin said, "The first thing I asked, as you would, was, 'What did I do wrong?'"

The Nation weighed real and faux causes. Channel 38 wanted an identity. Ned was "the absent-minded professor." At station parties he "showed up wearing a cardigan sweater and Hush Puppies." He didn't draw Montgomery out. Berkery could not explain how Martin's ratings were higher than the late 1970s; "tens of thousands," a critic wrote, "can barely remember Sox games without him, and don't care to try"; and *anyone* could more distill "the music of the game." Red Smith's *was* "a great line," Ned soliloquized, "because there *is* a music to the game, whether it's the crack of the bat at Winter Haven, a full house on Opening Day, the murmuration"—the perfect word—"of a meaningless game in July or the buzz you feel at a World Series."

There were "things about this game a beginner can understand," Martin continued, "and things about it none of us will ever understand. That's the beauty of baseball: It's never predictable, even thought it never changes." In 1988, Berkery, wanting "a young Bob Costas," tapped WSBK's studio host, post-game reporter, and *Ask the Manager* sidekick Sean McDonough to join Monty on 73 free games. NESN reached only one in nine—225,000 of greater Boston's 2 million—TV households. Most would no longer hear Ned quote *Hamlet* when the Townies failed: "O Gertrude, When sorrows come, they come not [as] single spies, but in battalions." Later, Booth wrote that "the Sox bounced him around, making him feel indebted to have a job."

The Bible calls it easier for a camel to fit through the eye of a needle than to enter the Kingdom of Heaven. It is almost as hard to replace a beloved Voice. Milo Hamilton followed Bob Prince. Better poison ivy. Someone will air the post-Scully Dodgers. Send a condolence card. Coleman and Martin did the Sox for 20 and 32 years, respectively. "Following them was like topping Paul Revere," said Mc-

Donough. "One if by Ken. Two if by Ned." Each had mentored the 1960s tyke. "You learned honesty, above all."

In 1986, the Syracuse University graduate, Triple-A Syracuse Chiefs Voice, and part-time official scorer gave an *E* to Marty Castillo, axed recently by Detroit.

"I'll hit 10 out there and see how many *you* stop!" steamed Marty.

"I'm not a Triple-A third baseman and you are," snapped McDonough. "You should have stopped it."

By 1988, the balding Sean was only 26. Dad Will was a *Globe* giant, likely to gild fils's press. McDonough might even curb defeatism: On Opening Day, new reliever Lee Smith yielded a tenth-inning homer to Detroit's Alan Trammell. Bannered the *Boston Herald*: "Wait 'Til Next Year." Piquing interest—thus, ratings—might offset Boston's rising payroll. "The Red Sox needed more revenue," Gammons said. "The park began to truly change, which pleased some and offended others."

Fenway was resodded, a souvenir store (The Lansdowne Shop) and restaurant (Diamond at Fenway) opened, and center-field color scoreboard built with a black-and-white message board. Ultimately, the new "600 [renamed .406] Club," a glassed-off section of 606 stadium club seats, moved the press box from just above the home-plate grandstand to the *roof*—so high, said Fox TV's Josh Lewin, "you should put numbers on the players' caps." The ticket office, dugouts, and several clubhouse rooms were built or renovated. "With more pressure," Joe C. added, "Mac didn't have much room for error."

Boston homered just eight times in its first 23 games. On July 1, Gedman hit the right-field pole in Kansas City, McDonough and the replay saying fair. Umpire Dale Scott ruled foul, whereupon Sox players began needling another Dale, Ford, the third-base umpire, who reciprocated. "Dale Scott made this call, not Dale Ford," McDonough noted, "but Ford did a Red Sox' game several weeks ago and ejected a couple players, and it's obvious that the Sox had some bad feelings."

Boston loses, 8-7. Next day Sean entered the clubhouse, finding McNamara's door closed. "What's going on?" said McDonough.

"Dale Ford's in there," said a bystander.

Sean: "Wow, they must have looked at the tape of the game, and he saw they missed it, and he's going to apologize."

The door finally opens, John and Dale chatting. McNamara points at Sean and says, "That's him right there."

"I heard what you said last night," Dale began. "Friends in Boston called and told me you said I have a running feud with the Red Sox and I don't like John. Nothing could be further from the truth."

"Wait a minute, that's not what I said," said Sean.

"Yes, it is, friends told me," Ford said.

"Here's what I said," McDonough said, offering to produce a tape of the game: convince, not kill, the ump.

"Oh, no, I don't need to do that. I know what you said."

The watercooler teemed after a night-before game with Sean. "If this is how you handle disputes on the field," he told Ford, "no wonder you have so many problems." Among Johnny Mac problem was a perceived double standard.

Evans, "the manager's pet," moved to first base: easier for a 36-year-old outfielder. In California, Rice missed a game ("injured ribs") but played 36 holes of golf at Pebble Beach. Meanwhile, Clemens shouldered 15 hits and nine earned runs before Mac relieved him. In June, Margo Adams of Costa Mesa, California, a former mortgage broker, filed a $6 million breach of oral contract suit against Boggs, charging that he broke a vow to repay her for time and wages lost traveling with him on the road. The media went kablooey. On TV's *Donahue*, Margo described the married Wade crashing teammates' rooms and shooting compromising photos of them with other women. "They called their maneuvers 'Delta Force.'" No force could save the skipper, radio talk crying, "Knife the Mac!"

McDonough decided "not to talk about it on the air unless it affected Wade's play or the Red Sox'." It did, after a long wait for a plane to Cleveland. "The team starts drinking, we land, and a fight broke out on the team bus between Boggs and Evans. At the hotel, the fight spilled into the lobby." Next day only Sean—the team's *Voice*—mentioned it. "At that time Wade hadn't admitted the affair, and there were rumors that players and players' wives would be depositioned."

A day later Dewey accosted him: "What are you *doing*?"

McDonough: "I'm embarrassed to be part of the traveling party."

Evans: "Fine. Don't travel with us."

McDonough: "I mentioned it because it hurt the Sox."

Evans: "Next plane, Sean, skip a parachute."

McDonough entered Fenway's press room, where Mrs. Yawkey called him over. "She was reclusive, we hadn't really talked, and I'm thinking, 'I'm barely here and I'm already in trouble.'" Instead, she took his hand: "I just want you to know there might be one or two players who don't think you're doing a good job, but their opinion doesn't matter much." Pause. "Mine is the one that matters. Keep up the great work." Sean felt as tall as Larry Bird.

Mrs. Yawkey convened a meeting, Mac leaving July 14—Bastille Day—with his head, if not job. Coach Joe Morgan—ex-hockey player, Massachusetts Turnpike worker, Walpole native, and Castiglione's best friend—became "interim manager." One Joe loved the other's line: "Interim is not in my vocabulary. I am the manager until they tell me otherwise." Morgan Magic began with a 12-game winning streak, 11-game homestand sweep, and AL record 24 straight wins at home. *This* skipper didn't cower. When Morgan pinch-hit Spike Owen to bunt, Rice yanked him into the dugout runway. Joe traded shoves, emulating Studs Terkel: "*I'm* the manager of this nine."

Margo's squeeze hit .366. Greenwell led the team with 8 triples, 22 homers, and 119 RBI. "The whole package," said Martin. "We thought, here's a star for years." Mike Boddicker left Baltimore to go 7-3. Clemens's eight shutouts were Boston's most since Ruth's 1916 nine. The Red Sox took first place on Labor Day, lost six of the last seven, but won their second title in three years for the first time since World War I. The playoff *v.* Oakland directly went awry. Hurst dropped Game One, 2-1. Longtime *Globe* writer Clif Keane threw out next day's first ball. "They've got to do it soon," he said. "I'm running out of time." The Sox were, too, again bowing in the Fens.

Boddicker blew a 5-0 lead at Oakland. Hurst then lost a 4-1 final, Boston toasting the A's four-game sweep by uncorking a bender on the flight home. In December, Clemens, on Hub TV, bemoaned having to carry his own luggage and how "there are a lot of things that are a disadvantage to a family here." Increasingly, the Sox made the Bronx Zoo look like Mayberry RFD.

To Castiglione, Morgan was "the most colorful-ever Red Sox manager"—the "original Honest Abe." By 1989, Boston platooned catchers: lefty Gedman, "a great guy," and righty Rick Cerone, "not a great guy." One night Chicago threw right-handed Shawn Hillegas. After the daily pre-game show, Mr. C. said, "Maybe I should have asked this on air, but why is Cerone, not Gedman, catching?"

"Hillegas is left-handed," Morgan said. "Therefore, Cerone's going to catch."

"Joe," said, "Hillegas is *right-handed*."

"Oh, geez, I screwed up," said Morgan, not saying *geez*. "What am I going to tell Gedman?" He went to find him and confess.

Naturally, Cerone took Hillegas deep to win the game, Castiglione asking, "Should I give the background, or not? No, Joe's my friend. What good would it do to say, 'Here's why Cerone's playing'? I let it go, we'll see what happens later."

Joe regularly played the track. Writers asked, "Did you have a hunch, like a horse, playing Cerone?"

Honest Joe said, "No, I screwed up. I thought Hillegas was a lefty. That's why Cerone played, and why I apologized to Gedman."

On second thought, said Castiglione, "Maybe Morgan is George Washington, who never told a lie."

By turn, Boyd filed for arbitration after winning 10 games since 1987, Clemens was booed at home and threatened to punch reporters if they wrote about his family, Ed Romero threw a container of Gatorade on the field after Morgan pinch-hit Gedman, and pitcher Wes Gardner was arrested for assaulting his wife. One day Gardner paid: "Pitch, swung on, grounded off Gardner, knocked him down, hit him in the face," said Joe. "He's lying down, Gardner rolls over! Oh, and [team doctor] Arthur Pappas is running out." Despite baseball's highest ticket scale, the third-place '89ers drew a record 2,510,012. A convert showed why.

Raised in Philadelphia, John A. Walsh had "a partner [grandma] in my [Baby Boom] Phillies fanaticism." One asked the other, "How's Richie Ashburn doing?" "Did Robin Roberts win today?" In 1988, *Inside Sports* magazine's founding editor moved to Bristol, Connecticut, as ESPN senior vice-president. Like Walsh, his son "became a card-carrying zealot of Red Sox Nation": dicey, since "he has a Nanna, just like I had a Gramma," and Nanna loved the Yanks. Seductive was Sox genius at making and being news.

Adams posed nude in *Penthouse* magazine. Boggs confessed he was addicted to sex, the helpful Boyd called him "a sex fiend," and in Tampa a bomb threat forced the club to change planes. Around the league, fans chanted, "Mar-go!" Her then beau is still first in franchise games at third base (1,521); second, average (.338); third, on-base percentage; fourth, doubles; fifth, hits; sixth, runs and total bases; and seventh, extra-base hits, at-bats, and games. At the time, however, Gorman, trying to trade him, fanned.

"You'd think the law of averages would sort of even out—that they would win one," said Bobby Doerr. Dewey could still hit. "Way back and over everything!"

said Joe. "Toward the Mass Pike! Tremendous home run by Dwight Evans!" Rice, who couldn't, was released: third in Red Sox hits, total bases, ribbies, and homers (382); fourth, games, runs, and extra-base hits; sixth, doubles; and eighth, slugging percentage.

On August 6, 1989, the team put another left-fielder's number—8—on the right-field facade, having retired Williams's No. 9 and Cronin's 4 on May 29, 1984, and Doerr's No. 1 on May 21, 1988. The list scrawled half-taunt and half-lament: 9-4-1-8, the month of the last Sox world title.

10 ONE MR. C. SUCCEEDS ANOTHER (1990–2001)

By 1989, Ken Coleman hosted radio's *Ken's Corner* of poetry and inspiration, had or would found the Bosox Club and the Red Sox Booster Club, and was an eight-time Ohio Sportscaster of the Year and a 12-time American Federation of Television and Radio Artists honoree. That offseason he had a heart attack, leaving Castiglione in the booth alone. "Other teams' announcers'd do one or two innings to spell me," said Joe. "Somehow we got through." In Florida, a Sox-Dodgers exhibition lasted 15 innings. "Before [1997] interleague play, you'd only see the other league's guys at a Series or spring training. This day Vin Scully called a couple innings, no airs." Joe never forgot 1986's unforgettable—"feeling Shea shake. I heard Vin describe Buckner: A passion to his voice—but restraint to his call."

In mid-1989, Coleman announced his retirement, Fenway's radio booth later named in his honor. He wrote variants of "Take Me Out to the Ball Game," sung by Broadway's and future Yankees' Voice Suzyn Waldman: "And if I can't actually be there, then give me the action by Curt, Ned, and Ken." He finished a fifth book: his favorite, *The Impossible Dream*. Doing Harvard football recalled 1968's last-quarter Crimson miracle—"This, of course," Coleman had said, "is *The* Play of *The* Game"—tying the score with seven seconds left. Half an hour later the student newspaper *Crimson* headlined: "Harvard Wins, 29 to 29." In 2000, the gentle man who never confused his tenses or ended a sentence with a preposition made the Red Sox Hall of Fame.

Hooraying was their Pawtucket mikeman: Don Orsillo, born Melrose, Massachusetts; raised on a Madison, New Hampshire, farm; watched the Sox on "one of our four TV stations, coverage not wall-to-wall like now"; and spent most nights by

156

the kitchen radio, with Ken. "He was everywhere," said Don of "1967, Clemens's 20-strikeout game, and Henderson's playoff blast." Growing up, Orsillo heard dad and mom insist he "reach for the stars." At 12 he did, "vowing to air the Sox." The family soon moved West, Don inhaling Angels' burly baritone Bob Starr. In 1987, he returned to Northeastern University, majored in communication studies, took a class from Castiglione, and as an intern became Fens booth statistician.

On October 1, 1989, Coleman ended his final game by thanking "the fans of New England for their support, their friendship, their patience and loyalty over the years," and for the Jimmy Fund, "which has been a most meaningful part of my professional life." He concluded, "This is Ken Coleman, rounding third and heading home," having also thanked the Sox statistician and future TV Voice. "Think that's surreal?" said Orsillo. "Consider who succeeded Ken"—1990–1992's Bob Starr.

Starr grew up in 1930s Oklahoma, wind burying farms in a half-moon of sand. Most of the state crossed Dogpatch and Hades. Bob knew little of economics: rather, a craving to get out. One day, a Braves scout invited a friend and him to a tryout in Kansas. Hitchhiking, they spied a sideboard truck with a winch and pulley system, Starr forgetting why it seemed familiar. "Little 'un, you get in the front," the driver said. "Big 'un [Bob], in the back." Boarding, Starr remembered. "This is a dead animal truck and this horse is expired and the aroma is pungent and little things are crawling on it that don't look too neat."

The trip resumes. Bob mounts his suitcase, leans over the edge, and fantasizes an autobiography titled *Forty Miles on a Dead Horse.* Later Starr was too busy, then ill, to pen a memoir: also bluff, dry, and unafraid. "I remember his deep piercing voice," said Castiglione—and lumbering into jams even Ripley would disbelieve. In 1972, Starr joined the NFL St. Louis Cardinals. "The only one who worked without a spotting board," Jack Buck said. "He knew the name, number, and information. Incredible." At KMOX, Bob Costas stared at "Bob using only a flip card roster. The best radio football guy I ever heard." As rare was the bigs' wishing upon a Starr.

"I'd never done baseball," Bob said. "I get to St. Louis, the Cardinals needed a number two," and he joined Buck and Mike Shannon on Anheuser-Busch's 14-state network. To Costas, Starr topped each "for baseball's greatest broadcast moment, surpassing Russ Hodges's call of Bobby Thomson's homer." National

Dairy Day, 1977: the Swifties host the Cubs. Starr, Buck, and Shannon call a ho-hum fourth inning, Costas, 25, nearby. Bored, Jack hails the dairy president, who precedes a buxom belle in high heels, bathing suit, and "Miss Cheesecake" sash. Below, Ken Reitz flies to left. The lass gives each Voice a cheesecake. A *Rashomon* moment nears.

In Starr's account, Buck asked, "Do you like cheesecake?" Bob said, "Yes, very much." Jack: "How do you like *this* cheesecake?" meaning dessert. Starr: "I haven't had any yet, but it looks good enough to eat." Costas recalls a rawer script. "Hey," Buck asks, "what do you think of Miss Cheesecake?" Starr thinks that Jack said "*this* cheesecake." He replies: "I'll tell ya, I'd like to try a piece of that right here."

In Pittsburgh, the Cardinals crowd a hotel bar, Starr keeping Napa Valley in the black. At 11 p.m., he goes to bed, nature calling near 2 a.m. Adrift, Bob finds the toilet, leaves, and opens the front door, which promptly closes—in the hallway, Starr is standing nude. He considers knocking on doors, asking a volunteer to hail a key, but instead tells a bellhop, "Uh, I have a little problem here." The worker finds a coat, gets a key, and returns the jaybird to his nest.

Starr relates his tale at breakfast. Buck phones popular KMOX talk host Jack Carney, who tells his audience. Listening, Bob's wife, Brenda, recalls Miss Cheesecake, later kidding him, "Tell me I didn't hear what I just heard on the air." One night, an ABC sports exec in town for *Monday Night Baseball* sees reporter Nancy Drew next to Brenda, asking, "Who are those good-looking babes in the KMOX booth?" Team publicist Jim Toomey didn't miss a beat. "You won't believe this, but that's Nancy Drew and Brenda Starr."

In 1980, Starr joined a team pining for Prince Valiant. "I loved [owner] Gene [Autry]," he said, called *Oklahoma Crude, Crude,* or *O.C.* after his boyhood and a 1974 film. "I wanted it to be white hats win—like the movies." In 1982, Bob brooked film noir: California blew a 2-0 game then-best-of-five LCS advantage. As we have seen, the Angels' 1986 playoff flick flopped, too. "You know what the poets say," mused Boston's McNamara. "Hope springs eternal in the human breast." It was a poem, and thought, with which either team could sympathize.

"Some Okie I am," Bob laughed of airing the Red Sox. "Just call me bi-coastal." Castiglione recalls "his wearing those plaid dotted shirts, loving golf, and Ken-like vintage music." In 1993, the at-heart West Coaster returned to "a franchise," wrote the *Los Angeles Times*, "that hasn't recovered [from 1986]." Before long he tried to recover from a lifetime of chain smoking.

Increasingly, Starr felt chest pains, took a leave of absence, fought cancer, and died August 3, 1998, at 65, of pulmonary fibrosis. "I had over four thousand games and no pennants," Bob told Joe C. near the end. "I must have loved the game." Nude, clothed, or eating cheesecake, the "big 'un" was easier to digest than his early '90s Townies, whose century's last decade began with a tale of man bites dog.

Seeking less to forget than redeem himself, Bill Buckner made the 1990 Red Sox: Cheered Opening Day, he was released in June, retiring. For a decade, another lefty, Wade Boggs, "was the very best I've seen at hitting the Wall—a healthy 25 times a season," said Castiglione, feeling "Wade had passed his prime when one year he didn't hit the Wall after May 22," suggesting "lost opposite-field power." Evans averaged .249 in his last Sox year, including an at-bat with 2,299 career hits. On ESPN, McDonough said, "Here's Dwight Evans, who's one shit high of 2,300 hits."

The production truck turned as quiet as a church mouse. Partner Ray Knight began cackling as loudly as a hen. "I did say he's one hit shy of 2,300, didn't I?" Sean hoped. "Absolutely," said Ray. Two weeks later a man greeted McDonough in Texas. "Will you do me a favor? Just say 'one hit shy' for me."

Soon after Will McDonough ripped Marty Barrett in a column. Seeing Sean in the clubhouse, Barrett visited his father's sins upon the son. "He can kiss my ass," Marty began, adding, "I laugh when I read comparisons about you and Bob Costas. You're as close to him as I am to Ryne Sandberg."

Sean flushed. "If that's supposed to be an insult, at least you know how far away you are from Sandberg." A while later he urged that Barrett be pinch-hit for in a game, Marty's wife phoning in a hissy fit: "Why do you *say* these things?"

McDonough, uncontrite: "You stand by your word."

In 1990, the word was no longer heard on WPLM, WRKO buying exclusivity. It etched 21-6 Clemens, Burks's best in eight team categories, and Astros reliever Larry Andersen acquired for future MVP Jeff Bagwell. The Sox led the AL East by 6½ games September 4, trailed by 1½ three weeks later, and like 1978 rallied—up one game with one to play—again one strike. With two on, behind, 3-1, Chicago's Ozzie Guillen lined to right. "If the Gods truly had it in for the Boston Red Sox, as New England has assumed for seven decades, Tom Brunansky would have lost . . . Guillen's drive in the full moon that hung over Fenway

Park last night," wrote the *Chicago Tribune*'s Andrew Bagnato. "Or he would have slipped as he stepped on the warning track. Or he would have dropped his glove as the ball hit the webbing."

ESPN's Voice was a Downeaster, Sox and Bruins fan, and University of Maine and Georgetown Law School graduate who paid tuition as a disc jockey/sportscaster. Gary Thorne then left the law—"It's dull compared to broadcasting"—for hockey in Augusta. In 1984, the co-owner of baseball's Triple-A Maine Guides named himself announcer. "My family thinks I'm out of my mind. But here I am, calling my two girls." Thorne did the Mets, White Sox, and O's, *National Hockey Night,* the Olympics, and 1997– World Series on MLB International to Armed Forces Radio in England, Israel, and Saudi Arabia. On one hand, "You have to explain the hit-and-run." Other: "People say 'hello from Bangladesh.'" At Fenway, Thorne said hello to Lewis Carroll.

Suddenly, on the monitor, Tom Brunansky vanished in the corner. "No camera showed whether he caught the ball," said the *New York Times*, "not even a slow-motion version of the original view." At sea, Thorne wavered. "Brunansky dives!" he said. "Did he get it? Yes, the Red Sox win [Eastern Division]! No, he dropped the ball! He dropped the ball!" amending, "Wait! He got it! Believe it, New England!" That spring ESPN had begun a four-year, $400 million, six-day-a-week pact. "Coverage went to cable," said Bob Costas, "because CBS [baseball's new network, replacing NBC] didn't want a *Game*," yearly airing a peewee 16 sets.

A decade later, ESPN head Steve Bornstein still disbelieved. "Murphy's Law struck. What used to happen to the Red Sox happened to us."

What happened in 1990's LCS was the Sox losing Games One–Three, then imploding. In the final, Clemens walked Willie Randolph, argued the call, shoved one umpire, and threatened another. Players scuffled, Andersen leaving the bull pen to restrain Rocket's ire. Boston lost the game, 3-1, and series, 4-0. A *Herald* cartoon drew Clemens as a baby on the mound, a bottle in one hand, shouting "Bleep!" The Sox scratched 23 hits, scored one run in each defeat, and stranded 21 of 22 runners in scoring position. Ex-Townie Carney Lansford sniffed, "The Red Sox are a disgrace." For relief, you could retrieve Brendan C. Boyd and Fred C. Harris's *The Great American Baseball Card Flipping, Trading and Bubble Gum Book*: "In 1955, there were 77,263,127 male American human beings. And every one of them in his heart of hearts would have given two arms, a leg, and his collection of Davey Crockett iron-ons to be Teddy Ballgame." Williams had brooked retirement and managing to less enter than own a room.

In 1990, George H. W. Bush, now president, wanted to give Ted the Medal of Freedom—America's highest civilian honor. Surgery delayed the event, starting a year of speculation, "like waiting for Godot," said a West Wing aide, "except Godot couldn't hit." Ultimately, Williams got the award that Lucille Ball, Omar Bradley, Warren Buffett, Martin Luther King Jr., Edward R. Murrow, and six U.S. presidents, including Bush, had or would receive. As Leigh Montville writes in his fine book, *Ted Williams: The Biography of an American Hero*, The Kid originally declined.

Startled, White House chief of staff John Sununu called to learn why.

"No thanks," Williams said.

"No thanks?" said Sununu.

"I don't want to do it."

Sununu called a longtime Bush family friend to ask Ted to change his mind, baseball commissioner Fay Vincent finding that Williams didn't want to wear a tuxedo. In turn, "Sununu said he didn't have to wear a tuxedo, but did have to wear a tie," wrote Montville. The Splinter did, Joe McCarthy somewhere smiling.

By July 1991 Sununu concocted another Ted Event, calling one day not to discuss a United Nations speech, Oval Office talk, or birthday message for the Dalai Lama. *This* was important: a tribute to Joe DiMaggio's and Teddy Ballgame's 1941 magic daybook—the Yankee Clipper's 56-game hitting streak, Williams's .406.

"The president wants to celebrate them," he told me, "and we've come up with a way." I was to write text for each's President's Award.

"When was the award last given?" I said.

"Never," said Sununu, nor since.

That week I joined other middle-aged teeny-/Teddy-boppers in the Rose Garden. Bush gave the award, praised DiMag's "grace and modesty," asked Williams's "help with my press relations," and cited his homer to win the 1941 All-Star Game. After lunch, numbers 41, 9, and 5 took Air Force One to a summit in Toronto with Canadian prime minister Brian Mulroney. "The idea behind the whole thing," Sununu told Montville, "was that we could ride on the plane for an hour and a half and have these two guys to ourselves and listen to them talk. It was wonderful."

Someday some administration may like the Sox more than Bush 41's, though it is hard to imagine how. Even Apple-born Sununu had learned, attending MIT: "horror of horrors, in Cambridge, in Boston, home of the hated Red Sox . . . and, as fate would have it, living on Commonwealth Avenue only four blocks from Fenway Park, that heaven for a right-handed pull hitter from Queens." The Wall itself tantalized, "and though I stayed ever faithful to the Yankees, I did fantasize about hitting."

Years later, the three-term New Hampshire governor and father of eight sons took the youngest to batting practice, where the ex–sandlot player's "same curiosity that killed a cat had to find out whether the old, tired body, the rusty reflexes, the bifocal eyes could meet the test." Challenging Iron Mike, père "started slowly," then hit line drive after line drive, almost all pulled to deep left-center: the 379-foot point in New England's pitch-and-putt arcade.

Back home, the newly impressed son said, "Mom, you should have seen Dad. He was really pounding the baseballs. He drew a crowd. If it had been at Fenway, he would have been loading the Screen over the Green Monster. He was great, really great!" Try finding such zeal at, say, Tampa Bay's Tropicana Field.

The then Devil Rays were born in 1998, by which time Butch Hobson, Kevin Kennedy, and Jimy Williams had succeeded Morgan, fired despite a 1991 second-place tie. "A dreary year," said Martin, presaging others. Even victory anesthetized. Once Ned went to NESN break, unaware the mike was live, telling Monty's 1988– successor Jerry Remy, "Boy, that [game] sucked." Next day the station general manager held a confab, saying, "I just wanted to know if you said it?" Ned said yes, and that he meant it. The GM said not to worry: "I don't blame you. It did."

Remy, 35, had edged Dick Radatz, Jim Lonborg, Rick Miller, and Mike Andrews to become NESN analyst: said head John Claiborne, "younger, more contemporary." In 1975, the Angels rookie stole 34 bases in 147 games. "Maybe this time," said the freshman, "will be OK again." Would the 1978–1984 Soxer be a know-it-all, shy-away, or homer? asked columnist Bill Doyle. "I want to be myself," said Remy, and was. He learned on the job, Martin writing down fluffs, then giving him the paper. Tutoring began in Jerry's first game. "I didn't know the score, or the count. I knew baseball, but I knew nothing about TV. I was totally lost." His first replay was a ground ball to short. Remy said, "There's a ground ball to short." Seeing Ned write, "I'd think, 'Uh-oh, what did I say [ungrammatically] now?' I'm sure some of the things I said just pierced his ears."

Martin sympathized, "sometimes confused," wrote Shaun L. Kelly, "as to whether he should fill [TV] silence with prose. It was as if Faulkner were suddenly ordered to write in haiku." Should Ned speak—or let the camera speak for him? Later, he ascribed "the game get[ting] away from me at times" to technology, making "the job of play-by-playman sterile"—*dull.* "Today the analyst is the star"—fine in football, not baseball—"usually a former player who sits there and watches the replay and tells you what you just saw." Alas, "the play-by-play man gets lost." Even on radio, Ned's "strengths became less and less important to the radio industry as it evolved from . . . the 1960s to what it is today," Art Martone wrote in the *Providence Journal.* "Quiet and intelligent doesn't play over the airwaves these days; modern radio execs like shrillness and hysteria. His profession changed, and Ned Martin couldn't"—wouldn't. Why, he must have marveled, would *anyone* dumb down?

Remy, a true Speed Boy, stole 208 bases in 1,154 games. Jody Reed's seven steals led 1992's last-placers. Having worked for the Red Sox and Yankees—"like changing sides as the Cold War grew frigid"—future Hall of Fame president Jeff Idelson "still tells Sox fans, 'Hey, I did my part. Your teams didn't cooperate.'" The Townies won only 73 games, 23 behind Toronto. Someone had to take the fall, and Sox management knew just the guy. After WSBK, Ned had said he was "not finished with baseball yet." In late September 1992, baseball finished with him.

Martin had hoped to work another year, "then go out with my head high and do it here." Instead, he got a day's notice, put Thoreau in a duffel bag, and "tried to hide his sadness," said Remy. The accused said he "never saw this coming." To the *Herald*'s Gerry Callahan, Ned differed from most mikemen "because he listened and he read and he asked and he never stopped learning." Shaughnessy wrote, "You've got to love those Red Sox. They give you the worst team in 26 years, the first last-place edition in 60 years, and their response is to fire . . . a man of infinite grace and dignity." NESN said Ned "resigned," fooling few but fearing he "might say something on the air," said Remy. "There was no chance of that. He went out with class."

Martin retired to an old farmhouse in Clarksville, Virginia, 12 miles from the North Carolina border. "This was his home," said daughter Caroline of the 15-acre plot. "He felt really at peace here," at a drop of the old English *B* cap showing a visitor family photos, Civil War cartoons, and books attesting, as Emerson said, how "every word was once a poem." For a decade Ned stayed away, Craig writing, "It's impossible to overestimate how much Red Sox fans loved him." Then, in 2000, like Coleman, Martin entered the Red Sox Hall of Fame, whose room shook on his introduction. "The ovation wouldn't end," said Castiglione. "The place just exploded. Until then, I don't think he knew how much he was loved. He was a most modest guy."

In 2002, The Kid, 83, died of cardiac arrest. On July 22, Ned attended the Ted Williams Tribute at Fenway Park—his first trip back since 1992. "He'd had a bad back and knee and hip replacement, but wouldn't miss it," said son Roley. "He just enjoyed the whole night, especially the videos at the end, the *Field of Dreams* song, [and] 'Taps.'" Martin, Yaz, and Gammons reminisced in the on-field ceremony. Ned saw longtime employees, again treating them like royalty, and spoke to Remy, Pesky, Gowdy, and Coleman, who said, "He had a style all his own. He loved the game, and the history of the game."

Castiglione called next morning by cell phone, finding Martin, 78, "very chipper." Ned flew to Raleigh-Durham Airport, caught a shuttle bus, and had a massive heart attack. The Sox were on NESN when his death reached Fenway. Red-eyed, Remy reported it, later saying, "I think what made it tougher is that I'd just seen him the day before." A moment of silence and video screen farewell preceded the next game.

"Those who always feel the 'good old days' were better than the present," wrote the *Globe*'s Bill Griffith, "might . . . this time . . . be right." Said Caroline, "From what he was as a husband and a dad, nothing you could ever say would capture papa. His love was his family [wife Barbara, of 51 years, three children, and nine grandchildren], and his dogs and cat, Emily, and the country." Mercy! Ned Martin was the cat's meow.

In 1978, the Hall of Fame began the annual Ford C. Frick Award. Unable to choose Mel Allen or Red Barber, its committee picked both. Allen was hot dogs, Ballantine Beer, and the U.S. Marine Band. Barber was white wine, Crepes Suzette, and bluegrass music. In 1984, Gowdy became the first Townie recipient, saying of Boston, "I could never tell you what happy days we had." A decade later, the Sox' 1954–1959 Bob Murphy joined him in Cooperstown. Most hailed him, Lindsey Nelson, and Ralph Kiner airing the 1962–1978 Amazin's. "Can you believe it?" Bob said. The early Mets had trouble turning two. All three announcers made the Hall.

The Greek poet Sophocles wrote, "One must wait until the evening to see how splendid the day has been." By 1994, Murphy's Okie twang had become a natural or belated taste in the ephemera capital of the world. The last four digits of his phone number—6-3-8-7—spelled Mets. Once, tired by a long trip, he signed into a hotel, "Robert E. Mets." Murphy's Law was as simple as the ex-Marine's love of country: "I tried to bring friendliness to the game."

After 2004, 1986 receded as a source of Sox pain. "Three-two the count," Murphy had said. "And the pitch by Stanley . . . And a ground ball trickling . . . it's a fair ball . . . it gets by Buckner! Rounding third is Knight! The Mets will win the ball game! They win! They win!" His 1988 Metsies took the East but lost the LCS. To *Bowling for Dollars*, the Gator Bowl, and the old AFL New York Titans, Bob added CBS Radio's *Game of the Week*. In July 1990, Philadelphia scored six ninth-inning runs. "Line drive! It's caught! It's over! The Mets win the ball game!" cried Murphy, who almost never swore. "They win the damn thing by a score of 10 to 9!"

Increasingly, Bob's voice was thicker than when he cried, "Hi, neighbor, have a 'Gansett!" Trimming workload bought another decade, his phrase *The Happy Recap* now a life. "I can't remember first saying it. I do remember thinking it was corny, dropping it, then mail on its behalf." The Mets' radio booth was named for Murphy in 2002. Next season he left, musing, "It was a lot easier to say hello 42 years ago than it is saying good-bye." Shea rocked to "Mur-phy! Mur-phy!" A giant card read, "Dear Bob. Wishing you all the best in your retirement. The Mets family." Thousands of friends signed, then mourned his next-year death at 79. Sophocles deserved a season's pass.

Bob's last two seasons were the Mets' Mo Vaughn's, barely resembling the decade-earlier Red Sox 6-foot-1, 240-pound first baseman—1993 his first of from four to six straight years leading the Townies in homers, RBI, and five other categories. A year before, McDonough had added CBS. "Jack Buck had just been let go on baseball," he said, "when [executive producer] Ted Shaker called about my interest." Hanging up, "I jumped up so high I . . . put a hole in the ceiling." World Series 1993 scoring was higher: "The Phillies have taken the [Game Four] lead by a field goal, 10 to 7!" Sean said. Game Six: "Well hit down the left-field line! Way back! Way back! And gone! Joe Carter with a three-run homer! The winners and still world champions! The Toronto Blue Jays!"

Next year, CBS, losing baseball, gave McDonough the Olympics, Masters, U.S. Open, hoops, and football. On Sox wireless, Missourian Jerry Trupiano, 42, replaced Bob Starr: St. Louis University, 14-year Houston talk host, and Voice of the Expos, CBS Radio *Game*, Southwest Conference, and Houston Astros, Oilers, Rockets, and Aeros. In 1989, Trupiano called a 22-inning game, lost by Montreal, 1-0: mascot Youppi, like 1903's Nuf Ced McGreevy, bounced for dancing on a dugout. Jerry once braved a four hour and 45 minute Yanks-Townies marathon, saying, "The Seven Year's War was shorter."

Trupiano liked puns, barbeque, saying "Way back!" of a homer, and—he knew the market—giving the stripes' score almost as often as Boston's. "Sharp [also excitable] voice, grasped baseball," said Castiglione, teaming with Mr. T. through 2006. "We loved North End [Boston] restaurants: two Italians chowing down." Meanwhile, ex-Sox reliever Mike Fornieles joined Hispanic play-by-play-men Martinez and Serano, trying, as Barber said, "to make a game played by two teams [into] a contest involving personalities who had families, trouble, blue or brown eyes." As Trupiano might pun, the 1993–1994 Sox finished "way back"— fifth and fourth, respectively.

On April 19, 1994, Mo and Tim Naehring twice hit back-to-back homers. "Whether it [the ball] is juiced or not, I don't know," said Naehring. "I missed that class in college." Castiglione's call hailed "a great day for the hitters!"—as FDR said, backing Hoey in 1937, "We both like a game with a lot of scoring." Short-stop John Valentin made only the bigs' tenth unassisted triple play. A mock Fen-way ceremony buried Dan Shaughnessy's book *The Curse of the Bambino*. None stopped a season-ending players lockout. A year later Kennedy became skipper, Vaughn was voted MVP, and Boston clinched a fourth AL East title in a decade. All-sports WEEI 850 replaced flagship talk WRKO, airing the LCS strike-delayed first "wild card" preamble: best-of-five Division Series (DS) *v.* Cleveland. A new Spanish Voice also called the Townies' eleventh straight postseason loss.

Juan Pedro Villaman, the youngest of nine children, was born in the Domini-can Republic in 1959, his mother dying giving birth. At 13, J. P. began calling baseball, aunt Orfelina Villaman, raising him, later watching two TVs at once: soap operas and his game. In 1986, Villaman immigrated to New York, then Law-rence, Massachusetts, like thousands of other Dominicans. In 1995, producer Bill

Kulick hired him for stations in Lawrence, Worcester, and the Hub. "He did selected games," said future partner Uri Berenguer, "loving the Sox so much. He saw
them as the Almighty." Passersby yelled *Papa Oso*—"Papa Bear"—and his game-
ending mot: "Keep the faith. God bless you. This game is *ours.*" *Si*: Vaughn's .326,
44 homers, and 143 RBI in 1996. *No*: Boston fired a Kennedy, unthinkable at the
ballot box. *Sorpresa*: In a designated hitter's league, Clemens singled May 23 "up
the middle," said Joe. "Can you believe it?"—a phrase he would use again.

On September 19, Roger encored 20 Ks at Detroit—to McDonough, "the
greatest individual performance I've seen"—still first, Sox all-time wins (192,
with Young), strikeouts, walks, shutouts, and 10-K games (68); second, walks and
games started; third, losses (111); sixth, games (383); seventh, winning percentage (.634); ninth, complete games; and tenth, ERA (3.06). Replacing Kennedy,
Braves coach Williams soon lost the single-game strikeout king. Rocket toddled
to Toronto, blaming new Sox GM Dan Duquette, late of Montreal, for calling
him washed up. Arriving: as *SI* might say, "a sign of the apocalypse," the first team
mascot, Wally the Walrus. Another: After 22 years, TV rights left Channel 38 for
WABU Channel 68, Warner Bros. 56, Fox 25, then back to 38 and Channel 4
before NESN 2006– exclusivity. "Viewers didn't know *where* we were," said Mc-
Donough. "Ironically, the Sox were the one thing I did where I really cared who
won and who lost."

In 1986, Seton Hall freshman Valentin hit ninth. In 1997, he clubbed an
AL-high hits (209), doubles (47), and triples (11). Ex–college mate Vaughn was
still the big Dog, or was he? A year earlier a former U.S. Olympic team walk-
on homered in his first full big-league game. "The dream finally came through,"
said Nomar Garciaparra. "It could have ended right there and would have been
enough." Enough was his 1997 30 homers, 98 RBI, and .306 average: also Sox
at-bat record (684), 30-game hit streak (trailing Dom D.'s 34), and 85 extra-base
hits (behind Foxx, Rice, and Williams)—first post-Fisk unanimous Rookie of the
Year. Said Duquette, "Nomar might be the best Sox rookie ever"—presumably
excluding The Kid.

Garciaparra signed a seven-year deal to keep him Boston's. "The Sox are back
in business!" vowed Duquette, upping 1998 payroll by 35 percent. The exception
brooked a drunk driving arrest, withdrawn contract offer, and psychological test
for alcoholism: acquitted, Vaughn felt insulted. "In baseball, you can't ignore the
human equation," said Castiglione. Montreal's Pedro Martinez had led the 1997

majors in ERA, complete games, and rival batting average. Now, dealt to his ex-GM, he threw a 1-0 complete game—"first at Fenway in a decade!" chorused Joe. Pro: Tom (Flash) Gordon had a bigs record 43 straight saves. Con: Vaughn said he hoped to follow Clemens to Toronto.

On August 30, 1998, Fenway sang "Happy [eightieth] Birthday!" to No. 9, watching on TV. Sans 1987– postseason victory, Boston plucked its first wild card, won the DS opener—"Deep again!" Castiglione said of Vaughn, homering twice—then began another losing streak. Worse, it spurned an exclusive free agent bargaining window. Mo took $80 million from the Halos. New York matched the Sox' seven-year $87.5 million to keep center-fielder Bernie Williams, whom Duquette thought all but signed.

"Where do we go now?" Dan said, sounding like Harry Frazee. "We'll probably take a look at pitching." Presently Clemens left Toronto—for the Yankees! The Nation, which thought it had seen everything, shook its head.

In 1999, the Sox hosted their first All-Star Game since 1961, thousands packing the week-long FanFest at downtown's Convention Center. The Cardinals' Mark McGwire, then less Snidely Whiplash than Dudley Do-Right, won the first round of Home Run Derby. Ken Griffey Jr. took the final. Nearly 40 nominees for MasterCard's Major League Baseball All-Century Team gathered. Griffey gravitated to Mays. Philadelphia's Curt Schilling left the pen to meet Mike Schmidt and Robin Roberts. Disable-listed Tony Gwynn flew from San Diego: "I finally got to see it! Fenway!" Before the game, The Kid rode a golf cart down the warning track, along the boxes, around the plate, and toward the mound, All-Stars circling Baseball's Grand Old Man. "Do you ever smell the wood burn?" he asked McGwire of bat on ball. Rafael Palmeiro refused to leave. "The game can wait. That's the chance of a lifetime." MVP Martinez struck out five of his six batters. Seldom had the sport seemed more certain of its place.

That fall two aces drew another Sox wild card: Nomar's .357 batting title and Pedro's 23-4 Cy Young. Trailing the DS, two games to 0, Boston rallied v. Cleveland, 9-3; 23-7, a 24-hit/largest postseason victory margin; and 12-8 "on the best pitcher in baseball's . . . six no-hit innings in relief coming off an injury, to send the Red Sox on to New York!" crowed Mr. C. of Martinez. LCS Game Three matched Pedro, 27, and Clemens, 37, Sr. leaving in the third. The Fens chanted, "Where is Roger?" Next night Jimy Williams was bounced, the crowd threw bottles, and

Yanks left the field. Steinbrenner said Jimy had "incited." Williams replied, "When Georgie-Porgie speaks, I don't listen." Boston braved bad umpiring, a record 10 series muffs, and clutch mojo falling, losing, four games to one. "Too bad it happened the first time we and the Yankees met in the postseason," Garciaparra said.

Karl Marx called religion "the opium of the people." Nomar's second straight title and Pedro's third Cy Young kept a new millennium's faith. Ex-Astro Carl Everett had 34 homers and Derek Lowe a league-high 42 saves. The 2000 stripes won the East for the fourth time since 1996. Irked, the Townies signed a Rorschach test in December—a mercurial and/or psychotic bopper, depending on your view. Next year Manny Ramirez led the team in average, hits, doubles, dingers, and RBI, if not yet dreadlocks. On April 4, 2001, in Baltimore, Hideo Nomo made his Sox debut—also the big-league coming out of a Voice we last met as Fenway booth statistician.

"He [Nomo] strikes out the side in the seventh!" said Don Orsillo, deeming horsefeathers baseball's superstition of not noting an at-work no-hitter. "He has not yet rendered a base hit . . . Nomo is flirting with a no-no!" Even more than usual, a road crowd had red hose on: "What a roar went up when . . . [Brian Daubach's eighth-inning homer] went over the wall"—Boston, 3-0.

Earlier Nomo had abided a 43-minute power delay. As play lagged, Orsillo now mused, "How will he do after such a long time on the bench?" The O's Brady Anderson answered in the ninth. "Right back at him [Nomo]! One out!" Don said. Next Mike Bordick hit "a little flare . . . shallow center. [Infielder Mike] Lansing will run it down!"—his somersaulting catch "keeps the no-hitter alive!" Delino DeShields then arced to left. "[Troy] O'Leary coming on. And Hideo Nomo has no-hit the Baltimore Orioles!" Remy added, "Welcome to Boston." It had "been awhile! 1965!" since Dave Morehead's last Sox official no-hitter, said Orsillo, who must have worried about peaking too soon.

Since 1991, Don had covered Springfield, Massachusetts, hockey, the 1994 AHL All-Star Game, and Pittsfield Mets, Double-A Binghamton, and Pawtucket, the last a bigs conveyor belt. (Riding it: the Mets' Gary Cohen, Giants' Dave Flemming, Rays' Andy Freed, and D.C.'s Dave Jageler.) Radio's child vowed to "reach for the stars." At 32, TV's adult got a three-game Fens tryout. "No matter what happened, I'd kept my promise." Three months later NESN made Orsillo a regular. For a time the '01ers contended despite Everett making Manny look as stable as Mr. Rogers.

Carl denied the existence of dinosaurs, grabbed his crotch after homering, was suspended 10 games for bumping an umpire, and said he "thrived on being hated." Inexplicably, Duquette backed him, firing Williams, the Townies henceforth 5-21. Jimmy had coined *Jimy*-wocky: "In retrospect, you are always looking back." "If a frog had wings, it wouldn't bump its booty." As future Astros skipper, Williams missed a malapropism of which even he would be proud.

In 2002, Theo Epstein, 28, became baseball's youngest-ever general manager: Brookline native; relatives including Boston University's creative writing program head, TV's *Homicide: Life on the Street* and *Tell Me You Love Me* writer, and *Casablanca*'s Academy Award–winning screenplay team. The *Yale Daily News* sports editor graduated '91 in American Studies, joined San Diego Padres publicity, headed Baseball Operations, got a law degree, returned East under new Sox head Larry Lucchino, and replaced interim GM Mike Port.

By 2004, as we shall see, Epstein had acquired Ramirez, Johnny Damon, Kevin Millar, Bill Mueller, David Ortiz, and Schilling, among others. Next year Texas made Jon Daniels, also 28, GM, one day guesting on Sox TV. Orsillo intended to note "the great success youthful GMs have had." Instead, he said, "Jon, in Boston we all know how much great sex young general managers can have."

Fearing this would be "my all-time blooper," Orsillo tried to pretend that nothing was amiss. A few batters later Jerry Remy couldn't help himself. "Don, that was a great point you made about young general managers."

Since 1912, the Sox had often been inferior to their park. The park now struggled to be as competitive as its club. The Townies began organized tours; renovated dugouts and restrooms; installed energy-efficient lighting, heating, and cooling; put a metal awning above the left- and right-field roof stands and a batting cage under the bleachers; added a 25-foot Coca-Cola bottle design on the left-field light tower; and donated to the Jimmy Fund when a drive hit the Screen or bottle. On August 22, 1998, Fenway hosted Jimmy Fund Fantasy Day, where a $1,250 gift got you 15 swings at the Monster and, *ESPN The Magazine* said, "a chance to tell your grandchildren how you felled the behemoth with one mighty stroke." Some despaired of revenue. "The Red Sox can't generate enough," wrote reporter Gerry Fraley of the park's size, "no matter how high they raise . . . tickets." Others felt cash contingent on success, and charm.

In 1990, the relocated-to-the-roof "600 Club" temporarily wrecked Fenway's home-plate camera shot—the viewer's picture window. "We had been right on the field," said Martin. "Now a viewer thinks he's in Providence": players resembled ants. A Soxaphile at the White House petitioned Ned, NESN, and the team VP, broadcasting and technology, Jim Healy, to return the camera to its old level, just above the angled backstop. Respecting feedback, the Red Sox next year built a TV catwalk there—Healy good-naturedly blaming me. "Give Red Sox fans something, and they'll give it back to you many times over," Carl Yastrzemski said. Increasingly, the Sox grasped Fenway's need to reciprocate.

As we have seen, Suburban-Ho threw baseball a post-1950s curve. Out: stands so near that you could almost know the players. In: generic clones, with freeway proximity, vast foul turf, bad sight lines, and seats in another county. "When I'm at bat, I can't tell where I am," Richie Hebner said, knowing that a great baseball franchise must have a baseball-only home. A born-in-1983 architectural firm Hellmuth, Obata, and Kassabaum (HOK Sport) knew, too. "The idea was laughed at," said chief architect Joseph Spear, "that a company could thrive by designing only sports." Revenue topped $7 million by 1988, the year that HOK's first major park opened: 19,500-seat Pilot Field, shoehorned into downtown Buffalo.

"Instead of building generically," said Triple-A Bisons owner Bob Rich, "they begin with a city's architecture and landscape." The 1980s Orioles noticed, vetoing a baseball/football plant to replace Memorial Stadium. Pittsburgh-born Lucchino had "loved Forbes Field as a kid and seen the damage done by Three Rivers Stadium." Now his O's razed an 85-acre site parallel to old trolley tracks, near the historic Camden Railroad Station of the old Baltimore & Ohio, on the site of Ruth's Cafe, owned by George Herman Ruth Sr., a pop fly from the Inner Harbor. "For once, they didn't build it at the intersection of interstates," said Michael Gershman of Oriole Park at Camden Yards, opened in 1992. "The city was part of the ballpark. The ballpark was part of the city," like a site born, 1912.

HOK's first design imitated bland new Comiskey Park. Lucchino hated it. Before his 1988 death from cancer, O's owner Edward Bennett Williams had, too. NL president–soon to be commissioner Giamatti said, "Why can't we have modern conveniences *and* idiosyncrasy? Give me sharper quirks and odder angles," recalling his first game, at age 10, with dad. Oakland seats half-circled each foul line. Camden's nuzzled them. Veterans Stadium braved height uniformity. The Yard rose from left field's seven feet to the right-field board's 25. New Comiskey's no-man's-land separated the seats and inner fence. Camden's wall and bleachers fused. "Fielders'll reach into the stands and grab a homer," said Lucchino—Dewey at Pesky's Pole. Three parks shaped the plot: Pilot, Forbes, and Fenway, most of all.

Many fences gently curve. The Yard leapt from 333 (left field) to 364 (left-center), hit 410 (deepest left-center), fell to 375 (right-center), and dropped to 318 (right). An arched facade mimed 1910–1990 Old Comiskey; ivy backdrop, Wrigley Field; right-field scoreboard, Ebbets Field, tying out-of-town score, ad, and blurb. A standing-room site topped it. Beyond, the Eastern Seaboard's longest building, a 1898 restored B&O Railroad Warehouse, enfolded Camden, like warehouses near Shibe Park. "Some wanted it torn down," said O's board member George Will. "Instead, they refurbished it," putting sports bars, souvenir stores, and team offices on or next to a 60-foot promenade extending Eutaw Street— think Yawkey Way. Camden's *feel* became the *Fens'*.

"When this park's complete, every team will want one," said Giamatti. "If you build it [right], they will come." Fenway came to Baltimore, then Arlington, Cleveland, Denver, Atlanta, Phoenix, Seattle, Houston, Detroit, San Francisco, Milwaukee, Pittsburgh, Cincinnati, San Diego, Philadelphia, St. Louis, Washington, New York (Mets and Yankees), Minneapolis, and Miami, chronologically—21 new sites in as many years. Houston's then Enron Field, said *SI*, had "more nooks and crannies than an English muffin." Safeco Field bared a pastiche of ferries, cargo ships, and sunsets from Albert Bierstadt. Boston had the Triangle, Williamsburg, and Yawkeys' Morse Code. "This is the capital of baseball," said Schilling, about to enter the Townies tale. Who moves a capital?

It was true that "Every time you see a new park," said Ted Williams, "remember who they're trying to imitate." It was also true that Fenway's infrastructure, facilities, and seats were small, cramped, and old. The Sox lot had sired going back to the future. Would it become a victim of its own success?

"The Red Sox tell us that what they need is luxury boxes, gourmet concession stands, nicer bathrooms, and more high-priced seats," the *Globe*'s Charles A. Radin wrote in 1998. "What they don't need, they say, is Fenway Park," fearing that Camden Etc. had devalued it. "The logic is bigger—and better—stadium, more revenue," a Sox exec said. "More revenue, better players, more success on the field; more success on the field, a more stable attraction, well into the future." Duquette would not detail a "spectacular plan" to replace Fenway, the team too busy with next year's All-Star Game, said Vice President Dick Bresciani to etch how, or when. "Everything [else] has slowed down right now, pretty much to a stop." In July, the *Globe* said that the Townies would at some point build a new park abutting Fenway on a triangular 14-acre parcel boarded by Yawkey Way, Brookline Avenue, and Boylston Street. The ersatz 44,130-seat site would "look and feel like Fenway." Most of the old park would crumble upon its birth.

"We need a *new* park," Duquette said. "Our fans complain about narrow seats and lack of modern amenities [e.g., rest rooms, ticket windows, and concession stands]. Without corporate boxes, there's just no way to get money to compete," cash accruing from suites, broadcasting, and likely a private partner. Red Sox now-CEO John Harrington vowed to "incorporate the old." Replicated: the Monster, Triangle, right-field pens, left-field ladder, arches, and brick facade. Money makers: a hundred luxury suites and five thousand club seats. Home plate would move 206 yards; Pesky Pole, to a new right-field line. Lengths: same, save right's 307, not 302. Shaughnessy wrote, "If they do what they say they are going to do, they'll be going new, without going modern."

A red seat would signify The Kid's 502-foot homer; Citgo sign, shroud left-center field; switchboard operator Helen Robinson, still connect the public. The infield, facade, original manual scoreboard, and part of the Wall would help form a museum, Sox Hall of Fame, and learning center. Envision walking from Kenmore Square down the old third-base line to a game. Diamond Vision would top the Monster; field lie 20 feet below street level; right's scoreboard crown two-tier bleachers; foul turf somehow *shrink*! "If the Sox'd varied from old Fenway more than this," wrote a columnist, "the cry would've killed a new."

The Sox hoped to transplant Fenway's *heart*. By 1998, hundreds carried "Save Fenway" signs and green bumper stickers, hoping to restore its *core*. Were they truthtellers or busybodies? Depended on who opined. The *Globe* home page asked why people visited. More than half (51.9 percent) said Fenway; 31.5 percent, Sox; 16.4 percent, opposition. Scott Hardy of Concord, New Hampshire, vowed to lie down in front of any bulldozer. Erika Tarlin, a Somerville librarian, said, "I'm almost more of a Fenway fan than a Red Sox fan." Each Monday night, she attended "Save Fenway" meetings. One plan, "WayFen," would rebuild it in two years, left-field's Wall becoming next season's right. Camdens were copycats, she ventured. *Here* was the original.

A new park might change the neighborhood, block a proposed Boylston Street shop boulevard, and/or move merchants from Yawkey Way and Brookline Avenue. "If they move we'd have to start over again," said David Paratore, manager and co-owner of the nearby bar Who's On First. Many doubted that a new Fenway could match the old. On the Internet, both sides hit away. "Taking away one of the jewels for money is wrong . . . RENOVATE!" The other: "There is no way the Sox would renovate." Increasingly, the latter's triumph seemed inevitable. Who knew the last laugh would be on it?

Even funding seemed resolved: $362 million privately, more than any club had raised, and $312 million publicly for design, land acquisition, construction, infrastructure, and 2,760-spot parking. The state legislature approved it in July 2000. "They did their job," wrote the *Globe*. "Now the pressure is on" the Townies. "Save Fenway"ers took solace in a World War I French general, Ferdinand Foch: "My center is giving way, my right is in retreat. Situation excellent. I shall attack."

11

MILLENNIUM IN THE MORN (2002–2006)

In his 1993 book, *President Kennedy: Profile of Power*, Richard Reeves writes, "There was an astonishing density of event during the Kennedy years": the Bay of Pigs, Berlin, the space race, civil rights, the Cuban Missile Crisis. Tom Wicker called JFK "the most fascinating might-have-been in American history." For the last decade, baseball's once-might-have-been has forged a vast density, too. On December 20, 2001, the Yawkey Trust accepted an estimated $660 million offer, plus $40 million in assumed debt, for Fenway Park, the Red Sox, and 80 percent of NESN from a group led by hedge-funds manager John Henry, Hollywood producer Tom Werner, Padres president and CEO Larry Lucchino, and other partners. The sale ended 69 years of Yawkey family rule. It also saved Fenway, though that was not then clear. Of six groups, "Ours was the only one committed to preserving and protecting [it]," claimed Lucchino. "We came in with the experience of building parks, so we knew the alternative." The Nation shrugged, having heard this all before.

At the time, as we have seen, conventional wisdom had Boston building a larger next-door park. "Plenty of naysayers thought this place should be destroyed, replaced," Lucchino recalled. In 1962, Richard Nixon held his "last press conference." A day after buying the Sox, the owners' triumvirate gave a first. Five pledges filled its core. One: "Field a team worthy of the fans' support." Two: "Preserve all that's good about Fenway Park and to take that experience to a higher level." Three: "Market aggressively to a new, broad region." Four: "Be active participants in the community," later adding "in terms of charitable and philanthropic activities." Five: "End the Curse of the Bambino and win world championships for Boston,

New England, and Red Sox Nation." Meat Loaf sang, "Two Out of Three Ain't Bad." Five out of five is better: the Sox spending $285 million to make Fenway over.

On September 8, 2008, the Boston American League Baseball Company broke the 1995–2001 Indians' major league record 455-game sellout streak. Even Fenway tours formed a waiting list, like pilgrims storming Lourdes. In a decade, Pedro Martinez prompted, "Who's your daddy?" David Ortiz became New England's *el padre*, and Kevin Youkilis's batting stance aped a Banshee line. Captain Ahab caught Moby Dick, taking the 2004 and 2007 World Series. A rolling rally hailed an Event worth waiting for. A 2011 collapse made even 1978 seem a joyride. In 1914, British foreign minister Sir Edward Grey eulogized World War I: "The lamps are going out all over Europe; we shall not see them lit again in our lifetime." New England's lamps went *on* in late 2001.

Baseball approved the sale January 16, 2002. It closed February 27 as pitchers and catchers prepped at 1993–2011 Ft. Myers training camp. John Henry knew Florida, as ex-Marlins chairman and sole owner; business, his firm a "recognized leader in alternative asset financial product innovation"; and baseball, as Yankees limited partner, Triple-A Tucson Toros chairman and majority owner, and Senior Professional Baseball League co-owner. Born in Illinois, raised in rural Arkansas, and educated by Harry Caray, the Townies new principal owner saw his first game at Sportsman's Park. Then and now, he felt baseball "an affair of the heart," the Nation's having shattered with metronomic rhythm.

Werner entered Harvard in 1967, his visual studies class documentary on Fenway presaging such TV hits as *The Cosby Show*, *Cybill*, *A Different World*, and *That '70s Show*, Robin Williams's *Mork and Mindy*, Billy Crystal's *Soap*, and Tony Danza and Danny DeVito's *Taxi*. He founded the Oxygen TV Network, began HBO's animated *The Life and Times of Tim*, and received multiple Peabody, Golden Globe, People's Choice, and Emmy awards. The Red Sox future chairman bought the Padres in 1990, headed baseball's TV committee, sired the wild card—think 2004—and swelled NESN baseball programming. Cliché: There's not a bad seat at Fenway. (See: behind a column.) Fact: there's not a bad camera angle. The bigs' highest network ratings are regularly Sox-Yankees—*especially* from the Fens.

Boston's baseball lynchpin was its new CEO and president. On October 13, 1960, Lucchino, 15, was walking home from school when Bill Mazeroski beat the Yanks, 10-9, in likely the World Series' greatest game. "I threw my radio toward the sky," he said, racing home "on air." Like Maz, Lucchino played second base—on Pittsburgh's high school title team. At Princeton, the ex-Pittsburgh All-City League basketball player made the Final Four. He graduated Yale Law School, joined founder Edward Bennett Williams's law firm, and was named a Williams and Connolly partner, Washington Redskins counselor, and team board director. In 1979, Williams bought the Orioles, naming Lucchino VP/general counsel. 1988: The protégé became prez. 1989: The now-part-owner bred Camden Yards. 1992: The 46,500-seat Yard—few call it "Oriole Park"—"the best plan for a . . . baseball park in more than a generation," said the *Times*, drew a team record 3,567,819.

In 1993, Peter Angelos bought the O's, Lucchino leaving a 41,000 paid and waiting season-ticket list to join San Diego. A 1998 referendum funded the Padres' $476 million PETCO Park—irregular, like the Yard: left field, 334 feet; center, 390; deepest right-center, 411; right field, 322. Design: HOK Sport. Plan: a Ballpark District of offices, homes, and retail shops—"vital," Lucchino said, "to making a seedy area a year-round jewel." Jacaranda trees, palm courts, and water malls conjured an early-Spanish mission. Nearly four thousand could stand or sit on an incline beyond center field. Bookending them: "[two-tiered left- and right-field] bleachers, like the grandstand individual sections, each facing the pitcher's mound," said Pads Voice and old Sox-killer Jerry Coleman. The Western Metal Supply Co. abutted left field, its corner painted yellow—"our standard foul pole," joked HOK's Joseph Spear, hoping, like Lucchino, for Baltimore redux.

An environmental dustup delayed PETCO till 2004, Lucchino by then having Williams's dream job. His vitae wowed the Nation but gave "Save Fenway"ers pause. Camden Yards. San Diego. What better postlogue than to replace Fenway Park? "I think Larry's past convinced some he was coming to put the park out of its alleged misery," said Ken Coleman. Walter O'Malley told son Peter that Dodger Stadium would be a "monument to the O'Malleys." Many expected a new Fenway to be Lucchino's.

In 1969, a former aide to the late Robert F. Kennedy, now press secretary for U.S. senator Charles Goodell, met Kennedy's successor as Congress's leading Viet Nam war critic. The two Georges, Mitrovich and McGovern, respectively, became friends. In 1972, Democratic presidential nominee McGovern won one state, Massachusetts. Mitrovich became a writer, speaker, and founder, the nonpartisan City Club of San Diego. At Chicago's 1996 Democratic National Convention, he encountered McGovern, in the visitor gallery, with Michael Dukakis, the party's 1988 losing nominee. "Have either of you addressed the convention—or been asked to speak?" Mitrovich asked. No, he was told: The party wanted to forget.

Riled, Mitrovich wrote a 2000 *New York Times* column on the eve of the Los Angeles Convention, scoring such ingratitude. Dukakis, in particular, was touched. A year later the visiting professor at UCLA's School of Public Affairs and member of Amtrak's board of directors accepted Mitrovich's invite to discuss "the state of American trains." A group met at Lucchino's oceanside La Jolla home, between L.A. and San Diego. "Larry was still with the Padres," said Mitrovich, whose City Club had backed ballpark funding, "and he and Dukakis started talking about stadia. I'll never forget what Mike told him: 'Anyone who wants to tear down Fenway Park should be criminally indicted.'"

As governor, Dukakis had confronted the future of the Fens. "The Sox kept saying the infrastructure was weak, maintenance prohibitive. Actually, they weren't maintaining the park so they'd have an excuse to leave." He said the price tag for a next-door Fenway "might have hit $850 million"—triple 2002–2011's renovation. "My allegedly fiscal conservative successor [William Weld] couldn't wait to climb aboard."

Dukakis was more skeptical, one day phoning several aides on his economic development staff.

"I said, 'Is this true? Is Fenway beyond saving?'"

"'Baloney,' they said. 'Of course it can be rebuilt.'"

In early 2002, Dukakis told Lucchino, "I hope you'll take a very serious look at saving Fenway." To "Save Fenway"ers' shock, the ex-governor met an open mind.

For one thing, Lucchino grasped Boston's loony bin cost of land. "The economics of renovation made much more sense than tearing [Fenway] down and building a new one," said Philip Bess, professor of architecture at the University of Notre Dame, who at the 2000 Future Fenway Design Symposium said a new park would mean bankruptcy. The triumvirate also heard New England: The Sox sans Fenway would not be the Sox. Business touts, but often ignores, its clientele. Antithetically, ownership had "a strong sense of how important Fenway was . . . to generations of Bostonians and New Englanders," Lucchino said. "We had a full-blown appreciation for its charm and appeal, and we thought it could be renovated, enhanced, expanded, modernized in certain ways." The group's task was to find how.

In Baltimore, Lucchino used architect Janet Marie Smith to "mastermind the Yard." Boston hired her, Smith hoping "to save a model for a generation of parks." She felt renovation doable—Fenway's steel frame structure had a concrete seating bowl, durable if maintained—and could occur offseason, if change were gradual: again, "Do no harm. We went in with an idea we were not going to make radical change"—some steps Big Foot; most, incremental. The Sox needed more seats, restrooms and concessions, concourse width, and high-tech boards—above all, sponsors. That meant buying adjacent property—renovation's key. The Dodgers left Flatbush, Vin Scully said, because "Ebbets Field could be expanded only up, not out." Fenway could expand out. "It became a 10-year unfolding cycle," Lucchino mused. "Each year we had a new Christmas present to be unwrapped on Opening Day."

Newer, larger began with 160 seats adjacent to each dugout. The 2003 Townies built 14 concession stands, 220 home plate and dugout seats, a hitters and pitchers board, and NL scoreboard, doubled concourse width, and opened a concourse behind first base and beneath outfield stands. Dicier was scrapping the Screen for Green Monster seats, in four rows atop the Wall. Said Sean McDonough, "They look like they could have been here a hundred years," topping *Boston* magazine's best Hub-seat list: so choice they are only sold online. 2004: Budweiser's Right Field Roof added 192 seats, in-seat service, and standing room. A Third Base Concourse aped the sub-outfield stands'. 2005: The First Base Deck expanded. AL East standings joined the Wall's Sox inning-by-inning score. At 80, actor Dick Van Dyke said he was "circling the drain." Fenway's new sand-based drainage system circled the field, let play continue longer, and ended how "when it rained very hard," Boston's Museum of Science said, "fish from the Charles would often swim out of the first base camera pit onto the field."

In particular, management fretted over the clubhouse's effect on signing and keeping players. "When it rained," said catcher Jason Varitek, "you reached the dugout on wood boards with water running underneath and wires [almost] falling on you." The Sox weight room was literally "a hallway," four feet wide; their then food area, now Ortiz's locker. Up went players and family lounges, a new dining area, and four rooms for weight training, hydrotherapy, coaching, and interview/video—"night and day compared to what it was," said pitcher Tim Wakefield. 2006: Each line's pavilion level grew. Nearly five hundred new speakers distributed sound. Glass came down between the field and .406 Club, adding 1,300 open-air seats in the second- and third-deck EMC Club and State Street Pavilion, respectively. 2007–2008: Standing room and State Street swelled, a Third Base Deck rose, visiting batting cage was relocated, and luxury suites gussied up.

A new 412-seat "Coca-Cola Corner" hailed the oldest (1912) Sox sponsor. Most of the original concrete lower seating bowl was repaired, waterproofed, and seats replaced or redone. Bolstered: stairways, utilities, and infrastructure. Succeeded: a single video scoreboard, by three high-definition boards. Added: a ticket booth and dugout, field box, loge box and right-field terrace seats. Night and day 37,495 and 37,067 capacity, respectively, included EMC Club/State Street Pavilion, 4,997; box, 13,650; grandstand, 11,929; bleachers, 6,448; Monster, 269; and Right Field Roof, 202. In 2009, having done more than "do no harm," Smith joined Lucchino and Jon Miller on the Baltimore-Boston shuttle, returning to Camden Yards as O's vice president of planning and development. *USA Today* named Fenway "a cathedral," rebuilt pew by pew.

In the last half-century, baseball has often snatched defeat from victory. Sentence commuted, Fenway snatched victory from defeat. Referencing the grim reaper's Yankee Stadium, Old Comiskey, and Tiger Stadium, Seth Livingstone wrote, "That Fenway is standing at all, let alone bustling at its seams nightly with patrons . . . is an amazing story of history and business savvy."

In *The Making of the President 1960,* Theodore W. White compared the sailor and navigator. The former "knows the winds and can brave the storm and recognizes the tide." The latter had "direction . . . knows and is guided by the stars." Less sailing than navigating, the triumvirate later formed the Boston-based New England Sports Ventures, renamed Fenway Sports Group, buying 50 percent of the Nascar auto racing team Roush Fenway Racing and the British football club Liverpool for $488 million. Subsidiary Fenway Sports Management, Inc., became a top marketing firm, "selling $60 million in sponsorships annually for properties it represents," said the *Wall Street Journal,* including its first individual, basketball's LeBron James. The gravy train's driver was baseball revenue. The Sox first topped 2.7, 2.8, and 2.9 million in 2003, 2004, and 2006, respectively, drew a still record 3,062,699 in 2009, and even hit 3 million in the walking wounded's 2010–2011—100.6 percent capacity.

Without blaspheming a Currier & Ives steeple, being a civic religion helped. Locally, each week 2 million heard Castiglione & Co. A normal game drew 25 per-

cent of the radio audience—"unheard of," said WEEI GM, sales, Jim Rushton—
almost triple the average share. Also helping: the region's young high-tech, high-
income, and highly educated workforce, Livingstone wrote, able "to pay the [game's]
highest prices": standing room, $20/25; infield grandstand, $52/55; loge box,
$95/99; field box, $130/135 (complete list, Appendix C). "People could afford
it," said Joe, "and the Red Sox dominate the area. So staying at Fenway worked."
Lucchino had liked former O's Brooks and Frank Robinson and Jim Palmer and
Boog Powell on the air, in the front office, even selling barbeque. "What's the good
of a home, if you're never in it?"comedian George Grossmith said. A new Legends
Suite helped Sox alumni revisit *their* old home—Tiant, say, watching a game with
groups or individuals. Ex-Townies festooned scouting, suits, or media: Eckersley,
Rice, Yaz, Evans, Malzone, Harper, and Jerry Stephenson joining Remy.

In 2004, Pesky and Doerr joined Boston mayor Thomas Menino near Gate
9A to dedicate The Kid's statue. Next year the Monster Pole was named for Fisk:
In August, Gowdy last visited Fenway. 2006: Right field's pole was renamed for
Pesky. Special nights feted 1946 and 1986. 2007: One event after another hailed
1967. 2009: The pre-1970 in-play flagpole was dedicated to recently deceased
Dom D. Each Father's Day thousands played Catch on the Professor's carpet.
"Red Sox Nation"'s forty thousand members home and abroad could watch bat-
ting practice from above the Wall. Fenway ambassadors, players, and alumni's
Winter Caravan ended with the team equipment truck leaving for Ft. Myers. Red
Sox Destinations scheduled trips, where you could get a seat. The Yard's color
scheme skewed red. Castig met a man who had seen every Sox game in Kansas
City since it got the A's in 1955. In Anaheim, the Nation filled seats of many leaving after the seventh inning to miss traffic. "We're the home team," Joe laughed,
"for half of our games away."

By 2011, the Red Sox Foundation, baseball's largest team charity, had raised
more than $50 million for the Dana-Farber Cancer Institute and earned the first
Commissioner's Award for Philanthropic Excellence. Vowing to raise $3 million,
the Home Plate Program helped veterans returning from Afghanistan and Iraq
with combat post-traumatic stress disorder and/or traumatic brain injury. The
franchise rebuilt a children's baseball field in a Dominican orphanage, helped the
Make-A-Wish Foundation, began a Japan-Youth Baseball Exchange, and funded
tutoring and mentoring in the Boston public school system. If a successful life
must include serving others, the Townies tried.

Theo Epstein and brother Paul founded the Foundation To Be Named Later, money collected from the Hot Stove, Cool Music concert series. Names to revisit this account fought childhood cancer, disability, and heart disease. Wakefield founded Wakefield Warriors; Mike Lowell, a Foundation; Varitek, Tek's 33s—his number; Youkilis, Hits for Kids; Ortiz, his Children's Fund. Any scoreboard message—birthday, wedding, Bar Mitzvah—helped charity. The team Yearbook reciprocated. Bank of America, Kraft Farm Foods, and Pulte Homes—"America's No. 1 Home Builder"—hailed "New England's No. 1 Team." A musical, *Johnny Baseball*, "shone a light on the ending of the so-called Curse." The Boston Pops produced *The Red Sox Album*, including "Casey at the Bat," "Suite from 'The Natural,'" and "Sweet Caroline," Fenway's eighth-inning ode.

In 1997, Amy Tobey began working for BCN Productions, a film and video communications firm: her job, choose the Fens' 1998–2004 music. Liking "Sweet Caroline," hearing it played elsewhere, she decided "to send the sweetness over the Fenway speakers," scheduling on a whim. In 2002, the triumvirate asked her to play the tune daily, "loving the crowd reaction." Not all agreed, saying it toadied to chic pink-capped Johnny-come-latelys there to appear, not cheer. "The wine-and-cheese crowd," said one Boston school teacher. "Even when we lose, they don't care. I hate that song. It's stupid."

Each side liked a yearbook ad quoting Updike's "[At Fenway] everything is painted green and seems in curiously sharp focus, like the inside of an old-fashioned peeping-type Easter egg." Which came first, the chicken *or* the egg? Sox charity, or popularity? Answer: a team very different from early '60s air horns sounding all over New England, Robert Creamer wrote, when Don Buddin and Pumpsie Green completed a double play.

In 1995, the Sox inked their first New Millennium building block: Wakefield, knuckling over three decades, four U.S. presidents, and two titles, seven times winning 10 or more games starting and relieving, his ERA and record as good as 2.81 and 17-8, respectively. In one year or another he Kd four batters in an inning, led the league in hit batsmen, and became second-oldest first-time All-Star (42, *v.* Satchel Paige's 45), first Townie to win the Roberto Clemente Award (Ortiz encored), and Red Sox all-time leader in innings pitched (passing Clemens). In 1997, Seattle's Varitek and Derek Lowe arrived for reliever Heathcliff Slocumb: less *North by Northwest* than *To Catch a Thief.* Varitek became the regular catcher,

Gold Glover, three-time All-Star, and fifth captain since 1923, hit as high as .296 with as many as 25 homers, and at one time made only eight errors in 268 games. "The rock," Castiglione said. "Day in and out, he played battered, beaten [like Wakefield, retiring in 2012]. The Red Sox didn't win without him in the lineup."

The Red Sox won after Manny Ramirez arrived in 2001 having already hit a single-year 45 homers, batted .333, and driven in a Cleveland-record *165* runs—baseball's most since Foxx. Manny now denotes faking injury, huffing, "Boston doesn't deserve a player like me"—teammates, sick of him, agreed—and slugging Sox 64-year-old traveling secretary Jack McCormick for not leaving "enough tickets" to a game. Then, he meant strength, plate discipline, and superb hand-eye skill. Ramirez could spray the ball, advance a runner, or hit 450 feet with one hand. Like Ruth, he was gluttonous. Like Pete Rose, his universe was him. Like Clemente, Manny was uncanny in the clutch: 555 regular-season and record 29 postseason homers, third-best 21 slams, and wall-to-wall top 10 Sox all-time in going deep, RBI, batting, slugging, and on-base percentage, extra and total bases, and walks. In 2004, he hit 44 doubles; 2005, parked 45 dingers; 2006, batted .321. His real adieu was 2007's LCS *v.* Cleveland, with nine walks and 10 RBI.

By 2008, mates *asked* Epstein to chart an L.A. trip-tick. Ramirez proceeded to flunk a Dodgers drug test, join the White Sox and Rays, and fail a second test in 2011. Rather than be suspended, he retired without telling Tampa Bay: Manny Being Manny, *SI* wrote, "meaning cowardice." In 2002, this all lay ahead, like free agent center-fielder Johnny Damon four straight years leading the Sox in steals. That season he, Nomar, and Manny paced the league in triples, doubles, and average, respectively. Boston had two 20-win pitchers for the first time since 1949: Lowe 21-8, Pedro 20-4, the club second a fifth straight time. In January 2003, Ortiz, a 6-foot-4, 230-pound Dominican who greeted people *bro* or *papi*—hence, named *Big Papi*—left Minnesota for the Fens: .288, 31 homers, and 101 RBI the *worst* of his next five years. Said Joe, "He and Manny may have been baseball's best duo since Hank Aaron and Eddie Mathews."

That August, Ken Coleman, 78, died, leaving sons Casey, since deceased, and William. Bill Mueller's batting title was Boston's fourth in five years. The wild-card Sox hit a franchise-record 238 homers, scored a second-best-to-1950 961 runs, beat Oakland in a five-game DS, then went forth to the 2003 LCS—the usual rival, with the usual result. At New York, Papi, Todd Walker, and Ramirez dinged: 5-2, Sox, Wakefield winning. Game Two: Andy Pettitte beat Lowe, 6-2. Three: At

Fenway, Martinez and Clemens met again, Pedro hitting the Yanks' Karim Garcia in the back, then berating catcher Jorge Posada. "I'll never forget Martinez jabbing a finger into the side of his head," said Castiglione. "Some [like now stripes coach Don Zimmer] thought it meant a beanball coming."

Next inning Manny, ducking a Rocket pitch, charged the mound as "both benches emptied," said Jerry Trupiano. Zimmer, 72, "threw a punch at Martinez," who, confused by role reversal, "threw him to the ground." A cop tried to keep Zim from again charging Pedro, 31. Joe: "Don Zimmer is down." Trupe: "You hate to see this, but emotions are running very high." Castig: "It wasn't that close." Jerry: "Manny overreacted." Mr. C. later took a longer view: "Zimmer, Clemens, changing teams: the whole Red Sox–Yankees intersection." The 4-3 Sox loss ended with the Yanks' Jeff Nelson and groundshelp fighting in the pen. In Game Six, Boston, down, 6-4, rallied to tie the LCS, 9-6, Trot Nixon homering in the ninth. "What a game!" Joe bayed. You ain't seen nothin' yet.

The final threatened to put the Curse in perpetuity. Pedro led, 4-0, then 5-2, at The Stadium. In his book, *Now I Can Die in Peace*, Bill Simmons claims Epstein and the triumvirate told second-year skipper Grady Little to yank Martinez when he a) threw a hundred pitches or b) finished the seventh inning. In the eighth, "I'm a little bit surprised to see Pedro out there," said Trupiano, Mike Timlin and Alan Embree warming. Castiglione nodded: "I think he'll have a very short leash here"—as it happened, not short enough.

Watching, Mike Dukakis saw that "it was clear Martinez had lost it. Where were the relievers?" Nick Johnson popped out on Pedro's 107th pitch. Derek Jeter then doubled, Castiglione saying, "The Yankees have new life"—livelier than he hoped. Bernie Williams batted, Trupe confident that "you'll see . . . Embree." We didn't, Bernie singling to score Jeter: 5-3. Joe announced, "Here comes Grady Little. Pedro does appear to be tiring." Then, Trupe, amazed: "*He's staying with him!*" Joe: "Pedro said he wanted to stay in there, and Grady Little's giving him the opportunity to do so." If this were an opportunity in disguise, as Churchill said, "it appear[ed] to be very effectively disguised."

Hideki Matsui doubled, Williams scoring. Joe: "Still, no sign of Grady Little." Trupiano: "The bull pen has been so dominant, I'm surprised that Pedro is still in the game." He had a lot of company. Posada hit a dunker "to shallow right-center—and it is going to drop for a hit!" said Mr. C. "We're tied at five!" Little had "rolled the dice," said Trupe, like McCarthy (1948), Darrell Johnson (1975), and Zim (1978). Joe: "This is stunning. Absolutely stunning." Jerry didn't "understand. The bull pen has been so good."

In the eleventh inning, still tied, Trupe noted Donald Trump and Regis Philbin three booths away "trying to incite the crowd." Few remember Nixon's, Kevin Millar's, Ortiz's, or Jason Giambi's two homers: only Aaron Boone, past midnight, lofting Wakefield's pitch. "There's a fly ball deep to left! It's on its way! There it goes!" howled the stripes' Charley Steiner. Joe was less a good-time Charlie: "Swing, a long drive to left field! Down the line! Deep toward the corner! If it's fair, it's gone! And it is—gone! A home run! The New York Yankees have won the pennant!"

As Bob Starr once said of Joe, the Nation had been "harpooned" again. "And the hands of fate have dealt New England baseball fans another very cruel and unbelievable ending," said Mr. C. The Yankees were "going to the World Series for the thirty-ninth time in their remarkable history!" Steiner added. Sox history was remarkable, too, if you could look past the pain.

Trupiano: "There's going to be a lot of conversation about how this game was handled over the next few days."

Joe: "Over the next several years, probably."

Just another fall in the Fens.

Think of postseason as a TV cliff-hanger—"cliff-dweller," Mets manager Wes Westrum malapropped—like *Dallas*'s "Who Shot J.R.?" Ought-three's segued to 2004 like two veins from a common mine. "Petey, I might not be here anymore," Little told Martinez after Boone's *touché*. He got that right. Next month new skipper Terry (Tito) Francona acquired a 2001–2002 45-13 bull. Curt Schilling led the 2004 Sox in ERA (3.26), innings, complete games, and victories (21-6), fanning six for each walk—he and Pedro first Sox teammates with 200 Ks in a year. (In 2009, Schilling retired with the best all-time K-walk ratio of anyone with 1,500 innings [more than four-to-one] and postseason percentage of at least 10 decisions [11-2's .846].) "We need guys who save runs," said Epstein, trading Garciaparra in July for first baseman Doug Mientkiewicz and shortstop Orlando Cabrera. Papi and Manny *meant* runs: first post-1931 AL mates to reach .300, 30 homers, and 100 RBI. "Papi'd hit the Wall," said Joe, "then the bleachers or right-field pole. Impossible to defend." Each home game sold out, one precedent preceding another.

By now, Castiglione taught broadcast journalism at Northeastern and Franklin Pierce Universities, was Jimmy Fund charity-club liaison, and grasped retired Jesuit priest and Boston College historian John Dillon Day's terming radio an apostolate to the shut-in, disabled, and elderly. "That showed me I was freeloading for life," Joe said, writing 2004's *Broadcast Rites and Sites*, a how-to for the road. It was not required reading. The October of its release is. Boston swept the DS: 9-3, Schilling tearing his right angle tendon sheath; Martinez, 8-3; and 8-6—"Swing and a fly ball to left field! Way back! Way back!" said Trupiano. "The Red Sox are going to the American League Championship Series on the back of David Ortiz who hits a two-run walkoff home run in the bottom of the tenth! And the Red Sox win it! Ortiz has sent this town into a delirium." The feeling would return.

Schilling lost the LCS opener—Yanks again—10-7. Next night Pedro pitched, having once said, "They beat me. I just tip my hat and call the Yankees my daddy." The Bronx crowd gave a Bronx cheer: "Who's Your Daddy?"—stripes, 3-1. A change of scenery further unhosed the Sox, 19-8: "a silver lining," said Joe, "how Wakefield gave up a next-game start, saying [in the fourth] 'Give me the ball. I'll give you some innings'"—a gift that kept on giving. Castiglione recalls thinking, "The Red Sox are better than this"—just not good enough to pivot an 0-3 game deficit, since no postseason team had. A night later "every pitch for the Yankees has the pennant riding on it," said Trupiano. It was an unforgettable five hour and two minute ride.

In the ninth, up, 4-3, reliever Mariano Rivera walked Millar, thrice threw to first base *v.* Dave Roberts, then fired outside as the pinch-runner tried to steal. "Here is the throw! Roberts dives, and he is *safe*!" said Joe. "Stolen base, Dave Roberts the hand tag. Jeter took the throw. It was close—*very* close at second"—as Castig later added, "the single most important steal in Red Sox history." Mueller then lined a single. "Here he [Roberts] comes. Bernie Williams's throw is cut off—the game is tied!" Three innings later Manny singled, followed by "Ortiz, so many times the hero for the Red Sox," said Trupe. "Trying to have the ball club jump on his back one more time." Papi channeled the right-field seats. "Jump on his back, fellahs, the Red Sox win! [6-4] David Ortiz, another walkoff home run! This one in the twelfth! And the Red Sox live to play again!"

Next night the Sox led, 2-0, trailed, 4-2, and "hung in there," Joe said, six relievers pitching eight scoreless innings. In the fourteenth, Ortiz added a bloop to his blast. "And a little flare, center field! The ball falls for a hit! Here comes Johnny

Damon with the winning [5-4] run!" Trupiano crowed after postseason's longest (5:49) game. "And David Ortiz has done it again! The Red Sox will play . . . tomorrow night in New York. Another wild celebration at Fenway Park!" The crowd chanted, "Who's Your Papi?" The poet Homer would have loved tales in which the Townies have been rich: 1941, .406; 1948, Denny Galehouse; 1960, The Final Swing; 1967, Yaz; 1975, Fisk; 1978, Jim Woods's "Suddenly the whole thing is turned around"; 1986, Scully's "through Buckner." Few top the Bloody Sock.

Doctors had vainly tried to stabilize Schilling's tendon, which kept popping out of place. Before Game Six, team doctor Bill Morgan's new procedure—"three sutures forming a wall to keep it intact"—helped Curt pitch seven innings, stirrup soaked in blood. In the eighth, ahead, 4-2, Sox reliever Bronson Arroyo got tying run Alex Rodriguez to tap near the mound, tagged him near the line, and had the ball jarred loose. "It rolls down the right-field line!" Joe said. "Jeter hits third, and he's going to score! A-Rod at second. He should have been out!" Later, he conceded thinking a "mental 'Not another Red Sox tragic moment!'" Instead, umpire Joe West ruled obstruction—"They're pointing to Jeter [to return to third]," said Castiglione, "and A-Rod's *out*!"—leading some to throw debris and Boston to leave the field.

Series tied, Joe previewed his LCS-ending call—"Before, why *would* I? The Yankees, way ahead, had history on their side." He found that Boston's last "significant victory" *v.* New York had been in 1904—"then-Highlander Jack Chesbro's wild pitch scoring a pennant-clinching run"—*one hundred years before*! The stripes won when it counted: "McCarthy relieving Kinder, Dent, Boone, always *someone*!" Next evening Ortiz "hammered a [first inning] drive deep to right field!" said Castig. "And this ball is gone": 2-0. Next inning Damon also lined "back toward the corner! [Gary] Sheffield looking up! Grand slam!" then later went deep again—"Way back! Upper deck!"—for the leadoffer, three hits and six RBI. An 8-1 lead gave Joe more time to think. "My call had to mention this unparalleled comeback, and how it beat the *Yankees*."

Boston's heart of darkness was not so easily assuaged. In Brookline, Dukakis turned to wife Kitty and said, "You know, we could still lose." At almost the same time, he later learned, Larry Lucchino turned to Tom Werner at The Stadium and said, "You know, we could still lose." Loathing statistics, Dizzy Dean called them *statics*. (It is doubtful he knew they derived from the Greek word *statikos*.) Despite

four regulars batting .300, the Sox were outhit, outscored, and outERAed in almost every LCS category—but games.

In the ninth, Embree, Boston's fourth pitcher, relieved Timlin. At 12:01 a.m.
October 21, pinch-hitter Ruben Sierra grounded to second base. "Pokey Reese
has it!" whooped Castiglione. "He throws to first! And the Red Sox have won the
American League pennant [10-3]—their greatest victory in team history! In the
104 years of the Boston Red Sox, this is the most *important* of them *all*!"—beating
"their archrival. Move over, Babe, the Red Sox are American League champions!"

Later, Joe termed his view fact, not opinion, "for without that victory what
happened next doesn't happen."

Garciaparra's trade helped transform the season. "He'd been hurt, was unhappy,
felt in a fishbowl," Trupiano said. On July 24, Varitek shoved his glove into Rodriguez's face after A-Rod was hit by a pitch, started for first, charged Arroyo, and
began a brawl on Fox's *Game of the Week*. Mueller's two-run ninth-inning belt beat
the Yanks' Rivera, 11-10. The 2004 World Series *v.* St. Louis lacked such a hinge.
Like the 1963 Dodgers, 1966 Orioles, and 1989 Athletics, Boston never trailed.
Still, Joe rebuffed thought of letdown, since "beating the Yankees would have
meant less if the Sox had lost the Classic"—another what-if. The Series scripted
what John Henry called "the biggest story in New England since the Revolutionary
War." Not wishing to contradict, Castiglione smiled. "I think he understates."

At Saturday's opener, Aerosmith sang the National Anthem, Yaz threw out
the first pitch, and a local band played "Tessie," from 1903. Four Sox errors blew
a 7-2 and 9-7 lead before Mark Bellhorn's "high fly ball deep down the right-field
line!" said Joe. "Down by the Pesky Pole! [Larry] Walker looking up! It hit the
foul pole!"—11-9. Next night Cabrera, Varitek, and Bellhorn each had two RBI,
Schilling tossing six shutout innings: Townies, 6-2. In politics, a bloody shirt is an
issue raised speciously. The again bloody sock was TV vérité. On Tuesday, Martinez blanked the Swifties for seven innings, Ramirez dinging—"This one is long
gone!"—and doubling Walker at the plate: "Manny coming in, still coming in,
still coming in! The runner tags! The throw to the plate! And he is out at home!"
said Trupe—4-1.

Unlike the LCS, Boston's 3-0 game edge let Joe anticipate a Series-ending
victory. Damon homered, leading off. Nixon added a fifth-inning bases-loaded
double: "a fly ball to deep right-center! It's off the wall!" said Trupiano. "Here

comes Ortiz! Here comes Varitek!"—Sox up, 3-0. Expecting the worst, since it invariably happened, Dukakis told his wife, "This is brutal. Turn the TV off." That morning Castiglione had decided the script must write itself: "I just hoped the final out would be definitive, no checked swing, trapped ball, did he or didn't he catch it?" In the seventh inning, he went to a restroom to change, expecting a post-game bath. Seeing an old friend, Cardinals farm director Bruce Manno, Joe explained why he was there, immediately regretting it: "Hey, Bruce is about to be swept. Thankfully, he understood."

By the ninth, Trupiano was in the clubhouse, Joe, alone, so focused "I wouldn't have heard a firecracker go off under me." Reliever Keith Foulke got Scott Rolen to fly out and Jim Edmonds fan. A lunar eclipse canopied Busch Stadium—a World Series first. Lightbulbs mimed a phalanx of fireflies. Before 2004, Joe's greatest call "hadn't happened yet." It did Wednesday, October 27, at 10:40 p.m. Central Time. "Two outs in the ninth inning here on the banks of the Mississippi River. They're all up on the railing by the top step of the dugout. Poised, some appear almost giddy." Edgar Renteria swung. "A ground ball, stabbed by Foulke! He has it! He underhands to first! And the Boston Red Sox are the world champions for the first time in 86 years! The Red Sox have won baseball's world championship! *Can you believe it?*" The question was rhetorical.

"The Boston Red Sox have forever put that 1918 chant to rest as this band of characters who showed great character all season have won the world championship for New England!" said Castiglione, who hushed, then recited, "And there's pandemonium on the field!"—feting "another person," he said of Ned, "never felt so good"—and *The Green Fields of the Mind*: Baseball "is designed to break your heart," except that now it sounded, as Fitzgerald wrote, "like a tuning-fork that had been struck upon a star." MVP Ramirez hit .412. Fox cheered the highest Series rating since 1996. Lowe said no crowd would ever chant "1918!" again. The *Globe* swelled the daily press run from 500,000 to 1.2 million, the headline "YES!" dwarfing its front page.

That Saturday a rolling rally of 17 amphibious vehicles began at Fenway, turned onto Boylston Street, then Tremont Street and Storrow Drive, before entering the Charles River. It passed under the Harvard Bridge, the Nation on each bank alight—more than 3 million of the devoted and deranged. Offseason the world champion Boston Red Sox took the Commissioner's World Series trophy to New York; Los Angeles; Atlanta; Washington, D.C.; Florida; the Dominican;

every New England state; and each of Massachusetts's 351 towns and villages—
Castiglione's signature now *Can you believe it?*

In New Haven, Lucchino, the Yale Law School alum, asked Joe to repeat it,
rapture all around. Shortly Castig began classes at Franklin Pierce. "Read, work,
build a reputation," New England's most recognizable voice told students. "Then
don't mislead. Above all, 'to thine own self be true.'" Hamlet would have liked the
'04ers showing how "the play's the thing."

In 1986, The Kid had vowed to drink a glass of milk and sleep soundly the night
the Sox won a Series. In 2004, sleep was optional, unlike other drinks of choice.
In Cooperstown, future Hall president and then publicity director Jeff Idelson recalled being "infatuated with baseball in grade school, from playing and following
the [1960s and '70s] Red Sox." Jeff visited Fenway on Opening Day and his June
birthday, "my parents having the foresight to assure I was born during the baseball
season." With only one in three regular-season games televised, radio and print
were his link to the outside. Idelson helped his "green-thumbed father" tend the
yard while listening to Coleman, Woods, and Martin. "We absorbed every word,
and our conversations were reserved for commentary about the game." Priorities
led granddad to desert Sunday's family barbeque for a Studebaker car radio, Jeff
joining him. At night, he "scored box scores on a legal-sized yellow pad of paper"
and heard the Sox from Anaheim and Oakland near midnight, "my radio quickly
moving to muffle the sound when the occasional parental check came to be sure
I was asleep."

Ultimately, Connecticut College '86 became Sox publicity intern, then Ken
and Castiglione's WRKO, WPLM, and in-booth research staff. He found statistic,
quote, and note, including "Chili Davis getting his nickname because his grandmother cut his hair with a chili bowl on his head." Jeff ran coffee, handled in-game
wire copy, and glided to station identification, "doing anything the two announcers needed." Coleman "was a storyteller and poet," Idelson trying to "stimulate
memories from years ago that related to [Ken's] game that day." Castig's brief
starred "unsurpassed preparation." Jeff left the Fens gasping why Voices become
beach bud, mountain messenger, and pillow pal: "A radio broadcaster has to re-
mind you of sitting around a fire, hearing tales."

Few warmed more than *Sports Illustrated* naming the Townies "2004 Sports-
men of the Year"—a professional team first. In another precedent, NESN "pen-

etration growing, soon [2006] there was no free local-team TV," said Orsillo, in '04 still sharing balls and strikes with McDonough. That December Sean was sacked, having kept his 1960s spring training scorebook, won a five-time New England "outstanding play-by-play" Sports Emmy, and led Boston's market with daily radio's *The McDonough Group*. "People tune in for the game. I'm not a television star," he said, next doing baseball for 2011 ESPN. McDonough thus missed 2004's coda: "as fine a [home 2005] Opening Day," said Orsillo, "as the old yard has known."

Each Townie got a Series ring, presented by soldiers wounded in Afghanistan and Iraq. An Indian yarn describes not "knowing another person" unless you "stand in his moccasins." The Yankees wore Boston's, watching from their dugout, giving the new titlist a hand. Pesky, Doerr, Yaz, and Dom D. helped current Sox raise the championship flag. Five red pennants on the Monster hailed 1903, 1912, 1915–1916, and 1918. A "2004 World Series Champions" banner dwarfed the rest of the Wall. Hub son James Taylor sang "America the Beautiful." The Boston Pops Orchestra played "The Star-Spangled Banner." Bobby Orr, Bill Russell, Tedy Bruschi, and Richard Seymour each threw a ceremonial first pitch. The Sox beat New York, 10-5: like a year earlier, the shoe on the other foot.

Family was the day's one-size-fit-all, with Castig's son Duke interviewing: ultimately, New York MY Fox 5 sports anchor and *Sports Extra* and WWOR MY 9 Yankees post-game host: once WHDH Hub anchor, ESPN *SportsCenter* and *Around the Horn* guest host, and *Sunday Night Baseball*, World Baseball Classic, and WCBS New York reporter. (Mr. C.'s other children: son Tom and daughter Kate.) Publicly, Duke copped Yankees pitcher Randy Johnson's first Big Apple interview, later grilling Kirk Radomski, ex-Mets employee, steroid dealer, and key source for 2007's (former U.S. senator George) Mitchell Report. Privately, he one-upped Fox TV's Joe Buck, whose dad aired baseball from 1954 to 2001.

"Joe," Castiglione said, "were you ever doing something in high school or college that you shouldn't be doing when you heard your father's voice on radio and told yourself, 'Whoops, I shouldn't be doing this?'"

Buck laughed knowingly: one broadcast junior to another. At a pool, in a convenience store, dad followed on one radio after another. "People talk about an inner voice," said Duke. "Mine was an outer voice. There was no escaping him." Pause. "Not that I'd want to, of course."

By 2005, there was no escaping Hispanic radio/TV in increasingly multilingual Boston. The 1953 Braves deserted the Jimmy Fund, which became the Sox official charity, whereupon Yawkey freed cash, The Kid visited countless children, and Gowdy, Coleman, and Castiglione Sr. took players from Fenway to see patients at the clinic. In 1994, Joe met 12-year-old Uri Berenguer, the nephew of Juan Berenguer, pitching for seven teams, notably Detroit—*Senor Smoke*. At three, Uri had been diagnosed with histiocytosis, a rare form of blood cancer, a Panamanian doctor wanting to amputate his leg. Instead, mother Daisy took Uri to Dana-Farber Cancer Institute, where "he didn't know till waking," said Castiglione, "that the leg had survived."

At 16, cured, Joe's intern learned to "keep out-of-town scores, do odd jobs, and keep statistics between treatment and playing high school ball." Uri graduated from Boston Latin School and Northeastern University, ran the Spanish Network board, and in 2003 became a mikeman, his idol J. P. Villaman, "so enamored with the team that he would hug, even kiss, players before interviewing them," read the *Globe*. In the 2004 World Series, Villaman's voice broke as Foulke underhanded to first baseman Mientkiewicz, screaming "*Boston gana!*" ("Boston wins!") seven times into the microphone—his "simplicity of heart," *The Great Gatsby* read, "its own ticket of admission."

In April 2005, Villaman got a Series ring. On May 30, Mother's Day in the Dominican, J. P. called his beloved 88-year-old aunt, not knowing that "he was saying good-bye," said cousin Susie Villaman. He and Berenguer broadcast at Yankee Stadium, got back to Fenway at 2 a.m., and laughed "how ESPN games take forever because of all the commercials," Uri said. "We gave each other a hug and I said, 'See you tomorrow, Papa.'" Driving home about 3:40 a.m., Villaman, apparently speeding, lost control of his Ford Explorer, hit a truck on Interstate 93, rolled down a slope, and hit a tree. He was 46.

Berenguer, 23, and Bill Kulik aired that night's game at Fenway. "I can say it is almost impossible to do this, but I have to . . . because I know that is what he would want," Uri said, crying about "a brother—every *hello* and *good-bye* a hug. It's Latino culture, and that's who he was: the most passionate broadcaster I've ever known." As the reader knows, Villaman ended each broadcast by saying, "This game is yours." Tonight Uri said, "J. P., this broadcast is completely yours, *companero*."

In 2010, Berenguer joined NESN TV and .com, next year rejoining 2002–Soxer Oscar Baez, of Bani, Dominican Republic; ex-Yankees minor leaguer and host of the *Conversando de Deportes* talk and *Calentando Brazo* Spanish *Beisbol* pre-game show. "Both are still close to the Jimmy Fund, especially Uri, running in its yearly Marathon," said Joe, citing a woman named Rosie Lonborg—to Berenguer, "my play lady"—a weekly volunteer at his clinic.

One day Uri saw a 1967 video of Jim Lonborg pitching. "Look," he said, "there's Rosie's husband!"

In 2005, the Fens looked to Wakefield: Sox-best in wins, ERA, innings, complete games, and strikeouts. Schilling got his two hundredth victory and three thousandth K. "Unbelievable control," said Castiglione, "could be a prima donna, but ice cold under pressure." An old cigarette ad puffed, "I'd walk a mile for a camel." Schilling walked that long for a camera. Boston won the wild card, losing the Division Series to Chicago. Halloween night Epstein resigned as general manager over what *Yahoo! Sports* Rick Blaine dubbed "a dispute over his level of authority" with, among others, mentor Lucchino. Theo avoided scrutiny by leaving his office in a gorilla costume. "Growing up in the shadow of Fenway Park," he said, "I never dreamed of having the chance to work for my hometown team during such an historic period. My affection for the Red Sox did not begin four years ago when I started working here, and it does not end today."

Next January Epstein returned as GM and new executive vice president, "resolving differences" with Lucchino, Blaine wrote, and getting "assurances about his role" from Henry. Offseason the '06ers lured Marlins Josh Beckett and Mike Lowell: 16-11 and team-high 47 doubles, respectively. Rookie regular Youkilis batted .279 at first and third. In his first full year, Jonathan Papelbon had a 0.92 ERA. On September 21, Papi's 51st home run broke Foxx's 1938 franchise-high 50. "There's a fly ball! Right-center field deep! Back by the bull pen!" said Joe. "And David Ortiz has set a Red Sox record!" Papi led the AL in homers (54) and RBI (137) and slugged a career-high .636, Boston's worst-since-1997 third place not keeping 2,930,588 away.

In February, Gowdy's death at 86 predeceased wife Jerre, daughter Cheryl Ann, and sons Curt Jr. and Trevor. A decade earlier the Cowboy had been feted by the Smithsonian Institution. Beforehand he did a radio interview in his room, the host phoning tardily. "I don't need this grief," Curt told me—yet did. In 2003 and

2008, Tim McCarver's seventy-eighth Classic TVcast and Joe Buck's thirteenth Series, respectively, topped Gowdy. "It's hard for a great broadcaster to let go," said Castig, "but Curt's legacy's intact"—more, say, than Trupiano's. Axed in fall 2006, Jerry was rumored by the *Herald* to be headed for the Cardinals. How could he? said the Missourian. "No talks took place." The Townies gave no reason, not even a release.

That year Entercom Communications bought Red Sox radio through 2016. Renamed flagship, WRKO tapped Glenn Geffner and ESPN's Dave O'Brien to replace Trupe in 2007. (Sister WEEI did weekend/weekday night.) Miami's Geffner graduated Northwestern University's Medill School of Journalism '90; did college, single, double, and triple-A, 1997–2002 Padres PR, radio, and *Padres Report* TV; became Sox VP, communications; and resumed broadcasting at the 2006–2007 Fens (NESN play-by-play and host, *Red Sox Report*, and WTIC Hartford *Red Sox Insider*). Born in suburban Quincy, raised in New Hampshire, O'Brien was pitch-perfect for Irish Boston. His way home began with Syracuse '86, Atlanta WSB talk radio, University of Georgia football/basketball, Falcons, Braves, and 1993–2001 Marlins, trying to make an upper deck tarp, statues of Dolphins owner Joe Robbie and coach Don Shula, and football sight lines baseball-cool.

Even large crowds got lost, or cheered a visitor: "Why are they *against* us?" a Marlin later said after a Red Sox game. "It feels as if we should be wearing gray uniforms." O'Brien and Joe Angel countered with "context, insight, situational nuances, [and] history," wrote Larry Lebowitz. In 1997, each added TV, Dave asking what Hall of Fame slugger Hack Wilson would make as a free agent—"Can you say Albert Belle times two?" At break, O'Brien joked, "Knowing what we know, we couldn't say on the air what he would have spent it on"—hooch. The '97 Fish won the Fall Classic. Next year Dave won the Achievements in Radio play-by-play award for Mark McGwire's 59th homer. In 1999, the now pathetic Marlins drew 8,628 to a game. "You have to be more creative," he said. "More storytelling and less play-by-play."

In 2002, O'Brien added more coverage: ESPN's regular season, DS and Series, soccer, including World Cup and *MLS Primetime Thursday*, and basketball. Next season he left Miami for a place christened in 1964 with Holy Water from Brooklyn's Gowanus Canal and the Harlem River at the spot it passed the Polo Grounds: To Dave, Shea Stadium would always be cursed. Was he still upset over

1986? Said the Mets' new TV Voice: "Upset doesn't cover it." In 2005, ESPN's refusal to release Dave kept him from joining the Cubs and its WGN TV super-station—and increasingly at its Bristol, Connecticut, campus. "A lucky break," he later said. "I was free when the Red Sox called."

By 2007, "*Monday Night Baseball* kept Dave from doing some [Sox] games," said Castiglione, "so Glenn helped us out." *Left* out was Trupiano. "Their [Boston] deciding so late [in 2006] kept me from a '07 job," he groaned, doing Minor League Baseball promotions, Westwood One NCAA College World Series color, and WBZ-FM *The Sports Hub* talk—an involuntary phased big-league withdrawal. In 2007, Trupiano and son Brian called a taped-delay cable access game between the Brockton Rox and Oil Can Boyd's Traveling All-Stars. Having vanished so suddenly, cryptically, Trupe taught at Young Broadcasters of America, buoyed the audio social media startup Lexy.com, and clutched a play-by-play lifeline of not being fired, just not rehired.

In the *Globe*, Ted Weesner mourned "The Lost Voice of the Red Sox. Many feel like a loved one has been stolen away," comparing the Townies to "Lenin [purging] Trotsky's image from official photographs." A blogger eulogized "The Joe and Jerry Show. They sounded so summer and so *Bahston*." The *Brockton Enterprise* noted "Trupiano on the Lookout." He still is, six years after his last big-league pitch. Websiter Jim Devlin explained the unexplainable: "Broadcasting is no less political than most other businesses."

The Sox liked Geffner. Entercom liked O'Brien, whose top ESPN twin-killing lay ahead: Barry Bonds's numbers 755 and 756 in 2007. As Gordon Lightfoot sang, Trupiano "walked away" like a "movie star who gets burned in a three-way script." By then, another ex-Sox Voice had become ESPN's TV 1990– *Sunday Night Baseball* prosopopeia. "It's an exciting opportunity," Jon Miller said, "if you consider standing on the edge of a cliff exciting."

In 1991, Miller won his first play-by-play cable ACE award. "I am incredibly honored to win this award with this room full of talented people," he said. "What am I? I go to games and my best lines are, 'low, ball one,' or probably the line I'm most proud of—'line drive, foul.'" Jon was still bonkers over Scully. "Vin's so great that young broadcasters emulate him. I hear it everywhere—'the 1-1 pitch, looww.' Even abroad you can't escape him," Miller reliving a trip to Japan: "One reason I went was to hear the Yomiuri Giants' Yoncharo Assami." Watching TV, Jon stared. "*He's* doing Scully! '*Atashiwa Carokwa in stadium neormas. Hagima Mashde dose-ruski llloowww.*' I go to Caracas. They're doing Vin in *Spanish*!"

A September 6, 1995, Orioles-Angels game historic in any tongue became official after 4½ innings. "For baseball, what great news!" said Miller on O's radio—Cal Ripken Jr.'s record 2,131st straight game. The Warehouse banner ditched "2-1-3-0." Cal tipped his cap on a hand-shaking/high-fiving voyage around Camden Yards. "My goal was always to be a Voice synonymous with one city," Jon later said, "like Ned, Harry Kalas in Philly, or Vin in L.A." He was happy, in his adopted burg, barbing and critiquing.

Jon's contact expired in 1996, three years after Peter Angelos bought the O's. "Jon's not much of an advocate," the new owner huffed—what Miller called "a homer." Agent Ron Shapiro called Angelos, who refused his call. "The Orioles never said we want you gone," said Jon. "They just never made an offer." Shapiro finally set a contract deadline, making Angelos phone the *Baltimore Sun*: "This is an employee, mind you, issuing an ultimatum to the owner." Finally, Miller friend George Will offered to intervene.

A day later the columnist phoned the soon-to-be-ex-O's announcer. "Well, Jon, I talked to Mr. Angelos."

"Yeah?" said Miller. "What'd he say?"

"If I were you, I'd start packing my bags."

In short order, Angelos proved the Law of Unintended Consequences by "letting me [Jon] go home." In 1965, Miller's father, returning from a trip to Minnesota, had told him, "The Twins got *nothing* on Russ [Hodges] and Lon [Simmons]. The *voices* of those Giants' two!" In 1997, Jon joined Lon at Candlestick Park, replaced by Pacific Bell Park three years later. "I grew up with these guys. Now it's like the early '60s. The Giants usually contend. Their new park is a showplace. I hated to leave Baltimore but am happy where I am."

Miller wrote *Confessions of a Baseball Purist*, made the National Association of Sportswriters and Sportscasters and Baseball Halls of Fame, built a Moss Beach house, could see his boyhood home across the bay, and studied ships in McCovey's Cove. Loving to sail, he flew a hundred thousand miles a year. One day: ESPN, from Puerto Rico. Next: Jints opener, as pre-game emcee. Yearly Jon took a post-season cruise. "By cruise's end, man, I'm juiced. Baseball! Forget spring training. I'm ready for the new season by New Year's Day."

In 2010, ESPN Radio's Series Voice aired the Giants first title since 1954. On November 3, Jon rode in San Francisco's victory parade, "hundreds of thousands of people . . . all joined in joyful celebration." At City Hall, he emceed a salute to "the whole panorama" of the post-1957 franchise: Willie Mays and Willie Mc-Covey hailing Buster Posey and Tim Lincecum. Miller then took a cruise to England, saying: "There won't be any parades with a million people along the route, I'm pretty sure." That week ESPN inexplicably ended his *Sunday Night Baseball* TV reign, Jon returning to local wireless.

Thirty years after Fenway Miller still loved baseball's "company. It comforts you, and you like it." *Dis*liked: peers panting for a shorter game. "'What?' 'This is in your way?'" Jon laughed. "'You need to be somewhere else? Man, we have the best job in history. What exactly *would* you rather do?' Baseball announcers are the world's most fortunate people. I say that even though I feel I'm underpaid." He paused, perhaps recalling late 1982: "We'll rectify that in our next negotiation."

12 ENCORE AND AFTERWORD (2007–)

"Two thousand and four was for our parents and grandparents and those people who suffered through eight decades before a world championship," Tom Werner said. "This [2007 World Series *v.* Colorado] was for us and for our children, and for everybody in Red Sox Nation." The encore had something for everyone.

Josh Beckett's 20-7 topped the league. Japan's Daisuke Matsuzaka—aka Dice-K—finished 15-12. Clay Buchholz, 23, threw the first Sox rookie no-hitter *v.* "the Orioles in his second major league start!" said Joe. "And the first one to greet him is Big Papi!" Mike Lowell led in RBI (120), played a Ft. Knox third base, and was a model citizen: to Castiglione, "maybe the most popular Red Sox since Yaz." Ortiz had a fifth straight year of at least 31 homers (35) and 101 RBI (117) or more. Dustin Pedroia hit .317, struck out 42 times in 520 ups, and had a dirty uniform by batting practice. Right-fielder J. D. Drew started a Sox tenure of consistency and mediocrity. Mirabile dictu: The 2007 Sox *became* the Speed Boys, stealing 96 bases in 120 attempts—80 percent. Jacoby Ellsbury, 23, stole 9 in 33 games, hit .353, and became a teenage heartthrob. "Some of the signs at our rolling rally proposed marriage," said Joe. Others would at one time have made mama wash her daughter's mouth out with soap.

The Sox led the East after April 17, drew a record 2,971,025 home (36,679 average) and 3,130,043 away (38,642), and pleased a new wireless sponsor— "Shaw's [Supermarkets six-state grocery store chain] WRKO Red Sox Radio Network." After a DS lark *v.* L.A.—Beckett, 4-0; Manny's "long drive to left!" said Joe. "Deep into the night. Three-run walkoff [6-3] home run!"; and Ramirez going "deep to center field [in 9-1's Game Three]!" O'Brien cheered. "This one is gone! Way, way back onto the rockpile!"—the LCS *v.* Cleveland was a closer-run thing. Papi and Ramirez reached base all 10 at-bats in a 10-3 opener. The Tribe then won, 13-6, 4-2, and 7-3. "Bad news: we're down three to one," said Castiglione. "Good: That's better than 2004."

Beckett won Set Five, 7-1. Back at the Fens, Drew earned his pay next game. "A fly ball, center field, hit well! Back goes [Grady] Sizemore to the warning track, by the fence. And it's gone!" Joe chimed—Boston, 12-2. Dice-K became the first LCS Game Seven rookie starter. Uke hit the Coke bottle. Pedroia "swings and a drive out to deep left-center field!" said Glenn Geffner. "[Kenny] Lofton is back at the wall! Good-bye!" A six-run eighth waved the flag, 11-2. Said Castig, "the first playoff series clinched at Fenway since 2004!" Not only chicks dug the long ball: The Townies slugged .521. The offensive series had a Gold Glove end. Joe: "High fly ball! [Center-fielder] Coco [Crisp] going back! Still going back! To the Triangle! Going back! He makes a great catch—the Red Sox have won the pennant! Falling down, he hangs on!"

Like 2004, the Fall Occasion debuted at Fenway, the AL taking July's home-field-deciding All-Star Game. Pedroia became the first Series rookie to homer, leading off. "Deep left-center field! Back by the wall it goes!" said Castiglione. "It is off the top of the wall! [No] It is a home run! The umpire got it right! It hit above the ledge, bounced back on the field!" Ortiz, Ramirez, and Julio Lugo each had three hits, Beckett breezing, 13-1. Game Two: Boston employed small, not long, ball, scoring on Varitek's sacrifice fly and Lowell's double; Schilling, 40, became the second oldest to start and win a (2-1) Classic game. Papelbon picked off the tying run, "firing over there and he [Matt Holliday] was out by plenty," said Castig. Game Three: Townies romped at Coors Field, 10-5, Ellsbury and Pedroia 7 for 10. Worth the wait: 12 pitchers forged a longest Series regulation 4:19 game.

"Want some history?" said Geffner on WRKO. "Ellsbury and Pedroia, first rookies to bat 1-2 in the order in a World Series game. Ellsbury, first with four hits [in a Classic game] since Joe Garagiola [*v.* Boston in 1946]." Lowell stole third base—first Townie in a Series since 1975. Said Castiglione, chuckling, "Mikey may not be the fastest runner, but he's among the smartest." On Sunday, October 28, Joe attended Mass in Denver with his family and Lowell's, a close friend who "in the Series was on fire." Leaning over, he told wife Jan, "If Mike gets a double and a home run tonight [Game Four], he'll be Series MVP." First, Lowell doubled.

Later homering—"ripped toward left!" Geffner said. "Back goes Holliday! Good-bye!"—he was voted Series MVP. Said Mr. C., "Maybe I should play Vegas."

In the ninth inning, ahead, 4-3, Boston's best fireman since Radatz faced Seth Smith. "Swing and a miss! It's over!" Castiglione said of Papelbon's K. "The Red Sox have swept the Colorado Rockies. The Red Sox are the world champions of baseball for 2007! And the Boston Red Sox become the first team in the twenty-first century to win two World Series titles!"—subtly knocking the Yankees, never far away. Townie hits (event-high 18 doubles; Terry Francona, second Sox skipper to win two Series; O'Brien's 2004–2009 MLB International's Classic gig) swamped their misses (Papelbon's idiosyncratic "Riverdance").

The duck boat ride through downtown was as sublime as the Sox .333 Series batting average, trailing only the 1960 Yanks' .338. "We won. They lost," Pirates fan Lucchino reminded you. The rivalry still went yard.

Castiglione had now won the Dick Young Award for excellence, entered the Italian-American Sports Hall of Fame, aired New England College and Northeastern hoops, had part of Franklin Pierce's ballpark named for him, and become a family member like Curt, Ned, and Ken. The New Englander knew that objectivity was in a listener's ears. "We don't openly root here—it's a little too sophisticated a market for that—but we do pull for the Red Sox." The history major knew that the Townies "are a historical team and that this whole region is filled with history." Ronald Reagan said that if you give a person 15 facts and one anecdote and "the story is told well, it's the story he remembers." Castig empathized: "a great story-teller," said WEEI's Jim Rushton, "and if you are, people listen."

As Joe would tell you, persona helps paddle baseball's dead air. A three-hour game may put the ball in play eight minutes. "Other sports carry the announcer," said the Bay Area's Hank Greenwald. "Baseball announcers carry their sport." Harry Kalas painted like a minimalist. Dick Enberg weds wearability and melody. Felo Ramirez says grace around the Marlins' tank. Whoever the Voice, they haul a story from the shelf. Castiglione used extempore prose to keep a listener. In 1960, Joe Garagiola wrote the seminal *Baseball Is a Funny Game*. Boston's Joe especially liked to call gotcha on himself.

One night O'Brien addressed how Castig was no, um, techie: retexting past messages, an accidental 3 a.m. phone call, a song about Joe somehow appearing on his iPod next to Taylor Swift's and Marvin Gaye's. He liked high-definition TV—assuming he could turn it on.

"I could really use a permanent Geek Squad," Joe confessed.

"You need a personal assistant," Dave agreed. "That's going to be my Christmas gift for you. A full-time PA."

Castiglione: "I'll take it."

After break, O' Brien praised Joe's "good-naturedness" about being technically challenged.

"I know my limitations."

No high-tech could save an especially slow game. "So we've played two really quick innings here," said Mr. C.

Dave: "Yeah, moving right along."

Joe: "You were clean shaven when this game began."

Like Werner, Castig grasped how 2004 and 2007 differed. The first "was for dead relatives and friends who hadn't lived to see a title," many putting bats and balls and Sox caps and pennants on a gravesite, including his brother-in-law on Joe's late dad's. Rolling rally signs cited a childhood frère, college classmate, Uncle Fred, "You won one for my grandma"—catharsis. Ought-seven hailed success. "We were baseball's best team," said Castiglione, not certain in 2004. Each year Fenway was "my office"—pals coming in and out; an usher, groundskeeper, vacationer from Nova Scotia, season-ticketer from the Cape; the "peanut vendor who's been there forever and sausage guy across the street." Inside, "most fans never see the passageways and shortcuts": ground equipment behind the Monster, door behind the scoreboard, staircase to an interview room, batting cage, or pen. To Mr. C., Fenway was a fine stage for hide-and-seek—as mysterious as Stephen King and unpredictable as Poe.

A Wallward belt made Joe pause, "never knowing if the ball might scrape the paint coming down." Hope a drive carries? "Pray the wind blows out." Want an outfielder exposed? "Hit to the Triangle." Like an inside-the-parker? "You've come to the right place." Everywhere were "nooks and crannies"—Giamatti's "eccentric angularities." Often Castig returned from the road in Sinatra's "In the Wee Small Hours of the Morning" to find a sudden magic place. "There'd be nobody there," he said. "I'd look out on the field, which was almost mystical. Imagine: a fabled ballpark to yourself. You walk alone up a gangway, view the field lit only by the clock, see lights on Ted Williams Way, and watch Fenway just before dawn—it's breathtaking." Less senior Sox mikemen nodded, hoping to match Castiglione's niche as New England personality of baseball in the flesh.

By 2007, Orsillo had called Cal Ripken's last game, been named Massachusetts Broadcaster of the Year, and twice helped the highest-rated regional sports network win a local play-by-play Emmy. NESN's Beanpot hockey, Boston College basketball, and Sox 60-minute pre- and post-game and twice weekly 30-minute *Monster Fenway* show popularized high-definition (HD) coverage. Don did ESPN's Big East, Cox Sports Providence hoops, the Farrelly Brothers' 2004 film *Fever Pitch* with Fox's Tim McCarver and future MLB Network's Harold Reynolds, and TBS 2007 wild card playoff and 2008–2011 DS—learning to his chagrin that some locales weren't as batty as Boston about ball.

"On the road," he said, "you rely on home-team camera people and stage managers, one of their jobs to complete the out-of-town score sheet with information from the ticker." One night in Texas, Rangers publicity director John Blake declared on the press-box intercom that a pitcher was tossing a no-hitter elsewhere. Hearing "no-hitter" with his headset on, Orsillo, removing it, asked a young lady, "Did you hear that announcement?"

She hadn't.

"Will you go and ask John Blake what he just said?" Don said.

"The no-hitter isn't happening in our game," said the baseball novice, returning.

"No kidding," he replied. This wasn't Yawkey Way.

Fox TV Voice Josh Lewin often laughs, "I know I'm not everyone's cup of tea." Lewin was scored for being slick; Orsillo, by some for lacking glitz. WEEI called him "Dynamic One," or "DO," for being *uber*programmed: "That's gonna grab some wall . . . the batter carves one foul . . . down by way of the K! . . . tardy on the cut!"—a home run "deep, far, gone!" In a NESN ad, Tim Wakefield called Don "announcer boy"—43 in 2011. Most found him solid and accurate, less Jim Britt than Curt Gowdy—"what the typical Red Sox fan wants," said Castiglione. Unlike Joe Scallan, Orsillo knew "the territory."

Home housed wife Lisa, daughters Sydney and Madison, and pets Knopfler the dog and Arthur the guinea pig. At NESN, Downeaster Tom Caron became Orsillo's pre- and post-game host, Dave McCarty, Ken Macha, Peter Gammons, Jim Rice, and Dennis Eckersley analyzing. In 2008, University of San Diego '03 and ex-Fresno ESPN Radio and Fox TV reporter Heidi Watney became Sox reporter, keying its *Ultimate Red Sox Show*.

Yin to Orsillo's yang was *SI*'s 2004 Massachusetts favorite TV Voice, that year's Bay State National Sportscasters and Sportswriters Association Announcer of the Year, and Fox Saturday *Game of the Week* commentator. Jerry Remy also made the Sox Hall of Fame and Red Sox Nation presidency, by online vote. As Martin said, "Today the analyst is the star"—e.g., "RemDawg."

Born in Fall Fiver, Remy lived a short time in Westport, played in the Swansea and Somerset Little Leagues, and starred at Somerset High School. Drafted at 18, he was a 1975–1977 Angels regular, joined the Townies, and in 1978 scored 87 runs, stole 30 bases, and made the All-Star team. Later Jerry got six hits in a game, led the AL in double plays, and twice topped .300. One knee injury after another—10 by 2010—ended his career at 31. He averaged .275, had 1,226 hits, and played Boston's best-extended second base since Doerr. In 2002, Bill James's *Historical Abstract* called him the one hundredth best all-time second sacker.

Retiring in 1986, Jerry worked with minor leaguers, then spent a year asking, "What the hell am I going to do?" He felt guilty, Remy and wife Phoebe's three children "coming in and saying, 'Dad, what do you do?'"

RemDawg: "I don't know, I just sit here."

"Do you work?"

"Actually, no."

As we have seen, Remy became Martin's 1988 color man, Gordon Edes later writing, "This cult status he now enjoys, no one in the family saw coming." He ran Web's theremyreport.com, opened a hot dog stand called RemDawg's on Yawkey Way and three other sports bars, and wrote six books, including a *Hello, Wally!* series about Wally the Green Monster. Said Edes, now of ESPNBoston.com, "He has his own catchy nickname . . . his own book on the local best-seller list, his own make-believe friend [Wally], and adoring fans who everywhere he goes call out his name, wear his face on their T-shirts and his hat on their heads. All that, and an honored place in [New England] . . . living rooms. And now we learn that Jerry Remy used to be a tap dancer," according to another dancer, mother Connie.

"I hated it," said Remy, "but I did it. She made me. I did it until I was 14."

Where, Edes wondered, "does it all end?"

In the Fens, a just marrieds' sign read, "Will Name First Child Remy." Five men in straw hats and grass skirts held a banner in Montreal blaring, "Straw Hat Guys Love Remy." In *New York*, he inscribed a "NESN/Remy" sign, having "developed a fervent following of his own, one that identifies Remy with the Red Sox almost as closely as it does Garciaparra, Martinez, and Ramirez," the *Globe's* Don Aucoin wrote. RemDawg even shaped coverage—"He sees everything before it happens, so the camera follows him," said producer Patrick Cavanaugh—the *Globe* feting Jerry's "more substance than style, a rational observer of a team about which Bostonians often get irrational." Aucoin distilled his core: "This guy knows his stuff. And he feels our pain."

In 2003, Remy inked a four-year pact as Orsillo's cable and McDonough's free TV pal. NESN coverage hit 125 games—to Don, "a throwback for me, working every day like the minors." By fall, Grady Little gone, Jerry was rumored next Sox skipper, asking a questioner, "Want to be my bench coach?" Why would he step down? – theremyreport.com's chat room the largest of 539 baseball groups with message boards on Yahoo. In 2008, NESN held Jerry Remy Day for "20 years of service"—*full* service beyond the mike. Remy tweeted endlessly. "Long flight home. Have I missed anything? Oh, yes, the Yankees lost." "Who looks the funniest? Jerry without his mustache or Don *with* Jerry's mustache." Remy liked pasta, playing tennis, *The Sopranos*, shorts and a T-shirt, Aruba, and family. He had everything—but health.

In November 2008, the once-steady smoker had surgery to remove a "very small, low-grade cancerous area" from his lung. Recovery progressed till an April 2009 West Coast trip, when overnight "I didn't want to get out of bed. The first thing you thought when you woke up was 'another lousy day is ahead of me.'" Remy flew back to Boston, fighting depression and fatigue. Next week Orsillo read a statement about Jerry taking an indefinite leave of absence, later adding, "I think he realized he came back too early." NESN got thousands of cards and e-mails. Pinch-Jerrys included writers Nick Cafardo, Edes, Gammons, and Tony Massarotti and on-field's or booth's Sean Casey, Ron Coomer, Brian Daubach, Evans, Jim Kaat, Kennedy, Buck Martinez, Montgomery, Rance Mulliniks, Dave Roberts, Frank Viola, and Eckersley, his "Eckspeak" terming a fastball "cheese."

In August, Remy trekked to Fenway, attended Francona's pre-game press conference, and visited the booth. The crowd cheered the scoreboard showing him, Don, and Eck, Boston.com columnist Chad Finn musing why Remy's vast "appeal relied so little on the fact he once played for the Red Sox?" The Internet helped explain. RemDawg played an imaginary air guitar, brought his Wally doll to Fenway, carted an Adirondack chair to booths around the league, and greeted Spanish viewers with *Buenos noches, amigos*. A *GQ* poll named Sox TV baseball's fourth-best team, behind the Dodgers, Mets, and Giants. "You spend a season with him [Remy]," Edes had written, "he thinks you're entitled to feel like you're with him, home and away. That's why he'll tell you a funny story about what happened on the team flight, or on the cab ride to the ballpark, or something in the clubhouse that strikes his fancy."

Even if he didn't "always get the syntax right," Remy "wants you to feel like you're sitting on the next stool beside him," said the then *Globe*ster. One year the four-time Emmy honoree caught pneumonia, a theremyreport asking, "Where Has RemDawg Been?" Seventy-five answered: "Miss your voice." "Get well, fast." "Watching the game on TV is just not the same." He returned to hear Orsillo note the visiting Angels' imminent cross-country flight. The "next stool"ers presently debated whether to pick up luggage at the airport.

"Some people get it right away," Don noted. Below, Kevin Youkilis eyed the mound.

Not Jerry. "You go to the hotel and go to bed. Some people wait for their bags."

"Right," said Orsillo. Youkilis fouled away

" 'Cause they're going to get their candles out."

"Right."

"Others go right to bed," said RemDawg. "Gives you an extra hour's sleep."

Orsillo didn't need it. "I have to have my stuff, know my stuff made it. I un-pack *everything*."

"I know that," Remy deadpanned. "I could care less if my junk makes it. It's only stuff." Pause. "I was gonna say something else."

"I wish you had," Don said. Below, Youk took a ball.

Luggage dismissed, Remy lugged on. "I want to challenge you to a game of ping pong," he said.

"*Now?*" said Orsillo. "What are you *talking* about?"

"Right now," said Remy. "I'll take my paddle"—he waved a hair brush—"and let's see your paddle."

"A brush?" said Don.

Remy: "I don't think any man in the world has as big a brush as yours."

Orsillo accused his analyst of "hair-envy," then began fencing: baseball's Hamilton and Burr. At that point, Youkilis tripled to center field, match to be resumed. Returning full-time in 2010, Remy still recalled his last *full* season as clearly as a walkoff homer.

In March 2008, RemDawg had flown to Japan, the Sox playing the Hanshin Tigers, Yomiuri Giants, and Oakland A's in the Ricoh Japan Opening Series at the Tokyo Dome. Franklin Roosevelt was accused of "breakfasting on grilled millionaire." At 6:07 a.m. Eastern Time the Nation breakfasted on ESPN. Boston returned to the Dodgers' fiftieth birthday exhibition at Los Angeles Memorial Coliseum—their 1958–1961 halfway house between Ebbets Field and Chavez Ravine. "There are generations of Angelenos who have grown up as Dodger fans and never had the opportunity to see a game [there]," said team owner, New Englander, and soon bankrupt Frank McCourt. Associated Press fancied a "field . . . reconfigured as close as possible to the original": a time impossible to relive, but not to miss living.

All ninety thousand seats sold almost instantly. The Dodgers then asked the Coliseum Commission, City, and fire department, said an official, "if there was any way we could accommodate additional fans." On March 29, baseball's largest-ever crowd, 115,300, including standees, jammed the amusement park built for football and track and field. Vin Scully voiced play-by-play, two years later visiting the Fens for the first time since 1989. "I always look at the roof. I keep remembering that dark day when I began at Fenway Park in 1949. Now all I see are luxury boxes."

Like Fenway, the Coliseum still had a short left-field porch, permanent seats having cut foul-pole footage to a *Bad News Bears* 201. To compensate, the wire screen once dubbed the Great Wall of China was raised 18 feet to 60. An outside "Baseball Festival" lured thousands, ex-Dodgers manning autograph booths. Live period music featured "California Dreamin'," T-shirts hyping "I Was There." Yankees-turned-new-Dodgers-skipper Joe Torre fed the flock: "It's a privilege to share this with the Boston Red Sox," he began. "Excuse me"—smile—"the *World Series champion* Boston Red Sox. For some reason, that doesn't bother me any more."

Jason Varitek prophesied a score: "Dodgers 85, Red Sox 81." (Boston won, 7-4.) Torre's five-man infield relived the Coliseum's late-'50s description of "having room for almost one hundred thousand people and two outfielders." Youkilis played *Screeno*. Sox shortstop Lugo played a drive off the *wall*. In Oakland, the Townies *re*opened their season. On one hand, Papi plunged from .332 to .264; 35 to 23 homers; 117 to 89 RBI. Other: Youk wed a career-best .312, 29, and 115; Dice-K was 18-3; and Papelbon had a career-high 41 saves. Pedroia was Sox-best in average (.326), at-bats (653), runs (118), hits (213), and doubles (54)—and AL MVP.

On September 9, Boston trailed Tampa Bay by ½ game. In the ninth, down, 4-3, Dan Johnson cleared Fenway's pen off Papelbon, the Rays then adding the winning run. Next night Tampa Bay won, in 14 innings, later clinching its first pennant. The wild card Townies again beat L.A. in the Division Series. On ESPN Radio's Sox-Rays LCS, Jon Miller noted a *St. Petersburg Times* pre–Game One primer: how many innings, outs to an inning, where field positions were. "I don't think they need that in Boston," he said slyly. Ahead, three sets to one, the Rays led Game Five, 7-0. "We're ready to clinch," said Voice Dave Wills. "I'm thinking of tidbits I can use to close the game, since we can't lose. When we do [8-7]"—Ortiz and Drew homered—"I felt closer than in any game to literally being sick."

The 2007 Red Sox had reversed a 3-1 deficit. Tampa Bay announcer Andy Freed feared they might again. "I said I didn't think this is how the Rays' tale was supposed to end," Wills differed after Boston tied the series: "their momentum against our destiny." Tampa Bay led the final, 3-1, Townie Jed Lowrie batting. "Swing and a ground ball to second, this should do it!" Wills said. "Aki [Akinori Iwamura] has it, takes it to second himself, this improbable season has another chapter to it! The Rays are going to the World Series!" The Sox went to the last year of their best decade in 90 years.

A proverb says, "East, west, home's best." In late 2008, Boston announced a new 2012 spring training complex in Lee County, Florida, six miles from its 1993– Ft. Myers site, Fenway South copying the Wall, Monster seats, a Yawkey Way–like concourse, and footage: 310, 379, 420, 302. Like the 1999 All-Star Game, 2009 began with a lion in winter riding into Fenway on a cart. Dying of brain cancer, Edward Kennedy, 77, threw the ceremonial pitch on his last visit to the Fens. In 1912, his grandfather, Mayor John (Honey Fitz) Fitzgerald, tossed out the first ball. Kennedy threw a fastball—"the thrill of a lifetime"—caught by Rice, whose uniform number 14 was retired July 28: seventh Townie after Cronin, Williams, Doerr, Yaz, Carlton Fisk (27, September 4, 2000) and Johnny Pesky (6, September 28, 2008). In 1997, each team retired number 42 on the fiftieth anniversary of Jackie Robinson breaking the color line.

Second again—the eleventh time since 1991—the '09ers drew a new attendance high 3,062,699. Beckett, top 10 AL best in six categories, and Lester earned pitching's Triple Crown: 15 victories, 200 innings, and a sub-4 ERA. Papelbon's 133rd save topped prior-high Bob Stanley's. The Old Man and the Sox: Wakefield made the All-Star team for the first time in a then 17-year career. Victor Martinez hit .336 after leaving Cleveland. Youkilis was fourth or better in league on-base percentage, hit by pitch, and slugging. Ellsbury had a Townie record 70 stolen bases. Lowell ended the decade first in third-basemen doubles (357) and second in games (1,380), hits (1,455), and RBI (860).

A doozy of a home 2009 again drew a wild card. April 24: An eleventh-inning belt was the Sox first 2004– walkoff homer *v.* New York. "A high fly ball! This one's gonna do it! Deep to left and she is *outta* here! This one's over! Kevin Youkilis has won it!" roared O'Brien. "He flips the helmet and goes crashing into the pile at home plate!" August 11: Lowell became first to twice homer off the bench since Joe Foy. August 25: Speed kills—unusually, not Boston. "There he goes," Joe referenced Ellsbury. "Taken for a strike! Stolen base! Number 55," breaking Tommy Harper's mark. Geffner might have called it, had he not returned to Florida. On May 4, 2010, Ernie Harwell, 92, died as the Giants' Tim Lincecum Kd 13 Marlins, including two on back-to-back called strike three. Rarely purloining prose, Glenn inexplicably used Ernie's line, "Both are out for excessive window shopping." Next day, learning Harwell's 7:30 p.m. time of death, Geffner found he copied him at 7:28.

Glenn did 2008– Marlins play-by-play, *Marlins on Deck*, *Tenth Inning*, and *Rain Delay Theater*. When O'Brien covered ESPN, Castig joined Boston College '94 Jon Rish, who also voiced B.C. men's hockey and women's hoops, ESPN baseball, the NBA, and college football. Each grew up on radio disc jockeys: "personalities with a theatre of the mind," Jon Miller said. On radio, Willie Mays conjured "a great catch, going yard." On TV, "I'd mention him," said Miller, "and you see some other guy spitting tobacco juice." In person, he sat pop-eyed at Willie McCovey's pop-up: "Would it ever come *down*? Same thing on radio—you *remember* it." On TV, "You never *see* the ball!—only bat hitting it, outfielder waiting, then catch." We are unlikely to forget No. 34.

Since 2003, Ortiz had sired "one clutch hit after another," said O'Brien, "legendary blasts to win unforgettable games; such a big bear, always smiling, mobbed everywhere"—*Big Papi*. Early in 2009, hitting under .200, he went homerless in 149 straight at-bats—"the magic gone"—stranding 12 runners in a game. On July 30, a getaway day at Fenway, Associated Press reported that, like Manny, the King of New England had once tested positive for performance-enhancing drugs: to Dave, "like someone erased the sun, news hitting like a hammer." Ramirez told reporters, "You want more information, *go ask the players' union*." Ortiz said the list "surprised" him because of how "I live," vowing to address details. O'Brien took refuge in "a presumption of innocence."

Getaway afternoon was hot, "little wind," said the husband (wife, Debra), dad (children Michael, Samantha, and Katie), and Rye, New Hampshire, resident. Dave recalls thinking about Cape Cod. "With the Sox, you're cognizant of the region's fans as they're listening. Are they sailing on the Vineyard, on beach blankets on the sand in Hampton, New Hampshire, or in the dunes at Rexhame Beach, near Boston?" How would the crowd respond? Had it even heard? Batting in the first inning—"awkward for me," said Dave, "trying to insert and explain the news"—Ortiz was greeted warmly, making O'Brien feel "some people didn't know."

In the seventh, Sox behind, Papi hit with two runners on. "When they needed him, he'd always delivered," said Dave. "Now, in a day of great embarrassment, huge mistakes, and so many questions, I recall seconds before he swung, thinking, 'Well, this is what he does. He's going to hit one just like you expect him to.' And damned if he didn't crush a monstrous three-run homer to right-center to put Boston ahead [final, 8-5]." On air the Irishman used British understatement: "What a way to cap an absolutely fascinating day for David Ortiz, to say the least."

That spring Scully said that "if I come back, I'd like to come back looking like Cary Grant, dancing like Gene Kelly, and singing like Bing Crosby." O'Brien was as smooth as Donald O'Connor, describing Papi. By late afternoon, "everyone *knew* the story. It *had* been a fascinating day. I hope my voice and delivery expressed how even in these conditions, the baseball gods were still in play."

Ultimately, Ortiz left the critical list, leading the post–June 5 AL in homers (27) and RBI (78). His 270th dinger as a designated hitter topped Frank Thomas: Big Papi, trumping the Big Hurt. The Angels swept the 2009 Division Series, 5-0, 4-1, and 7-6, Boston blowing a 5-1 lead. It was like old times again: a toothache that wouldn't stop.

In late 2009, *TSN* named the Sox and Epstein "Team" and "Executive" of the last decade, respectively. Free agent John Lackey joined the '10ers, forgetting how he once went 19-9. Another Hessian, Adrian Beltre, had an MVP-type year, leading Boston in batting (.321), hits (189), doubles (AL-high 49), and RBI (102, with Ortiz) before taking $96 million from Texas through 2016. Rookie Ryan

Kalish grand-slammed twice. On June 12, 2010, a former Santa Clara University team equipment manager, minor-league journeyman, and 27-year-old Sox rookie crashed the show. On pre-game, Joe suggested Daniel Nava "swing on the first pitch, because you only get one chance." In a bases-full second inning, Nava did.

"[Joe Blanton's] pitch. A deep drive! Right field!" O'Brien, like Fenway's 37,061, pinched himself. "It is gone! It's outta here! A grand slam!"—into the Sox pen. "Daniel Nava, on the first pitch that he sees in the major leagues, has just hit a grand slam! Wow! You gotta be kidding me!"—only the second to slam on his first bigs pitch. Learning of his call-up, Daniel's parents had almost missed a flight to see him play. "I told the girl at the desk that my son was going to be playing left field in Boston, in front of the Green Monster," said Don Nava. "They had to get us on," and did. In the stands, camera flashing, dad and mom's Kodak moment was caught by Fox's *Game of the Week*, moving its announcer, old Sox friend Dick Stockton, to muse, "There's just *something* about Fenway Park."

That month a statue *Teammates*—based on David Halberstam's book on No. 9, Pesky, Doerr, and the Little Professor—was unveiled outside Gate B. Otherwise, 2010's "something" was injuries. Ellsbury crashed into Beltre, broke five ribs, and hit .192 in 18 games. Tearing a thumb muscle, Youkilis played in 102. Beckett made just 21 starts. A June weekend in San Francisco was more lost than Ray Milland's. Pedroia, Buchholz, and Victor Martinez broke bones and tore tendons: limited to 302 at-bats, 17-7, and leaving for Detroit, respectively. Twenty-four trips by 19 players to the disabled list cost a likely big-league record 1,018 games. Somehow Boston finished 89-73—"Tito's greatest job," Castig said. Lowell retired, Joe noting Hemingway's "grace under pressure." Surprisingly, radio/TV ratings fell sharply, suggesting less Sox diminution than, as we will see, general baseball malaise.

In late 2010, Epstein obtained slugger Adrian Gonzalez and speedster Carl Crawford from San Diego and Tampa Bay, respectively. "I wish titles were won on paper," a friend told Joe. "We'd be planning the rolling rally." The 2011 paper titlist began 0-6, hit 2-10, and reached .500 May 15: the latest Sox date since 1996. Boston swept the first six games at—The Stadium. Later, going 37-16, it tied for first place with—the Yanks. O'Brien and Garciaparra gave ESPN's *Wednesday Night Baseball* a Townie tilt. "Together again," Dave joked of the Sox and stripes—and/or his team and No. 5. Crawford struggled to find a comfort zone, batting first, second, seven, and ninth. One four-for-four day, dinging, he was greeted on the bench like a rock star or royalty. It didn't last. The former Ray batted .255 and treated left field like the gout.

The year's rarest play was a 5-4-3 three for the price of one. "Well, the Red Sox may not be great at double plays turned," laughed Joe, "but triple plays are another matter." Francona's "greatest play" ended a game in the Fens: "A line drive and a great catch by Pedroia, racing up the middle into the outfield!" said O'Brien: Sox, 3-1. The most bizarre was at the park whose name implied sun, breeze, and Ricky Ricardo but which linked faux grass, a roof, and cable rings, or catwalks. Once a foul soared above a zip code of empty seats. "That hits one of those lights up there!" Dave said of Tropicana Field. "And here comes glass raining down onto the infield! The crowd loves it—it's like a fireworks display. That's like a scene out of *The Natural*"—sadly, the Trop not "the best there ever was."

Gonzalez was as advertised: .338, 27 homers, and 117 RBI. Ellsbury had a .321, 32, 105, 39 stolen base, Lynn-like fielding year—fourth player with same-season 200 hits, 30 dingers, 100 RBI, and 35 steals. Ortiz and Pedroia topped .300. *Medical Center* was again full. Dice-K missed most of 2011, Buchholz went down in June, and Lackey, Youkilis, Papi, and Crawford were disabled. The Sox had "a $170 million payroll and three rotation soft spots," said *USA Today*. Wakefield won his two hundredth game, 186 with Boston: final score, 18-6. "It's over [an eight-start wait]!" said O'Brien. "Nineteen years in the making, he's done it." Another starter had eight scoreless innings in a 5:29 Trop marathon before waiting three hours—"like two games," Beckett said—for Pedroia's sixteenth-inning single to score Josh Reddick. Varitek, 39, caught each inning, Francona vowing to carry him on the plane. The 1-0 game ended at 1:54 a.m., Boston flying to Baltimore, where at 7:05 p.m. it began a 15-10 rout.

Week after week Rudy York–style ball kept the Yanks and Red Sox twinned. In one game New York thrice grand-slammed Oakland. By August, the Townies *20* times had scored in double digits. "Boy, if you're going to tell me that Youkilis [having homered in a game] is going to get hot, those [games] are going to be commonplace," said O'Brien. Youk promptly *re*homered. "The Red Sox continue to tear the cover off the ball!" That month Fenway drew *five* of its all-time 15 largest crowds, including 76,803 for August 16's Tampa Bay day-night double-header. Dan Shaughnessy had called the 1978 Sox "collapse [the worst] against which all others must be measured." Without warning, a ruler came out of storage.

On August 31, the Red Sox thumped the Yankees, 9-5: to Mike Dukakis, "really the last good game they played all year." Walking 20 minutes home, his wife said, "How can you beat this? The crowd, the team, the atmosphere?" On September 2, Boston led the East, Yanks second, Rays nine games back, then went 2-9, 5-18, and ended the regular-season 7-20: a fold worse than 1972, 1974, 1977–1978, 1986, 1988, 1990, and 2000, among others. Stripes Voice Michael Kay was sympathetic: "What's going on is hard to explain—and for the Red Sox hard to believe." Said ESPN's Rick Sutcliffe, "The Dream Team [like "SuperTeam"] is living a nightmare now."

September 13: Boston led the wild card by three games. 21: It blew a lead to Baltimore—Fenway abloom with boos. Starting pitchers came, and went. Relievers worked, and reeled. The month's staff ERA was 7.08. 25: The soon-named AL Comeback Player of the Year applied a tourniquet. "A long [fourteenth-inning three-run 7-4] drive!" said Joe at The Stadium. "Ellsbury has done it again!" Had the Red Sox made postseason, he later said, "It would've been the year's big hit." Instead, next day Boston lost at Baltimore as Tampa Bay beat New York, wild card tied for the first time since May. On Wednesday, September 28, the Sox played the year's final game to avoid having "*this* over our head," as Remy said of 1978, "for the rest of our lives."

Even at the time, the night felt magical. "Cellphones, split screens, three TVs at home [NL wild card Braves and Cardinals also tied], a [Boston] rain delay in Baltimore," said the Associated Press. It was hard to keep up—harder to keep track. New York led the Rays, 7-0. Marco Scutaro scored on a balk and Pedroia homered: Townies, 3-2. A one hour, 26 minute rain delay then began, Shaughnessy telling NESN, "The one thing eliminated is that the Red Sox season ends tonight. They live to play another day." Tampa scored six eighth-inning runs, including Evan Longoria's three-run blast: Yanks, 7-6. Dan Johnson's 2008 Fenway jolt had pivoted the East. The .108 average reserve now dinged a 7-all two-out ninth-inning pitch—like 1986, *one strike to go.* When Boston resumed, ESPN showed cut-ins at the Trop. ESPN2 aired Atlanta, *it* losing a thirteenth-inning wild card, too.

Earlier Scutaro was thrown out at the plate. In the ninth inning, Sox rookie Ryan Lavarnway banged into a bases-full double play—still 3-2. In Baltimore's half, Chris Davis doubled after Papelbon Kd the first two men. A 2-2 pitch to Nolan Reimold—*again,* one strike to go—became "Hit in the air toward the gap in right-center!" ESPN's Sean McDonough said. "It is a hit! The tying run scores for Baltimore!" Boston had won each game—77—it led after eight innings. Robert Andino now lined Papelbon's 1-1 pitch to left. "Crawford plays shallow! Can't get it!"—Carl's missed diving catch opening his ex-club's door. "Reimold comes to the plate—he scores! And the Baltimore Orioles stun the Boston Red Sox!"—4-3. Three minutes later Longoria again homered to win the wild card, 8-7: "the Sox the first team to miss postseason," said Elias Sports Bureau, "after leading by . . . nine games for a playoff entering September."

Shocked, the crowd at Camden Yards—another Red Sox "home game"—sat frozen: some having seen the plot before; post-2003 trendies spoiled by success; all (re)learning the Calvinist lesson that life is hard. "Ahhhh, the good old days," Grant McQuillan told the *Wall Street Journal*'s Jennifer Levitz, who rhapsodized, "After seven years of baseball euphoria . . . the city is back to being heartbroken by its team." As Leigh Montville wrote in 1974, we "had almost forgotten [our] inbred pessimism, [our] rooting heritage. [We] had stuffed it in the drawer."

Some felt the collapse might help Sox marquee: epic defeat richer than robotic triumph. Ortiz had none of it, hating "about the worst thing I've been part of." The *Herald* bannered, "Choke's On Us," as if the Nation needed to be told. Blame attitude, in-game clubhouse drinking and video games, or free agent busts Lackey, Drew, Crawford, and Julio Lugo, among others: next day management scrapped Francona's option—"arguably the best manager in franchise history," said Tim Kurkjian. NESN left post-news conference analysis to cover Liverpool-Wolverhampton soccer. "While NESN rival Comcast went knee-deep into analysis," Shaughnessy wrote, "the Sox flagship TV station went to soccer. Wow."

From its start, Fenway Sports Group, like NESN, had relied on a pecking order: all depended on wall-to-wall Red Sox interest. Putting soccer first—Liverpool was an FSG team—threatened to turn a full house into a house of cards. Shaughnessy couldn't forget how, "as the Sox fought [September 28] for their playoff lives, NESN . . . virtual ads [touted] next day's soccer at 4 p.m."—the exact time a one-game playoff *v.* Tampa Bay on TBS would start! "Got that?" he marveled. "On Thursday, Sept. 29, at 4 p.m., the geniuses at NESN wanted you to watch soccer—instead of a one-game playoff involving the Red Sox."

Next month Epstein resigned to become Cubs president of baseball operations, not telling if he would bring his gorilla costume. Aide Ben Cherington replaced Theo as Sox GM, in a cycle of irony saying that Tommy John Surgery would shelve Lackey in 2012. In mid-September Orsillo said, "The question had been, who'll win the East. Now it's who'll make the playoff." By mid-October the question was, "Can the Sox reverse a free-fall?" said former WITS talk host Tom Shaer. "I think the people who remain can do that in a hurry." That would await offseason: our time to *pass* the time, until the Red Sox returned.

On December 2, 2011, the Townies named Francona's successor: the voluble/ volatile Bobby Valentine, who, saying "I hate the Yankees," showed his instincts to be in sync. The hiring further raised the Red Sox' Richter scale of 24/7 buzz. "Besides winning championships," the *Wall Street Journal*'s Jason Gay gaped, "it is the [franchise's] organizational mission to absorb every last drop of attention and oxygen out of baseball's atmosphere until an astronaut on Mars is wearing a 'B' logo cap and a third of all babies born (male and female) are named Pedroia—or at least Youkilis."

Accordingly, that fall the Sox announced a 2012 centennial to remember: a visitors open house in the dugout and clubhouse; throwback uniform days; commemorative tickets baring a 1912 photo of the Gate A entrance; All-Fenway Team online voting; Mayor Menino's "Fenway Park 100 Essay" contest; "100 Acts of Kindness" to benefit charities and other non-profits; plaques, displays, historical markers, and a "Preserve Fenway Park [Archives] Fund"; and a coffee-table book, *Fenway Park*. Also scheduled: football, soccer, and "Frozen Fenway," a 16-day hockey blizzard, including community skates, high school games, and a Hockey East Massachusetts–Vermont and Maine–New Hampshire double-header.

Walt Whitman wrote, "I hear America singing, the varied carols I hear." Fenway's carol is baseball. The Braves played the 1914 Series, 1915 early season, and yearly preseason game there before moving to Milwaukee. On September 8, 1942, the Philadelphia Stars edged the Baltimore Elite Giants, 8-7, in the Fens' first African American exhibition. Quincy's Fore River Shipyard played the Negro League's New York Black Yankees, New York Cuban Stars, Kansas City Monarchs, and Birmingham Black Barons. Fenway has hosted the state high school tournament, biennial all-star game between the Cape Cod League and Athletic Collegiate Baseball League, and 1990– four-college annual Beanpot Tournament among Boston College, Harvard, Northeastern, and Boston University, then UMass.

Richard Johnson, curator, the Sports Museum in Boston, recalls other carols at 1912–1960s Fenway: less Mt. Rushmore than "a 'people's park,' where high school and college baseball and football was as much a part of the schedule as the mostly hopeless Sox." The NFL 1933–1936 tenant Boston Redskins exited for Washington. The 1944–1948 Boston Yanks became the Indianapolis (née Baltimore) Colts after stops in New York and Dallas. The AFL 1963–1968 then Boston Patriots holed up in the Fens. At one 1940s and '50s time or another, Frank Leahy–coached B.C. and Harry Agganis's B.U. Terriers rented it. The end zone almost touched boxes beyond first and third base. Even soccer shot, missing (1968–1969 North American Soccer League Boston Beacons) and scoring (July 8, 1968, Pele's Brazilian team, Santos, beat them, 7-1). Soccer returned in 2010: Celtic FC 2, Sporting Lisbon 1.

In 2011, Johnson gave *USA Today* Fenway's non-baseball top 10 list of hits and runs. 10) July 29, 1954. Harlem Globetrotters 61, George Mikan All-Stars 41. 9) September 6, 1932. Super featherweight Kid Chocolate aka the Cuban Bon Bon melted Steve Smith in a 10-round decision. 8) August 21, 2005. The Rolling Stones (twice) started Fenway up, like Bruce Springsteen, Jimmy Buffett, the Black Eyed Peas, Dave Matthews Band, the Police, Neil Diamond, and Paul McCartney. 7) January 1, 2010. The NHL Winter Classic: see below. 6) Pele: see above. 5) November 19, 1927. Babe Ruth's Knights of Columbus South Boston Lodge sponsored a football game: ten thousand watched a 34-7 New York Giants romp. 4) December 5, 1934. Beating Oak Park, Illinois, 80-0, Everett, Massachusetts, capped a 600-0 year as "America's best high school team." 3) June 6, 1914. Three circus elephants for which Hub schoolchildren raised $6,700 to buy brought fifty thousand to the Franklin Park Zoo. 2) November 16, 1940. In overwhelmingly Catholic Boston, forty thousand saw one school of the Cross, 11-0 Boston College, edge another, Georgetown, 19-18. 1) November 4, 1944. Like 1932, 1936, and 1940, Franklin Roosevelt campaigned in Boston, which supported him each time he ran for president. Frank Sinatra wowed bobby-soxers. Orson Welles spoke, FDR once telling him, "You and I are the best actors in America." Ten thousand listened by speaker outside Fenway.

As a child, I saw Guy Lombardo become New Year's Eve, his clientele so posh it had to inhabit a separate planet from mine. The 2010 NHL Winter Classic starred a sport so different from baseball as to frequent a separate orb. Fenway's remade rink sardined a crowd of 38,112. More than 6.5 million watched on North American TV and nhl.com, hearing NBC's Mike Emrick's *brio* prose. The game ended Bruins 2, Flyers 1: Mark Recchi tying late in the third period; Marco Sturm scoring in overtime; ice positioned between first and third base, players entering from each dugout.

Towers lit the rink. Seats behind the goals paralleled each foul line. A week later the Fens hosted a college men's and women's double-header. Like 2012's "Frozen Fenway," public skates scent of small towns and frozen ponds—the New England winter of *Yankee* magazine. It was still hard to forget the summer game, the Nation viewing the pastime through itself. Some year the Red Sox might again find a final strike.

13 POSTLOGUE

Boston likes to be thought of as different—*attitude*, you might say. In baseball, the difference works, the Hub and its exterior a big-league redoubt. In 2009, Entercom Communications again made WEEI Red Sox flagship. Two years later, WEEI FM 93.7 became co-flagship—"making sure," said Castiglione, "you can get us anywhere on the dial." Their network listed 69 stations by 2012: Maine 17, Massachusetts 13, New Hampshire 13, Vermont 10, New York 6, Connecticut 5, Florida 2, and Rhode Island, Colorado, and Wyoming 1 each. Nashville Predators Voice Pete Weber says of hockey's *bleu, blanc et rouge,* "Montreal Canadiens fans care *too* much." That can be true of the Olde Towne Team. Some ask what the Red Sox mean. Visit New England in the summer, as my parents did Fenway on their 1949 honeymoon. Read the *Globe* and *Herald*. Listen to Joe and Dave and Don and Jerry at an ice cream stand, on the street, in a car. At a diner, inhale what Gene Kirby dubbed "baseball's patter." On the beach, hear a thousand radios, as ubiquitous as body oil. Have a priest, preacher, or rabbi ask, "How about those *Sawx?*" You will understand what the team—what Fenway—means.

It is true that baseball's health affects—how could it not?—the Townies'. It is also true that if every franchise were the Red Sox, baseball would be far nearer a Baby Boomer's sun, moon, and stars than a partial or full eclipse. In 2011, Cambridge University released the book *The Cambridge Companion to Baseball*. Research for my keynote chapter saddened me. As Bob Costas said, "Baseball's place in society is not nearly what it should be." At worst, the game is in cultural decline, especially among the young.

In a 1960 Gallup poll, baseball routed football, 39 to 17 percent, as America's "favorite game." The 2009 pastime trailed, *43 to 11* percent, losing each demographic: white, black, brown, rich, poor, middle class, small town, city, and suburban: "in every metric," said *SI*, "the NFL's stance as America's game is undisputed." In 1952, each World Series game averaged 1 in 2 U.S. TV viewers; 1980, 1 in 5; 2011, 1 in 16. The 2012 Super Bowl lured 1 in 3, or 111 million: the most-watched show ever. A year earlier football forged 19 of the 20 top-rated sports events, the Pro Bowl outrating the *All-Star Game*. Dallas Cowboys owner Jerry Jones says, correctly, "The most popular *TV* sport is America's most *popular* sport."

Baseball commissioner Bud Selig says that "our game has never been near this popular," ignoring falling attendance and football's wide lead in video game sales, licensed garb, unique Internet users, and "marketable athletes" lists. Hollywood once meant *Bull Durham* and *Eight Men Out*. In 2009, football's *The Blind Side* became sport's all-time highest-grossing film. Long-term, the *Wall Street Journal* cites "gloomy studies suggest[ing] kids are losing interest"—7- to 17-year-old baseball players down 24 percent, hockey and football up 38 and 21 percent, respectively, in a decade—noting municipal parks turning baseball fields into soccer, football, and lacrosse. The decline has been over time, not overnight. Recovery is not inevitable—also not impossible.

A good person with whom to start is actor James Earl Jones. "America has rolled by like an army of steamrollers," he mused in *Field of Dreams*. "It's been erased like a blackboard, rebuilt, and erased again. But baseball has marked the time." America's army steamrolls battlefields, historic shrines, even homes under eminent domain. "Wow," Steve Martin said, mocking transience in another movie, *L.A. Story*. "Some of these buildings are more than 20 years old."

Fenway's renovation will let the Red Sox stay an estimated 30 to 40 years. "That doesn't mean the next stewards of the franchise will want to stay and play here," said Lucchino, "but this will be an alternative." One alternative was not another name. "I don't think you will ever see—at least during our time period"—a Geico Park, he added. Antithetically, the 2009 Yankees left one Stadium for another, keeping its name. A saw says you can't buy tradition. The stripes vainly tried to transfer it, not grasping what they had.

Since 1923, Yankee Stadium had meant a drop-dead look of monuments and sloping shadows and steep-ridged seats. Until 1974–1975's generic makeover, The Big Ballpark in the Bronx's numbers wrote a feel-good shrine: left field, 301 feet: left-center, 457; center, 461; right-center, 407; right field, 296. Acreage and triple tiers *built* the stage. Winning—27 pennants there through 1964—*filled* it. If The Stadium wasn't broke, why fix it? Pricey ticket, concession, and luxury suite *greed*.

Wall Street's Gordon Gekko says, "Greed is good." It can be blind, too. The 57,000-seat Stadium's last four years drew 4 million, including 2007's record 4.2 million and 2008's selling out after June. A year later the House That Greed Built opened to bile reserved for Sarah Palin—except at least she grasped the middle class. Prices for the 52,325-seat venue included $525 to *$2,625* home plate and dugout-to-dugout boxes, making the Sox seem like Tobacco Road. Associated Press once counted only 37 of 146 posh seats filled. Selig "broke down all the prices of all the seats, and they are affordable." That is true, if you're Warren Buffett.

TV's center-field shot showed first-row boxes behind the plate emptier than a politician. A top-that insult was Major League *Soccer's* head twitting the Yankees' gate: Charles Atlas, decked by the 98-pound weakling. The Old Stadium had first- and third-base camera wells: "a must for a new park," said the *New York Post's* Phil Mushnick. The New junked them for vacant stands. The Old's exquisite low home-plate camera was unobscured by an angled backstop. The New's vertical screen blocked half the infield, like peering through prison bars. Yogi Berra said he observed a lot by watching. We rarely watch what we cannot see.

Old Stadium decks perched one atop another. *New* right field's upper tier seemed remote as Jersey City, the design helping sound leave between the grandstand and bleachers. "You guys call yourselves Yankee fans?" the *Times* quoted a patron. "Make some noise!" Renovation could have restored The Stadium to, say, 1964. "No ballpark could hold a Louisville Slugger to that place," Scott Pitoniak wrote in *Memories of Yankee Stadium*. Castig recalls how "like Fenway, anything could happen. A 300-foot homer, a 450-foot out. They could have made the Stadium like it was for Mick." Instead, baseball's flagship team paved paradise for those in the counting house. Disraeli said, "It was worse than a crime. It was a blunder."

Few liken the $1.5 billion New Stadium to PNC Park, AT&T Park, or Camden Yards. Edward Bennett Williams compared his Redskins and Orioles, asking, "What's dumber than the dumbest *football* owner? The smartest *baseball* owner." Even the post-1970s Old Stadium was the game's *primus inter pares*—Latin for "first among equals." As a recent visit shows, Fenway Park is now.

In 1960, at age nine, I thought Fenway massive. Half a century later it seems closer to a den. As *SI* once wrote, few come by car, parking limited to gas stations, private lots, or crowded on-street spots. Most still use public transportation, bus routes and commuter trains ending at the park or Kenmore Square. Emerging, you pass shops, apartments, and industrial buildings, see Fenway's two decks and light towers, and read a poster, "Bleachers Straight Ahead." Taxis jam one-way streets. Charter buses from outposts of the Nation pack bars and eateries from The Diamond at Fenway to Cask 'n Flagon. As Dick Stockton said, "There's just something about Fenway Park." In 2011, certain Sox pitchers conceded drinking in-game "Rally Beer." On Opening Day 1998 (Good Friday), Jimy Williams said of a ban on alcohol, "I make it a point never to drink on the bench."

Senses mix: fried dough and Cajun chicken and hot pretzels. Stores sell baseball cards and jackets and jerseys and pennants and photographs. Fenway's diagram fills a local building window. Across Yawkey Way, hopefuls tangle for standing room. Tykes with baseball gloves and Red Sox pants and caps take dad's hand, spy the Sox, league, and American flag, enter through ground-level archways in Fenway's brick facade, and walk into the tunnel, up a walkway, and toward the field. "When I made the big leagues in 1967," Russ Gibson said, "my hometown [Fall River] tossed a day for me. I was a rookie." Like then, Fenway is the Towne Team's hearth.

At his first game there, Lyme, New Hampshire's Jared Duval, age six, learned the ballpark's etiquette: "You stood and sang, not just for the national anthem, but for all the songs; you actually watched the game; you freely shared the rules and history of the game with any newcomers around you; you were generous to the kids; you high-fived complete strangers; you stood and cheered as loud as possible for home runs and diving catches; and, yes, you booed players when they needed it." Most of all, he said, "we were all in it together."

Some left-field stands still turned back toward center—"at least giving a good angle into the [Sox first-base] dugout to see what's going on," one patron said. Another, columnist Brenda Kelley Kim, occupied "by far the best seats anywhere in the park, anywhere in the world"—the front row behind the dugout. Dad, a former Triple-A umpire, sat next to her, each hooked less by on-base percentage than by the yard. "Fenway is about the sausages you can smell a block away from the park," she wrote. "It's about the big envelope that came every February with the tickets for all the home games. Red Sox baseball is about Fenway Franks, the

Green Monster, and the little baseball-shaped car that used to bring the pitchers in from the bull pen." Brenda missed the car, but reverie kept it close.

One night Jon Lester served a curve—or was it Ellis Kinder or the Gentleman? Another day a fielder neared the Pesky Pole—but was he the Golden Boy or Dewey? The Prudential Building, Citgo sign on Beacon Street, and Monster remained real as any relative, yesterdays buzzing like cicadas around the scoreboard. Baseball's sole "in-play" ladder evoked Jim Lemon's 1950s fly ricocheting for an inside-the-park homer. Above, seven players hit pre-Monster seat uprights: Conigliaro, Jensen, Brooks Robinson, Malzone, Mantle, Mike Easler, and Gene Conley. Center field's roped-off seats, once Conig's Corner, still elicited Tony C. "It's all here," Brenda marveled. "An entire century."

Envision baseball at Lambeau Field. You can't. Put basketball in Montreal's Bell Centre. Square pegs don't fit in round holes. Here the flag still whips in or out—a pitcher's or hitter's wind. The message board still bays, "Welcome to Fenway Park: Home of the Red Sox," tying average, player photo, and ads to pay the bills. The sound system blares Madonna, not Lawrence Welk, but the Wave still seems wayward. After a game the crowd scatters around and from the Hub. Police corridor the field. Ushers hurry stragglers. Depending on score, standing, and time of year, Fenway casts sweetest air or saddest thought.

Alexander Chase said, "Memory is the thing we forget with." In the Fens, we remember. "Fenway's not old, but sacred," the Sports Museum's Richard Johnson said in 1998. "For the city or state to tear it down would be like the government of Greece tearing down the Parthenon." It was the Greeks, he recalls, who said, "Let the games begin." They still do, a hundred years after Fenway's birth.

"In life, you try to learn from the best in their field," Curt Gowdy said in 2005. "Why doesn't baseball try to emulate the Red Sox?" In 1965, his question would have seemed absurd. Today most teams would kill to be as popular. Below, several thoughts on the game: some, generic: others, specific—if not to "emulate" Fenway and the Red Sox, at least to learn.

1) Hire announcers who are harmonic with the market. Harry Caray spun existential pleasure in St. Louis and Chicago. New England might have deported him. Dizzy Dean said, "Pod-nuh, you ain't just a woofin.'" Boston might have felt Ol' Diz a dog. Popular in New York, John Sterling might land in stocks in the Hub. Different folks like different strokes.

2) If baseball is a great *talking*, it is a greater *writing*, game. Few teams can duplicate the Nation's academic and literary lineage. All can serve 2012's print media, including Internet. Imagine the Sox sans the *Globe*: unthinkable. Even radio's company ends on sign off. Print's can be endlessly reread.

3) Only hockey and college football even approach baseball's history. Tradition runs deeper through The Kid, Silent Captain, El Tiante, and Pudge than clubs born after they retired. At the same time, any franchise's former players can be strung like popcorn around a tree.

4) A park should be a participant, not spectator. "You *cared* about players because you *knew* them," Harmon Killebrew said of his Metropolitan Stadium, the Fens, Tiger Stadium. "See 'em sweat, hear 'em curse"—he never did—"it only happens with real parks": a watercooler, not library. For Dolphin Stadium to stir interest, Miami would have had to blow it up.

5) A local cult must precede America's. Brooklyn made the Dodgers a national team; Midwest, Cardinals; ChiTown, Cubs. The Townies' century-old Connecticut to Maine proprietary ownership "forms an aura," said Castiglione, "that charms the neutral fan"—thus, Red Sox Nation. This possibility may not apply to the Arizona Diamondbacks.

6) Even Boston needs big-league marketing. "Football works no matter who's on TV," said NFL Films' David Plaut. The majors rely on the Sox and Yanks. ESPN's 2011 large-market Cubs-Mets drew *half* of same-month Florida International-Louisville football—to *USA Today*, "Yikes!" *Brooklyn Bridge* creator David Goldberg said, "Life used to stop" for a Boomer's World Series. Unless your club qualifies, does today's Series even count?

7) Each team, including the deep-count Sox, must quicken a glacial pace. America took Normandy, split the atom, reached the moon. Baseball won't enforce the strike zone, batter in the box, or bases-empty rule mandating a pitch each 12 seconds. A 2-1 game often tops three hours. The 1960 Series final scored 19 runs in two hours and 36 minutes. As culture turns less patient, baseball turns more inert.

8) Duplicate Fenway's close-up coverage—especially home plate's low, yet above a wire backstop, shot. Avoid putting the camera booth above swanky suites, and/or behind a sight-blocking screen. What a recipe for losing a generation: little happens, and you can't see what does.

As the prologue notes, I am glad the Sox term Fenway "America's Most Be-loved Ballpark." I would be happier if baseball grasps what makes the Sox the Sox—"Fenway kills you, thrills you, but never bores you," said Costas—fueling deep-down caring in a skin-deep age, whether a Dante of damnation or next-year Christmas Eve.

October 2003. Aaron Boone joins Dent and Buckner. The Sox then wooed Deliverance: Like the British, Alex Rodriguez was coming! "Three-quarters of me was already wearing a Sox uniform," he later said. The other quarter won. John Henry blamed no salary cap for A-Rod joining the stripes. Irked, George Steinbrenner mocked Boston's "failure." When would it end?

October 2004. The earth turned flat. Tiny Tim sang bass. For the first time since 1918, the Sox shed ghouls and ghosts and spooked-up nights, the diaspora communing by phone, mail, in person, by Internet, observing, like fife and drum had at Yorktown, *The World Turned Upside Down*.

Such passion is hard to find.

A 1943 novel proclaimed *A Tree Grows in Brooklyn*. A park stays in Boston: play-ers, under a cloudless sky, with the moon over baseball's Oz. Castiglione says, "We travel well." So does Fenway—for me, to a place 240 miles away, near "the mountains [that] stood in their native dress, dark, rich, and mysterious," James Fenimore Cooper wrote in *The Deerslayer*, "while the sheet glistened in its solitude, a beautiful gem of the forest."

On July 23, 1989, the year *Sports Illustrated* called Williams "the patron saint of Cooperstown," Yaz and Johnny Bench joined him in the Hall of Fame. A then record twenty-five thousand packed Cooper Park, their accent more North End or Plymouth than Zanesville or Columbus. Hosting his only Induction Day, Bart Giamatti, 51, died 39 days later, precluding his becoming the gold standard by which a commissioner is judged.

Some recalled Bench's '70s Big Red Machine. More invoked 1967's Adair on Revere Beach, or Lonborg that August—"The fans here in New York," Coleman said. "You'd think you were in Boston!"—or Roger Angell attributing to Fisk's homer a Nation "for once at least utterly joyful and believing in that joy," or tomb-like silence after Dent, or the rolling rally in 2004, people literally hanging from trees: so, here.

Suddenly, a tune wafted from near the Hall of Fame Library. In 1967, Boston radio/TV's Jess Cain wrote and performed "Yastrzemski Song": music, by Henry Fillmore; adapted from ragtime's "Shoutin' Liza Trombone." Much later I introduced it to my then five-year-old son, saying, "I want you to learn high culture." He especially liked "We Fenway fans, we stop and clap our hands at Yaz's jazz." We still do.

Singing, the 1989 Induction Mass recalled No. 8—as today it would his field: born 1912, beloved, nearly dead, gloriously reborn. "Sure, they could probably draw more people," Gowdy had said. "Some of those Yankee–Red Sox games I did could have had a hundred thousand people a game. That doesn't matter, only this: The Red Sox without Fenway are no longer the New England Red Sox."

Shakespeare coined a "Little Touch of Harry in the Night." More than ever, baseball needs a Touch of Fenway Park.

APPENDIX A: BOSTON RED SOX

Franchise history: named the Boston Americans, Plymouth Rocks, Puritans, Speed Boys, Somersets (after original owner Charles W. Somers), or Pilgrims, 1901–1907; Boston Red Sox, 1908–present. The latter reflected Boston's 1907 National League Red Stockings manager Fred Tenney's decision to ditch red hosiery, fearing red dye in socks would cause a spike wound infection. As noted, Sox owner John I. Taylor said, "From now on, we'll wear red stockings, and I'm grabbing that name Red Sox." He did, as the Sox grabbed us.

Franchise home: *Huntington Avenue Grounds* (AL, 1901–1911). First game: May 8, 1901. Boston 12, Philadelphia 4. Last game: October 7, 1911. Boston 8, Washington 1. *Fenway Park* (AL, 1912–present). First game: April 20, 1912. Boston 7, New York 6.

World Series title: 1903, 1912, 1915, 1916, 1918, 2004, and 2007.

American League pennant: 1903, 1904, 1912, 1915, 1916, 1918, 1946, 1967, 1975, 1986, 2004, and 2007.

Division title: 1975, 1986, 1988, 1990, 1995, and 2007.

Wild card: 1998, 1999, 2003, 2004, 2005, 2008, and 2009.

Year	Position	W	L	Pct.	GA/GB	Attendance
1901	2	79	57	.581	4	289,448
1902	3	77	60	.562	6 ½	348.567
1903	1 ***	91	47	.659	+14 ½	379,338
1904	1	95	59	.617	+1 ½	623,295**
1905	4	78	74	.513	16	466,828
1906	8	49	105	.318	45 ½	410,209

Year	Position	W	L	Pct.	GA/GB	Attendance
1907	7	59	90	.396	32 ½	436,777
1908	5	75	79	.487	15 ½	473,048
1909	3	88	63	.583	9 ½	668,965
1910	4	81	72	.529	22 ½	584,619
1911	5	78	75	.510	24	503,961
1912	1 ***	105	47	.691	+14	597,096
1913	4	79	71	.527	15 ½	437,194**
1914	2	91	62	.595	8 ½	481,359**
1915	1 ***	101	50	.669	+2 ½	539,885
1916	1 ***	91	63	.591	+2	496,397
1917	2	90	62	.592	9	387,856
1918	1 ***	75	51	.595	+2 ½	249,513
1919	6	66	71	.482	20 ½	417,291
1920	5	72	81	.471	25 ½	402,445
1921	5	75	79	.487	23 ½	279,273
1922	8	61	93	.391	33	259,184
1923	8	61	91	.401	37	229,688
1924	7	67	87	.435	25	448,556
1925	8	47	105	.309	49 ½	267,782
1926	8	46	107	.301	44 ½	285,155
1927	8	51	103	.331	59	305,275
1928	8	57	96	.373	43 ½	396,920
1929	8	58	96	.377	48	394,620
1930	8	52	102	.338	50	444,045
1931	6	62	90	.408	45	350,975
1932	8	43	111	.279	64	182,150
1933	7	63	86	.423	34 ½	268,715
1934	4	76	76	.500	24	610,640
1935	4	78	75	.510	16	558,568
1936	6	74	80	.481	28 ½	626,895
1937	5	80	72	.526	21	559,659
1938	2	88	61	.591	9 ½	646,459
1939	2	89	62	.589	17	573,070
1940	4 (tie)	82	72	.532	8	716,234
1941	2	84	70	.545	17	718,497
1942	2	93	59	.612	9	730,340
1943	7	68	84	.447	29	358,275
1944	4	77	77	.500	12	506,975

Year	Position	W	L	Pct.	GA/GB	Attendance
1945	7	71	83	.461	17 ½	603,794
1946	1	104	50	.675	+12	1,416,944
1947	3	83	71	.539	14	1,427,315
1948	2	96	59	.619	1	1,558,798
1949	2	96	58	.623	1	1,596,650
1950	3	94	60	.610	4	1,344,080
1951	3	87	67	.565	11	1,312,282
1952	6	76	78	.494	19	1,115,750
1953	4	84	69	.549	16	1,026,133
1954	4	69	85	.448	42	931,127
1955	4	84	70	.545	12	1,203,200
1956	4	84	70	.545	13	1,137,168
1957	3	82	72	.532	16	1,181,087
1958	3	79	75	.513	13	1,077,047
1959	5	75	79	.487	19	984,102
1960	7	65	89	.422	32	1,129,866
1961	6	76	86	.469	33	850,589
1962	8	76	84	.475	19	733,080
1963	7	76	85	.472	28	942,642
1964	8	72	90	.444	27	883,276
1965	9	62	100	.383	40	652,201
1966	9	72	90	.444	26	811,271
1967	1	92	70	.568	+1	1,727,832**
1968	4	86	76	.531	17	1,940,788
1969	3	87	75	.537	22	1,833,246**
1970	3	87	75	.537	21	1,595,278**
1971	3	85	77	.525	18	1,678,732**
1972	2	85	70	.548	½	1,441,718
1973	2	89	73	.549	8	1,481,002
1974	3	84	78	.519	7	1,556,411**
1975	1 <<	95	65	.594	4 ½	1,748,587**
1976	3	83	79	.512	15 ½	1,895,846
1977	2 (tie)	97	64	.602	2 ½	2,074,549
1978	2	99	64	.607	1	2,320,643
1979	3	91	69	.569	11 ½	2,353,114
1980	4	83	77	.519	19	1,956,092
1981	5/2 (tie)	59	49	.546	5 ½	1,060,379
1982	3	89	73	.549	6	1,950,124

Year	Position	W	L	Pct.	GA/GB	Attendance
1983	6	78	84	.481	20	1,782,285
1984	4	86	76	.531	18	1,661,618
1985	5	81	81	.500	18 ½	1,786,633
1986	1 >>	95	66	.590	5 ½	2,147,641
1987	5	78	84	.481	20	2,231,551
1988	1 <<	89	73	.549	+1	2,464,851
1989	3	83	79	.512	6	2,510,012
1990	1 <<	88	74	.543	+2	2,528,986
1991	2 (tie)	84	78	.519	7	2,562,435
1992	7	73	89	.451	23	2,468,574
1993	5	80	82	.494	15	2,422,021
1994	4	54	61	.470	17	1,775,818
1995	1 <	86	58	.597	+7	2,164,410
1996	3	85	77	.525	7	2,315,231
1997	4	78	84	.481	20	2,226,136
1998	2 <	92	70	.568	22	2,343,947
1999	2 > <<	94	68	.580	4	2,446,162
2000	2	85	77	.525	2 ½	2,586,024
2001	2	82	79	.509	13 ½	2,625,333
2002	2	93	69	.574	10 ½	2,650,063
2003	2 > <<	95	67	.586	6	2,724,162
2004	2 ***	98	64	.605	3	2,837,304
2005	1 (tie) <	95	67	.586	+15	2,847,888
2006	3	86	76	.531	11	2,930,588
2007	1 ***	96	66	.593	+2	2,971,025
2008	2 > <<	95	67	.586	2	3,048,248
2009	2 <	95	67	.586	8	3,062,699
2010	3	89	73	.549	7	3,046,444
2011	3	90	72	.556	7	3,054,001

GA/GB means games ahead of the second-place team, signified by +, or behind the champion. Other symbols follow:

**	Led AL in attendance.
***	Won World Series.
>>	Won League Championship Series – thus, pennant.
<<	Lost League Championship Series.
>	Won Division Series.
<	Lost Division Series.

Note: In 1981, player stoppage divided the regular season into two halves. The Red Sox finished 30-26 (fifth, four games behind) and 29-23 (tie, second, 1½ games behind), respectively: thus, 5½ games behind with a 59–49 record. In 1904, Boston won the pennant, but the World Series was canceled.

CAREER BATTING LEADER

All statistics are with Red Sox only.

Games. Carl Yastrzemski, 3,308; Dwight Evans, 2,505; Ted Williams, 2,292; Jim Rice, 2,089; Bobby Doerr, 1,865; Harry Hooper, 1,646; Wade Boggs, 1,625; Rico Petrocelli, 1,553; Jason Varitek, 1,546; Dom DiMaggio, 1,399; Frank Malzone, 1,359; David Ortiz, 1,287; Mike Greenwell, 1,269; George Scott, 1,192; Duffy Lewis, 1,184.

At-bats. Yastrzemski, 11,988; Evans, 8,726; Rice, 8,225; T. Williams, 7,706; Doerr, 7,093; Hooper, 6,270; Boggs, 6,213; DiMaggio, 5,640; Petrocelli, 5,390; Malzone, 5,273; Varitek, 5,099; Ortiz, 4,738; Greenwell, 4,623; Billy Goodman, 4,399; Du. Lewis, 4,325.

Runs. Yastrzemski, 1,816; T. Williams, 1,798; Evans, 1,435; Rice, 1,249; Doerr, 1,094; Boggs, 1,067; DiMaggio, 1,046; Hooper, 988; Ortiz, 844; Johnny Pesky, 776; Manny Ramirez, 743; Jimmie Foxx, 721; Nomar Garciaparra, 709; Tris Speaker, 703; Goodman, 688.

Runs batted in. Yastrzemski, 1,844; T. Williams, 1,839; Rice, 1,451; Evans, 1,346; Doerr, 1,247; Ortiz, 1,028; Ramirez, 868; Foxx, 788; Petrocelli, 773; Varitek, 757; Mo Vaughn, 752; Joe Cronin, 737; Jackie Jensen, 733; Greenwell, 726; Malzone, 716.

Hits. Yastrzemski, 3,419; T. Williams, 2,654; Rice, 2,452; Evans, 2,373; Boggs, 2,098; Doerr, 2,042; Hooper, 1,707; DiMaggio, 1,680; Malzone, 1,454; Greenwell, 1,400; Ortiz, 1,367; Petrocelli, 1,352; Goodman, 1,344; Speaker, 1,328; Varitek, 1,307.

Batting average (1,500 at-bats). T. Williams, .344; Boggs, .338; Speaker, .337; Garciaparra, .323; Pete Runnels, .320; Foxx, .320; Bob Johnson, .313; Pesky, .313; Ramirez, .312; Fred Lynn, .308; Goodman, .306; Dustin Pedroia, .305; Vaughn, .304; Greenwell, .303; Doc Cramer, .302.

Doubles. Yastrzemski, 646; T. Williams, 525; Evans, 474; Boggs, 422; Doerr, 381; Rice, 373; Ortiz, 348; DiMaggio, 308; Varitek, 306; Garciaparra, 279; Greenwell, 275; Cronin, 270; John Valentin, 266; Ramirez, 256; Du. Lewis, 254.

Triples. Hooper, 130; Speaker, 106; Buck Freeman, 90; Doerr, 89; Larry Gardner, 87; Rice, 79; Hobe Ferris, 77; Evans, 72; T. Williams, 71; Jimmy Collins, 65; Freddy Parent, 63; Du. Lewis, 62; Chick Stahl, 62; Yastrzemski, 59; DiMaggio, 57.

Home runs. T. Williams, 521; Yastrzemski, 452; Rice, 382; Evans, 379; Ortiz, 320; Ramirez, 274; Vaughn, 230; Doerr, 223; Foxx, 222; Petrocelli, 210; Varitek,

193; Garciaparra, 178; Jensen, 170; Tony Conigliaro, 162; Carlton Fisk, 162.

Extra-base hits. Yastrzemski, 1,157; T. Williams, 1,117; Evans, 925; Rice, 834; Doerr, 693; Ortiz, 681; Boggs, 554; Ramirez, 537; Varitek, 513; Garciaparra, 507; Petrocelli, 469; DiMaggio, 452; Foxx, 448; Greenwell, 443; Vaughn, 439.

Total bases. Yastzemski, 5,539; T. Williams, 4,884; Rice, 4,129; Evans, 4,128; Doerr, 3,270; Boggs, 2,869; Ortiz, 2,701; DiMaggio, 2,363; Ramirez, 2,324; Hooper, 2,303; Petrocelli, 2,263; Varitek, 2,220; Garciaparra, 2,194; Greenwell, 2,141; Malzone, 2,123.

Multi-homer games. T. Williams, 37; Ortiz, 35; Rice, 35; Ramirez, 28; Yastrzemski, 27; Foxx, 23; Evans, 22; Vaughn, 22; Garciaparra, 17; Doerr, 14; Vern Stephens, 13; Lynn, Malzone, G. Scott, and Reggie Smith, 12.

Slugging percentage (1,500 at-bats). T. Williams, .634; Foxx, .605; Ramirez, .588; Ortiz, .570; Garciaparra, .553; Vaughn, .542; Lynn, .520; Rice, .502; Kevin Youkilis, .492; Vern Stephens, .492; Brian Daubach, .488; Conigliaro, .488; Cronin, .484; Speaker, .482; Fisk, .481.

Stolen bases. Hooper, 300; Speaker, 267; Jacoby Ellsbury, 175; Yastrzemski, 168; Heinie Wagner, 141; Gardner, 134; Parent, 129; Tommy Harper, 107; Bill Werber, 107; C. Stahl, 105; J. Collins, 102; Du. Lewis, 102; DiMaggio, 100; Johnny Damon, 98; Jerry Remy, 98.

Walks. T. Williams, 2,021; Yastrzemski, 1,845; Evans, 1,337; Boggs, 1,004; Hooper, 826; Doerr, 809; Ortiz, 769; DiMaggio, 750; Rice, 670; Petrocelli, 661; Ramirez, 636; Foxx, 624; Varitek, 614; Cronin, 585; Jensen, 585.

On-base percentage (1,500 at-bats). T. Williams, .482; Foxx, .429; Boggs, .428; Speaker, .414; Ramirez, .411; Runnels, .408; Pesky, .401; Vaughn, .394; Cronin, .394; R. Ferrell, .394; Youkilis, .391; Ortiz, .387; R. Johnson, .386; Goodman, .386; DiMaggio, .383; Lynn, .383.

SINGLE-SEASON BATTING LEADER

Games. Jim Rice, 163 (1978); Bill Buckner, 162 (1985); Dwight Evans, 162 (1984); Evans, 162 (1982); Carl Yastrzemski, 162 (1969); George Scott, 162 (1966); Mo Vaughn, 161 (1996); Wade Boggs, 161 (1985); Yastrzemski, 161 (1970); Yastrzemski, 161 (1967).

At-bats. Nomar Garciaparra, 684 (1997); Rice, 677 (1978); Buckner, 673 (1985); Rick Burleson, 663 (1977); Doc Cramer, 661 (1940); Jacoby Ellsbury, 660

(2011); Garciaparra, 658 (2003); Cramer, 658 (1938); Rice, 657 (1984); Dustin Pedroia, 653 (2008); Boggs, 653 (1985).

Runs. Ted Williams, 150 (1949); T. Williams, 142 (1946); T. Williams, 141 (1942); Jimmie Foxx, 139 (1938); Tris Speaker, 136 (1912); T. Williams, 135 (1941); T. Williams, 134 (1940); Dom DiMaggio, 131 (150); T. Williams, 131 (1939); Foxx, 130 (1936 and 1939).

Runs batted in. Foxx, 175 (1938); Vern Stephens, 159 (1949); T. Williams, 159 (1949); David Ortiz, 148 (2005); T. Williams, 145 (1939); Manny Ramirez, 144 (2005); Walt Dropo, 144 (1950); Stephens, 144 (1950); Vaughn, 143 (1996); Foxx, 143 (1936).

Hits. Boggs, 240 (1985); Speaker, 222 (1912); Boggs, 214 (1988); Pedroia, 213 (2008); Rice, 213 (1978); Adrian Gonzalez, 213 (2011); Ellsbury, 212 (2011); Boggs, 210 (1983); Garciaparra, 209 (1997); Johnny Pesky, 208 (1946); Vaughn, 207 (1996); Boggs, 207 (1986); Pesky, 207 (1947).

Batting average (400 at-bats). T. Williams, .406 (1941); T. Williams, .388 (1957); Speaker, .383 (1912); Garciaparra, .372 (2000); Dale Alexander, .372 (1932); T. Williams, .369 (1948); Boggs, .368 (1985); Boggs, .366 (1988); Speaker, .365 (1913); Boggs, .363 (1987).

Doubles. Earl Webb, 67 (1931); Garciaparra, 56 (2002); Pedroia, 54 (2008); Speaker, 53 (1912); Ortiz, 52 (2007); Garciaparra, 51 (2007); Boggs, 51 (1989); Joe Cronin, 51 (1938); Adrian Beltre, 49 (2010); Pedroia, 48 (2009); six tied with 47.

Triples. Speaker, 22 (1913); Buck Freeman, 20 (1903); Larry Gardner, 19 (1914); Freeman, 19 (1904); Chick Stahl, 19 (1904); Freeman, 19 (1902); Speaker, 18 (1914); L. Gardner, 18 (1912); Russ Scarritt, 17 (1929); Harry Hooper, 17 (1920); Jimmy Collins, 17 (1903); Freddy Parent, 17 (1903).

Home runs. Ortiz, 54 (2006); Foxx, 50 (1938); Ortiz, 47 (2005); Rice, 46 (1978); Ramirez, 45 (2005); Vaughn, 44 (1996); Yastrzemski, 44 (1967); Ramirez, 43 (2004); Tony Armas, 43 (1984); T. Williams, 43 (1949).

Multi-homer games. Foxx, 10 (1938); Ortiz, 9 (2005); Ramirez, 7 (2002); Rice, 7 (1977); Ortiz, 6 (2006); Ortiz, 6 (2003); Vaughn, 6 (1996); Armas, 6 (1983); Rice, 6 (1983); Ramirez, 5 (2001); Garciaparra, 5 (1999); Rice, 5 (1979); Carlton Fisk, 5 (1977); Yastrzemski, 5 (1967).

Slugging percentage. T. Williams, .735 (1941); T. Williams, .731 (1957); Foxx, .704 (1938); Foxx, .694 (1939); T. Williams, .667 (1946); Babe Ruth, .657 (1919); T. Williams, .650 (1949); T. Williams, .648 (1942); Ramirez, .647 (2002); Fred Lynn, .637 (1979).

Extra-base hits. Foxx, 92 (1938); Ortiz, 91 (2004); Ortiz, 88 (2007); Ortiz, 88
   (2005); Ramirez, 87 (2004); Rice, 86 (1978); T. Williams, 86 (1939); Ortiz,
   85 (2006); Garciaparra, 85 (2002); Garciaparra, 85 (1997); T. Williams, 85
   (1949).

Total bases. Rice, 406 (1978); Foxx, 398 (1938); Rice, 382 (1977); Vaughn, 370
   (1996); Rice, 369 (1979); Foxx, 369 (1936); T. Williams, 368 (1949); Garciaparra, 365 (1997); Ellsbury, 364 (2011); Ortiz, 363 (2005).

Stolen bases. Jacoby Ellsbury, 70 (2009); Tommy Harper, 54 (1973); Speaker, 52 (1912);
   Ellsbury, 50 (2008); Speaker, 46 (1913); Otis Nixon, 42 (1994); Speaker, 42
   (1914); Billy Werber, 40 (1934); Hooper, 40 (1910); Ellsbury, 39 (2011).

Walks. T. Williams, 162 (1949); T. Williams, 162 (1947); T. Williams, 156 (1946);
   T. Williams, 147 (1941); T. Williams, 145 (1942); T. Williams, 144 (1951);
   T. Williams, 136 (1954); Yastrzemski, 128 (1970); T. Williams, 126 (1948);
   Boggs, 125 (1988).

Pinch-hits. Cronin, 18 (1943); Rick Miller, 16 (1983); Dick Williams, 16 (1963);
   R. Miller, 14 (1984); Lenny Green, 14 (1966); Dalton Jones, 13 (1967); D. Jones,
   13 (1966); Lou Finney, 13 (1939); Bing Miller, 13 (1935); two tied with 12.

On-base percentage. T. Williams, .553 (1941); T. Williams, .526 (1957); T. Williams,
   .499 (1947); T. Williams, .499 (1942); T. Williams, .497 (1948); T. Williams,
   .497 (1946); T. Williams, .490 (1949); T. Williams, .479 (1956); Boggs, .476
   (1988); three tied with .464.

BATTING CHAMPION

Dale Alexander: 1932 (.367, including 23 games with Detroit). Jimmie Foxx: 1938
   (.349). Ted Williams: 1941 (.406), 1942 (.356), 1947 (.343), 1948 (.369), 1957
   (.388), and 1958 (.328). Billy Goodman: 1950 (.354). Pete Runnels: 1960
   (.320) and 1962 (.326). Carl Yastrzemski: 1963 (.321), 1967 (.326), and 1968
   (.301). Fred Lynn: 1979 (.333). Carney Lansford: 1981 (.336). Wade Boggs:
   1983 (.361), 1985 (.368), 1986 (.357), 1987 (.363), and 1988 (.366). Nomar
   Garciaparra: 1999 (.357) and 2000 (.372). Manny Ramirez: 2002 (.349). Bill
   Mueller: 2003 (.326).

HOME RUN CHAMPION

Buck Freeman: 1903 (13). Jake Stahl: 1910 (10). Tris Speaker: 1912 (12, tie with
   Frank Baker). Babe Ruth: 1918, (11, with Tilly Walker) and 1919 (29). Jimmie

Foxx: 1939 (35). Ted Williams: 1941 (37), 1942 (36), 1947 (32) and 1949
(43). Tony Conigliaro: 1965 (32). Carl Yastrzemski: 1967 (44, with Harmon
Killebrew). Jim Rice: 1977 (39), 1978 (46), and 1983 (39). Dwight Evans:
1981 (22, with Tony Armas, Bobby Grich, and Eddie Murray). Tony Armas:
1984 (43). Manny Ramirez: 2004 (43). David Ortiz: 2006 (54).

RUNS BATTED IN CHAMPION

Buck Freeman: 1902 (104) and 1903 (104). Babe Ruth: 1919 (114). Jimmie
   Foxx: 1938 (175). Ted Williams: 1939 (145), 1942 (137), 1947 (114), and
   1949 (159, with Vern Stephens). Vern Stephens: 1949 (159, with Ted Williams) and 1950 (144, with Walt Dropo). Walt Dropo: 1950 (144, with Vern
   Stephens). Jackie Jensen: 1955 (116, with Ray Boone), 1958 (122), and 1959
   (112). Dick Stuart: 1963 (118). Carl Yastrzemski: 1967 (121). Ken Harrelson:
   1968 (109). Jim Rice: 1978 (139) and 1983 (126, with Cecil Cooper). Tony
   Armas: 1984 (123). Mo Vaughn: 1995 (126, with Albert Belle). David Ortiz:
   2005 (148) and 2006 (137).

CAREER PITCHING LEADER

All statistics are with Red Sox only.

Games. Bob Stanley, 637; Tim Wakefield, 590; Jonathan Papelbon, 396; Mike Timlin, 394; Derek Lowe, 384; Roger Clemens, 383; Ellis Kinder, 365; Cy Young,
   327; Ike Delock, 322; Bill Lee, 321; Mel Parnell, 289; Manny Delcarmen, 289;
   Greg Harris, 287; Mike Fornieles, 286; Dick Radatz, 286.

Innings. Wakefield, 3,006.0; Clemens, 2,776.0; C. Young, 2,728.1; Luis Tiant,
   1,774.2; Parnell, 1,752.2; Stanley, 1,707.0; Bill Monbouquette, 1,622.0;
   George Winter, 1,599.2; Joe Dobson, 1,544.0; Lefty Grove, 1,539.2; Tom
   Brewer, 1,509.1; Frank Sullivan, 1,505.1; B. Lee, 1,503.1; Bill Dinneen,
   1,501.0; Bruce Hurst, 1,459.0.

Games started. Wakefield, 430; Clemens, 382; C. Young, 297; Luis Tiant, 238; Par-
   nell, 232; Monbouquette, 228; Brewer, 217; Hurst, 217; Dobson, 202; Pedro
   Martinez, 201; F. Sullivan, 201; Dennis Eckersley, 191; Grove, 190; Willard
   Nixon, 177; Winter, 176.

Complete games. C. Young, 275; Dinneen, 156; Winter, 141; Joe Wood, 121; Grove,
   119; Parnell, 113; Tiant, 113; Babe Ruth, 105; Clemens, 100; Tex Hughson,
   99; Dutch Leonard, 96; Ray Collins, 90; Dobson, 90; Carl Mays, 87; Jesse
   Tannehill, 85.

Wins. Clemens, 192; C. Young, 192; Wakefield, 186; Parnell, 123; Tiant, 122; P. Martinez, 117; J. Wood, 116; Stanley, 115; Dobson, 106; Grove, 105; Hughson, 96; Monbouquette, 96; B. Lee, 94; Brewer, 91; Leonard, 90; F. Sullivan, 90.

Losses. Wakefield, 168; C. Young, 112; Clemens, 111; Stanley, 97; Winter, 97; Red Ruffing, 94; Jack Russell, 94; Monbouquette, 91; Dinneen, 85; Brewer, 82; Tiant, 81; F. Sullivan, 80; Danny MacFayden, 78; Parnell, 75; Hurst, 73.

Winning percentage (100 decisions). P. Martinez, .760; Jon Lester, .691; J. Wood, .674; Ruth, .659; Josh Beckett, .641; Hughson, .640; Clemens, .634; C. Young, .632; Grove, .629; Kinder, .623; Parnell, .621; Tannehill, .620; Wes Ferrell, .608; Tiant, .601; Dobson, .596.

Earned run average (1,000 innings). J. Wood, 1.99; C. Young, 2.00; Leonard, 2.14; Ruth, 2.19; Mays 2.21; R. Collins, 2.51; P. Martinez, 2.52; Dinneen, 2.81; Winter, 2.91; Hughson, 2.94; Clemens, 3.06; Kinder, 3.28; Grove, 3.34; Tiant, 3.36; Sad Sam Jones, 3.39.

Strikeouts. Clemens, 2,590; Wakefield, 2,046; P. Martinez, 1,683; C. Young, 1,341; Tiant, 1,075; Hurst, 1,043; Beckett, 1,014; J. Wood, 986; Monbouquette, 969; Lester, 894; F. Sullivan, 821; Ray Culp, 794; Jim Lonborg, 784; Eckersley, 771; Leonard, 771.

Walks. Wakefield, 1,095; Clemens, 856; Parnell, 758; Brewer, 669; Dobson, 604; Jack Wilson, 563; W. Nixon, 530; Delock, 514; Maurice McDermott, 504; Tiant, 501; Fritz Ostermueller, 491; Earl Wilson, 481; Hurst, 479; F. Sullivan, 475; Stanley, 471.

Shutouts. Clemens, 38; C. Young, 38; Wood, 28; Tiant, 26; Leonard, 25; Parnell, 20; R. Collins, 19; Hughson 19; S. Jones, 18; Dobson, 17; Ruth, 17; Dinneen, 16; Monbouquette, 16; Rube Foster, 15; Grove, 15.

Ten-strikeout games. P. Martinez, 72; Clemens, 68; J. Wood, 18; Lester, 16; Hurst, 13; Culp, 10; Lonborg, 10; Dave Morehead, 10; Tiant, 9; C. Young, 8; Curt Schilling, 7.

Saves. Papelbon, 219; Stanley, 132; Radatz, 104; Kinder, 91; Jeff Reardon, 88; Lowe, 85; Sparky Lyle, 69; Tom Gordon, 68; Lee Smith, 58; Bill Campbell, 51; Ugueth Urbina, 49; Fornieles, 48; Heathcliff Slocumb, 48; Keith Foulke, 47; Jeff Russell, 45.

Home runs allowed. Wakefield, 401; Clemens, 194; Monbouquette, 180; Hurst, 173; Tiant, 170; Eckersley, 167; Beckett, 137; B. Lee, 136; Delock, 134; Dennis Boyd, 126; Brewer, 126; F. Sullivan, 123; Earl Wilson, 123; Stanley, 113; Lonborg, 105.

Relief wins. Stanley, 85; Radatz, 49; Kinder, 39; Mark Clear, 35; Delock, 34; Fornieles, 31; Timlin, 30; Campbell, 28; Jack Wilson, 26; Mike Ryba, 26.

SINGLE-SEASON PITCHING LEADER

Games. Mike Timlin, 81 (2005); Greg Harris, 80 (1993); Dick Radatz, 79 (1964); Timlin, 76 (2004); Heathcliffe Slocumb, 75 (1996); Derek Lowe, 74 (2000); Lowe, 74 (1999); Rob Murphy, 74 (1989); Daniel Bard, 73 (2011); Manny Delcarmen, 73 (2008); Tom Gordon, 73 (1998).

Innings. Cy Young, 384.2 (1902); C. Young, 380.0 (1904); Bill Dinneen, 371.1 (1902); C. Young, 371.1 (1901); Joe Wood, 344.0 (1912); C. Young, 343.1 (1912); C. Young, 341.2 (1903); Dinneen, 335.2 (1904); Babe Ruth, 326.1 (1917); Ruth, 323.2 (1916).

Games started. C. Young, 43 (1902); Dinneen, 42 (1902); Ruth, 41 (1916); C. Young, 41 (1904); C. Young, 41 (1901); Jim Lonborg, 39 (1967); Howard Ehmke, 39 (1923); seven tied with 38.

Complete games. C. Young, 41 (1902); C. Young, 40 (1904); Dinneen, 39 (1902); C. Young, 38 (1901); Dinneen, 37 (1904); Ruth, 35 (1917); J. Wood, 35 (1912); C. Young, 34 (1903); C. Young, 33 (1907); Dinneen, 32 (1903).

Wins. J. Wood, 34-5 (1912); C. Young, 33-10 (1901); C. Young, 32-11 (1902); C. Young, 28-9 (1903); C. Young, 26-16 (1904); Mel Parnell, 25-7 (1949); Dave Ferriss, 25-6 (1946); Wes Ferrell, 25-14 (1935); Roger Clemens, 24-4 (1986); Ruth, 24-13 (1917).

Losses. Red Ruffing, 10-25 (1928); Ruffing, 9-22 (1929); Slim Harriss, 14-21 (1927); Joe Harris, 2-21 (1906); C. Young, 13-21 (1906); Dinneen, 21-21 (1902); Milt Gaston, 13-20 (1930); Jack Russell, 9-20 (1930); Ehmke, 9-20 (1925); Sad Sam Jones, 12-20 (1919).

Earned run average. Dutch Leonard, 0.96 (1914); C. Young, 1.26 (1908); J. Wood, 1.49 (1915); Ray Collins, 1.62 (1910); C. Young, 1.62 (1910); Ernie Shore, 1.64 (1915); J. Wood, 1.68 (1910); Rube Foster, 1.70 (1914); Pedro Martinez, 1.74 (2000); Carl Mays, 1.74 (1917).

Strikeouts. P. Martinez, 313 (1999); Clemens, 291 (1988); P. Martinez, 284 (2000); J. Wood, 258 (1912); Clemens, 257 (1996); Clemens, 256 (1987); P. Martinez, 251 (1998); Lonborg, 246 (1967); Clemens, 241 (1991); P. Martinez, 239 (2002).

Walks. Parnell, 134 (1949); Mickey McDermott, 124 (1950); Mike Torrez, 121 (1979); Don Schwall, 121 (1962); Bobo Newsom, 119 (137); Jack Wilson, 119 (1937); W. Ferrell, 119 (1936); Ehmke, 119 (123); Ruffing, 118 (1929); Ruth, 118 (1916).

Shutouts. J. Wood, 10 (1912); C. Young, 10 (1904); Ruth, 9 (1916); Clemens, 8 (1988); Mays, 8 (1918); Clemens, 7 (1987); Luis Tiant, 7 (1974); Joe Bush, 7 (1918); Leonard, 7(1914); C. Young, 7 (1903).

Ten-strikeout games. P. Martinez, 19 (1999); P. Martinez, 15 (2000); Clemens, 12 (1988); P. Martinez, 9 (2002); P. Martinez, 9 (2001); Clemens, 9 (1987); P. Martinez, 8 (1998); Clemens, 8 (1996); Clemens, 8 (1986); Lonborg, 8 (1967).

Saves. Gordon, 46 (1998); Lowe, 42 (2000); Jonathan Papelbon, 41 (2008); Ugueth Urbina, 40 (2002); Jeff Reardon, 40 (1991); Papelbon, 38 (2009); Papelbon, 37 (2010); Papelbon, 37 (2007); Papelbon, 35 (2006); Jeff Russell, 33 (1993); Bob Stanley, 33 (1983).

Home runs allowed. Tim Wakefield, 38 (1996); Earl Wilson, 37 (1964); Josh Beckett, 36 (2006); Wakefield, 35 (2005); Bruce Hurst, 35 (1987); Rick Wise, 34 (1975); Bill Monbouquette, 34 (1964); Gene Conley, 33 (1961); Dennis Boyd, 32 (1986); John Tudor, 32 (1983); Tiant, 32 (1973); Monbouquette, 32 (1965).

Relief wins. Radatz, 16 (1964); Radatz, 15 (1963); Mark Clear, 14 (1982); Stanley, 13 (1978); Bill Campbell, 13 (1977); Stanley, 12 (1982); Ike Delock, 11 (1956); seven tied with 10.

CY YOUNG AWARD WINNER

Jim Lonborg: 1967 (22-9, 3.16 earned run average). Roger Clemens: 1986 (24-4, 2.84), 1987 (20-9, 2.97), and 1991 (18-10, 2.62). Pedro Martinez: 1999 (23-4, 2.07) and 2000 (18-6, 1.74).

TWENTY-GAME WINNER

Cy Young: 1901 (33-10), 1902 (32-11), 1903 (28-9), 1904 (26-16), 1907 (21-15), and 1908 (21-11). Bill Dinneen: 1902 (21-21), 1903 (21-13), and 1904 (23-14). Tom Hughes: 1903 (20-7). Jesse Tannehill: 1904 (21-11) and 1905 (22-9). Joe Wood: 1911 (23-17) and 1912 (34-5). Hugh Bedient: 1912 (20-9). Buck O'Brien: 1912 (20-13). Ray Collins: 1914 (20-13). Babe Ruth: 1916 (23-12) and 1917 (24-13). Carl Mays: 1917 (22-9) and 1918 (21-13). Sad Sam Jones: 1921 (23-16). Howard Ehmke: 1923 (20-17). Wes Ferrell: 1935 (25-14) and 1936 (20-15). Lefty Grove: 1935 (20-12). Tex Hughson: 1942 (22-6) and 1946 (20-11). Dave Ferriss: 1945 (21-10) and 1946 (25-6). Mel Parnell: 1949 (25-7) and 1953 (21-8). Ellis Kinder: 1949 (23-6). Bill Monbouquette: 1963 (20-10). Jim Lonborg: 1967 (22-9). Luis Tiant: 1973 (20-13), 1974 (22-13), and 1976 (21-12). Dennis Eckersley: 1978 (20-8). Roger Clemens: 1986 (24-4), 1987

(20-9), and 1990 (21-6). Pedro Martinez: 1999 (23-4) and 2002 (20-4). Derek
Lowe: 2002 (21-8). Curt Schilling: 2004 (21-6). Josh Beckett: 2007 (20-7).

EARNED RUN AVERAGE CHAMPION
Cy Young: 1901 (1.62). Dutch Leonard: 1914 (1.00). Joe Wood: 1915 (1.49). Babe
Ruth: 1916 (1.75). Lefty Grove: 1935 (2.70), 1936 (2.81), 1938 (3.08), and
1939 (2.54). Mel Parnell: 1949 (2.77). Luis Tiant: 1972 (1.91). Roger Clemens: 1986 (2.48), 1990 (1.93), 1991 (2.62), and 1992 (2.41). Pedro Martinez:
1999 (2.07), 2000 (1.74), 2002 (2.26), and 2003 (2.22).

STRIKEOUT CHAMPION
Cy Young: 1901 (158). Tex Hughson: 1942 (113, tie with Bobo Newsom). Jim Lonborg: 1967 (246). Roger Clemens: 1988 (291), 1991 (241), and 1996 (257).
Pedro Martinez: 1999 (313), 2000 (284), and 2002 (239). Hideo Nomo: 2001
(220).

GOLD GLOVE AWARD (BEGUN 1957)
Frank Malzone: third base, 1957–1959. Jim Piersall: center field, 1958. Jackie Jensen: right field, 1959. Carl Yastrzemski: outfield, 1963, 1965, 1967–1969, 1971,
1977. George Scott: first base, 1967–1968, 1971. Reggie Smith: outfield, 1968.
Carlton Fisk: catcher, 1972. Doug Griffin: second base, 1972. Fred Lynn: outfield, 1975, 1978–1980. Dwight Evans: outfield, 1976, 1978–1979, 1981–
1985. Rick Burleson: shortstop, 1979. Mike Boddicker: pitcher, 1990. Ellis
Burks: outfield, 1990. Tony Pena: catcher, 1991. Jason Varitek: catcher, 2005.
Kevin Youkilis: first base, 2007. Dustin Pedroia: second base, 2008, 2011. Adrian Gonzalez: first base, 2011. Jacoby Ellsbury: center field, 2011.

ROOKIE OF THE YEAR
Walt Dropo: 1950 (.322, 34 home runs, and 144 runs batted in). Don Schwall:
1961 (15-7, 3.22 earned run average). Carlton Fisk: 1972 (.293, 22, 61). Fred
Lynn: 1975 (.331, 21, 105). Nomar Garciaparra: 1997 (.306, 30, 98). Dustin
Pedroia: 2007 (.317, 8, 50).

MOST VALUABLE PLAYER
Tris Speaker: 1912 (.383 average, 10 home runs, and 98 runs batted in). Jimmie
Foxx: 1938 (.349, 50, 175). Ted Williams: 1946 (.342, 38, 123) and 1949

(.343, 43, 159). Jackie Jensen: 1958 (.286, 35, 122). Carl Yastrzemski: 1967 (.326, 44, 121). Fred Lynn: 1975 (.331, 21, 105). Jim Rice: 1978 (.315, 46, 139). Roger Clemens: 1986 (24-4, 2.48 earned run average). Mo Vaughn: 1995 (.300, 39, 126). Dustin Pedroia: 2008 (.326, 17, 83).

APPENDIX B: RED SOX RADIO/TV

The Red Sox debuted on radio and television in 1926 and 1948, respectively. Cable and Hispanic play-by-play started in 1984 and 1988, respectively. The Sox eventually began using separate Voices for radio, TV, and later cable aka the New England Sports Network. The table below cites Townie flagship stations, announcers, and milestones in order of appearance: radio (R), free over the air TV (channel number), NESN (N), and Hispanic (S) coverage. On first mention, flagship call letters, dial position, and channel number are listed. Play-by-playmen—for instance, Ned Martin, 1975 radio—are cited first, unless the analyst has seniority: e.g., Jerry Remy (1988) preceding Don Orsillo (2001) on NESN.

Year	Radio	Television	Broadcasters	Miscellany
1926	WNAC (1230 AM)		Gus Rooney	Opening Day only.
1927	WNAC		Fred Hoey, Gerry Harrison	Fred Hoey, 42, starts 12-year Sox reign: "The man who does the games."
1928	WNAC		Fred Hoey	WNAC flagship of Yankee—also later Colonial—Network.
1929	WNAC		Fred Hoey	Network ties six states and 22 stations.
1930	WNAC		Fred Hoey	"His mail," says *The Sporting News*, "keeps the postman loaded down."
1931	WNAC		Fred Hoey	Fred gets Day—and gold, pipe, and $3,000.
1932	WNAC		Fred Hoey	Airs 1927–1938 Braves. Like Sox, their sponsors are Kentucky Club tobacco and Mobil Oil.

Year	Radio	Television	Broadcasters	Miscellany
1933	WNAC		Fred Hoey	Sloshed, Hoey yanked off CBS Radio World Series opener.
1934	WNAC		Fred Hoey	Sox crack first division for first time since 1918.
1935	WNAC		Fred Hoey	Region chimes, "He throws to first and gets his man."
1936	WNAC		Fred Hoey	Hoey airs Mutual's All-Star Game from Braves Field.
1937	WNAC		Fred Hoey	Yankee head John Shepard III fires, then rehires, Fred after public and FDR protest.
1938	WNAC		Fred Hoey	Hoey demands raise: instead, is sacked.
1939	WAAB (1440 AM)		Frankie Frisch, Tom Hussey	Fans, new angels General Mills and Socony Oil tire of Frankie Frisch's "Oh, those bases on balls."
1940	WAAB		Jim Britt, Tom Hussey	Erudite Jim Britt begins first three-year Sox and Braves suzerainty.
1941	WAAB		Jim Britt, Tom Hussey	Each game pre-empted for 15 minutes by radio's *Superman*.
1942	WAAB/ WNAC (1260 AM)		Jim Britt, Tom Hussey	Britt does Mutual All-Star Game, then enters navy.
1943	WNAC		Tom Hussey, George Hartrick	Tom Hussey re-creates Sox and Braves away: to Leo Egan, "a warm glass of milk."
1944	WNAC		Tom Hussey George Hartrick	Sound effects shunned: just the balls and strikes, ma'am.
1945	WNAC		Tom Hussey, George Hartrick	War ends, Britt returning from Pacific Theater.
1946	WNAC		Jim Britt, Tom Hussey	Sox wonderyear: first post-1918 flag; longest Fenway homer; Britt does Mutual Radio Mid-Summer and Fall Classic.
1947	WHDH (850 AM)		Jim Britt, Tom Hussey	WHDH becomes flagship through 1975.
1948	WHDH	WBZ (Channel 4), WNAC (Channel 7)	Jim Britt, Tom Hussey. Leo Egan (R only). Bump Hadley (TV only)	Britt telecasts Hub's first game, from Braves Field, then airs AL playoff and Series.
1949	WHDH	WBZ/ WNAC	Jim Britt, Tom Hussey, Leo Egan	Hoey, 64, dies. Sox lose last-day pennant. Britt does first TV Classic, for NBC. Vin Scully starts career at Fenway.
1950	WHDH	WBZ/ WNAC	Jim Britt, Tom Hussey. Leo Egan (R only). Bump Hadley (TV only)	Britt calls homer "*under* the fence," then covers his final Mutual World Series.

Year	Radio	Television	Broadcasters	Miscellany
1951	WHDH	WBZ/ WNAC	Curt Gowdy, Tom Hussey, Bob Delaney	Braves return to Yankee Network, Britt leaving Sox to air them. Also does TV All-Star Game and Classic.
1952	WHDH	WBZ/ WNAC	Curt Gowdy, Tom Hussey, Bob Delaney	Curt Gowdy begins to bloom as Townies' prosopopeia— ultimately, *The Cowboy At the Mike*.
1953	WHDH	WBZ/ WNAC	Curt Gowdy, Tom Hussey, Bob Delaney	Ted Williams spends his second year in Korea: to Curt, "the most competent person I've ever met."
1954	WHDH	WBZ/ WNAC	Curt Gowdy, Tom Hussey, Bob Murphy	One gentleman joins another: Gowdy hires Bob Murphy, each having trained in Oklahoma.
1955	WHDH	WBZ/ WNAC	Curt Gowdy, Bob Murphy	Sox stay alive post–Labor Day for only year of the 1950s.
1956	WHDH	WBZ/ WNAC	Curt Gowdy, Bob Murphy	Williams spits, fined $5,000 by the Sox: announcers caught between The Kid and Tom Yawkey.
1957	WHDH	WHDH (Channel 5)	Bob Murphy, Bill Crowley. Don Gillis (TV only)	Reinjuring back, Gowdy misses season. Yawkey pays salary and medical bills.
1958	WHDH	WHDH	Curt Gowdy, Bob Murphy, Bill Crowley	With Mel Allen, Curt telecasts his first network event: NBC TV's World Series.
1959	WHDH	WHDH	Curt Gowdy, Bob Murphy, Bill Crowley	Pumpsie Green becomes first Sox African American player. The Kid hits .254, demands that Yawkey cut his salary.
1960	WHDH	WHDH	Curt Gowdy, Bill Crowley, Art Gleeson	Murphy joins the Orioles. Curt emcees Williams's final game tribute, then airs "home run . . . in his last time at-bat in a Red Sox uniform!"
1961	WHDH	WHDH	Curt Gowdy, Art Gleeson, Ned Martin	Ned Martin calls Carl Yastrzemski's debut and Roger Maris's No. 61, buoying Sox through 1992.
1962	WHDH	WHDH	Curt Gowdy, Art Gleeson, Ned Martin	Gowdy does his fifth All-Star Game since 1959.
1963	WHDH	WHDH	Curt Gowdy, Art Gleeson, Ned Martin	Dick Stuart gets standing ovation at Fenway for picking up hot dog wrapper.
1964	WHDH	WHDH	Curt Gowdy, Art Gleeson, Ned Martin	Hint of things to come: Curt calls NBC's Yankees-Cardinals Classic. Art Gleeson, 58, dies.
1965	WHDH	WHDH	Curt Gowdy, Ned Martin, Mel Parnell	Attendance worst since 1945. Ratings survive Townies' 62-100 record.

Year	Radio	Television	Broadcasters	Miscellany
1966	WHDH	WHDH	Ken Coleman, Ned Martin, Mel Parnell	Quincy-born Ken Coleman replaces Gowdy. Martin says of Sox, "When sorrows come, they come not [as] single spies but in battalions."
1967	WHDH	WHDH	Ken Coleman, Ned Martin, Mel Parnell	Yaz. Gentleman Jim. The Impossible Dream last-day pennant. Coleman and Gowdy air the Series. A supercalifragalistic year.
1968	WHDH	WHDH	Ken Coleman, Ned Martin, Mel Parnell	Boston's 1967 "garrison finish," says Ned, transforms the franchise. Attendance and radio/TV audience soar.
1969	WHDH	WHDH	Ken Coleman, Ned Martin, Johnny Pesky	Johnny Pesky replaces Mel Parnell. Martin, Coleman, and young Sean McDonough score a spring training game in Florida.
1970	WHDH	WHDH	Ken Coleman, Ned Martin, Johnny Pesky	Gowdy becomes first sportscaster to win George Foster Peabody award.
1971	WHDH	WHDH	Ken Coleman, Ned Martin, Johnny Pesky	Like the 1950s: also-ran team, first-rate booth. Martin almost fired for saying "bullshit."
1972	WHDH	WBZ (Channel 4)	Ned Martin, John MacLean, Dave Martin (R). Ken Coleman, Johnny Pesky (TV)	Wyoming dedicates Curt Gowdy State Park. Coleman shifts to TV. Martin becomes radio's No. 1.
1973	WHDH	WBZ	Ned Martin, Dave Martin (R). Ken Coleman, Johnny Pesky (TV)	Dave (no relation) Martin fails to remotely approach his namesake.
1974	WHDH	WBZ	Ned Martin, Jim Woods (R). Ken Coleman, Johnny Pesky (TV)	Whiskied Jim Woods aka the Possum joins Ned to form "the best play-by-play combination in the history of American sport," Clark Booth says.
1975	WHDH	WSBK (Channel 38)	Ned Martin, Jim Woods (R). Dick Stockton, Ken Harrelson (TV)	UHF flagship change swells coverage, costing Coleman his job. Dick Stockton and Ken Harrelson voice. Dick, Ned, and Gowdy do NBC radio/TV Series. "Home run! The Red Sox win!"
1976	WMEX (1510 AM)	WSBK	Ned Martin, Jim Woods (R). Dick Stockton, Ken Harrelson (TV)	To afford $450,000 pact, weak signal WMEX radio ups ad inventory. Prostitution widens gulf between station and Poss & Ned.

Year	Radio	Television	Broadcasters	Miscellany
1977	WMEX	WSBK	Ned Martin, Jim Woods (R). Dick Stockton, Ken Harrelson (TV)	Martin does second of three straight CBS Radio LCS.
1978	WITS (1510 AM)	WSBK	Ned Martin, Jim Woods (R). Dick Stockton, Ken Harrelson (TV)	Flagship renamed WITS. The Collapse. Boston Massacre. Bucky (Bleepin') Dent. Playoff is Martin and Woods's finale, despite grand coverage.
1979	WITS	WSBK	Ken Coleman, Rico Petrocelli (R). Ned Martin, Ken Harrelson (TV)	Coleman hired for Sox wireless. Woods joins USA TV, and Stockton CBS. Loving radio, Martin moves to TV, where opposites don't attract.
1980	WITS	WSBK	Ken Coleman, Jon Miller (R). Ned Martin, Ken Harrelson (TV)	Jon Miller replaces Rico Petrocelli. Coleman gets him to mimic Scully and Sherm Feller on radio. Later Miller calls Ken "almost like a brother." Britt, 70, dies.
1981	WITS	WSBK	Ken Coleman, Jon Miller (R). Ned Martin, Ken Harrelson (TV)	Players' lockout splinters regular season. Martin does CBS Radio postseason.
1982	WITS	WSBK	Ken Coleman, Jon Miller (R). Ned Martin, Bob Montgomery (TV)	Distressed by dysfunctional Sox front office, Harrelson trades Red for Pale Hose. Late in year, Miller joins Orioles.
1983	WPLM (1390 AM/ WPLM (99.1 FM)/ WRKO (680 AM)	WSBK	Ken Coleman, Joe Castiglione (R). Ned Martin, Bob Montgomery (TV)	Joe Castiglione succeeds Miller. Plymouth's WPLM AM/FM named flagship. Real anchor: Hub's WRKO.
1984	WPLM AM & FM/ WRKO	WSBK, New England Sports Network (NESN)	Ken Coleman, Joe Castiglione (R). Ned Martin, Bob Montgomery (Channel 38). Mike Andrews, Kent Der Divanis (NESN)	Gowdy becomes first Red Sox announcer to enter Cooperstown. Townies add NESN cable to free TV coverage.
1985	WPLM AM & FM/ WRKO	WSBK, NESN	Ken Coleman, Joe Castiglione (R). Ned Martin, Bob Montgomery (TV)	Martin calls free and cable video. Gowdy joins CBS Radio's *Game of the Week*, often from Fenway.
1986	WPLM AM & FM/ WRKO	WSBK, NESN	Ken Coleman, Joe Castiglione (R). Ned Martin, Bob Montgomery (TV)	Ken calls Stevie Nicks a boy. Coleman and Castiglione air Series radio. Bigs policy bans Ned's local-team TV. After Bill Buckner muff, John McNamara asks Joe, "Why me? I go to church."

Year	Radio	Television	Broadcasters	Miscellany
1987	WPLM AM & FM/ WRKO	WSBK, NESN	Ken Coleman, Joe Castiglione (R). Ned Martin, Bob Montgomery (TV)	Martin does last year of Channel 38 play-by-play—and 27th on free radio/TV.
1988	WPLM & FM/ WRKO, WRCA (1330 AM Spanish)	WSBK, NESN	Ken Coleman, Joe Castiglione (R). Sean McDonough, Bob Montgomery (38). Ned Martin, Jerry Remy (N). Hector Martinez, Bobby Serano (Spanish)	McDonough, 26, succeeds Ned on WSBK. Jerry Remy joins NESN. Spanish network debuts, Hector Martinez and Bobby Serano voicing. Woods, 71, dies.
1989	WPLM AM & FM/ WRKO, WRCA	WSBK, NESN	Ken Coleman, Joe Castiglione (R). Sean McDonough, Bob Montgomery (38). Ned Martin, Jerry Remy (N). Hector Martinez, Bobby Serano (S)	Like 1988, announcers walk tightrope on Margo Adams's suit against married Wade Boggs. Coleman retires to head Jimmy Fund.
1990	WRKO, WROL (950 AM Spanish)	WSBK, NESN	Joe Castiglione, Bob Starr (R). Sean McDonough, Bob Montgomery (38). Ned Martin, Jerry Remy (N). Hector Martinez, Bobby Serano (S)	Bob Starr succeeds Coleman. McDonough and Marty Barrett clash. Sean adds ESPN big-league coverage. Network's Gary Thorne loses division-clinching catch.
1991	WRKO, WROL	WSBK, NESN	Joe Castiglione, Bob Starr (R). Sean McDonough, Bob Montgomery (38). Ned Martin, Jerry Remy (N). Hector Martinez, Bobby Serano (S)	A year earlier booth put on the roof to accommodate the 600 Club made the home plate shot remote. A low catwalk is built to restore best big-league coverage.
1992	WRKO, WROL	WSBK, NESN	Joe Castiglione, Bob Starr (R). Sean McDonough, Bob Montgomery (38). Ned Martin, Jerry Remy (N). Hector Martinez, Bobby Serano (S)	Martin fired after team-record 32 straight years on radio/TV. McDonough replaces Jack Buck on CBS TV baseball.

Year	Radio	Television	Broadcasters	Miscellany
1993	WRKO, WROL	WSBK, NESN	Joe Castiglione, Jerry Trupiano (R). Sean McDonough, Bob Montgomery (38). Jerry Remy, Bob Kurtz (N). Hector Martinez, Bobby Serano, Mike Fornieles (S)	Sean does CBS *Game of the Week*, All-Star Game, LCS, and Series. Jerry Trupiano joins Sox radio through 2006.
1994	WRKO, WROL	WSBK, NESN	Joe Castiglione, Jerry Trupiano (R). Sean McDonough, Bob Montgomery (38). Jerry Remy, Bob Kurtz (N). Hector Martinez, Bobby Serano (S)	Players' lockout begins, killing World Series for first time since 1904, delaying till 1995 "wild card" expanded postseason.
1995	WEEI (850 AM), WROL	WSBK, NESN	Joe Castiglione, Jerry Trupiano (R). Sean McDonough, Bob Montgomery (38). Jerry Remy, Bob Kurtz (N). Hector Martinez, Bobby Serano, J. P. Villaman (S)	After 12 years as flagship, WRKO yields to WEEI. Sox English and Spanish radio air first Division Series. J. P. Villaman becomes Hispanic Voice.
1996	WEEI, WROL	WSBK, NESN	Joe Castiglione, Jerry Trupiano (R). Sean McDonough, Jerry Remy (38). Remy, Bob Kurtz (N). Hector Martinez, Bobby Serano, J. P. Villaman (S)	Remy replaces Bob Montgomery as Channel 38 analyst. With NESN, he does virtually every Red Sox game.
1997	WEEI, WROL	WABU (Channel 68), NESN	Joe Castiglione, Jerry Trupiano (R). Sean McDonough, Jerry Remy (68). Remy, Bob Kurtz (N). Hector Martinez, Bobby Serano, J. P. Villaman (S)	Sign of the times: After 22 years, WSBK loses Sox free television rights, starting flagship merry-go-round.
1998	WEEI, WROL	WABU, NESN	Joe Castiglione, Jerry Trupiano (R). Sean McDonough, Jerry Remy (68). Remy, Bob Kurtz (N). Hector Martinez, Bobby Serano, J. P. Villaman (S)	Gowdy's greatest thrill: reading "Casey at the Bat," with Boston Pops, at Tanglewood. Bob Starr, 65, dies.

Year	Radio	Television	Broadcasters	Miscellany
1999	WEEI, WRCA (1330 AM Spanish)	WLVI (Channel 56), NESN	Joe Castiglione, Jerry Trupiano (R). Sean McDonough, Jerry Remy (56). Remy, Bob Kurtz (N). Bobby Serano, J. P. Villaman (S)	Channel 56 named free TV flagship. Hispanic coverage returns to WRCA.
2000	WEEI, WRCA	WFXT (Channel 25), NESN	Joe Castiglione, Jerry Trupiano (R). Sean McDonough, Jerry Remy (25). Remy, Bob Kurtz, Bob Rodgers (N). Bobby Serano, J. P. Villaman (S)	Coleman and Martin enter Red Sox Hall of Fame. Fox becomes third free TV outlet in as many years.
2001	WEEI, WRCA	WFXT, NESN	Joe Castiglione, Jerry Trupiano (R). Sean McDonough, Jerry Remy (25). Remy, Don Orsillo (N). Bobby Serano, J. P. Villaman, Bill Kulik (S)	Don Orsillo of New England and Triple-A Pawtucket named NESN cable Voice.
2002	WEEI, WLYN (1360 AM Spanish)	WFXT, NESN	Joe Castiglione, Jerry Trupiano (R). Sean McDonough, Jerry Remy (25). Remy, Don Osillo (N). J. P. Villaman, Oscar Baez, Luis Tiant (S)	Martin, 78, dies, on return to North Carolina from No. 9's memorial service at Fenway Park.
2003	WEEI, WROL (950 AM Spanish)	WSBK (Channel 38)/WBZ (Channel 4), NESN	Joe Castiglione, Jerry Trupiano (R). Sean McDonough, Jerry Remy (38/4). Remy, Don Orsillo (N). J. P. Villaman, Uri Berenguer, Oscar Baez, Luis Tiant (S)	Coleman, 78, dies. "They keep changing [free] flagships," says McDonough. NESN's percentage of coverage grows.
2004	WEEI, WROL	WSBK/WBZ, NESN	Joe Castiglione, Jerry Trupiano (R). Sean McDonough, Jerry Remy (38/4). Remy, Don Orsillo (N). J. P. Villaman, Uri Berenguer, Oscar Baez (S)	Deliverance. Sox rally v. Yankees in LCS, then win their first world title in 86 years. After Series sweep, Mr. C. asks, "Can you believe it?" McDonough axed six weeks later.

Year	Radio	Television	Broadcasters	Miscellany
2005	WEEI, WROL	WSBK, NESN	Joe Castiglione, Jerry Trupiano (R). Jerry Remy, Don Orsillo (38, NESN). J. P. Villaman, Uri Berenguer, Oscar Baez (S)	Villaman killed in car accident, replaced by Uri Berenguer as lead Hispanic Voice. Local free TV's final season of Red Sox play-by-play.
2006	WEEI, WROL	NESN	Joe Castiglione, Jerry Trupiano, Jon Rish (R). Jerry Remy, Don Orsillo (TV). Uri Berenguer, Oscar Baez (S)	Gowdy, 86, dies: a generation's sports paradigm. Trupiano is released after 14 years as Castiglione's No. 2. Entercom Communications buys radio through 2016.
2007	WRKO (680 AM)/ WEEI, WROL	NESN	Joe Castiglione, Dave O'Brien, Jon Rish, Glenn Geffner (R). Jerry Remy, Don Orsillo (TV). Uri Berenguer, Oscar Baez (S)	Joe, Dave O'Brien, and Glenn Geffner divide radio. Remy observes twentieth year. WEEI sister WRKO becomes second flagship. Sox take LCS and Series for second title in four years.
2008	WEEI/ WRKO, WROL	NESN	Joe Castiglione, Dave O'Brien, Jon Rish, Dale Arnold (R). Jerry Remy, Don Orsillo (TV). Uri Berenguer, Oscar Baez (S)	Fifty-thousand-watt WTIC Hartford celebrates 52nd year on Townies radio network—longest continuous play-by-play coverage.
2009	WEEI/ WRKO, WROL	NESN	Joe Castiglione, Dave O'Brien, Jon Rish, Dale Arnold (R). Jerry Remy, Don Orsillo (TV). Uri Berenguer, Oscar Baez (S)	Boston makes postseason for sixth time since 2003—Castiglione's Sox-record 12th since 1986.
2010	WEEI, WWZN (1510 AM Spanish)	NESN	Joe Castiglione, Dave O'Brien, Jon Rish, Dale Arnold (R). Jerry Remy, Don Orsillo (TV). Uri Berenguer, Oscar Baez (S)	Jon Miller enters Hall of Fame. Ironically, Hispanic flagship WWZN has same 1510 AM frequency as English 1976–1982 WMEX/WITS.

Year	Radio	Television	Broadcasters	Miscellany
2011	WEEI AM/ FM 93.7/ WRKO, WWZN	NESN	Joe Castiglione, Dave O'Brien, Jon Rish, Dale Arnold (R). Jerry Remy, Don Orsillo (TV). Uri Berenguer, Oscar Baez (S)	Sox add WEEI FM flagship to WEEI AM and WRKO. Five stations form Spanish Beisbol Network.
2012	WEEI AM/FM, WWZN	NESN	Joe Castiglione, Dave O'Brien, Jon Rish (R). Jerry Remy, Don Orsillo (TV). Uri Berenguer, Oscar Baez (S)	English radio 10-state network boasts 69 outlets. Castiglione's thirtieth consecutive year on Townies air trails only Ned Martin. Voices adjust to life with Bobby Valentine.

RED SOX ON THE AIR

What follows, alphabetically, are play-by-play, color, and studio Voices since Red Sox radio's and television's 1926 and 1948 debut, respectively. Names, years, and affiliate(s) are listed. Radio is AM, unless noted:

Mike Andrews, 1984, New England Sports Network (NESN) TV; Dale Arnold, 2008–2009 WRKO, 2010–2011 WEEI AM/FM; Oscar Baez, 2002 WLYN, 2005–2009 WROL, 2010–present WWZN; Uri Berenguer, 2003–2009 WROL, 2010–present WWZN; Jim Britt, 1940–1942 WAAB, 1942 and 1946 WNAC, 1947–1950 WHDH, and 1948–1950 WBZ TV-4, WNAC TV-7; Tom Caron, 2004–present NESN; Joe Castiglione, 1983–1989 WPLM AM/FM, 1989–1994 WRKO, 1995–present WEEI, 2011–present WEEI FM, 2007–2009 and 2011 WRKO; Ken Coleman, 1966–1971 WHDH, 1979–1982 WITS, 1983–1989 WRKO, 1966–1971 TV-5, and 1972–1974 TV-4; Bill Crowley, 1957–1960 TV-5; Bob Delaney, 1951–1953 WHDH and TV-4, TV-7; Jenny Dell, 2012 NESN; Kent Der Divanis, 1984 NESN; Dennis Eckersley, 2003–present NESN; Leo Egan, 1948–1950 WHDH and 1948–1949 TV-4, TV-7; Mike Fornieles, 1993 WROL; Frankie Frisch, 1939 WAAB; Peter Gammons, 2010–present NESN; Glenn Geffner, 2007, WEEI and WRKO; Don Gillis, 1957 TV-5; Art Gleeson, 1960–1964 WHDH and TV-5; Curt Gowdy, 1951–1965 WHDH and 1951–1956 TV-4, TV-7 and 1957–1965 TV-5; Bump Hadley, 1948 and 1950 TV-4, TV-7; Ken Harrelson, 1975–1981, WSBK TV-38; Gerry Harrison, 1927 WNAC; George Hartrick, 1943–1945

WNAC; Fred Hoey, 1927–1938 WNAC; Tom Hussey, 1939–1942 WAAB, 1942–1946 WNAC, 1947–1954 WHDH and 1948–1954 TV-4, TV; Bill Kulik, 2001 WRCA; Bob Kurtz, 1993–2000, NESN; David McCarty, 2005–2008 NESN; Ken Macha, 2007–2008 NESN; Dave Martin, 1972–1973 WHDH; Ned Martin, 1961–1975 WHDH, 1976–1977 WMEX, 1978 WITS, and 1961–1971 TV-5, 1979–1987 WSBK TV-38, and 1988–1992 NESN; Hector Martinez, 1988–1989 WRCA and 1990–1998 WROL; Sean McDonough, 1988–1996 and 2003–2004 WSBK TV-38, 1997–1998 WABU TV-68, 1999 WB Channel 56, 2000–2002 FOX 25, 2003–2004 WBZ TV-4; John MacLean, 1972 WHDH; Jon Miller, 1980–82 WITS; Bob Montgomery, 1982–1995 WSBK TV-38, 1985–1987 NESN; Bob Murphy, 1954–1959 WHDH and 1954–1956 TV-4 and TV-7 and 1957–1959 TV-5; Dave O'Brien, 2007–present WRKO or WEEI, 2011–present WEEI FM; Don Orsillo, 2001–present NESN, 2005 WSBK TV-38; Mel Parnell, 1965–1968 WHDH and TV-5; Johnny Pesky, 1969–1971 WHDH and 1969–1971 TV-5, 1972–1974 TV-4; Rico Petrocelli, 1979 WITS; Jerry Remy, 1988–present NESN, 1996 and 2003–2005 WSBK TV-38, 1997–1998 WABU TV-68, 1999 WB Channel 56, 2000–2002 FOX 25, and 2003–2004 WBZ TV-4; Jim Rice, 2003–present NESN; Jon Rish, 2006–present WEEI, 2011–present WEEI FM, 2007–2009 and 2011 WRKO; Bob Rodgers, 2000 NESN; Gus Rooney, 1926 Opening Day, WNAC; Bobby Serano, 1988–1989 and 1999–2001 WRCA, 1990–1998 WROL; Matt Stairs, 2012 NESN; Bob Starr, 1990–1992 WRKO; Dick Stockton, 1975–1978 WSBK TV-38; Luis Tiant, 2002 WLYN, 2003 WROL; Jerry Trupiano, 1993–1994 WRKO, 1995–2006 WEEI; J. P. Villaman, 1995–1998 and 2003–2005 WROL, 1999–2001 WRCA, 2002 WLYN; Heidi Watney, 2008–2011 NESN; Jim Woods, 1974–1975 WHDH, WMEX 1976–1977, WITS 1978.

RED SOX RADIO NETWORK

"Lots of New England is remote," said Ned Martin. "Radio matters more for the Sox than most teams." Historically, their radio network has linked the six New England states. Today, Boston's 69-station English-speaking arrangement serves 10 states from Wyoming to Florida. Following: the network by state, city, outlet, and frequency, courtesy flagships WEEI AM 850 and WEEI FM 93.7. Affiliates are AM, unless noted:

Massachusetts (13 stations). Boston flagships WEEI 850 and WEEI FM 93.7; Beverly, WBOQ 104.9 FM; Fall River, WSAR 1480; Fitchburg, WPKZ 1280;

Hyannis, WEII 96.3 FM; Milford, WMRC 1490; New Bedford, WBSM 1420; North Adams, WNAW 1230; Pittsfield, WBEC 1420; Springfield, WWEI 105.5 FM; Worcester, WCRN 830 and WVEI 1440.

Colorado (1). Salida, KVRH, 1340.

Connecticut (5). Greenwich, WGCH 1490; Hartford, WTIC 1080; New Haven, WQUN 1220; Putnam, WINY 1350; Willimantic, WILI 1400.

Florida (2). Ft. Myers, WWCN 770; Palm Beach, WSVU 960.

Maine (17). Augusta, WFAU 1280; Bangor, WZON 620; Calais, WQDY 92.7 FM; Camden, WCME 96.7 FM; Dover/Foxcroft, WDME 103.1 FM; Ellsworth, WDEA 1370; Farmington, WKTJ 99.3 FM; Gray, WJJB 96.3 FM; Houlton, WHOU 100.1 FM; Madison, WIGY 97.5 FM; Machias, WALZ 95.3 FM; Millinocket, WSYY 1240; Portland, WLOB 1310; Presque Isle, WEGP 1390; Rockland, WRKD 1450; Saco, WPEI, 95.9 FM; Topsham, WGEI 95.5 FM.

New Hampshire (13). Franklin, WFTN 1240; Hanover, WTSL 1400; Hillsboro, WTPL 107.7 FM; Keene, WKBK 1290 and WKNE 103.7 FM; Laconia, WEMJ 1490; Manchester, WGAM 1250; Nashua, WGHM 900; New London, WCFR 1480 and WNTK 99.7 FM; Plymouth, WPNH 1300; Rochester, WQSO 96.7 FM; and Wolfeboro, WASR 1420.

New York (6). Albany, WOFX 980; Johnstown, WIZR 930; North Syracuse, WTLA 1200 and 97.7 FM; Oswego, WSGO 1440 and 100.1 FM.

Rhode Island (1). Providence, WVEI 103.7 FM.

Vermont (10). Bennington, WBTN 1370; Brattleboro, WKVT 1490; Burlington, WJOY 1230; Middlebury, WFAD 1490; Newport, WIKE 1490; Randolph, WTSJ 1320; Rutland, WSYB 1380; St. Albans, WRSA 1420; St. Johnsbury, WSTJ, 1340; Woodstock, WMXR 93.9 FM.

Wyoming (1). Jackson, KJAX 93.3 FM.

The Red Sox Spanish Network consists of Boston flagship WWZN 1510 and Lawrence, Massachusetts, WCEC 1490.

APPENDIX C: FENWAY PARK

Fenway Park's address is 4 Yawkey Way, Boston, Massachusetts 02215. Administration number: (617) 226-6000. General information: 877-REDSOX9. Tour information: (617) 266-6666. E-mail address: http://www.redsox.com. As we have seen, baseball's oldest field was named by then Red Sox owner John I. Taylor. "It's in the Fenway section [of Boston], isn't it?" he barbed. "Then name it Fenway Park." The park debuted April 20, 1912, with a 7-6 11-inning victory over the New York Highlanders. Fenway was rebuilt in 1934 by new owner Thomas Yawkey, renovated, and enlarged by the 2002– Henry-Werner Group. On May 15, 2003, the Red Sox sold every home ticket for a game with Texas. In September 2008, Boston set a new big-league record of 456 consecutive sellouts—712, entering 2012.

Dimensions: left field, 310 feet; left-center field, 379; center field, 390; deep center field, 420; deep right field, 380; right field, 302. Outfield wall height: left field, 37 feet, 2 inches; center field, 17; bull pens, 5; right field, 3 to 5. The left field wall is 231 feet long, 228 in fair territory. Seating capacity: EMC Club/State Street Pavilion, 4,997 seats; box, 13,650; grandstand, 11,929; bleachers, 6,448; Green Monster, 269; right field roof deck, 202. Daytime total: 37,067. Nighttime total: 37,495.

Ticket information: By phone, 24-hour automated ticketing (888-RED SOX6). Accessible seating: (877-REDSOX9). In person: Red Sox Ticket Office, 4 Yawkey Way. Hours: Monday–Friday, 10 a.m. to 5 p.m. Additional hours on game days. Prices: Green Monster, $165; field box, $130/135; roof deck, $115; loge box, $95/99; pavilion box, $90; right field box, $52; right field roof box, $52;

infield grandstand, $52/55; outfield grandstand, $30; bleacher, $28; pavilion level standing room, $25; lower level standing room, $20; upper bleacher, $12.

FENWAY PARK ATTENDANCE

In 2004, 2004, and 2006, Boston drew 2.7, 2.8, and 2.9 million, respectively, for the first time. The 2008 Townies topped 3 million. Next year's team hit a still franchise high 3,062,699—a record for a nonpareil big-league tenth straight season. In 2011, Boston sold out its 81-game schedule another record eighth year in a row. Current capacity tops 1912's 35,000; 1953, 34,824; 1965–1967, 33,524; 1968–1970, 33,375; and 1971–1975 33,437, but is smaller than pre-fire limit size. All-time record: 47,726 (New York, double-header, September 12, 1935); 46,995 (Detroit, DH, August 19, 1934); 46,766 (New York, DH, August 12, 1934). Postwar day game record: 38,525 (Tampa Bay, August 16, 2011). Postwar night game: 38,477 (Cleveland, August 4, 2011). Postseason single-game: 39,067 (Los Angeles Angels, LCS Game Three, October 5, 2008). Opening Day: 37,440 (New York Yankees, April 4, 2010).

LEAGUE-LEADING ATTENDANCE

At Huntington Avenue Grounds: 1904, 634,295. At Fenway Park: 1914, 481,359; 1915, 539,885; 1967, 1,727,832; 1969, 1,833,246; 1970, 1,595,278; 1971, 1,678,732; 1974, 1,566,411; 1975, 1,748,587.

BEST ATTENDANCE BY YEAR

1. 3,062,599 (2009). 2. 3,054,001 (2011). 3. 3,048,248 (2008). 4. 3,046,444 (2010). 5. 2,971,925 (2007). 6. 2,930,588 (2006). 7. 2,847,888 (2005). 8. 2,837,304 (2004). 9. 2,724,162 (2003). 10. 2,650,063 (2002). 11. 2,625,333 (2001). 12. 2,586,024 (2000). 13. 2,562,435 (1991). 14. 2,528,986 (1990). 15. 2,510,012 (1989).

BEST SINGLE-GAME 1967– CROWDS

Six of Fenway Park's top 15 single-game crowds occurred in 2011, including five that August. 1. 38,525, Tampa Bay, Game One, August 16, 2011. 2. 38,477, Cleveland, August 4, 2011. 3. 38,422, San Diego, June 21, 2011. 4. 38,347, Toronto, May 21, 2009. 5. 38,304, Los Angeles Angels, August 17, 2010. 6. 38,294, Oakland, July 6, 2009. 7. 38,278, Tampa Bay, Game Two, August 16, 2011. 8. 38,266, Baltimore,

April 17, 2009. 9. 38,239, Oakland, August 26, 2011. 10. 38,238, New York Yankees, April 4, 2010. 11. 38,228, Tampa Bay, Game One, September 13, 2009. 12. 38,196, Florida, June 17, 2009. 13. 38,193, Oakland, July 29, 2009. 14. 38,189, Kansas City, July 9, 2009. 15 (tie): 38,189, New York Yankees, August 7, 2011.

FENWAY 2002– AL ATTENDANCE RANK
Each year is listed first to fifth. 2011: New York, Minnesota, Los Angeles, *Boston,* Texas. 2010: New York, Los Angeles, Minnesota, *Boston,* Texas. 2009: New York, Los Angeles, *Boston,* Detroit, Minnesota. 2008: New York, Los Angeles, Detroit, *Boston,* Chicago. 2007: New York, Los Angeles, Detroit, *Boston,* Chicago. 2006: New York, Los Angeles, Chicago, *Boston,* Detroit. 2005: New York, Los Angeles, *Boston,* Seattle, Baltimore. 2004: New York, Anaheim, Seattle, *Boston,* Baltimore. 2003: New York, Seattle, Anaheim, *Boston,* Baltimore. 2002: Seattle, New York, Baltimore, *Boston,* Cleveland.

RED SOX ROAD ATTENDANCE
In 2011, the Red Sox drew 2,591,963 in 81 games away from Fenway Park—a 31,999 average—their forty-fifth straight year above 1 million. Boston has drawn more than 2 million road in the following years, including each non-players' lockout season since 1988. 1978, 2,183,113. 1979, 2,132,807. 1986, 2,266,765. 1988, 2,200,047. 1989, 2,394,851. 1990, 2,398,449. 1991, 2,331,280. 1992, 2,359,528. 1993, 2,542,249. 1996, 2,113,889. 1997, 2,139,097. 1998, 2,427,873. 1999, 2,395,593. 2000, 2,524,776. 2001, 2,700,881. 2002, 2,474,060. 2003, 2,443,539. 2004, 2,880,236. 2005, 3,054,438. 2006, 2,924,019. 2007, 3.130,043. 2008, 3,107,743. 2009, 2,743,392. 2010, 2,615,214. 2011, 2,591,963.

ALL-TIME RED SOX TEAM
1969 Fan Voting. Catcher: Birdie Tebbetts. First base: Jimmie Foxx. Second base: Bobby Doerr. Shortstop: Joe Cronin. Third base: Frank Malzone. Outfield: Ted Williams, Tris Speaker, and Carl Yastrzemski. Right-handed pitcher: Cy Young. Left-handed pitcher: Lefty Grove. Greatest player: Ted Williams.

1982 Fan Voting. *First team.* Catcher: Carlton Fisk. First base: Jimmie Foxx. Second base: Bobby Doerr. Shortstop: Rick Burleson. Third base: Rico Petrocelli. Outfield: Ted Williams, Carl Yastrzemski, and Dwight Evans. Right-handed pitcher: Cy Young. Left-handed pitcher: Babe Ruth. Relief pitcher: Dick Radatz.

Manager: Dick Williams. *Second team*: Catcher: Birdie Tebbetts. First base: George Scott. Second base: Jerry Remy. Shortstop: Johnny Pesky. Third base: Frank Malzone. Outfield: Jim Rice, Carl Yastrzemski, and Fred Lynn. Right-handed pitcher: Luis Tiant. Left-handed pitcher: Lefty Grove. Relief pitcher: Sparky Lyle. Manager: Joe Cronin. Greatest player: Ted Williams.

THE ALL-STAR GAME

What Curt Gowdy called "New England's night club" has hosted three All-Star Games. On July 9, 1946, Ted Williams had a walk, two singles, four runs scored, five batted in, and two home runs, one *v*. Rip Sewell's blooper pitch: the American League won, 12-0, outhitting the Nationals, 14-3. Seven other Sox made the All-Star team: Bobby Doerr, Dom DiMaggio, Dave Ferriss, Mickey Harris, Johnny Pesky, Hal Wagner, and Rudy York. In 1959–1962, two games were yearly played to benefit the Players Pension Fund. On July 31, 1961, Fenway hosted the second game, stopped by rain after nine innings: score 1-1. Boston boasted only manager Mike Higgins, as AL coach, and rookie pitcher Don Schwall. The Americans scored on Rocky Colavito's homer. In 1999, the Fens hosted the July 13 Mid-Summer Classic. Before the game, Williams rode a golf cart down the warning track, along the boxes, around the plate, and toward the mound, All-Stars greeting him like parishioners might the Pope. Pedro Martinez fanned five of his six batters, the AL winning, 4-1. Townies Nomar Garciaparra, Jose Offerman, and coaches Jim Rice and Jimy Williams also made the team. Fan voting has chosen each 1947–1957 and post-1969 starting team.

THE HALL OF FAME

Eighteen members of the Baseball Hall of Fame and Museum in Cooperstown played much or most of their career with the Red Sox. In order of their induction: Babe Ruth: pitcher, outfield, 1914–1919, 391 games with A.L. Boston (entered 1936). Tris Speaker: outfield, 1907–1915, 1,065 games (1937). Cy Young: pitcher, 1901–1908, 327 games (1937). Jimmy Collins: third base, 1901–1907, 741 games (1945). Lefty Grove: pitcher, 1934–1941, 214 games (1947). Herb Pennock: pitcher, 1915–1922, 201 games (1948). Jimmie Foxx: first base, 1936–1942, 887 games (1951). Joe Cronin: shortstop, 1935–1945, 1,134 games (1956). Ted Williams: outfield, 1939–1960, 2,292 games (1966). Red Ruffing: pitcher, 1924–1930, 237 games (1967). Harry Hooper: outfield, 1909–1920,

1,646 games (1971). Rick Ferrell: catcher, 1933–1937, 522 games (1984). Bobby Doerr: second base, 1937–1951, 1,865 games (1986). Carl Yastrzemski: outfield, 1961–1983, 3,308 games (1989). Carlton Fisk: catcher, 1969, 1971–1980, 1,076 games (2000). Dennis Eckersley: pitcher, 1978–1984 and 1998, 241 games (2004). Wade Boggs: third base, 1982–1992, 1,625 games (2005). Jim Rice, 1974–1989, 2,089 games (2009). Two longtime Sox executives join them: Eddie Collins, 1933–1951 (entered 1939), and Thomas A. Yawkey, 1933–1976 (1980).

Many other Hall of Famers wore the Boston uniform. In order of induction: Jesse Burkett: outfield, 1905, 149 Sox games (1946). Jack Chesbro: pitcher, 1909, 1 game (1946). Al Simmons: outfield, 1943, 40 games (1953). Heinie Manush: outfield, 1936, 82 games (1964). Waite Hoyt: pitcher, 1919–1920, 35 games (1969). Lou Boudreau: shortstop, 1951–1952, 86 games (1970). George Kell: second base, outfield, 1952–1954, 235 games (1983). Juan Marichal: pitcher, 1974, 11 games (1983). Luis Aparicio: shortstop, 1971–1973, 367 games (1984). Ferguson Jenkins: pitcher, 1976–1977, 58 games (1991). Tom Seaver: pitcher, 1986, 16 games (1992). Orlando Cepeda: designated hitter, 1973, 142 games (1999). Tony Perez: first base, 1980–1982, 304 games (2000). Dick Williams: infield and outfield, 1963–1964, 140 games (2008). Rickey Henderson: outfield, 2002, 72 games (2009). Andre Dawson: outfield, 1993–1994, 196 games (2010).

Eleven inductees managed the Red Sox. In order of induction: Cy Young: 1907, 6 games (1937). Jimmy Collins: 1901–1906, 842 games (1945). Hugh Duffy: 1921–1922, 308 games (1945). Frank Chance: 1923, 154 games (1946). Ed Barrow: 1918–1920, 418 games (1953). Joe Cronin: 1935–1947, 2,007 games (1956). Joe McCarthy: 1948–1950, 369 games (1957). Lou Boudreau: 1952–1954, 463 games (1970). Bucky Harris: 1934, 153 games (1975). Billy Herman: 1964–1966, 310 games (1975). Dick Williams: 1967–1969, 477 games (2008).

In 1984, Curt Gowdy received the Hall of Fame's Ford C. Frick Award for broadcast excellence. Former Sox Voices Bob Murphy and Jon Miller joined him in 1994 and 2010, respectively. Inexplicably, they have not been joined by the late Ken Coleman, Ned Martin, and Jim Woods.

RED SOX HALL OF FAME
In 1995, the Red Sox formed a Hall of Fame, chosen by a 14-member committee of Townie Voices and executives, past and present media, and The Sports Museum in Boston and the BoSox Booster Club. All Sox in Cooperstown—players, man-

agers, executives, and broadcaster Curt Gowdy—were automatically enshrined. Fifty-two other players, managers, coaches, broadcasters, executives, owners, or scouts have been elected by the committee. All follow, alphabetically:

Wade Boggs, third base; Dick Bresciani, executive; Rick Burleson, shortstop; Bill Carrigan, catcher/manager; Ken Coleman, broadcaster; Eddie Collins, executive; Jimmy Collins, third base/manager; Tony Conigliaro, right field; George Digby, scout; Dom DiMaggio, center field; Bobby Doerr, second base/coach; Dennis Eckersley, pitcher; Dwight Evans, right field; Rick Ferrell, catcher; Wes Ferrell, pitcher; Boo Ferriss, pitcher/coach; Carlton Fisk, catcher; Jimmie Foxx, first base; Larry Gardner, third base; Billy Goodman, infield/outfield; Lou Gorman, executive; Curt Gowdy, broadcaster; Mike Greenwell, left field; Lefty Grove, pitcher; Tommy Harper, outfield/coach; John Harrington, executive; Tex Hughson, pitcher; Bruce Hurst, pitcher; Jackie Jensen, right field; Eddie Kasko, executive/manager; Ed Kenney Sr., executive; Ellis Kinder, pitcher; Bill Lee, pitcher; Duffy Lewis, left field; Jim Lonborg, pitcher; Fred Lynn, center field; Frank Malzone, third base; Ned Martin, broadcaster; Bill Monbouquette, pitcher; Ben Mondor, executive, Pawtucket Red Sox; Joe Morgan, manager; Dick O'Connell, executive; Mel Parnell, pitcher; Herb Pennock, pitcher/coach; Johnny Pesky, shortstop/third base; Rico Petrocelli, shortstop/third base; Jimmy Piersall, center field; Rick Radatz, pitcher; Jerry Remy, second base; Jim Rice, left field; Red Ruffing, pitcher; Pete Runnels, first base/second base; Babe Ruth, pitcher/outfielder; Everett Scott, shortstop; George Scott, third base/first base; Reggie Smith, center field/right field; Tris Speaker, center field; Bob Stanley, pitcher; Vern Stephens, shortstop; Frank Sullivan, pitcher; Haywood Sullivan, executive; Luis Tiant, pitcher; John Valentin, shortstop/third base; Mo Vaughn, first base; Dick Williams, infielder/outfielder/manager; Ted Williams, left field; Smoky Joe Wood, pitcher; Jean Yawkey, owner; Tom Yawkey, owner; Carl Yastrzemski, left field; Cy Young, pitcher; Don Zimmer, coach/manager.

RED SOX RETIRED NUMBERS

In 1931, the Red Sox put numbers on their uniform. Seven have been retired: 4 (Joe Cronin) and 9 (Ted Williams) on May 29, 1984; 1 (Bobby Doerr), May 21, 1988; 8 (Carl Yastrzemski) August 6, 1989; 27 (Carlton Fisk), September 4, 2000; 6 (Johnny Pesky), September 28, 2008; and 14 (Jim Rice), July 28, 2009. In 1997, every major league team retired number 42 on the fiftieth anniversary of Jackie Robinson cracking baseball's color line. Each of these numbers drapes Fenway's right-field grandstand facade.

FENWAY RANK IN HOME RUNS

The Fens rank second among all major-league parks in most regular-season home runs. 1. Wrigley Field, 12,236 (1914–present). 2. Fenway Park, 11,379 (1912–present). 3. Yankee Stadium. 11,270 (1923–2008). 4. Tiger Stadium, 11,111 (1912–2000). Kevin Millar poked number ten thousand August 9, 2003, *v.* Baltimore. The Red Sox have hit 5,994 homers at Fenway.

BEST HOME AVERAGE (200 AT-BATS)

Unsurprisingly, Ted Williams's .428 average led in 1941. The Kid also batted .403 in 1951 and 1957. Wade Boggs hit .418 (1985), .411 (1987), .397 (1983), and .389 (1991). Jimmie Foxx averaged .405 (1938), Dom DiMaggio .397 (1950), and Tris Speaker .392 (1912).

FENWAY LIFETIME HOMERS

Ted Williams hit 248 of his 521 career Red Sox home runs at Fenway Park. There: Carl Yastrzemski belted 237 of 452; Jim Rice, 208 (382); Dwight Evans, 199 (379); David Ortiz, 150 (320); Bobby Doerr, 145 (223); Manny Ramirez, 136 (222); Rico Petrocelli, 134 (210); Jimmie Foxx, 126 (222); Mo Vaughn, 118 (230); Carlton Fisk, 90 (162); George Scott, 90 (154); Tony Conigliaro, 87 (162); Nomar Garciaparra, 86 (178); Jackie Jensen, 86 (170); Jason Varitek, 85 (193); Reggie Smith, 76 (149); Joe Cronin, 74 (119); Vern Stephens, 70 (122); Fred Lynn, 69 (124); Frank Malzone, 68 (131); Dick Gernert, 66 (101); Mike Greenwell, 64 (130); Kevin Youkilis, 63 (129); John Valentin, 61 (121); Troy O'Leary, 61 (117).

RIVAL LIFETIME HOMERS

Each of these dingers was hit in the Fens. Babe Ruth: 38, 1920–1934. Mickey Mantle: 38, 1951–1968. Harmon Killebrew: 37, 1954–1975. Lou Gehrig: 30, 1923–1939. Al Kaline: 30, 1953–1974. Joe DiMaggio: 29, 1936–1942 and 1946–1951. Gus Zernial: 28, 1949–1959. Rocky Colavito: 26, 1955–1968. Willie Horton: 26, 1963–1980. Reggie Jackson: 25, 1967–1987. Roy Sievers: 25, 1949–1965. Vic Wertz: 25, 1947–1958 and 1961–1963. Note: Ruth and Wertz also hit 11 and 24 homers at Fenway, respectively, for 1914–1919 and 1959–1961 Boston.

SOX SINGLE-SEASON HOMERS

Jimmie Foxx holds Fenway's single-season home run record: 35 in 1938. In 1979, Fred Lynn's 28 set its left-handed mark. Other Fens dingers hit, by whom, and when follow. 28: Jim Rice (1978). 27: Carl Yastrzemski (1967), Rice (1977 and 1979), and Mo Vaughn (1996). 25: Dick Stuart (1963). 24: Walt Dropo (1950). 23: Ted Williams (1949), Tony Conigliaro (1965), and Manny Ramirez (2004). 22: Rico Petrocelli (1969), Yastrzemski (1970), Ramirez (2001), and David Ortiz (2006). 21: Foxx (1936), Vern Stephens (1949), Yastrzemski (1969), Tony Armas (1984), and Ramirez (2001). 20: Petrocelli (1970), Vaughn (1997), and Ortiz (2005). Away, Ortiz's 32 (2006) and 27 (2005) homers lead. Williams hit 26 in 1957. Next: 24: Vaughn (1995) and Ortiz (2004). 23: Rice (1983) and Ramirez (2005). 22: Armas (1984) and Don Baylor (1986). 21: Vaughn (1998) and Jason Bay (2009). Five players, including Williams thrice, have hit 20 homers, the last 2004's Ramirez.

RIVAL SINGLE-SEASON HOMERS

Each home run was hit at Fenway. Babe Ruth: 8, 1927, New York. Joe Carter: 7, 1987, Cleveland. Vic Wertz: 7, 1957, Cleveland. Harmon Killebrew: 6, 1963, Minnesota. Mickey Mantle: 6, 1961, New York. Pat Seerey: 6, 1944, Cleveland. Hank Greenberg: 6, 1937, Detroit. Lou Gehrig: 6, 1927, New York.

SOX HITTING FOR THE CYCLE

Twenty times a Red Sox player has singled, doubled, tripled, and homered in the same game. (Bobby Doerr cycled twice.) Eleven have occurred at Fenway Park. Buck Freeman: June 6, 1903, at Cleveland. Patsy Dougherty: July 29, 1903, v. New York. Tris Speaker: June 9, 1912, at St. Louis. Roy Carlyle: July 21, 1925, at Chicago. Julius Solters: August 19, 1934, at Detroit. Joe Cronin: August 2, 1940, at Detroit. Leon Culberson: July 3, 1943, at Cleveland. Bobby Doerr: May 17, 1944, v. St. Louis and May 13, 1947, v. Chicago. Bob Johnson: July 6, 1944, v. Detroit. Ted Williams: July 21, 1946, v. St. Louis. Lu Clinton: July 13, 1962, at Kansas City. Carl Yastrzemski: May 14, 1965, v. Detroit. Bob Watson: September 15, 1979, at Baltimore. Fred Lynn: May 13, 1980, v. Minnesota. Dwight Evans:

June 28, 1984, *v.* Seattle. Rich Gedman: September 18, 1985, *v.* Toronto. Mike Greenwell: September 14, 1988, *v.* Baltimore. Scott Cooper: April 12, 1994, at Kansas City. John Valentin: June 6, 1996, *v.* Chicago.

THREE HOMERS IN GAME
Twenty-five times a Red Sox player has thrice homered in a game. The 13 at Fenway are listed, as follows. Ted Williams: July 14, 1946, *v.* Cleveland. Bobby Doerr: June 8, 1950, St. Louis. Clyde Vollmer: July 26, 1951, Chicago. Norm Zauchin: May 27, 1955, Washington. Jim Rice: August 29, 1977, Oakland. Tom Brunansky: September 29, 1990, Toronto. Jack Clark: July 31, 1991, Oakland. John Valentin: June 2, 1995, Seattle. Mo Vaughn: September 24, 1996, Baltimore, and May 30, 1997, New York Yankees. Nomar Garciaparra: May 10, 1999, Seattle, and July 23, 2002, Tampa Bay. Kevin Millar: July 23, 2004, New York Yankees.

RIVAL THREE HOMERS IN GAME
Twenty-three times a player has homered thrice *v.* Boston. The 14 dinging at Fenway are listed, as follows. Lou Gehrig: June 23, 1927, New York. Ken Keltner: May 25, 1939, Cleveland. Bobby Avila: June 20, 1951, Cleveland. Harmon Killebrew: September 21, 1963, Minnesota. Boog Powell: August 15, 1966, Baltimore. Bill Freehan: August 9, 1971, Detroit. Fred Patek: June 20, 1980, Kansas City. Joe Carter: August 28, 1986 and May 28, 1987, Cleveland. Tim Raines: April 18, 1994, Chicago. Mark McGwire: June 11, 1995, Oakland. Frank Thomas: September 15, 1996, Chicago. Adam Lind: September 29, 2009, Toronto. Mark Teixeira: May 8, 2010, New York Yankees.

SOX NO-HIT GAMES
Surprisingly for a "pitcher's graveyard," Fenway has hosted 13 of Boston's 20 no-hit games, 19 official. (Rain curtailed Devern Hansack's 2006 no-no.) Listed are those that happened there. 1904: May 5, Cy Young *v.* Philadelphia, 3-0. 1905: September 27, Bill Dinneen *v.* Chicago, 2-0. 1911: July 29, Joe Wood *v.* St. Louis, 5-0. 1916: June 21, George Foster *v.* New York, 2-0; August 30, Dutch Leonard *v.* St. Louis, 4-0. 1917: June 23, Eddie Shore *v.* Washington, 4-0. 1956: July 14, Mel Parnell *v.* Chicago, 4-0. 1962: June 26, Earl Wilson *v.* Los Angeles, 2-0. 1965: September 16, Dave Morehead *v.* Cleveland, 2-0. 2002: April 27, Derek Lowe *v.* Tampa Bay, 10-0. 2006: October 1, Devern Hansack, *v.* Baltimore, 9-0, five

innings, rain. 2007: September 1, Clay Buchholz, *v.* Baltimore, 10-0. 2008: May 19, Jon Lester *v.* Kansas City, 7-0.

NO-HIT GAMES *V.* SOX

Credit home-field advantage. Only four of 13 no-hitters *v.* Boston have occurred in the Fens. (Twelve are official, rain curbing Dean Chance's in 1967.) They are listed, as follows. 1917: April 24, New York's George Mogridge, winning, 2-1. 1920: July 1, Washington's Walter Johnson, 1-0. 1926: August 21, Chicago's Ted Lyons, 6-0. 1958: July 20, Detroit's Jim Bunning, 3-0.

SOX LEFT-HANDED PERCENTAGE

When the 1949–1960 Yankees visited Fenway, southpaw Whitey Ford rarely pitched. "That damn Wall is too close," explained skipper Casey Stengel. Some Sox lefties thrived, anyway, listed by winning percentage of at least 25 decisions. Lefty Grove: .764 (55-17, 1934–1941). Roger Moret: .720 (18-7, 1970–1975). Babe Ruth: .710 (49-20, 1914–1919). Jon Lester: .706 (36-15, 2006–2011). Mel Parnell: .703 (71-30, 1947–1956). Joe Hesketh: .643 (18-10, 1990–1994). Sparky Lyle: .640 (16-9, 1967–1971). John Tudor: .639 (23-13, 1979–1983). Bruce Hurst: .629 (56-33, 1980–1988). Bill Lee: .623 (48-29, 1969–1978). Herb Pennock: .597 (37-25, 1916–1922). Ray Collins: .585 (24-17, 1912–1915). Dutch Leonard: .564 (44-34, 1913–1918). Bob Ojeda: .541 (20-17, 1980–1985).

MOST GAMES BY POSITION

Designated hitter: David Ortiz, 1,135 (2003–2011). First base: George Scott, 988 (1966–1971 and 1977–1979). Second base: Bobby Doerr, 1,852 (1937–1944 and 1946–1951). Shortstop: Everett Scott, 1,093 (1914–1921). Third base: Wade Boggs, 1,520 (1982–1992). Outfield: Ted Williams, 2,151 (1939–1942 and 1946–1960); Dwight Evans, 2,079 (1972–1990); and Carl Yastrzemski, 2,076 (1961–1983). Catcher: Jason Varitek, 1,488 (1997–2011). Pitcher: Bob Stanley, 637 (1977–1989). Tim Wakefield, 411 games started (1995–2011). Jonathan Papelbon, 396 games relieved (2005–2011).

SOURCES

Brief portions of this book have appeared in slightly different form in *Our House, Storied Stadiums,* and *What Baseball Means to Me* by Curt Smith. Grateful acknowledgment is made for permission to reference brief excerpts from the following:

A Great and Glorious Game: Baseball Writings of A. Bartlett Giamatti, by A. Bartlett Giamatti, 1998, Algonquin Books.
Boston Red Sox, by Henry Berry, 1975, Rutledge Books.
"Fenway: From Frazee to Fisk," by Martin F. Nolan, 1986, *Boston Globe.*
"From Father, with Love," by Doris Kearns Goodwin, 1986, *Boston Globe.*
"Rapt by the Radio," by John Updike, 1986, Alfred A. Knopf.
Rhubarb in the Catbird Seat, by Red Barber with Robert Creamer, 1968, Doubleday.
Sports Illustrated, issues of April 15, 1957; April 13, 1959; April 11, 1960; and April 10, 1961.
Ted Williams: The Biography of an American Hero, by Leigh Montville, 2005, Doubleday.
The Great American Baseball Card Flipping, Trading and Bubble Gum Book, by Brendan C. Boyd and Fred C. Harris, 1973, Little, Brown.
"TV's 50 Greatest Sports Moments," July 11–17, 1998, *TV Guide.*
When It Was a Game, 1991, Home Box Office.
"Yaz, to the End, True to Himself," by Peter Gammons, 1983, *Boston Globe.*
Play-by-play commentaries in *Mercy!* are reprinted with the permission of the Miley Collection, Boston Red Sox, and WEEI and WHDH Radio. Grateful acknowledgment is also made to CBS and ESPN Radio and CBS, ESPN, and NBC Television.

BIBLIOGRAPHY

Angell, Roger. *Five Seasons: A Baseball Companion.* New York: Simon and Schuster, 1977.

Ballou, Bill. *Behind the Green Monster: Red Sox Myths, Legends, and Lore.* Chicago: Triumph Books, 2009.

Beach, Jerry. *Fighting Words: the Media, the Red Sox, and the All-Encompassing Passion for Baseball in Boston.* Burlington, MA: Rounder Books, 2009.

Berry, Henry. *Boston Red Sox.* New York: Collier Books, 1975.

Castiglione, Joe. *Broadcast Rites and Sites: I Saw It on the Radio with the Boston Red Sox.* With Douglas B. Lyons. Lanham, MD: Taylor Trade Publishing, 2004.

Chadwick, Bruce. *Boston Red Sox: Memories and Mementoes of New England's Team.* Photography by David M. Spindel. New York: Abbeville Press, 1992.

Coleman, Ken. *So You Want to Be a Sportscaster: The Techniques and Skills of Sports Announcing by One of the Country's Most Experienced Broadcasters.* New York: Hawthorn Books, 1973.

Frost, Mark. *Game Six: Cincinnati, Boston, and the 1975 World Series: The Triumph of America's Pastime.* New York: Hyperion, 2009.

Gammons, Peter. *Beyond the Sixth Game.* Boston: Houghton Mifflin, 1985.

———. "Game Six." *Sports Illustrated,* April 6, 1989.

Giamatti, A. Bartlett. *A Great and Glorious Game: Baseball Writings of A. Bartlett Giamatti.* Edited by Kenneth S. Robson. Foreword by David Halberstam. Chapel Hill, NC: Algonquin Books, 1998.

Goodwin, Doris Kearns. *Wait Till Next Year.* New York: Simon and Schuster, 1998.

Gowdy, Curt. *Cowboy at the Mike.* With Al Hirshberg. Garden City, NY: Doubleday, 1966.

———. *Seasons to Remember: The Way It Was in American Sports, 1945–1960.* With John Powers. New York: HarperCollins, 1993.

Greenwald, Hank. *This Copyrighted Broadcast.* San Francisco: Woodford Press, 1997.

Halberstam, David. *Summer of '49*. New York: W. Morrow, 1989.

Hirshberg, Al. *What's the Matter with the Red Sox?* New York: Dodd, Mead, 1973.

Holmes, Tommy. *The Dodgers*. New York: Collier Books, 1975.

Hubbard, Donald. *The Red Sox before the Babe: Boston's Early Days in the American League, 1901–1914*. Jefferson, NC: McFarland Books, 2009.

Lewine, Harris, and Daniel Okrent, eds. *The Ultimate Baseball Book*. With historical text by David Nemec. Boston: Houghton Mifflin, 1979.

Miller, Jon. *Confessions of a Baseball Purist: What's Right, and Wrong, with Baseball, As Seen from the Best Seat in the House*. With Mark Hyman. New York: Simon and Schuster, 1998.

Montville, Leigh. *Ted Williams: The Biography of an American Hero*. New York: Doubleday, 2005.

Nowlin, Bill. *Mr. Red Sox: The Johnny Pesky Story*. Edited by Jim Prime. Foreword by Ted Williams. Burlington, MA: Rounder Books, 2004.

———, and David Vincent. *The Ultimate Red Sox Home Run Guide*. Burlington, MA: Rounder Books, 2009.

Oliphant, Thomas. *Praying For Gil Hodges: A Memoir of the 1955 World Series And One Family's Love of the Brooklyn Dodgers*. New York: Thomas Dunne Books, 2005.

Pitoniak, Scott. *Memories of Yankee Stadium*. Chicago: Triumph Books, 2008.

Powers, Ron. *SuperTube: The Rise of Television Sports*. New York: Coward-McCann, 1984.

Remy, Jerry. *Jerry Remy's Red Sox Heroes: The RemDawg's All-Time Favorite Red Sox, Great Moments, and Top Teams*. With Corey Sandler. Guilford, CT: Lyons Press, 2009.

Riley, Dan, ed. *The Red Sox Reader: 30 Years of Musings on Baseball's Most Amusing Team*. Thousand Oaks, CA: Ventura Arts, 1987.

Seidel, Michael. *Ted Williams: A Baseball Life*. Chicago: Contemporary Books, 1991.

Shannon, Bill, and George Kalinsky. *The Ballparks*. New York: Hawthorn Books, 1975.

Shaughnessy, Dan. *The Curse of the Bambino*. New York: Penguin Books, 1991.

Snyder, John. *365 Oddball Days in Boston Red Sox History*. Cincinnati, OH: Clerisy Press, 2009.

Vecsey, George, ed. *The Way It Was: Great Sports Events from the Past*. New York: McGraw-Hill, 1974.

Walton, Ed. *Red Sox Triumphs and Tragedies*. New York: Stein & Day, 1980.

Williams, Ted, and Jim Prime. *Ted Williams' Hit List*. Indianapolis, IN: Masters Press, 1996.

Wood, Bob. *Dodger Dogs to Fenway Franks: And All the Wieners in Between*. New York: McGraw-Hill, 1988.

INDEX

ABOUT THE AUTHOR

Curt Smith is America's leading baseball radio/TV historian: to *USA Today*, "the voice of authority on baseball broadcasting." The columnist, radio host, and senior lecturer of English at the University of Rochester wrote more speeches than anyone for George H. W. Bush during his time as president (1989–1993). Bob Costas says, "Curt Smith stands up for the beauty of words."

A longtime Red Sox fan, Smith is a columnist for Gatehouse Media, Major League Baseball's official website MLBlog.com, and *Jewish World Review*'s PoliticalMavens.com, and host of the National Public Radio affiliate series *Perspectives*. Associated Press and the New York Broadcasting Association have voted his radio commentary "Best in New York State."

Smith's 15 books include *Voices of The Game*, *A Talk in the Park*, *What Baseball Means To Me*, *Long Time Gone*, and *Pull Up a Chair*. Recent book essays include the Memoir As Art, 32 Greatest Presidential Speeches, 32 Greatest TV/film Presidential Portrayals, 1959 White Sox, 1960 Pirates, and 1969 Mets. His essay on the media keynoted Cambridge University's 2011 *The Cambridge Companion to Baseball*.

Raised in Upstate New York, Smith was a Gannett reporter, speechwriter for John B. Connally, and *The Saturday Evening Post* senior editor before joining the Bush White House in 1989. He wrote the forty-first president's "Just War" Persian Gulf speech, Margaret Thatcher Medal of Freedom address, and speech aboard the USS *Missouri* on Pearl Harbor's fiftieth anniversary. The *New York Times* terms his work "the high point of Bush familial eloquence."

Leaving the White House in 1993, Smith headed the former president's speech staff, writing Bush's moving 2004 eulogy to Ronald Reagan. He has keynoted the Cooperstown Symposium on Baseball and American Culture, hosted Smithsonian Institution and XM Satellite Radio Baseball Hall of Fame series, and helped write ABC/ESPN's *SportsCentury* and ESPN's *Voices of The Game*. The latter title has become shorthand for baseball radio/TV.

Smith has written for, among others, the *Boston Globe*, *Newsweek*, the *New York Times*, *Reader's Digest*, *Sports Illustrated,* and the *Washington Post*—and appeared on such network radio/TV programs as ABC's *Nightline*; Armed Forces Radio; BBC; *CBS This Morning*; CNN, ESPN, and MSNBC TV; Fox News Channel; History Channel; Mutual Radio's Jim Bohannon; and Radio America. His website is curtsmithusa.com.

The State University of New York at Geneseo alumnus has been named among the SUNY system's "100 Outstanding Alumni." He is a member of the Judson Welliver Society of former White House speechwriters; Baseball Hall of Fame Ford C. Frick Award committee; and National Radio Hall of Fame committee, creating its Franklin D. Roosevelt Award in Political Communication. In 1999, Smith joined the University of Rochester faculty, teaching Presidential Rhetoric and Public Speaking. He lives with his wife and their two children in Upstate New York.